DAILY STRENGTH

DAILY STRENGTH

A DEVOTIONAL FOR MEN

SAM STORMS

GENERAL EDITOR

 **CROSSWAY**®

WHEATON, ILLINOIS

Daily Strength: A Devotional for Men

Copyright © 2022 by Crossway

Published by Crossway
    1300 Crescent Street
    Wheaton, Illinois 60187

Cover design: Dan Farrell and Jordan Singer

First printing 2022

The daily devotionals were first published as part of the *ESV Men's Devotional Bible* (Crossway, 2015) and are reprinted by permission.

Printed in China

Hardcover ISBN: 978-1-4335-7340-8
ePub ISBN: 978-1-4335-7342-2
PDF ISBN: 978-1-4335-7341-5
Mobipocket ISBN: 978-1-4335-7342-2

Library of Congress Cataloging-in-Publication Data

Names: Storms, C. Samuel, 1951- editor.

Title: Daily strength : a daily devotional for men / Sam Storms, general editor.

Description: Wheaton, Illinois : Crossway, 2021. | "The daily devotionals were first published as part of the ESV Men's Devotional Bible (Crossway, 2015)" | Includes bibliographical references and index.

Identifiers: LCCN 2020019824 (print) | LCCN 2020019825 (ebook) | ISBN 9781433573408 (hardcover) | ISBN 9781433573415 (pdf) | ISBN 9781433573422 (mobi) | ISBN 9781433573422 (epub)

Subjects: LCSH: Men--Religious life. | Devotional calendars.

Classification: LCC BV4528.2 .D3435 2021 (print) | LCC BV4528.2 (ebook) | DDC 242/.642--dc23

LC record available at https://lccn.loc.gov/2020019824

LC ebook record available at https://lccn.loc.gov/2020019825

Crossway is a publishing ministry of Good News Publishers.

RRDS		31	30	29	28	27	26	25	24	23	22
15	14	13	12	11	10	9	8	7	6	5	4	3	2	1

Contents

Introduction

THE AUTHOR OF the epistle to the Hebrews reminds us that "it is good for the heart to be strengthened by grace" (13:9). *Daily Strength: A Devotional for Men* is uniquely designed for men to achieve that very goal. Based on the daily devotionals originally appearing in the *ESV Men's Devotional Bible*, this new book presents those devotionals in a "one a day" format for regular reading throughout the calendar year.

This resource does more than inform the mind. Its aim is to equip and encourage men who long to experience spiritual and moral transformation in the depths of their heart. More than fifty men who serve as pastors, professors, and Christian leaders have contributed 365 daily devotional studies on biblical themes of practical importance to the lives of men today.

Perhaps never before in the history of the church have men faced the intensity of temptation and relentless assault from the world, the flesh, and the devil that we are witnessing in our day. The essence of biblical masculinity is being undermined as we are repeatedly told that a "real man" must be wealthy, influential, autonomous, self-made, sexually liberated, and self-reliant. The result is that marriages are being destroyed, families are in crisis, and countless men are increasingly losing their sense of identity in Jesus Christ. *Daily Strength* speaks pointedly to men who long for lives of integrity, self-sacrifice, love, and passionate devotion to their families and, above all, to the Lord Jesus Christ.

Our goal is to strengthen and transform the hearts of men through the power of the Spirit-inspired word of God. *Daily Strength* provides daily insights into Scripture that not only enlighten the mind but especially feed, nurture, and empower the hearts of men to enjoy all that God is for them in Jesus Christ. Each daily devotional study is tied to a particular biblical passage that speaks to the most pressing needs and concerns that men face today. The contributors are themselves men who understand the unique challenges we encounter in today's world, and they have written with an eye to the application of Scripture to our most practical needs. Their insights are theologically rich, honest, vulnerable, penetrating, and always gospel-centered.

The devotionals included in *Daily Strength* follow the biblical text from Genesis through Revelation. The devotionals are not arranged topically or thematically but rather are tethered closely to the text on which each is based. To get the most out of the devotional readings, we strongly recommend that you read the Bible text for each day before you read the related devotional. There is at least one devotional for each book of the Bible, connected with the passages that most clearly capture key themes of that book. If the 365 devotionals are read consecutively throughout the year, along with the passages on which they are based, beginning in Genesis and ending in Revelation, the reader will have gained by the end of the year an extensive overview of Scripture and the history of salvation.

May the Lord's grace strengthen and encourage you as you immerse yourself in his life-changing word.

Sam Storms
General Editor

Contributors

CHRISTOPHER ASH
Writer-in-Residence, Tyndale House, Cambridge University; pastor, speaker, writer; former Director, Cornhill Training Course, London

ALISTAIR BEGG
Senior Minister, Parkside Church, Cleveland, Ohio

JON BLOOM
Cofounder, Desiring God

MIKE BULLMORE
Senior Pastor, CrossWay Community Church, Bristol, Wisconsin

KEVIN CAWLEY
Directional Leader, Redeemer Fellowship, Kansas City, Missouri

BRYAN CHAPELL
Pastor Emeritus, Grace Presbyterian Church, Peoria, Illinois; President Emeritus, Covenant Theological Seminary; President, Unlimited Grace Media; leader, administrative committee of the Presbyterian Church in America

SAM CRABTREE
Pastor for Small Groups, North Campus, Bethlehem Baptist Church, St. Paul, Minnesota; Chairman of the Board, Bethlehem College and Seminary

ANDREW M. DAVIS
Senior Pastor, First Baptist Church, Durham, North Carolina

JASON S. DEROUCHIE
Research Professor of Old Testament and Biblical Theology, Midwestern Baptist Theological Seminary

DAN DORIANI
Professor of Biblical and Systematic Theology, Vice President at Large, Covenant Theological Seminary

ZACK ESWINE
Pastor, Riverside Church, Webster Groves, Missouri

GREG GILBERT
Senior Pastor, Third Avenue Baptist Church, Louisville, Kentucky

AARON J. GOLDSTEIN
Adjunct Professor of Old Testament, Covenant Theological Seminary

GRAEME GOLDSWORTHY
Former lecturer in Old Testament, Biblical Theology, and Hermeneutics, Moore Theological College, Sydney, Australia

JAMES M. HAMILTON JR.
Professor of Biblical Theology, The Southern Baptist Theological Seminary; Pastor, Kenwood Baptist Church, Louisville, Kentucky

JOHN D. HANNAH
Department Chairman and Distinguished Professor of Historical Theology, Dallas Theological Seminary

JUSTIN S. HOLCOMB
Canon for Vocations, Episcopal Diocese of Central Florida; Adjunct Professor, Reformed Theological Seminary

PAUL R. HOUSE
Professor of Divinity, Beeson Divinity School of Samford University

R. KENT HUGHES

Senior Pastor Emeritus of College Church in Wheaton, Illinois; former professor of practical theology at Westminster Theological Seminary; cofounder of the Charles Simeon Trust

RYAN KELLY

Pastor for Preaching, Desert Springs Church, Albuquerque, New Mexico

JULIUS J. KIM

President, the Gospel Coalition; Visiting Professor, Westminster Seminary California

DAVE KRAFT

Life/leadership coach; leadership seminar presenter; blogger on leadership issues at www.dave kraft.org

MICHAEL LUMPKIN

Pastor, teacher, Fort Worth, Texas

JASON C. MEYER

Pastor for Preaching and Vision, Bethlehem Baptist Church, Minneapolis

GARY MILLAR

Principal, Queensland Theological College, Brisbane, Australia

PAUL E. MILLER

Founder and Executive Director, seeJesus

ANDREW DAVID NASELLI

Associate Professor of Systematic Theology and New Testament, Bethlehem College and Seminary in Minneapolis; member of pastoral staff, Bethlehem Baptist Church

TOM NELSON

Senior Pastor, Christ Community Church, Kansas City, Kansas; President, Made to Flourish

DOUGLAS SEAN O'DONNELL
Senior Vice President of Bible Publishing, Crossway

DANE C. ORTLUND
Senior Pastor, Naperville Presbyterian Church, Naperville, Illinois

ROBERT L. PLUMMER
Chairman, New Testament Department; Collin and Evelyn Aikman Professor of Biblical Studies, The Southern Baptist Theological Seminary

MICHAEL REEVES
President and Professor of Theology, Union School of Theology

PHILIP RYKEN
President, Wheaton College

J. J. SEID
Pastor of Leadership Development, Frontline Church, Edmond, Oklahoma

JAY SKLAR
Professor of Old Testament, Vice President of Academics, Covenant Theological Seminary

COLIN SMITH
Senior Pastor, The Orchard Evangelical Free Church, Arlington Heights and Barrington, Illinois; President and Bible teacher, Unlocking the Bible

SCOTTY WARD SMITH
Founding Pastor, Christ Community Church, Franklin, Tennessee; Teacher in Residence, West End Community Church, Nashville

SAM STORMS
Lead Pastor of Preaching and Vision, Bridgeway Church, Oklahoma City

BRIAN J. TABB
Academic Dean, Associate Professor of Biblical Studies, Bethlehem College and Seminary; General Editor, *Themelios*

ERIK THOENNES
Professor of Theology; Chair, Undergraduate Theology, Biola University/ Talbot School of Theology; Pastor of Congregational Life, Grace Evangelical Free Church, La Mirada, California

JOE THORN
Lead Pastor, Redeemer Fellowship, St. Charles, Illinois

STEPHEN T. UM
President and Executive Director of the Center for Gospel Culture

MILES V. VAN PELT
The Alan Hayes Belcher Jr. Professor of Old Testament and Biblical Languages, Director of the Summer Institute for Biblical Languages, Academic Dean, Reformed Theological Seminary, Jackson

R. FOWLER WHITE
Retired pastor, professor, academic administrator

JARED C. WILSON
Assistant Professor of Pastoral Ministry, Spurgeon College; Author in Residence, Midwestern Baptist Theological Seminary; Director of the Pastoral Training Center, Liberty Baptist Church, Kansas City, Missouri

TODD WILSON
Cofounder and President, the Center for Pastor Theologians

ROBERT W. YARBROUGH
Professor of New Testament, Covenant Theological Seminary

God's Purpose in Marriage

R. KENT HUGHES

IT WAS GOD, not Adam, who knew that it was not good for the man to be alone; it was God who honed Adam's awareness of his need by having him provide a name for every living creature, so that he would become aware that there was no helper among them who was fit for him. And it was God who caused a deep sleep to fall upon Adam and removed one of his ribs, moist with Adam's fluids and warm with his marrow and DNA, and literally *built* it into a woman. And then, it was God (like an earthly father) who presented her to Adam.

Adam's ecstatic response contains the first human words recorded in the Bible, and the first poetic couplet:

This at last is bone of my bones
    and flesh of my flesh;
she shall be called Woman,
    because she was taken out of Man. (Gen. 2:23)

Because God had honed Adam's naming powers, Adam restated his own name embedded in the woman's. He saw her as a mirror of himself, with some very agreeable differences! He had found his companion and his longed-for love. He was no longer alone. Such intimacy—all of God.

Adam's voice subsides, and Moses immediately declares, "Therefore a man shall leave his father and mother and hold fast to his wife, and they shall become one flesh" (v. 24). One-flesh intimacy is the marital ideal, the marital pursuit. Men, understand that we are to be the keepers of this intimacy, rooted in the very act of creation on the culmination of the sixth day.

Such a high calling. But there is more, because, in Ephesians chapter 5, the apostle Paul concludes his teaching on marriage by referencing the declaration, "the two shall become one flesh," and then adding, "This mystery is profound, and I am saying that it refers to Christ and the church"

(Eph. 5:31–32). When God created "one-flesh" intimacy it was a creational prophecy of the intimacy of Christ and the church. Therefore, all who name the name of Christ must understand that the relationship of a man and his wife is meant to be a window into the relationship of Christ and the church—a gospel window going all the way back to creation.

The call, "Husbands love your wives, as Christ loved the church and gave himself up for her" (Eph. 5:25), is ultimately a call to preach the gospel.

JANUARY 2 • GENESIS 3

The Urgency of Hearing and Heeding God's Word

R. KENT HUGHES

THE FALL OF MANKIND began when the serpent/Satan asked, with feigned incredulity, "Did God actually say, 'You shall not eat of any tree in the garden?'" (Gen. 3:1). This "innocent" question was actually a calculated slur on God's goodness, implying that he is ungenerous. In truth, God had told Adam, "You may surely eat of *every* tree of the garden" (2:16). But no matter, a seed of doubt had been planted in Eve's heart that would bear immediate fruit in her response.

First, Eve *diminished* God's word by leaving out the word "every" in her own response: "And the woman said to the serpent, 'We may eat of the fruit of the trees in the garden'" (3:2a). Her inexact, shrunken rendition of God's word discounted God's generosity. Second, Eve *added to* God's word. God had told the first couple that *eating* of the tree of the knowledge of good and evil would bring death (2:17), but Eve told Satan that merely *touching* the tree was forbidden (3:3). Thus, she magnified God's harshness: an inadvertent touch, and "you're history." Lastly, Eve *softened* God's word as she left out the word "surely" from God's original statement, "you shall surely die" (2:17). Her omission removed the certitude of death for eating from the tree.

With that, Satan was emboldened to declare God's word a deception: "The serpent said to the woman, 'You will not surely die'" (3:4). "Eve," he seemed to say, "the threat of death is a divine scare tactic: God is repressive and he's jealous; he's afraid that you might ascend too high."

It was too much for Eve. She should have run screaming from the serpent. But instead she reached forth a lovely hand and resolutely took the fruit, believing that divinity would soon be hers. Shocking! But here's the real shocker: Adam was *with* her (v. 6). And, moreover, Adam was *not* deceived by the snake (see 1 Tim. 2:14). Adam sinned with his eyes wide open. He had watched Eve take the fruit, and nothing happened to her. So, he sinned willfully, assuming there would be no consequences.

Everything was upside down: *Eve followed the snake, Adam followed Eve, and no one followed God.*

Men, if there ever was a call to be a man of the word, this is it. And here is what the ultimate Man says: "Man shall not live by bread alone, but by every word that comes from the mouth of God" (Matt. 4:4). Feed on it and live it—for the glory of God in your life, your family, the church, and the lost world.

JANUARY 3 · GENESIS 12:1-9

The Life of Faith

R. KENT HUGHES

THE PROMISES OF blessing that God made to Abram amid pagan, moon-worshiping Ur were immense in their personal and global scope. The personal promises were staggering: "And I will make of you a great nation, and I will bless you and make your name great, so that you will be a blessing" (Gen. 12:2). The parallel *global* promise of blessing was equally overwhelming: "I will bless those who bless you, and him who dishonors you I will curse, and in you all the families of the earth shall be blessed" (v. 3). The immensity of these promises was beyond imagination.

Nevertheless, Abram believed and obeyed the word of God, and by faith led his entire family and entourage on an eight hundred–mile journey to the land of Canaan—where his sojourn in the Promised Land gives us wisdom about the life of faith.

The life of faith calls God's people to be *pilgrims* in this world, as the writer of Hebrews says of Abram, "By faith he went to live in the land of promise, as in a foreign land, living in tents. . . . For he was looking forward to the city that has foundations, whose designer and builder is God" (Heb. 11:9–10). Father Abram personally understood and believed that "this world is not my home, I'm just a passing through." What a challenge to the dominant earth-bound ideologies of our age!

The truth is, Abram never did build a home in the Promised Land. The only land that he owned was a cave that he purchased as Sarah's grave (Genesis 23). But he did become a builder, building not a tower, nor a city, nor a house—but *altars* for worship across the land. The first was in Shechem (12:6–7) and the second was in Bethel (vv. 8–9), both prominent places of pagan worship; and there he offered sacrifices to the true God.

How beautiful: the only architecture that remained after Abram's life was altars to the Lord, the artifacts of a worshiping heart. Faithful Abram worshiped wherever he went.

Today, "if you are Christ's, then you are Abraham's offspring, heirs according to the promise" (Gal. 3:29)—and pilgrims who are called to build altars not of stone but of the heart, wherever you are, to "present your bodies as a living sacrifice, holy and acceptable to God, which is your spiritual worship" (Rom. 12:1).

JANUARY 4 • GENESIS 15

By Faith Alone

R. KENT HUGHES

CONSIDERABLE TIME HAD passed since Abram first obeyed God's call to leave Ur, which had opened with the dazzling promise, "I will make of you a great nation." But Sarai, his wife, was barren, and the shadow of barrenness had only deepened through the ups and downs of the couple's sojourns. Thus it was on a dark, fearful night that God met Abram in a vision, and Abram poured out his fear that his servant Eliezer would, of necessity, become his heir. God's response to Abram that dark night was a revelation: a son would come from his own body.

As Abram reeled from the revelation, God took him outside and directed his vision upward, saying, "Look toward heaven, and number the stars, if you are able to number them. . . . So shall your offspring be" (Gen. 15:5). Alone under the silent stars with God Almighty, with the incredible promise still ringing, Abram was speechless.

What was happening in the heart of silent Abram? Though Abram does not tell us, the Scripture does: "he believed the Lord, and he counted it to him as righteousness" (v. 6). Abram's soul uttered a silent "amen." He *rested everything* on God's word of promise, and God counted (or reckoned, or imputed) Abram's faith to him as righteousness. Faith alone had brought Abram the free gift of righteousness—salvation.

No other biblical text has exercised such an influence on our understanding of faith, or, indeed, such an influence on the New Testament in its entirety. For example, the fourth chapter of Romans is an extended exposition of Genesis 15:6; in fact, Paul quotes verse 6 three times and repeats the key word "counted" eleven times as he drives home the glorious truth that salvation has always been by faith alone.

Faith alone is the vocabulary of rest. We are called to cease from our works and rest everything on the promise of the finished work of Christ. Here is the gospel of rest: "For by grace you have been saved through faith. And this is not your own doing; it is the gift of God, not a result of works, so that no one may boast" (Eph. 2:8–9). Faith's refrain is,

Jesus, I am resting, resting
In the joy of what Thou art.

Laughter!

R. KENT HUGHES

HERE IS AN ACCOUNT filled with laughter—all kinds of laughter—and ultimately the laughter of heaven.

God Almighty had just renamed Abram *Abraham* ("father of a multitude"), promising him that kings would come from him. And here God changes Sarai ("princess") to *Sarah*, which also means "princess," as a doubled affirmation that royalty would come from her barren ninety-year-old womb (Gen. 17:15–17). When Abraham heard God say, "I will give you a son by her," he fell on his face and laughed! But it wasn't necessarily the laughter of unbelief; perhaps it was simply incredulous hilarity. After all, the Bible tells us that he never wavered concerning the promise (see Rom. 4:18–21). God directly informed Abraham (with a smile?) that his and Sarah's son would be named *Isaac*, literally "laughter."

Abraham then received three mysterious visitors, whom he entertained with a sumptuous feast (Gen. 18:1–9). In retrospect, Abraham would understand that his guests were the Lord himself, along with two attending angels. God came to dinner! And the covenantal function of the meal with the Lord and his angels was to restate the promise of a son through Sarah, and for the old princess to hear it herself as she listened at the door of the tent and heard the Lord say, "I will surely return to you about this time next year, and Sarah your wife shall have a son." Sarah's response was inward and silent: "So Sarah laughed to herself" (18:12). It was melancholy, hopeless, unbelieving laughter. Happily, her silent, hopeless humor would soon be transformed into the laughter of belief.

The epilogue in 21:3–6 chronicles the old couple's mirth: "Abraham called the name of his son who was born to him, whom Sarah bore him, Isaac [Laughter]. And Abraham circumcised his son [Laughter] when he was eight days old, as God had commanded him. Abraham was a hundred years old when his son [Laughter] was born to him. And Sarah said, 'God has made laughter for me; everyone who hears will laugh over me.'" There was laughter everywhere. The old man and his wife laughed and continued to laugh as they held tiny Laughter in their arms. Heaven smiled.

Abraham and Sarah had indeed birthed a royal dynasty of kings through their son Isaac, from which would come the King of kings amid peals of merriment as the angels proclaimed,

> Glory to God in the highest,
> and on earth peace among those with whom he is pleased.
> (Luke 2:14)

God Will Provide

R. KENT HUGHES

ABRAHAM WAS INTENTIONALLY vague when he said to his servants, "Stay here with the donkey; I and the boy will go over there and worship and come again to you" (Gen. 22:5). "Worship" veiled his intention to offer up Isaac as a burnt offering, and "come again to you" indicated his belief in the resurrection. The writer of Hebrews tells us that Abraham believed that God was able to raise Isaac from the dead (Heb. 11:19), when as yet there was nothing in history to suggest that such a thing could happen. What bold, original, amazing faith!

As father and son ascended the mount in silence, Isaac's piercing question, "My father! . . . Behold, the fire and the wood, but where is the lamb for a burnt offering?" (Gen. 22:7), led to Abraham's immortal answer, "God will provide for himself the lamb for a burnt offering, my son" (v. 8), which is the turning point in the account. *God will provide* states Abraham's absolute trust in God. Abraham believed that nations and kings would come from Isaac, and he left everything in God's good hands.

Abraham's often-told obedience and God's astonishing provision came together as Abraham prepared the pyre, bound his beloved Isaac so that he might not flee in sudden fear, took the knife in his trembling hand, and tightened his grip for the sacrificial cut—only to hear God roar his name twice from the heavens with the command, "Do not lay your hand on the boy" (v. 12). In the same instant, Abraham saw the substitute provision: the account says that "Abraham lifted up his eyes and looked, and behold, behind him was a ram, caught in a thicket by his horns. And Abraham went and took the ram and offered it up as a burnt offering instead of his son" (v. 13). Never was there a more joyous and eager sacrifice!

In ecstasy, "Abraham called the name of that place, 'the Lord will provide [*Jehovah Jireh*]'; as it is said to this day, 'On the mount of the Lord it shall be provided'" (v. 14). Abraham's declaration of faith—*God will provide*—as he and Isaac ascended the mountain had now become the wondrous conclusion. We see that the God who tests is the God who provides. When God tests you, he will always provide for you.

JANUARY 7 · GENESIS 24

The Beauty of Divine Providence

R. KENT HUGHES

FOR ABRAHAM, SARAH'S death was a fresh awakening to his own advanced age and his responsibility to make sure that his forty-something son, Isaac, would marry well and produce heirs. So he called his most trusted servant and had him take a formal vow that he would return to Abraham's country and his kindred to find a wife for Isaac. He assured the servant of divine guidance, saying that God "will send his angel before you, and you shall take a wife for my son there" (Gen. 24:7). Abraham believed that God's unseen hand would do it all. He rested in God's providential guidance.

There would be no miracle in this account (as we usually think of miracles)—no suddenly barren rivers, no solar pauses, no healings. Rather, God would bring about the discovery of Isaac's bride through the "normal" events of life.

The positioning of this story here at the end of Abraham's life serves, in effect, to tell us that this is the way God works in our everyday lives. The God of Scripture is not simply a God of miracles who occasionally injects his power into life. He is far greater, because he arranges all of life to suit and effect his providence.

The servant's search spanned hundreds of miles as his caravan traveled north and then east to Nahor in Mesopotamia. There in the slanting rays of dusk, when women come out to draw water, Abraham's servant directed his camels to kneel near the town well, where he offered this extraordinary prayer: "Let the young woman to whom I shall say, 'Please let down your jar that I may drink,' and who shall say, 'Drink, and I will water the camels'—let her be the one whom you have appointed for your servant Isaac" (v. 14). To be sure, the criteria were demanding! But it was not a request for a miraculous sign. He did not ask for a fleece (see Judg. 6:36–40). He did not ask for the normal effects of nature to be suspended. Nevertheless, it was a "mundane miracle"—a glimpse behind the everyday curtain of life.

This story means that we must live in full consciousness of the miracle of divine providence, understanding that God has total hands-on control of the world—and that all of life is to be lived for him without fear and with increasing expectation.

JANUARY 8 · GENESIS 27

Resting in God's Sure Word

R. KENT HUGHES

GOD'S PROPHETIC WORD to the matriarch Rebekah, as her twin boys struggled in her womb, was that "the older shall serve the younger" (Gen. 25:23). And, indeed, though her firstborn, Esau, did initially inherit the birthright, he sold it to Jacob for a bowl of stew. "Thus Esau despised his birthright" (25:34). One would think that this disgraceful event would seal Jacob's position once and for all in the family's mind. But Genesis 27 chronicles two in-house responses to the prophetic word that indicate that neither Isaac and Esau, on the one hand, nor Rebekah and Jacob, on the other, believed that God's sure word would stand.

To begin with, old, visually impaired Isaac believed that he could nullify God's word when he asked Esau to hunt game and then prepare a meal for him, during which he would then bless Esau and thus restore Esau's birthright (vv. 1–4). He actually thought that his willful opposition to the stated word of God could thwart it.

The patriarch's attempt to nullify God's word then brought about Rebekah and Jacob's collusion and the absurd theater of deception that followed, as Jacob (lying three times) fooled Isaac into blessing him (v. 23), so that Isaac was compelled to pronounce an "anti-blessing" on Esau, thus sealing the blessing for Jacob (vv. 39–40). But there is a deeper absurdity here, namely, the matriarch and her son's belief that their sinful theatrics were necessary to make God's word come true and, by implication, that their lying and deception were justified.

Everyone sinned—and suffered. Old Isaac tossed a relational torch into his families' tents by attempting to nullify God's sure word about Jacob's prominence. The patriarch's attempt to thwart God's word then gave rise to Rebekah and Jacob's disgraceful machinations—which ultimately resulted in Jacob's flight from Esau to Mesopotamia, where he suffered long under the duplicities of double-dealing Laban. Rebekah never saw her beloved Jacob again. And Esau, who had despised his birthright, lost everything.

How much better, how good life would have been, if the patriarchal family had simply believed and rested in God's sure word. The sinful attempts to thwart it and the sinful attempts to help it would never have taken place. Men, believe and rest in this today: "Every word of God proves true" (Prov. 30:5; cf. Isa. 55:10–11).

JANUARY 9 • GENESIS 29:1-30

The Pruning of a Patriarch

R. KENT HUGHES

AT NIGHTFALL, after fleeing the wrath of Esau, Jacob in exhaustion lay his head on a stone pillow and dreamed of a ladder reaching from earth to heaven, where the Lord stood as angels ascended and descended (Gen. 28:10–13)—indicating that there was commerce between heaven and earth on his behalf. It was, and is, an apt symbol of God's providential direction of his elect children's lives. Fittingly, Jacob named the place Bethel, the "house of God."

Some five hundred miles later, having arrived at his destination, Jacob encountered what he must certainly have regarded as a smiling providence when he met lovely cousin Rachel at a well (his mother, Rebekah, had also been discovered at a well; 24:10–21!). Jacob uncovered the well, watered his uncle Laban's sheep, and then "kissed Rachel and wept aloud" (29:11). Jacob no doubt saw this as the beginning of the promised blessing. God was directing the commerce of heaven in his behalf. And this was profoundly true, but not as Jacob expected. The young patriarch-to-be (this deceiver!) needed the benefits of a frowning providence—some divine pruning. Jacob needed to experience pain and disappointment and humiliation. He needed to become compassionate. He needed to stop trusting himself and learn to rest everything in God.

Enter the archdeceiver, Uncle Laban, and the infamous matrimonial "bait and switch" of the less appealing older sister Leah for the beautiful young Rachel—after Jacob had worked seven years for her hand! On top of this, Jacob was forced to labor seven more humiliating years to finally earn Rachel. Where was the ladder of angels now? Actually, it was in full operation, and behind the palpable frown of God was his smiling providence indeed. Jacob's nemesis and greatest antagonist was God's gracious instrument in shaping him. Jacob was going to change, not overnight but over time. He would become Israel, a prince of God.

Today, the ladder of God's providential care is administered by the ascended Son of Man, as Jesus explained to Nathanael: "Truly, truly, I say to you, you will see heaven opened, and the angels of God ascending and descending on the Son of Man" (John 1:51). In Christ, there is continual, graced commerce between heaven and earth for all of God's children, especially in the difficulties of life. In the words of William Cowper,

Judge not the Lord by feeble sense
But trust him for his grace;
Behind a frowning providence
He hides a smiling face.[1]

When God Rehabilitates Your Name

R. KENT HUGHES

IT TOOK THIRTY YEARS of stormy, humbling existence before Jacob was ready to heed and obey God's word to return to Bethel, where God had revealed himself when he had fled from his brother, Esau. But once there, Jacob worshiped, offering joyful sacrifices to God in fulfillment of his thirty-year-old vow (Gen. 35:7; cf. 28:21). At last, Jacob was in the place where he was supposed to be—worshiping God in whole-hearted obedience.

Jacob's obedience was rewarded by a theophany, as "God appeared to Jacob again . . . and blessed him" (35:9). God's blessing confirmed Jacob's change of name from Jacob ("deceiver") to Israel ("strives with God")—a name change that had originally occurred at Peniel on the other side of the Jordan (32:28). Now, at Bethel in the Promised Land, the obedient patriarch has his new name validated and rehabilitated by the audible voice of God. He is, indeed, Israel.

God's blessing of Jacob/Israel continues as God identifies himself to the patriarch as *El Shaddai*, saying, "I am God Almighty: be fruitful and multiply" (v. 11). The divine title *El Shaddai* was first used in Scripture to confirm God's promise to Abraham of fruitfulness, a nation, kings, and the land (17:1–8), and here the promise to Jacob continues in concert with that to Father Abraham (35:11–12). *El Shaddai* identifies God as the one who fulfills every promise by means of his sovereign might.

God Almighty's stunning blessing evoked Jacob's deeper consecration: "And Jacob set up a pillar in the place where he had spoken with him, a pillar of stone. He poured out a drink offering on it and poured oil on it. So Jacob called the name of the place where God had spoken to him Bethel" (vv. 14–15). The fact that the consecration went beyond the oil-anointing of some thirty years earlier (now, by pouring out a drink offering on the pillar) indicates that Jacob was investing the pillar with fresh new meaning. This was Bethel, "the house of God." Jacob understood the place with a depth of devotion that he had not been capable of in his youth.

Jacob's experience of expanded understanding is common to us all. As new, inexperienced believers, we came to learn some new truth, and it did us much good. Then, years later, after the ups and downs of spiritual life, and some progress in obedience and consecration, we had cause to reflect on the same truth—but with a far deeper level of understanding and application.

The Energizing Power of God's Presence

R. KENT HUGHES

JOSEPH WAS SO extraordinary that, even in the context of the greats of the Bible, he towers like a skyscraper. As to why this is so, the story of Joseph and Potiphar's wife leaves no doubt: Moses's narrative voice-over at both the beginning and end of the account states that Joseph was successful because the Lord was *with* him (stated twice at the beginning of the story [Gen. 39:2–3] and three times at the end [vv. 21–23]). So we must understand that the unseen hand in the story is God's, who was present and working on Joseph's behalf in his phenomenal rise, his humiliating downfall, and his quick restoration to prominence.

But it is one thing to be outside the story and observe that God was with Joseph, and quite another to be *Joseph* inside the story and believe that God is with you, when all you have worked for is being ripped from you because of your integrity. And here Joseph shines because he knew that God was with him as he refused Mrs. Potiphar's advances, declaring to her, "How then can I do this great wickedness and sin against God?" (v. 9). The grand deterrent to the seductive pleas was Joseph's awareness that God is present and sees all, and that a sin that no one else knows about, committed behind locked doors in a dark room, is actually committed in the presence of a holy God.

Such a temptation! Joseph was seventeen or eighteen years old (see 37:2), and surely his hormones were raging, so that he brimmed with sexual curiosity and drive. The rationalizations were so natural and logical. No one would ever know (see 39:11). He was a slave. His life was not his own. And besides, a little strategic fornication could benefit his career. But Joseph said no!

What a towering figure Joseph had become. Never once, whether in prosperity or adversity, had Joseph doubted God. He sensed and appropriated God's presence in every circumstance. And never had Joseph been more of a success than now. He dwarfed the monuments of the Nile.

How does the story of Joseph intersect our lives today? It does so beautifully and powerfully in the incarnation of Christ the Messiah, who is Immanuel, "God with us" (Matt. 1:23). Brothers, the key to our day-to-day success is to believe this with all our being, and conduct every moment of life in the dazzling reality of Christ's presence.

JANUARY 12 · GENESIS 41:37-57

From the Pit to the Palace

R. KENT HUGHES

THINK OF IT. Joseph went from the pit to the palace in a single day. In the morning he was an imprisoned slave, and by nightfall he was second only to Pharaoh, dressed in fine linen, a golden chain about his neck, and Pharaoh's signet ring on his hand. And more, Joseph would become an astonishing success from day one—ultimately rescuing Egypt and the surrounding lands.

But his sudden elevation was infused with peril. It is one thing to remain believing and God-centered and faithful in the pit; it is quite another to be faithful at the pinnacle. While in the pit, there was only one way for Joseph to look, and that was up—to God. But at the top, looking up was not so natural. The truth was that this newly minted thirty-year-old viceroy of Egypt (a handsome man with acute mental capacity) was in real danger.

But as we look at Joseph here, and at the whole of his life, it is clear that the "Oval Office" never did get to Joseph. He knew who he was and who God was. He knew that there was no power in himself. His own God-infused rhetoric in interpreting Pharaoh's dreams, as he repeatedly asserted variations of "God has revealed to Pharaoh," provides glimpses of his God-focused existence. Joseph stood alone, and above every soul in the world, in his profound understanding of God. No one on earth saw God as he did, or believed in God as he did!

Fellow believers, lay this to heart: *the most important thing about you is what you believe about God*, because what you believe about God will not only determine the way you live; it will determine your eternal destiny. This side of the cross, the revelation of God is immense: "No one has ever seen God; the only God, who is at the Father's side, he has made him known" (John 1:18). "He [Jesus] is the radiance of the glory of God and the exact imprint of his nature, and he upholds the universe by the word of his power" (Heb. 1:3). Jesus is the supreme revelation of God. The revelation is massive, and if you believe it with all your heart, your eternal destiny is sealed, and you will navigate the pits and pinnacles of life knowing who God is and who you are—to the glory of God.

JANUARY 13 · GENESIS 45

The Natural, Supernatural Work of God

R. KENT HUGHES

WHEN JOSEPH CALLED his brothers to him and revealed his identity, it is apparent that he had spent years praying, thinking, and rethinking what had gone on between them, and God had given him wisdom. So, with all eleven brothers assembled, Joseph stripped away the superficial surface of human activity to reveal the hand of God, with four explicit references to God's overriding of the brothers' selling him into slavery: "God sent me before you to preserve life" (Gen. 45:5); "God sent me before you to preserve for you a remnant" (v. 7); "So it was not you who sent me here, but God" (v. 8); and "God has made me lord of all Egypt" (v. 9).

These lines provide a magisterial declaration of divine providence: God works his will in and through the actions of all people, be they good or bad.

Joseph understood that every episode in his life's story, and in that of his brothers, was under God's direct rule—the robe of many colors; the offending dreams of his youth; the sudden appearance of a caravan bound for Egypt; his rise and fall in the house of Potiphar; Pharaoh's imprisonment of his baker and his cupbearer; their strange dreams and Joseph's supernatural interpretation; his summons to interpret Pharaoh's terrifying dreams; the astonishing elevation of Joseph to power in Egypt; the drought in Egypt—all these things were brought about *naturally* by the supernatural work of God in everyday life.

The providential events of Joseph's life have been written large on the canvas of patriarchal history for our benefit. And, if we could pull back the curtain of natural life, we would see that this is the way God works in all of our lives.

The God of Joseph is our God, and therefore everyday life brims with his providential care: "And we know that for those who love God all things work together for good, for those who are called according to his purpose" (Rom. 8:28).

Believe it, and rest in it, because it is eternally true.

JANUARY 14 · GENESIS 49:1-27

The Wine of the Coming King

R. KENT HUGHES

WHEN JACOB ASSEMBLED his twelve sons at his deathbed and blessed them, the transcending blessing went to Judah, as Jacob pronounced upon him an astonishing oracle that established the kingly role of the tribe of Judah until the Messiah would come.

The oracle announced the tribe's dominance (Gen. 49:8), its lion-like might (v. 9), its messianic mission (v. 10), and the future reign of the Messiah:

Binding his foal to the vine
    and his donkey's colt to the choice vine,
he has washed his garments in wine
    and his vesture in the blood of grapes.
His eyes are darker than wine,
    and his teeth whiter than milk. (vv. 11–12)

In that day, there will be such an abundance of grapes that the Messiah will tether his donkey to a choice grapevine with no concern as to his ride helping itself to the vintage. There will be such a surplus of wine that clothes will be washed in it. He, the Messiah, will be altogether lovely.

What dizzying, evocative imagery! And when the Messiah came, he announced the age to come using just this imagery when he changed the water into wine at the wedding in Cana of Galilee. The apostle John tells us, "This, the first of his signs, Jesus did at Cana in Galilee, and manifested his glory. And his disciples believed in him" (John 2:11). For a shimmering, golden moment, donkeys were hitched to grapevines, and wine was as abundant as water. In fact, water was turned into wine! Jesus's disciples knew that the scepter-bearing Messiah would come out of the tribe of Judah. And when he changed the water into wine, his disciples knew that he was the Messiah. It was a day of intoxicating, exuberant abundance—and a taste of the eternal day.

This side of the cross, we know that the path to that joy led through the cross. Jesus, on the eve of the crucifixion, offered a different wine to his followers—the cup of the new covenant in his blood that was shed for his people.

So we understand that the exuberant, endless wine of the kingdom can be ours only through the shed blood of the Lion of the tribe of Judah:

Worthy is the Lamb who was slain,
to receive power and wealth and wisdom and might
and honor and glory and blessing! (Rev. 5:12)

God's Good Plans for His People

R. KENT HUGHES

JOSEPH'S BROTHERS were pathetic. They actually thought that, with Jacob dead and buried, Joseph would avenge himself for the evil they had done to him. Their groveling pleas for mercy wounded Joseph so deeply that he wept. Joseph told his brothers not to fear. He comforted them by letting them know that he had no desire to play God. And more, in addition to his having no desire to stand in the place of God, he discerned God's good providence in their evil: "As for you, you meant evil against me, but God meant it for good, to bring it about that many people should be kept alive" (Gen. 50:20). This is the mysterious heart of the Joseph story: God works good through the sins of wicked people. Indeed this truth informs all of Genesis. God created everything "good" (1:4–31) and then—through all his dealings with his people's sins and machinations before and after the flood—he worked out his good plan.

The prophet Jeremiah voiced this same truth to encourage his people when they were about to go into captivity in evil Babylon: "For I know the plans I have for you, declares the LORD, plans for welfare and not for evil, to give you a future and a hope" (Jer. 29:11). "Welfare" here is the Hebrew word *shalom*. It means peace, or "wholeness"; it means God's good plans for us. God can have no evil thoughts toward his children— no thoughts of calamity. He has never had an evil thought toward a child of his, and he never will. This doesn't mean that his people are shielded from hardship or misery (consider Joseph's life!). What it does mean is that God's plans are never for evil in the believer's life, but with an eye to their well-being and wholeness—always. The apparent evil that we suffer is for our good.

The grand New Testament expression of this truth is, of course, Romans 8:28: "And we know that for those who love God all things work together for good." This means that everything that happens to those who love God (both the good things and the bad) works for their good.

Now, when we add these great texts together (Gen. 50:20 + Jer. 29:11 + Rom. 8:28), when we stack them theologically, they teach that the God of the Bible is so great that he is involved concurrently and confluently in the flow of his children's lives so as to work out his good plans for them.

If you have never understood or believed this, taking it to heart will change your life.

JANUARY 16 · EXODUS 2:1-10

The Birth of a Savior

PHILIP RYKEN

DESPERATE TIMES call for desperate measures. Worried by the rising tide of immigration, Pharaoh tried everything he could to stop the Israelites from flooding over Egypt, until finally he resorted to genocide.

During these desperate times a young Jewish man dared to marry. When the couple celebrated the uniting act of their love covenant, God produced a son, whom they tried desperately to hide from their deadly enemies.

Elsewhere we learn that the child's mother was called Jochebed, and that she was married to Amram (Ex. 6:20). But here in chapter 2 the mother and father are left unnamed, anonymous. They were ordinary people with extraordinary confidence in God. In Hebrews 11—the Faith Hall of Fame—we read that "by faith Moses, when he was born, was hidden for three months by his parents, because they saw that the child was beautiful, and they were not afraid of the king's edict" (Heb. 11:23).

This brave couple feared God more than they feared other people. They were determined to live by faith. But then, raising the next generation is always an act of faith! By faith a husband and wife pray for a child, share sexual relations, and give birth. By faith they train their children and then send them out into the world. Children do not flourish to their full potential unless they are raised by faith, and not in fear.

Raising this particular child was part of God's plan for triumphing over evil and bringing salvation to his people. For when the child became a man—the man called Moses—he would set God's people free.

The story of baby Moses points us toward the birth of a child "worthy of more glory than Moses" (Heb. 3:3). This baby was born in Bethlehem, and he, like Moses, was a beautiful child. Indeed, he was the Son of God incarnate. Like Moses, Jesus was born under a death sentence. Another genocidal maniac—Herod the Great—tried to kill him before he could do his saving work. But God preserved his life in infancy so that he could deliver us from the Egypt of our sin by dying and rising again.

The best way to face our own life-or-death challenges is by trusting this Savior. Trust God as much as Amram and Jochebed did when they put baby Moses in a basket and believed that God would rescue him from Pharaoh.

JANUARY 17 · EXODUS 3

Called by God

PHILIP RYKEN

MOSES WAS IN the wilderness—barefoot at the burning bush—cowering in the presence of a holy God. The man had led his flocks to Horeb, the mountain of God. There he saw a strange sight: a bush that kept burning without burning up.

When he went over to investigate, Moses had a close encounter with the glory of the eternal God. He heard the voice of God speaking to him from the bush, explaining that he had seen the misery of his people Israel and heard their cry to be delivered out of Egypt. Because he remembered his covenant with Abraham, God was coming down to save his people.

At this point the conversation took a surprising turn. Apparently, God would accomplish his salvation through the person and work of Moses. "Come," the Lord said, "I will send you to Pharaoh that you may bring my people, the children of Israel, out of Egypt" (Ex. 3:10).

Here we encounter a paradox of grace: God uses ordinary people—even sinful people—to carry out his saving purpose. Earlier, Moses had tried to save the Israelites all by himself, by dealing with one Egyptian at a time. That attempt was such a complete disaster that Moses had to leave the country. But God used the events of the prophet's life to prepare him to be a great spiritual leader. Now the time of preparation was over, and God was commissioning Moses to lead his people out of slavery.

This is the way God (almost) always does his work: through ordinary people. The eternal, holy Lord accomplishes his purpose through the willing obedience of his faithful servants.

The call of Moses is a reminder that every godly man has a job to do. God's call includes not only our *salvation*, but also our *vocation*—the specific task that God has called us to accomplish for his glory. The God who saves is a God who sends. Thus every Christian man has two callings: first to salvation, and then to service.

What is your calling? Whether you are a preacher or a postman, a banker or a bridge builder, the God of the burning bush has work for you to do. As you do his good work, he gives you the same promise that he gave Moses: "I will be with you" (Ex. 3:12).

River of Blood

PHILIP RYKEN

THE NILE RIVER meant everything to the Egyptians. Thus there was no better way for the God of Israel to show that he was the Lord of Egypt than by turning the river into blood. This was the first of ten plagues, or miraculous "signs and wonders," that afflicted the Egyptians and their gods (Ex. 7:3).

The plagues began with Moses going to the banks of the Nile and waiting for Pharaoh to come and pay homage to the river gods. On this particular day, Moses struck the Nile with the rod of justice and God turned life-giving water into a blood-red river of death. This started a chain reaction: the blood killed the fish, and as they began to decompose, the whole river was putrefied.

To understand how distressing this was for the Egyptians, we have to appreciate how dependent they were on the Nile. The river was the life-blood of their civilization. It enabled them to satisfy their thirst, irrigate their fields, and move their goods from place to place. The land of Egypt was the gift of the Nile.

Since the Egyptians practically owed their existence to the Nile, it is not surprising that they worshiped the great river as their creator and sustainer. Yet with one single blow God punished the Egyptians for this idolatry. Later, when the Israelites marched out of Egypt and Moses tried to explain what God had done, he proclaimed that the Lord had "executed judgments" on their gods (Num. 33:4).

One day God will do the same thing to the gods of our own age. What we count on, what we work for, what we play at, what we dream about—these are the gods we worship. Today most people depend on the economy every bit as much as the Egyptians depended on the Nile. They worshiped the Nile; we follow the stock market. But these are simply two different names for the same god.

Can you imagine what life would be like if our economy collapsed, our drinking water was contaminated, and our grocery stores started running out of food? Yet one day God will glorify himself in every nation the way he glorified himself in Egypt. He will triumph over every false god.

If we trust in other deities for our peace and prosperity, we are bound to be disappointed. But if we place our confidence in God alone as our Creator and Provider, then even when everything else is taken away, we will stand secure.

JANUARY 19 • EXODUS 12:1-28

The Blood of the Lamb

PHILIP RYKEN

ON THE SAME NIGHT that God brought death to every house in Egypt, he also visited the home of every Israelite. He did not come to destroy them but to teach them salvation from sin through the gift of atonement by blood.

Like the Egyptians, the Israelites deserved divine judgment; but unlike the Egyptians, they were saved by grace through faith. What they needed was a sacrifice, which God provided in the form of a perfect lamb. When God saw the blood of the lamb on the doorpost of each house, the angel of death would pass over and the firstborn son would be saved.

The importance of the lamb as a substitute would hardly have been lost on the firstborn son. Once the lamb was chosen, it was kept in the home for four days, during which time the family fed it, cared for it, played with it, and perhaps even named it. In that short time they would have identified with the lamb, so that it almost became part of the family. "This is our Passover lamb," they would have said.

Then the lamb was slaughtered, which was a messy, bloody business. The head of the household took the lamb in his arms, pulled back its head, and slit its throat. Red blood spurted onto the lamb's white wool. "Why, Daddy?" the children would ask. Then their father would explain that the lamb was a substitute. The firstborn son did not have to die, because the lamb had died in his place.

We have a substitute, too, and the sign of our deliverance is the blood of Jesus Christ. When we look at the cross, we see that payment has been made for our sin. The cross is stained with the blood of God's firstborn Son. When God sees this blood, he says, "It is enough. My justice has been satisfied. The price for sin is fully paid. Death will pass over you, and you will be safe forever."

If you had been present for the first Passover, would you have sacrificed a lamb and put its blood on the door? Of course! So, will you trust in the blood that Jesus shed on the cross? God has provided the Lamb who takes away sin, and everyone who trusts in his blood will be saved.

JANUARY 20 · EXODUS 14

Out of Egypt

PHILIP RYKEN

GOD IS NOT MERELY a character in the drama of redemption; he is the author, producer, and director. His grand purpose is to display his glory, and this is what he did in the exodus; he saved his people for his glory.

First, God sent his people into the wilderness, where they were surrounded by an impassable desert, with their backs against an uncrossable sea. Any sound military strategist would have recognized that God's people were trapped. But the whole thing turned out to be a ruse. God was enticing Pharaoh to press what seemed to be a strategic advantage. But once he attacked, his army would be destroyed. Then it would be obvious to everyone that God had planned the whole thing all along. Thus the glory of God's victory came at Pharaoh's expense. God said, "I will get glory over Pharaoh and all his host" (Ex. 14:4).

God used a similar strategy when he sent his Son to the cross. To Satan it must have seemed like Jesus was trapped. God the Son allowed himself to be handed over to sinful men, who stripped him, beat him, and crucified him. At the cross, Satan thought he had the strategic advantage, so he pressed it to the death. But of course this was his fatal mistake. The cross was not a defeat for Jesus, but a victory. By making atonement through the sacrifice of his death, Jesus gained eternal victory over sin, death, and Satan, triumphing over all of them through the cross (see Col. 2:15).

Israel's great escape points us to the greatest escape of all: we are saved from our bondage to sin through the death and resurrection of Jesus Christ. The New Testament describes Christ's saving work in terms of the exodus. Shortly after Jesus was born, his parents fled to Egypt. Their eventual return fulfilled the words of the prophet Hosea: "Out of Egypt I called my son" (Matt. 2:15; cf. Hos. 11:1). In its Old Testament context, this prophecy referred to the original exodus. But Jesus is the perfect Israel, whose death was the ultimate exodus (see Luke 9:31). He is the new Moses, who leads us out of our bondage to sin and into the Promised Land of eternal life. Anyone who believes this gospel "has passed from death to life" (John 5:24).

JANUARY 21 • EXODUS 16

Grumble, Grumble

PHILIP RYKEN

AFTER THEIR MIRACULOUS exodus from Egypt, the Israelites camped by the springs of Elim for several weeks, lingering under the palm trees and taking long drinks of cool water. Then it was time to move on. They were on a spiritual journey—a pilgrimage that reveals the pattern of the Christian life.

The spiritual geography of Israel's exodus from Egypt can be mapped onto the experience of our own souls. Although there are times of refreshing, usually they do not last for long. Soon it is time to head back into the desert, which is a place of testing and spiritual growth.

The Israelites headed deeper into the wilderness. Soon they were tired and hungry, and once again they started to complain. Whining was Israel's besetting sin. It started when Moses first went to Pharaoh and people complained that he was making their job harder instead of easier (Ex. 5:21). They grumbled at the Red Sea, where they accused Moses of bringing them out into the desert to die (Ex. 14:11–12). The grumbling continued more or less for forty years, as they became a nation of malcontents.

Our own complaints are not caused by our outward circumstances; rather, they reveal the inward condition of our hearts. Really, the Israelites had nothing to complain about. They were *not* running out of food, but were confusing what they *wanted* with what they *needed*. This is often the source of our discontent: thinking that our "greeds" are really our needs.

The Israelites also exaggerated the advantages of their former situation. "Remember the good old days?" they said. Looking back with longing on their time in Egypt, they imagined themselves bellying up to Pharaoh's buffet. Yet it is doubtful that, as slaves, they were ever treated so lavishly.

Israel's attitude is a warning against the great sin of complaining. Although they complained to Moses, they were really grumbling against God. By saying that it would have been better for God to let them die back in Egypt, they were really saying that they wished they had never been saved.

We need to be honest about the fact that all of our dissatisfaction is discontent with God. Usually we take out our frustrations on someone else. But God knows that when we grumble, we are finding fault with him. A complaining spirit indicates a problem in our relationship with God.

The irony, of course, is that God always gives us exactly what we need. For the Israelites, this meant manna in the wilderness. For us it means the true Bread of Life, Jesus Christ.

On Eagles' Wings

PHILIP RYKEN

UNDER THE LEADERSHIP of Moses, the Israelites came out of bondage, across the sea, and through the wilderness. Three months later they reached the mountain of God.

The mountain was a place for the people to meet with God, and also for God to speak to his people. "You yourselves have seen what I did to the Egyptians," he said, "and how I bore you on eagles' wings and brought you to myself" (Ex. 19:4).

The beautiful image of eagles' wings is richly symbolic. The eagle is a fierce bird of prey; it attacks its enemies the way God attacked Egypt. It is also a bird of rescue. This is wonderfully portrayed near the end of J. R. R. Tolkien's fantasy *The Hobbit*. When the heroes are surrounded by hordes of vicious goblins, just at the moment when all hope seems to be lost, one of them "gave a great cry: he had seen a sight that made his heart leap, dark shapes small yet majestic against the distant glow. 'The Eagles! The Eagles!' he shouted. 'The Eagles are coming!'"[2]

The wings of eagles depict God's protective nurture and tender care. The same image appears again in Deuteronomy 32, where Moses sings of God's love for his people. In caring for their daily needs in the wilderness, he was "like an eagle that stirs up its nest, that flutters over its young, spreading out its wings, catching them, bearing them on its pinions" (Deut. 32:11).

Eaglets are virtually helpless. They remain in the nest for as many as a hundred days. When it is time for them to fly, the mother eagle disturbs the nest but does not abandon her young. If they experience difficulties on their fledgling voyage, she swoops below them and lifts them back up.

This is precisely what God did for his people in the wilderness: he lifted them up on his mighty wings, providing food, water, and victory in battle. God has done the same for us. He has delivered us from bondage to sin through the death and resurrection of Jesus Christ. Since then, he has carried us on eagles' wings. Every day he provides what we need, and whenever we are in danger of falling, he catches us and lifts us back up.

The Mercy Seat

PHILIP RYKEN

DOWN THROUGH THE MILLENNIA, human beings have constructed many remarkable buildings: the Great Pyramids, the palace at Machu Picchu, the Parthenon, the Taj Mahal, the World Trade Center. But the most important structure ever built was the tabernacle of God.

The tabernacle was not very large. The whole thing would have fit inside any decent-sized church building. Nor was it especially ornate. Although it was beautiful, it was not dazzling. Nevertheless, the tabernacle was the only building ever specifically designed by Almighty God and constructed according to his plan. More importantly, it was laid out in such a way as to teach the plan of salvation.

The most important thing in the tabernacle was the ark of the covenant. This ornate box was the exact place where God would descend to dwell with his people, which of course was the main purpose of the whole tabernacle.

The ark of the covenant was an earthly symbol of a heavenly reality. The cherubim on top of the ark represented the burning angels who worship at God's throne in heaven. The space above the cherubim was left empty, to be filled with the living presence of God. Under the cherubim were two tablets containing the words of the Ten Commandments. In effect, these tablets were placed under God's feet.

There was only one problem with this arrangement: God's people were not able to keep God's law—not perfectly. This is why the lid of the ark, the "mercy seat," was so important. Once a year, the high priest would sprinkle sacrificial blood on the lid of the ark to show that atonement for sin had been made. The sacrificial blood covered transgression by coming between the holy God and his lawbreaking people.

The principle holds true for us as well. If we are to be saved, something has to come between God's perfect holiness and our unholy sin. That "something" is the blood of a sacrifice acceptable to God. This is precisely what Jesus was doing on the cross: he was offering a sacrifice in blood, poured out for sinners. Our mercy seat—the place where atonement was made for our sin—is the cross where Jesus shed his own perfect blood.

JANUARY 24 • EXODUS 33:12–23

This Passing Glory

PHILIP RYKEN

MOSES APPROACHED GOD with two of the most audacious demands that any man has ever made: "Please show me now your ways" (Ex. 33:13) and "Please show me your glory" (v. 18).

In order to lead people effectively, Moses needed to know the mind of God. He didn't want God simply to send down orders; he wanted to know the purpose behind God's plans. To that end, Moses wanted to remain in constant communication with his Maker. This was essential to his leadership as a man of God.

Any man who seeks God's calling should pray the way Moses prayed. We should ask God to give us intimate knowledge of him. The things we do will be successful only if God is in them. Whenever we do something that God has called us to do—whether it is serving in our singleness, learning how to be married, working at a job, or getting involved in ministry—we need to pray that God will show us his way to go about things.

Moses also wanted something more: he wanted to see God's glory. This request was not as imperious as most translations make it sound. In the original Hebrew it comes across more like an entreaty; Moses was saying "Please . . ." Still, it was an audacious request. The prophet was asking to see the splendor and radiance of God.

Mercifully, God did not show Moses the full brightness of his divine glory, because this would have been fatal (see v. 20). But God did consent to show Moses his goodness. In order to protect his prophet from deadly exposure to his radiant glory, God made special arrangements. He put Moses in a cleft in the rock and covered him with his hand until his glory had passed by. Then Moses saw the contrails of God's glory—the luminous clouds that streamed from his divine being. Although the prophet was not allowed to look God in the face, he was able to catch a fleeting glimpse of the back of his glory (v. 23).

Someday we will get to see what Moses wanted to see: the glory of God. We will look Jesus right in the face and will not be destroyed but will be filled with glorious joy. In the heart of every man there is a yearning—yet unsatisfied—to see this promise fulfilled. We know that there is more for us to see, and so we long to gaze upon the beautiful face of Jesus Christ.

JANUARY 25 · EXODUS 40:34-38

When Glory Came Down

PHILIP RYKEN

THE EXODUS WAS all for the glory of God. This theme reaches its glorious climax at the end of the book. The people had seen God's glory in their deliverance from Egypt. They had seen it as well in the fire and smoke on Mount Sinai. But they had not yet seen a close, visible manifestation of God's almighty majesty.

And so, on the anniversary of Israel's exodus from Egypt, God told Moses to set up a tabernacle. Moses set up the tabernacle piece by piece. As each piece was put in place, the suspense built: Would God really come down in glory?

Moses began with the tabernacle itself—the tent of meeting (Ex. 40:34). Inside he put the ark of the covenant, where blood was sprinkled to atone for sin, as well as the fellowship table for bread, the golden lampstand of life, and the altar of incense for prayer. Outside he set up the altar of sacrifice and the basin for cleansing.

Once everything was in place, the only thing missing was the one thing that everyone was waiting to see: the glorious presence of God. Moses could build a tabernacle, but only God could fill it with his glory. And that is precisely what God did. The glory cloud of God descended on the tabernacle, filling that sacred space with brilliant rays of divine majesty.

Everything that Moses saw on that glorious day finds its fulfillment in Jesus Christ. Jesus is our golden lampstand, the source of our light and life. He is the basin of our cleansing, the sanctifier of our souls. He is our Great High Priest, who prays for us at the altar of incense. And he is the blood on the mercy seat, whose atonement reconciles us to God.

Jesus is also the glorious dwelling place of God: "The Word became flesh and dwelt among us, and we have seen his glory, glory as of the only Son from the Father, full of grace and truth" (John 1:14). The Greek word that John uses here for "dwelt" is drawn from tabernacle vocabulary. It is a way of saying that Jesus *is* our tabernacle, full of the glory of God.

We live in the hope of seeing the glory of God in the bodily tabernacle of the risen Christ. After our long journey from life to death, through a wilderness of suffering, we will enter the dwelling place of God and see the glorious person of Jesus.

Restoring Fellowship with God

JAY SKLAR

WE OFTEN USE special ceremonies to show that a person is taking up a new role. In a wedding, the bride and groom begin the ceremony as single people and finish it as husband and wife. The ceremony involves various rites that symbolize the change in role, such as vowing faithfulness to each other and exchanging rings as symbols of their love and commitment.

In Leviticus 8, we have an ordination ceremony that also results in new roles. Aaron and his sons begin the ceremony as laypeople and finish it as ritually holy priests. This ceremony also involves various rites symbolizing the change in role, such as Aaron and his sons putting on priestly uniforms and going through various cleansing rites to bring them into a state of ritual holiness.

But why is this ceremony needed? On the one hand, it shows that the Israelites have a deep need for a holy mediator between themselves and their holy Lord. Their sin and impurity is like a wall that stands between them and God. If they were to try to breach this wall by themselves, the Lord's holiness would consume them just as light consumes darkness. They need holy mediators who can go before the Lord on their behalf and present atoning sacrifices to cleanse them of sin and impurity and restore them to fellowship with God.

It is the Lord himself who commands this ceremony for the Israelites. Why? Because he does not want them to remain in their sin and impurity; he wants them to deal with these things properly so they can have fellowship with him. The Lord's desire in creation was for people to walk with him, to know him, and he therefore does what is necessary to make this possible for sinful and impure people.

By sending Jesus, God demonstrates in the clearest possible way his desire for sinful and impure people to be restored to relationship with him. Jesus is the ultimate and final priestly Mediator, the one who has gone "into heaven itself . . . to appear in the presence of God on our behalf" (Heb. 9:24). And he is the ultimate and final atoning sacrifice, who atoned for our sin and impurity "once for all when he offered up himself" (Heb. 7:27). It is in Jesus, through Jesus, and because of Jesus that we can be restored to relationship with God. Have we committed our lives to him?

JANUARY 27 • LEVITICUS 16

The Day of Atonement

JAY SKLAR

KNOWN IN JEWISH circles as Yom Kippur, the Day of Atonement was one of the most important ceremonies in ancient Israel. It was a once-a-year spiritual housecleaning, a way of making sure that the Israelites' sins and impurities were dealt with properly so that their holy Lord could continue to dwell in their midst.

During the ceremony, sin was pictured in different ways. Sometimes it was pictured as a defiling substance that needed to be cleansed (Lev. 16:11–19) and sometimes as a lethal burden weighing down on the head of the guilty (vv. 20–22). We can identify with these pictures: sin often makes us feel dirty and leaves us feeling condemned.

In both instances, God provided a solution. The defiling sins and impurities of verses 11–19 were cleansed away (vv. 16, 19), and the lethal burden of sin in verses 20–22 was transferred to the head of another who bore it away (vv. 21–22). The parallels to Jesus are clear. By his sacrifice, Jesus has made "purification for sins" (Heb. 1:3), and in his sacrifice, he has offered himself to "bear the sins of many" (Heb. 9:28; see also Isa. 53:11–12). In Jesus, our sin and impurity has been dealt with fully and finally.

What is the proper response? On the Day of Atonement, the Israelites were to "afflict" themselves (Lev. 16:29, 31), which likely refers to fasting (Ps. 35:13). This is something Israelites did as a way of showing humble repentance for their sin (1 Sam. 7:6; Dan. 9:3–5). And they did so because they knew that it did not matter what the priests did on their behalf if they themselves did not look to God in humble and repentant faith. God had provided a solution for sin and impurity, but he also called for a response of faith.

In the same way, Jesus has provided a solution for our sin and impurity, and he has also called for a response of faith. "Come to me, all who labor and are heavy laden, and I will give you rest. Take my yoke upon you, and learn from me, for I am gentle and lowly in heart, and you will find rest for your souls" (Matt. 11:28–29). It is by entering into this yoke that we become truly free, as Jesus himself releases us from the burden of our sin and teaches us to live in fellowship with the God who has made us to walk with him.

Living a Life Reflective of God's Own Character

AARON J. GOLDSTEIN

"HOLY, HOLY, HOLY is the LORD of hosts; the whole earth is full of his glory!" (Isa. 6:3). These are the words of the angelic beings around God's throne, as they emphatically proclaim his holiness. It is this same holiness that is the subject matter at hand. The guiding exhortation for the whole of Leviticus 19 occurs in verse 2: "You shall be holy, for I the LORD your God am holy." That is to say, the instructions in our text are about living holy lives in imitation of a holy God. In fact, each grouping of instructions is punctuated with a common refrain: "I am the LORD (your God)," emphasizing that the life of holiness commanded is in some way reflective of God's own character. The Lord has redeemed his people and is calling them to be set apart by the way in which they embody his values.

Many different values of the Lord are on display here. God shows his concern for the poor by instructing that food that falls to the ground during harvest be left for those in need (vv. 9-10). In a similar manner, we should be quick to share our time and our possessions. God's people are to deal honestly with one another, and those in authority should never use power to abuse those in vulnerable situations, because the Lord never deceives, and he protects the weak (vv. 11-14). Because the Lord himself is the ultimate Judge, our compass of justice and fairness should reflect his own (vv. 15-16). When mistreated, God's people should not respond with hatred and anger (vv. 17-18) but with love for neighbor, because the Lord shows his covenant love to his people despite their unfaithfulness. And in the person of Jesus, God loves to the uttermost those who would crucify him.

This idea of imitating God's holiness is admittedly intimidating, as we are well aware of our personal failings. We must remember, however, that we are not on our own in this task. As Christians, the Holy Spirit dwells within us, continually leading us (Rom. 8:1-17) and producing godly fruit in our lives (Gal. 5:22–25). He is the one who will help us to imitate the Lord, our holy King, in all things. This is what a watching world needs to see—the glory of God's holiness reflected by his people.

Jesus, Our Perfect Sacrifice

JAY SKLAR

MANY CHRISTIANS STRUGGLE to find contemporary relevance in the book of Leviticus, but the truths found here are of utmost importance for us today.

In the first section of this passage, the Lord gives commands about the proper animals the Israelites must bring for sacrifices (Lev. 22:17–25), and in the second, he gives commands about the proper procedure for making the sacrifices (vv. 26–30). The Israelites were to follow these commands in order that they might be "accepted" before the Lord (v. 29), that is, in order that they may experience his grace and favor.

On the one hand, the fact that the Lord would even give the Israelites these commands shows that he wants them to know his grace and favor. He is a King who delights to show these things to the world. Indeed, as the New Testament makes clear, he is a King who would go to the greatest lengths to make his grace and favor freely available by sending Jesus—the ultimate sacrifice, "without blemish"—on our behalf (1 Pet. 1:18–19). At the same time, the very fact that these commands exist also shows that this is a holy King who must be approached on his terms, not our own. For this reason, the New Testament makes it equally clear that it is only in Jesus that we may be accepted by the Lord, because it is only in Jesus that our sins are taken away (John 14:6; Heb. 10:19–22).

In the third section of our passage (Lev. 22:31–33), the Lord emphasizes the importance of obedience in two different ways. First, he reminds the Israelites that he is holy (v. 32), that is, utterly distinct in his power, purity, and love. For this reason alone, the Israelites were to "sanctify" him—acknowledge his holiness—by their full-hearted obedience and love. To do otherwise would be to "profane" the Lord, that is, to deny his holy character and to treat him as an ordinary thing, unworthy of their full-hearted devotion.

Second, the Lord reminds the Israelites that he is their Redeemer, the one who rescued them so that they would be his people and he would be their God (v. 33). Significantly, the Lord makes clear that his redemption is not simply deliverance *from* slavery but also a calling *to* holiness. He is the God who "sanctifies" them, that is, who sets them apart to live holy lives by obedience to his holy commands. The Lord's redemption always involves both deliverance from sin and a call to righteousness (1 Pet. 1:14–20). And what a great privilege it is to reflect the glorious character of this Redeemer into the world, so that the world might know him (1 Pet. 2:9).

JANUARY 30 · LEVITICUS 26

The Lord's Resilient Faithfulness

JAY SKLAR

WHEN A KING entered into a covenant with a people in the days of ancient Israel, he would often list blessings and curses near the end of the covenant document. It is therefore no surprise to find blessings and curses here, near the end of Leviticus, since its laws are part of the covenant that the Lord, the heavenly King, has entered into with the Israelites at Mount Sinai.

The blessings begin with various types of material provision (Lev. 26:4–10). This is no surprise. The Lord has made us material creatures and knows we have material needs. But the blessings peak with the Lord's promise that, "I will make my dwelling among you. . . . And I will walk among you and will be your God, and you shall be my people" (vv. 11–12). Indeed, when we take together all the blessings of verses 4–12, what we have is a return to Eden: the Lord's people, living in a lush land, with all their material needs met, walking in rich fellowship with their heavenly King. All the Israelites need to do is show faithfulness to this King by obedience to his gracious laws.

If they fail to do this, the curses will follow (vv. 14–39). The key word in these curses is "discipline" (vv. 18, 23, 28). A good father does not have children just so that he can punish them, but so that he can raise them to be people of character; when necessary, he will use discipline to correct wrong and harmful ways and to instill good and life-giving ways. In all of this, he has in view their good. Similarly, the Lord's goal with these curses is not punishment for punishment's sake; it is to bring his people back to himself and his life-giving instructions. He has not created us for curse but for blessing.

The chapter ends with a glorious promise that contrasts the Israelites' faithlessness with the Lord's faithfulness. Even after the Israelites are cursed with exile for "spurning" and "abhorring" the Lord's laws (v. 43), once they cry out to him with repentant hearts (v. 40), the Lord will not "spurn" and "abhor" them (v. 44). Instead, he will be faithful to his covenant promises and restore them—to the land and to himself, so that the glorious vision of Eden may be realized.

This chapter therefore serves as a warning: we must hate sin so much that we do not do it and cause the Lord to discipline us for it. But it also serves as an encouragement: if the Lord disciplines us for sin, he does so to bring us back to him, and he will gladly take us back as we turn to him with hearts that mourn our sin and recommit to walking in his ways.

JANUARY 31 · NUMBERS 9:15-23

Making Our Way through the Wilderness

R. FOWLER WHITE

ISRAEL HAD BEEN camped for a year at Sinai, receiving God's law and preparing to march to Canaan. All was now ready and in accord with the Lord's command: the tabernacle (Num. 9:15; Ex. 40:34–38), the priests (Numbers 1–4), and the people (Numbers 5–9). The march was at hand. The people were to proceed just as they had prepared: only at the Lord's command (Num. 9:18, 20, 23). The Lord—the Holy Spirit (Isa. 63:10–14)—would lead his people, dwelling with them in the cloud of glory, the pillar of cloud and fire. When he moved, they were to move; when he rested, they were to rest. In effect, they were to believe God and "walk by the Spirit" (Gal. 5:16). They were to "keep in step with the Spirit" (Gal. 5:25), embracing his promises, trembling at his warnings, and obeying his commands.

Although Israel's march started well, it did not end well. Although God's promise of rest in Canaan had been preached to them, in the years to come they would fail to move as he directed, and so they would fall in the wilderness. As they hardened their hearts in unbelief, their faith would prove to be not a saving faith after all, but only a temporary faith. Later on, David would exhort subsequent generations not to harden their hearts as the exodus generation did (Ps. 95:7–11).

As we in the visible church make our way through the wilderness of this world to the world to come, we too are warned not to imitate that generation's example of disbelief and disobedience. We have had God's promise of rest in a new homeland (the new earth; Rev. 21:1) preached to us. That promise is made good to us in Christ, who is better than Moses, Joshua, and David. And "we have come to share in Christ, if indeed we hold our original confidence firm to the end" (Heb. 3:14).

Knowing these things, let's be sure to "take care, . . . lest there be in any of [us] an evil, unbelieving heart, leading [us] to fall away from the living God" (Heb. 3:12). Let's also "exhort one another every day, as long as it is called 'today,' that none of [us] may be hardened by the deceitfulness of sin" (Heb. 3:13). In other words, let's believe God and "walk by the Spirit." Let's "keep in step with the Spirit," embracing his promises, trembling at his warnings, and obeying his commands.

FEBRUARY 1 • NUMBERS 13:1–14:38

What Kind of Man Will You Be?

R. FOWLER WHITE

THE PEOPLE OF ISRAEL were "this close" to the Promised Land. It was there for the taking—or, we should say, it was "there for the receiving" from the Lord, who was giving it to them (Num. 13:2). And so, at the command of the Lord, Moses sent twelve men, married with children

(14:2–3) and heads of their tribes (13:2–3), to spy out the land. Their specific mission was to assess the prosperity of the land and the strength of its occupants. To fulfill their mission, they were called on to be men of courage (13:20).

So how did their mission go? The twelve spies got the lowdown on the land and its occupants alright. The land was prosperous indeed. And the occupants? The twelve all agreed on certain details: they were renowned for their strength, there were lots of them, and they were living in huge, fortified cities. Beyond those facts, however, the spies were divided in their assessment, and by no small margin. Two of the spies—Caleb and Joshua—saw victory ahead and urged the congregation to go up to Canaan; the other ten spies saw only defeat at hand and urged the people to go back to Egypt.

What was the difference between the Two and the Ten? Why were two men courageous and ten men cowardly? The Two were men of "a different spirit" (14:24): they were men of faith; the Ten were men of fear. The Two, through eyes of faith, praised the surpassing greatness of God (14:8); the Ten, through eyes of fear, only lamented the surpassing greatness of their enemies. The two men of faith took the Lord at his word and saw a future of victory and life in the land; the ten men of fear disobeyed the Lord's word and saw only a future of defeat and death in the land. The fear-filled majority incited the congregation to fear and wickedness in grumbling and rebelling against the Lord and his servants. The faith-filled minority interceded for the fearful, wicked congregation and exhorted them to faith. The Ten led their own generation to death in the desert; the Two would lead a new generation to life in the land.

At the command of the Lord, Moses sent twelve men—husbands and fathers—on a mission. Two were men of faith; ten were men of fear. What kind of man will you be?

High-Sounding Words, Hard-Hearted Apostasy

R. FOWLER WHITE

KORAH AND HIS BAND of 250 malcontents claimed to know who was qualified to enter God's presence: everyone, they said, without exception or distinction. After all, "all in the congregation are holy, every one of them, and the LORD is among them" (Num. 16:3). High-sounding words, but words revealing hard-hearted apostasy.

We learn the reality of the situation in Leviticus: it is, first of all, the Lord who is holy, and his people are called to imitate that holiness (Lev. 11:44; 19:2; 20:26; Num. 15:40). As role models for the people, the priests especially are called to be holy: "The man whom the LORD chooses shall be the holy one" (Num. 16:7).

So Moses saw through the words of Korah and his rebel gang: far from being holy, they were despising the Lord. To Korah the Levite, it was not enough that the Lord had made distinctions between Levites such as himself and the rest of the people. It was not enough that the Lord had granted the Levites a special appointment as his own possession, his tabernacle ministers (Num. 8:14; 18:21). No, Korah wanted what Aaron and his sons had: he wanted the priesthood. He wanted to be a priest, not just an "assistant priest."

And what of Korah's allies Dathan and Abiram? They were dissatisfied with Moses. To them, it was deceptive of Moses to have led the people out of their Egyptian "paradise" into the desert. It was deceptive of Moses *not* to have led the people, as he had promised, into that new paradise in Canaan. No, Dathan and Abiram would not be fooled by Moses any longer: they would not have Moses make himself a prince over them. They wanted what Moses had: they wanted leadership, and they wanted it without any conditions attached.

Korah and his apostate companions were motivated not by God's glory but by selfish ambition. They were disqualified from the priesthood and from acting on behalf of God's people. Consumed in God's fiery judgment, the men became a warning to the people that, for them to qualify to enter God's presence, they must find that priest who had humbled himself and sought God's glory at the expense of his own. Thanks be to God, we find just such a priest in Jesus (Phil. 2:5–8; Heb. 5:1–10). In him alone we are holy, qualified to enter God's presence.

FEBRUARY 3 · NUMBERS 21:4-9

Dead to Egypt, Alive to God

R. FOWLER WHITE

A NEW GENERATION was emerging in Israel. Yet how "new" were they, really? Impatient with their progress, they were repeating the same old grumblings. They protested God's purpose. They detested his provisions. So the Lord had to do as he had done before: he took them to the woodshed. He sent them serpents whose bite was fatal to the faithless. Happily, however, divine chastisement yielded its proper fruit. The new generation did something new. They learned obedience through what they suffered. They confessed their sin to the Lord, and he provided them a remedy: a snake on a pole. So where was the remedy in that?

For one thing, the snake reminded those with the eyes of faith that they were dead to Egypt. They remembered the serpent as a symbol of Egyptian supremacy, a supremacy celebrated in the legendary cobra image in Pharaoh's crown. Yet Israel had an even better memory too: the Lord had overpowered that Egyptian snake in the exodus. The snake on a pole, then, was a signal that Israel was dead to Egypt.

But there was more. A snake on a pole also reminded those with the eyes of faith that they were now alive to God. That serpent emblem echoed the story of Adam, in which they learned the origins of their sin, death, desert wanderings, and new life. Death in the desert was the wage of human sin, not the failure of divine power. In fact, new life was God's gift through a Son of Man who would crush the serpent's head. Even the pole that lifted the snake was itself an Egyptian symbol of

God's life-giving power. A snake on a pole, then, spoke of the Lord as the giver of new life.

The snake on the pole was not magical, however. The healing to which it bore witness had to be received by faith. Those bitten and dying could live only as they gazed with the eyes of faith on the snake and saw the Lord their healer (Num. 21:9; Ex. 15:26).

Sometimes we Christians find ourselves taken to the woodshed just as our ancestors under Moses were. When that happens, look back in faith to that serpent on the pole and realize anew that you are dead to the world and alive to God in Christ. See there your healer, the Son of Man lifted up to bring you eternal life: "As Moses lifted up the serpent in the wilderness, so must the Son of Man be lifted up, that whoever believes in him may have eternal life" (John 3:14–15).

Training God's People to Look to the Future

R. FOWLER WHITE

BY THIS POINT in Numbers, it is painfully obvious that the redemption and covenant that Moses brought were not enough to overcome the nation's sin. They were no longer slaves to Pharaoh, but they were still slaves to sin. They were required to obey God, but they were unable to do so. Numbers tells us then that if the people were ever to have freedom from sin and new hearts for obedience, they needed to find a prophet greater than Moses. Numbers tells us even more, however, for the Levites were ineffective too. Their sacrifices simply could not put away sin once and for all. So, if the people were ever to finish with sin and sacrifice, they needed to find a priest greater than the descendants of Levi. Clearly, the people's need went well beyond Moses and Levi, so God was training them to look to the future for a better prophet and a better priest.

Then, in the story of Balak and Balaam, we see God training his people to look to the future not only for a better prophet and a better priest, but also for a better king. Despite their evil scheming, God over-rules Balak and Balaam to create Israel's future according to his promise: "I see him, but not now; I behold him, but not near: a star shall come out of Jacob, and a scepter shall rise out of Israel" (Num. 24:17). This future king will put himself in harm's way to make the people secure and pure for fellowship with God in the land. This king will fulfill God's promise to the patriarchs to bless them with dominion (v. 19), just as the nation itself had fulfilled God's promise to bless them with descendants, and the gift of Canaan will fulfill his promise to bless them with land. All this will be according to grace. At every point, God will show Israel that it owes its blessedness not to its own faithfulness but to the faithfulness of others. In faith, then, they should look to the future for the coming prophet, priest, and king.

Later Scriptures encourage us as we see God fulfill Balaam's predictions, especially under David and finally under David's son, Jesus. Indeed, like David and the other kings, Jesus put himself in harm's way for God's people. As Christians, we rejoice supremely in Jesus, for he suffered even death for us and, through death, he conquered sin, surpassing not just all other kings, but all other prophets and priests as well.

FEBRUARY 5 · DEUTERONOMY 4:29-31

Marveling at Mercy

JASON S. DEROUCHIE

LIKE THE IDOLS they would someday worship (Deut. 4:28), the majority of Moses's listeners had eyes that didn't see and ears that didn't hear. They were ignorant of God's greatness, blind to his glory, and deaf to his word (29:4; cf. Ps. 115:4–8). Their rebellion and unbelief had led to four decades of discipline in the wilderness (Deut. 1:26, 32, 35), and even most of those from the new generation were stubborn, unbelieving, and rebellious (9:6–7, 23–24). Their obstinacy would lead to enactment of the covenant curses, climaxing in exile from the Promised Land (4:25–28; cf. 30:1; 31:16–17, 27–29).

How amazing, therefore, is Moses's promise of new covenant redemption (4:29–31; cf. parallel promises in 30:1–10). After experiencing curse in the latter days, the people would seek the Lord and actually find him (4:29). They would return to God and obey his voice (v. 30). Verse 31 declares the reason why: "For the LORD your God is a merciful God." Mercy stands at the forefront of Yahweh's character (Ex. 34:6). It identifies God's deep compassion for his people and often expresses the withholding of a judgment that they deserve. Without mercy, there would be no new covenant—no victory, no hope, no life. But mercy has come, and Moses stresses in Deuteronomy 4:31 that this new covenant mercy means that God's presence as provider and protector is now sure ("He will not leave you"), that his wrath is now appeased ("[He will not] destroy you"), and that both Jews and Gentiles can rejoice in salvation. God has remembered "the covenant with your fathers" that through Abraham all the world would be blessed (i.e., justified; Gen. 12:2–3; 22:18; cf. Gal. 3:8, 14).

Like Israel of old, we begin our lives with a sensory disability: we are spiritually ignorant, blind, and deaf. We need God to overcome our illness. If you have sought the Lord and found him (Deut. 4:29), then marvel at his mercy. If, "according to his great mercy," God has caused you "to be born again to a living hope" (1 Pet. 1:3), then make much of his mercy. If you find yourself today worshiping something worthless, then plead for more mercy, and by these same mercies present your body "as a living sacrifice, holy and acceptable to God" (Rom. 12:1).

The decisive cause of all new covenant relationship is blood-bought mercy. Stand in awe today of the mercy-filled *gifts* of justification (Rom. 3:24), sanctification (Rom. 6:17, 22), and eternal life (Rom. 6:23). "The Father of mercies and the God of all comfort" has entered into our world in Christ (2 Cor. 1:3). May we marvel at mercy—such free, undeserved, yet costly love.

Why Must I Obey?

JASON S. DEROUCHIE

HAVE YOU EVER heard a child ask, "Why do I have to obey?" Moses expects that parents who love and obey God (Deut. 6:4–6) and are calling their children to do so as well (v. 7) will get this kind of question (v. 20). In these verses, he shows us how to reply.

First, *we should recall the context of obedience* (vv. 21–23). Specifically, we should (1) stress our desperate situation apart from God; (2) highlight God's saving activity that freed us; and (3) emphasize that God is faithful to the end.

We see the first two steps in the statement, "We were Pharaoh's slaves in Egypt. And the LORD brought us out" (v. 21). God delivered Israel from bondage through the exodus. They were slaves; God was the Savior. Following God is a response to past grace, and heeding God's rules is about freedom, not slavery. The same is true in a deeper way in the new covenant, as Jesus our Savior frees us from slavery to sin and God's wrath through the cross.

Next, "He brought us out from [Egypt], that he might . . . give us the land" (v. 23). While many Israelites, by their unfaithfulness, forfeited the opportunity to enter the Promised Land (2:14–15), God himself is always faithful both to bless and to curse. With God is life and victory; apart from him is death. In Christ, all who believe find real rest now (Matt. 11:28) and have the sure hope of complete rest in eternity (Heb. 4:1–13). This fact should motivate our loyalty.

Second, *we should recall the benefits of obedience* (Deut. 6:24). Moses motivates obedience by emphasizing the blessings that it brings: "The LORD commanded us to do all these statutes, to fear the LORD our God, for our good always, that he might preserve us alive, as we are this day" (v. 24). Like the circle of blessing that surrounds a child who obeys and honors her parents (Eph. 6:1–3), there is a deep connection between heeding God's word and enjoying life: "Man does not live by bread alone, but

. . . by every word that comes from the mouth of the Lᴏʀᴅ" (Deut. 8:3; cf. Matt. 4:4; Deut. 32:47).

Jesus's perfect obedience secures our pardon, purchases God's promises, and provides the power to enjoy life (Rom. 8:1–4, 13; 2 Cor. 1:20). When your children ask you the point of following God, point them to God's past grace and faithfulness and remind them of the blessings enjoyed by all who say no to sin and yes to God.

FEBRUARY 7 · DEUTERONOMY 7:17–26

Defeating Fear

JASON S. DEROUCHIE

Tʜᴇ Lᴏʀᴅ ᴄᴀʟʟᴇᴅ Isʀᴀᴇʟ to "devote . . . to complete destruction" the nations inhabiting the Promised Land (Deut. 7:1–2; cf. 20:17). These pagans and their wares would easily become snares to Israel, turning them from God and making them his enemy (7:4, 26; cf. 8:19–20; 20:18). Failure to overcome obstacles to God-centered living is a serious and dangerous offense against the Lord, who deserves all our love (6:5).

In this passage, the new generation of Israelites is facing the same "greater and taller" people who had terrorized their parents (1:28), and Moses anticipates that some in his audience will fear defeat (7:17). Moses calls for a fearless attack (v. 18a) and clarifies the nature and reason for boldness. First, *a valiant assault starts by recalling God's past grace and his future promises* (vv. 18–20). For Israel, this meant remembering (1) how Yahweh saved them by defeating the greatest earthly power (vv. 18b–19a) and (2) that he who freed them from both shackles and flood in Egypt would certainly secure victory for them over their present lesser foes (vv. 19b–20). The old covenant pattern of redemption and provision finds its climax in Christ, in whom every promise is now "Yes" for Christians (2 Cor. 1:20): "He who did not spare his own Son but gave him up for us all, how will he not also with him graciously give us all things?" (Rom. 8:32).

Second, *we gain confidence in battle from knowing that our God, who is with and for us, is both able and willing to fight victoriously* (Deut. 7:21–24).

Israel's present help was "a great and awesome God" (v. 21b), and he would "clear away these nations" (v. 22a). While victory would not come immediately (v. 22), it would be complete, for Yahweh would fight for them (vv. 23–24). Like Israel, Christians must believe that the great and awesome God exists and that he rewards all who earnestly seek him (Heb. 11:6). Faith in God fuels courage.

Christians stand in a different redemptive period than Moses. Physical wars are not part of the church's mission. This is because Christ's kingdom is not yet of this world (John 18:36), and it expands spiritually through suffering, not by a sword (Mark 10:45; Col. 1:24), and by preaching, not by a pistol (Matt. 28:19–20; Acts 1:1–8). Nevertheless, Christians are engaged in a spiritual battle against the same enemy forces that derailed both the Canaanites and the Israelites (2 Cor. 10:3–6; Eph. 6:10–12; 1 Pet. 5:6–11), and we move ahead confident that Christ is greater and has already triumphed (1 John 4:4; Col. 2:15). Faith in God's faithfulness helps defeat our fears (1 Thess. 5:23–24).

FEBRUARY 8 · DEUTERONOMY 9:6

No Longer Stubborn

JASON S. DEROUCHIE

WE CAN BE slow learners. After decades of discipline, Israel should have known that God takes sin and his glory seriously and that they should too. Yahweh's "consuming fire," which either incinerates sinners or ignites holiness (see Lev. 9:23–10:3), was about to destroy the "wicked" nations of Canaan (Deut. 9:3–5). Nevertheless, Israel was ignoring the gravity of the moment, for the same "wickedness" that had been apparent in them forty years previously remained unchanged. The lack of God-dependence evident at Mount Sinai (vv. 12–21) and in the initial journey to Kadesh (vv. 22–23) continued, for they were still "stubborn" (v. 6) and "rebellious against the Lord" (vv. 7, 24).

This obstinacy revealed the people's unrighteousness: "Know, therefore, that the LORD your God is not giving you this good land to possess because of your righteousness, for you are a stubborn people" (9:6). Righteousness is about keeping everything in its right order, which means putting God above everything else. Fearing, following, loving, and serving the Lord (10:12–13) would have proven Israel's righteousness (6:25; cf. 24:13), but their failure to do so revealed a heart problem requiring surgery: "Circumcise therefore the foreskin of your heart, and be no longer stubborn" (10:16).

The internal nature of stubbornness and ignorance makes it impossible for us to perform the necessary operation on our own hearts. So without the divine Surgeon mercifully healing (29:4), Israel's fate would be the same as that of their pagan enemies (see 31:27–29).

Amazingly, God promised that, on the other side of judgment, he would accomplish for his people what they could not do on their own. He would remove their callousness, empower their love, and bring them new life: "When all these things come upon you, the blessing and the curse, . . . the LORD your God will circumcise your heart and the heart of your offspring, so that you will love the LORD your God with all your heart and with all your soul, that you may live" (30:1, 6; cf. 4:30–31). Moses had equated Israel's stubbornness with ignorance, unrighteousness, and uncircumcised hearts (9:3, 6; 10:16); now, he says, with God's new covenant heart surgery, they will enjoy knowledge, righteousness, and healing.

Let us rejoice today, for the great Healer of all spiritual disability has come in the person of Jesus. By his Spirit, he circumcises our hearts (Rom. 2:29; Col. 2:11), helps us to know him (John 17:3; Heb. 8:11), declares us righteous (Rom. 5:19; Phil. 3:9), and empowers us to live righteously (Rom. 8:4; 1 John 3:7). "Let us offer to God acceptable worship, with reverence and awe, for our God is a consuming fire" (Heb. 12:28–29).

Love God and Live

JASON S. DEROUCHIE

DEUTERONOMY PORTRAYS life and blessing as being conditional: "the blessing, if you obey . . . and the curse, if you do not obey" (Deut. 11:27–28; cf. ch. 28; 30:15). Moses says that God "keeps covenant and steadfast love with those who love him and keep his commandments . . . and repays to their face those who hate him" (7:9–10; cf. 5:9–10). How should Christians think about God's conditional love?

First, we must distinguish God's *unconditional elective* love from his *conditional covenant* love. God sets his elective love on certain individuals before they are even born or do anything good or bad (Rom. 9:11–13, 16). He also chose and set his affection on Israel, not because of anything about them but only because he loved them and was remaining true to his promises to the patriarchs (Deut. 7:7–10). In contrast, God's conditional covenant love assumes that a relationship exists that requires sustained loyalty in order to enjoy the covenant Father's kindness instead of his severity (Rom. 11:22; cf. Rom. 8:28).

Second, Jesus underscores the priority of love by describing Moses's call to "love the Lord" (Deut. 6:5) as "the great and first commandment" (Matt. 22:37–38). Jesus also stresses that those who love him will follow him (John 14:15, 21); and, like Moses, he emphasizes, "If you keep my commandments, you will abide in my love, just as I have kept my Father's commandments and abide in his love" (John 15:10). As such, Jude urges, "Keep yourselves in the love of God" (Jude 21), while also stressing that God keeps every individual he electively loves (Jude 1).

Third, while the nation of Israel's hard-heartedness doomed them to destruction (Deut. 31:27, 29), God promised a day when he would generate in his people the love he commanded (30:6). This happens through Jesus, whose perfect obedience fulfills for us the law's demands (Rom. 5:18–19; Col. 2:14) and thus secures for us every spiritual blessing as we await our full inheritance (Eph. 1:3, 13–14). God justifies us in Christ (Rom. 3:24;

8:1–3) in order to give us his Spirit, by whom we are enabled to fulfill the law of love (Rom. 8:4; 13:8–10), putting "to death the deeds of the body" and meeting the covenant conditions for life (8:13; cf. 6:22). While "the Lord [still] disciplines the one he loves" (Heb. 12:6), we rest in the certainty that every promise of blessing is already "Yes" for us in Christ (2 Cor. 1:20), and we now know that *nothing* in all creation "will be able to separate us from the [covenant] love of God in Christ Jesus our Lord" (Rom. 8:39).

FEBRUARY 10 · DEUTERONOMY 26:16–19

Fickle Promises and a Faithful God

JASON S. DEROUCHIE

EARLIER IN DEUTERONOMY, Moses declared that loving God (Deut. 6:4–5; 10:12) and their neighbors (10:16–19) was *what* God called Israel to do. Now in chapters 12–26 the various "statutes and rules" clarify *how* they are to do that (12:1; 26:16). The central thrust of this unit is captured in 16:20: "Righteousness, and only righteousness, you shall follow, that you may live" (author's translation). Our God, who is passionate about right order, wants his people to display righteousness in three spheres: righteousness in community worship (12:1–16:17), righteousness in community oversight (16:18–18:22), and righteousness in daily community life (19:1–26:15). By keeping the "statutes and rules" with all their heart and soul (26:16), Israel will show that they love God with all their heart and soul (6:5).

Drawing his second sermon to an end, Moses now details in 26:16–19 the formalizing of the Moab covenant between Yahweh and Israel. Verse 17 describes the people's declaration, and verses 18–19 describe Yahweh's response. The people first assert their allegiance to Yahweh as their God, and then they spell out the implications of their commitment: to follow his ways, to remain faithful to his instruction, and to heed his voice (v. 17). Yahweh in turn expresses his expectation that they should live as his treasured possession and follow his commands, and then he promises that such living will result in their being elevated in the eyes of the nations and set apart as a holy people (vv. 18–19).

Four decades earlier at Mount Sinai, Yahweh made a comparable commitment (Ex. 19:4–6) and the people a similar promise: "All that the LORD has spoken we will do" (Ex. 19:8). But while Yahweh is "a God of faithfulness and without iniquity" (Deut. 32:4), history had proven Israel's faithlessness, and it would do so again (31:27, 29; 2 Kings 17:13–15; Rom. 11:7–8). How fickle human promises can be, and how much we need God's grace in order to live out our commitment to love and righteousness (Deut. 29:4)! Apart from such grace, right order in corporate worship, in the public square, and in our daily lives is impossible.

We should celebrate that Christ has secured our pardon and that his Spirit bears the fruit of love and faithfulness in us, helping us by faith to become who we could not be on our own (Gal. 2:20; 5:22–23). The Lord promises that he will complete the work that he has begun in us (Phil. 1:6), and we can rest today, trusting a faithful God who has committed to sanctify us completely, readying us for the coming of our Lord Jesus Christ (1 Thess. 5:23–24).

FEBRUARY 11 · DEUTERONOMY 30:19-20

God Is Your Life

JASON S. DEROUCHIE

"I HAVE SET BEFORE you life and death, blessing and curse. Therefore, choose life . . . for [God] is your life" (Deut. 30:19–20). Moses's logic here is breathtaking. May the Lord help us feel and respond appropriately to these truths.

First, spiritual life does not happen on its own (see John 3:36; Eph. 2:1–3). We must *choose* life. In the Sermon on the Mount, Jesus notes, "For the gate is wide and the way is easy that leads to destruction, and those who enter by it are many. For the gate is narrow and the way is hard that leads to life, and those who find it are few" (Matt. 7:13–14). Impurity, dishonesty, selfishness, arrogance, laziness, rash responses, and the like— these characterize the natural, easy way, but they lead to death. In contrast, purity, honesty, service, humility, discipline, and self-control distinguish the more difficult way that leads to life, and such traits are realized only when God by his Spirit creates new desires (Gal. 5:16–17).

Second, the choices we make reveal our deepest longings and wants. Desires drive action, for our highest motivations always move us one way or another. Sin results when temporary, empty pleasures become more desirable than pleasing God. With this in mind, notice how, in Deuteronomy 30:19–20, Moses does more than call for a decision. He also motivates people to choose life by grounding his charge in the most awe-inspiring truth: to choose life is to gain God, *"for he is your life."* "The Rock, his work is perfect. . . . A God of faithfulness and without iniquity, just and upright is he" (32:4). This one who stands distinct above all else (4:35; 33:26) and who controls all things (4:39; 10:14)—this one becomes ours. Supreme power and worth wrapped in tender care . . . only for those who choose life.

Third, Moses clearly believes that the quest for joy, life, and blessing is itself not sin (see Rom. 2:7). The sin comes when we settle too quickly for fleeting, empty pleasures instead of embracing lasting pleasures of substance, all of which are found only in relation to God (see 2 Pet. 1:4; 1 John 2:16–17). "You make known to me the path of life; in your presence there is fullness of joy; at your right hand are pleasures forevermore" (Ps. 16:11). Paul stresses his conviction that he will glorify Christ most when Christ is his deepest satisfaction, both in life and in death (Phil. 1:20–21). As such, he declares, "Indeed, I count everything as loss because of the surpassing worth of knowing Christ Jesus my Lord" (Phil. 3:8). I exhort you today, *choose life and gain God.*

FEBRUARY 12 · DEUTERONOMY 32:39

The Hope of Resurrection

JASON S. DEROUCHIE

MOSES'S SONG in Deuteronomy 32:1–47 captures in poetic verse what the rest of the book declares: Israel had "dealt corruptly" with God (32:4–6), making him jealous by idolatry, arousing his anger and the promise of destruction (vv. 21–22). Nevertheless, for the sake of his reputation (vv. 26–27),

God "will vindicate his people and have compassion on his servants, when he sees that their power is gone" (v. 36). Yahweh said the song itself was to stand as a lasting "witness for me against the people" (31:19). In it Moses proclaims "the name of the LORD" (32:3), describing Yahweh's character as it will show itself in the people's history of sin, destruction, and restoration (see Rev. 15:3–4).

In Deuteronomy, the Old Testament's most common terms for exile are remarkably scarce. Instead, the terms used relate to extermination and death. For example, God warns Israel that he will "destroy [them] from off the face of the earth" (Deut. 6:14–15) and that they will "perish" (8:19–20; 11:16–17; 30:17–18) if they persist in idolatry. While passages like 4:29–31 and 30:1–10 underscore that a remnant will continue to exist physically in exile, the people as a national entity and the old covenant they embody will die. Anything that continues will be substantially discontinuous with the past.

Yahweh declares in 32:39,

> See now that I, even I, am he,
>   and there is no god beside me;
> I kill and I make alive;
>   I wound and I heal;
>   and there is none that can deliver out of my hand.

The Lord's use of the word "heal" after "wound" highlights that the ordering of elements within the pairs is significant. God portrays his curse as death and injury, whereas the restoration blessing that follows is nothing less than resurrection and healing. Deuteronomy 32:39 marks Scripture's first clear witness to the new covenant as rebirth, inaugurated by resurrection from the dead.

Because only "in [Abraham's] offspring shall all the nations of the earth be blessed" (Gen. 22:18), the world's hopes rested on God's willingness to "make alive" after Israel's death-judgment. Christ's resurrection marks him as "the beginning, the firstborn from the dead" (Col. 1:18), "the firstfruits of those who have fallen asleep" (1 Cor. 15:20). New creation dawns in Jesus (2 Cor. 5:17), and we who were "dead in our trespasses" are "made alive" together with him (Eph. 2:5; cf. 1 Cor. 15:22). Thank God for such great love.

God Is with Us!

SAM STORMS

THE YEAR WAS 1406 BC. Moses was dead. The reins of leadership in Israel had passed to Joshua. Knowing the challenges he faced, we could understand if he would hesitate or perhaps even ask that God find someone else more worthy of the task. But he embraced the call of God on his life and the opportunity at hand because he knew that God was with him. The divine promise was unmistakable: "Just as I was with Moses, so I will be with you" (Josh. 1:5; cf. v. 9).

Joshua likely had to fight against the fear of being overshadowed by Moses's acknowledged greatness. Feelings of inadequacy, even inferiority, must be resisted. "Who am I," Joshua must have often asked himself, "that I should be expected to lead the people into the land?" I suspect that Moses would have reminded his young protégé of what God had said to him at the burning bush: "I will be with you" (Ex. 3:12). And now this *same God* reassured Joshua with the *same promise*.

Whereas God is always and everywhere present in his divine being, we can also count on the manifestation of his abiding presence in times of difficulty and challenge. What God promised to Moses, to Joshua, and to us as well, is the unshakable and liberating knowledge that we belong to him and nothing will ever separate us from his love. This is the reassuring promise that we are the recipients of his saving favor and grace, based not on anything we have done but solely on what he does. This is the experiential joy of feeling his nearness and knowing that, no matter how dark it may become, no matter how perilous the circumstances may be, no matter how powerful the opposition we face, God is at our side (Psalm 23). This is the gracious guarantee that nothing will come our way that God cannot providentially turn for our ultimate good and his glory. This is the unshakable assurance that, whatever God requires us to do, he will more than abundantly supply the strength and power to obey.

In the New Testament book of Hebrews we are exhorted to live free from the love of money and to be content with what we have, because what God said to Joshua he now says to us: "I will never leave you nor forsake you" (Heb. 13:5b). The God who sustained Moses and Joshua, the God who entered our world in the person of Jesus and died and rose again for our sins, this very God "will never leave" us or "forsake" us. "So we can confidently say, 'The Lord is my helper; I will not fear; what can man do to me?'" (Heb. 13:6).

It's stunning to consider what we could accomplish for the sake of God's kingdom if we lived daily in the strength and assurance of that simple truth: God is with us.

FEBRUARY 14 · JOSHUA 2

The Remarkable Reach of God's Saving Grace

SAM STORMS

THE GREATEST LESSON for us in the remarkable story of Rahab and the Israelite spies is not whether it is ever permissible to lie (Josh. 2:4–7; cf. Heb. 11:31; James 2:25). The most important thing to see is that God's saving grace can extend beyond the borders of Israel, into the depths of the worst of human sin and depravity, and save even the vilest of sinners, even you and me!

According to the apostle Paul, Rahab, as a Gentile living before the time of Christ, was "separated from Christ, alienated from the commonwealth of Israel and [a stranger] to the covenants of promise, having no hope and without God in the world" (Eph. 2:12). Moreover, she was a woman in a man's world, vulnerable and without rights, unmarried and childless. Worse still, she was a prostitute and a polytheist, until she encountered the one true God of Israel.

Rahab's story reminds us that God often works in mysterious ways. Clearly he had revealed himself to Rahab apart from the expected means.

What she knew about Yahweh would have been useless, however, had it not been for the Holy Spirit giving her eyes to see and a heart broken with repentance. The story also teaches us how important it is to move beyond first impressions. Rahab would likely have been offensive to the moral convictions of the spies. Their instinctive reaction would be to distance themselves from someone so immoral and pagan, yet they saw in her the evidence of God's Spirit at work.

Some might think that God had altogether abandoned a woman given to such chronic sexual sin. The damage to her soul from repeated encounters with total strangers would lead many to write her off as a reprobate for whom there was no hope. But we must never conclude that someone is "too far gone" and thus beyond the possibility of salvation. If we had known Rahab and were familiar with her lifestyle and her religious beliefs, would you or I have ever bothered to take the risk and invest the time to speak to her of redemption and forgiveness and the grace of God?

Regardless of what your life has been up until this very moment, regardless of how far you have strayed, or how deeply you have immersed yourself in sensuality, rebellion, or self-indulgence, the Lord God of Israel calls upon you to come to him. He redeemed a harlot like Rahab and orchestrated history in such a way that she became the great-great-grandmother of King David, from whom Jesus descended according to the flesh.

Amazing grace indeed!

FEBRUARY 15 • JOSHUA 3

The God of the Unlikely Time

SAM STORMS

OFTEN OUR SCHEDULE and God's seem out of sync. He acts earlier than we had expected, or later than we had hoped, or when it seems most awkward and inconvenient. The result is that sometimes we are impatient with God or choose to act impetuously, while on other occasions we are lazy and inactive.

I suspect that's how the Israelites must have felt as they stood on the banks of the Jordan River, prepared to enter the Promised Land of Canaan. They learned a lesson there that all of us must learn sooner or later. The lesson is simply that the God we love and serve is often the God of the unlikely time.

When the two spies returned from Jericho, Joshua received the news he had been waiting for: "And they said to Joshua, 'Truly the LORD has given all the land into our hands. And also, all the inhabitants of the land melt away because of us'" (Josh. 2:24). But God then forced them to stand and watch the raging waters of the Jordan River for three days! The torrent was unabated. They could only look across the rising waters into Canaan, on the other side. The river seemed utterly impassable. Their long journey to the Promised Land appeared to have ended just short of their goal. Why did God bring them to the edge of the river and compel them to look with longing and frustration at the land he had promised to their forefathers? His reason seems clear: to drive home to their hearts the seeming impossibility of tomorrow!

God compelled them to wait three days to allow their feelings of helplessness and hopelessness and inadequacy to reach the highest level possible. He forced them to wait until the waters of that river had risen to such a height that virtually all hope had been washed away.

We often find ourselves asking, What does God expect of me? What does he want? The answer is that he wants a people who will faithfully respond to his call to act in the pursuit of his promises, even at the most unlikely time.

Perhaps you are only moments away from seeing the fruition of a dream that you've nurtured for years. Perhaps there is some massive problem that is on the verge of being solved, or a fractured relationship that is close to being healed, or a lifelong prayer that may finally be answered. God may be speaking to you in much the same way that he was speaking to the Israelites, saying, "Stand up! Be firm in your faith! The day of inheritance is here. The moment for fulfillment has arrived. As difficult as it may be for you to understand, I've actually chosen this challenging and demanding moment precisely because it affords the greatest opportunity for my power and love to be seen when I finally step into the situation and bring it all to pass!"

Who Really Fought the Battle of Jericho?

SAM STORMS

WE READ IN HEBREWS 11:30 that "by faith the walls of Jericho fell down after they had been encircled for seven days." The walls of this formidable city fell because Joshua and the people of Israel honored God by trusting him to act on their behalf. Whenever God is honored, God acts.

Their faith certainly wasn't a blind leap into the dark. This couldn't have been an ill-founded act of desperation on their part. So what exactly did they believe?

First, the ark of the covenant was the place of God's presence, and it appears no fewer than ten times in Joshua 6. Above all else, the Israelites put their confidence in the unassailable truth that God was with them, to which the ark bore witness.

Second, they trusted in God's power. I grew up singing a silly little song that went something like this: "Joshua fit the battle of Jericho, Jericho, Jericho; Joshua fit the battle of Jericho, and the walls came a tumblin' down!" Technically speaking, that's not true. Joshua never raised so much as a hand against Jericho. He never launched an arrow or even threw a rock in the direction of the city. *God* "fit" the battle of Jericho! It was his power and his alone that accounts for what we read in this chapter.

Third, they had faith in God's promise. According to Joshua 6:2, the Lord said to Joshua, "See, I have given Jericho into your hand, with its king and mighty men of valor." This was simply one more affirmation of the promise that God originally gave to Abraham, that he would grant Israel entrance into Canaan and possession over its cities, including Jericho.

It was their faith in God's presence and power, and above all else in God's promise, that accounted for the victory. Despite overwhelming odds and against all reason, contrary to what could be seen from a purely human point of view, they clung tenaciously to God's promise that he had already given them Jericho.

Whether it be a seemingly overwhelming obstacle, a relational struggle, or a circumstance that defies explanation, much of life comes down to a question of faith. As with the people of Israel, so also with us today, the issue is whether or not we will invest our faith and hope in God's presence (that he will never leave us nor ever forsake us), in his power (that we serve a God who is able to do exceedingly, abundantly beyond all that we ask or think, according to the power at work in us), and in his promises to us in Christ (that our God cannot lie or fail to fulfill his word).

FEBRUARY 17 · JOSHUA 10:1–15

"Big God-ers" vs. "Little God-ers"

SAM STORMS

SOME TWELVE YEARS following his graduation from Princeton Theological Seminary, Donald Grey Barnhouse, pastor at Tenth Presbyterian Church in Philadelphia, was invited to preach in chapel. His former professor, Robert Dick Wilson, sat attentively on the first row. After Barnhouse had concluded his message, Wilson approached him and said,

> If you come back again, I will not come to hear you preach. I only come once. I am glad that you are a big God-er. When my boys come back to the seminary, I come to see if they are big God-ers or little god-ers, and then I know what kind of ministry they will have.

Barnhouse was confused and asked him to explain himself:

> "Well," said Robert Dick Wilson, "some men have a little god, and they are always in trouble with him. He can't do any miracles. He can't take care of the inspiration of the Scriptures and their preservation and transmission to us. They have a little god, and I call them little god-ers. Then there are those who have a great God. He speaks, and it is done. He commands, and it stands fast. He knows how to show himself strong on behalf of those that fear him. You have a great God, and he will bless your ministry. You are a big God-er!"[3]

How big is your God? Is he big enough to create the universe and uphold it by the word of his power, and to providentially govern its direction and bring about the consummation of all things in precisely the way that he planned? Or do you worship and love and serve a tiny god, a pygmy god, a diminutive deity, a wee little god who easily fits in your back pocket or in a box of your own making, a so-called god who is unsure of himself and can't guarantee that anything he desires to accomplish will ever ultimately be brought to pass?

Joshua was a big God-er! He knew that his God was big enough to work all things together for good, big enough to defeat the enemies of Israel and to grant Israel their inheritance in the Promised Land.

You can't understand Joshua 10 if you aren't a big God-er. Little god-ers are confused by the events in this chapter. Big God-ers, on the other hand, love Joshua 10. If you know God to be great and big and immeasurable and majestic, such miracles are but the fringes of his power, the mere droplets in an ocean of divine omnipotence.

Are you a big God-er? If so, come to him with big requests. Come to him with impossible tasks. Come to him asking for the unlikely. Come and ask!

FEBRUARY 18 · JOSHUA 23

Cling to the Lord Your God

SAM STORMS

THE TEMPTATION to forget God is always present. But there is a way to maintain one's devotion to the Lord. Joshua's counsel in 23:6–11 is especially helpful and can be summarized using four *As*.

First, give *attention* to God's word (v. 6). God never blesses disobedience. A mind filled with Scripture can critically evaluate secular society and can see through the empty values of the modern world and resist assimilation.

An unmistakable sign of impending abandonment of God is a diminishing respect for the authority of his word. A disregard for biblical inspiration is always the first step toward spiritual rebellion. Joshua is talking about "keeping" and "doing" God's word, not simply giving tacit consent to its claims. We must be "strong" to keep it and do it and not deviate from it either to the right or to the left.

Second, *avoid* pagan influence (v. 7). Note the relationship between verses 6 and 7. The way one avoids being shaped after the image of pagan society is precisely by keeping and doing God's word. There will always be a temptation to think the world has it better than we do (see Ex. 23:13). But if you have Scripture on your lips and the praise of God's name in your mouth, you won't have room or time for even so much as acknowledging anything else.

Third *attach* yourself to God (Josh. 23:8). The word "cling" in this verse is translated "hold fast" or "cleave" in Genesis 2:24, where God says a man should leave his father and mother and "cleave" to his wife (compare its use in Deut. 10:20–21; 11:22; and 13:4).

Envision a young child holding fast to his father's hand. To "cling" to God is to stay so close to him that no sin can get between you and him. To "cling" to God is to strategically plan for time alone with him for prayer and praise and the study of his word. To "cling" to God is to trust his promises, to seek his favor, to care only for his approval and not for that of men, to invest time in his service, and to always keep his praise on your lips (Ps. 63:7–8).

Finally, cultivate a deep *affection* for God in every way (Josh. 23:9–11). "Be very careful . . . to love the LORD your God" (v. 11). The emphasis is on a relationship of intimacy: "I am yours and you are mine!" God is not just God. He is "your" and "my" God. His passion for us is undying.

Although the enemies we face today are not those that Joshua and the people of Israel encountered, the strategy for confronting them remains much the same: Be *attentive* to God's word. *Avoid* pagan influence. *Attach* yourself to God. Cultivate a deep *affection* for him.

The Urgency of Commitment

SAM STORMS

JOSHUA 24 IS ALL ABOUT the urgency of commitment: to one's family; to truth and moral virtue; and above all else, to God.

We should note a few things about making a commitment to God. First, you must choose. Straddling the fence and wavering between options is impossible. There is no such thing as neutrality when it comes to your relationship with God. Indecision is a decision! It's all or nothing. These words from Joshua are a call for undivided loyalty and complete commitment.

Second, you must choose for yourself. No one can make this choice for you. Joshua couldn't make it on behalf of the Israelites. Some try to live vicariously through their pastors, thinking that, if a respected leader is totally committed, that means they are as well, since they attend that particular church. That's also why, when a pastor or leader fails, such people may suffer irreparable spiritual and psychological damage. You can't serve the Lord on someone else's coattails.

Third, although everyone eventually reaches the age when they must choose for themselves, Joshua also took responsibility for his entire family. Men, you are not responsible for, nor do you have the power to determine, whether or not your children believe and pursue God. But you do have an obligation to lead them and teach them and explain the gospel to them. It isn't your business to save them, but it is your calling to put them in an atmosphere at home and in the church where *God* can save them. Some of you stand alone for God in your family. Your wife may mock you, despise you, and even ultimately walk out on you. Your children may never embrace the Christian faith. But God is calling you, no less than he called the Israelites, to commit yourself wholeheartedly and unreservedly to him.

Finally, we should take note of Joshua's determination. Paraphrasing verse 15, it is as if he says (and may we do so as well), "No matter what anyone else does, even if it means standing alone, God can count on me. I

75

will not succumb to the pressure of the majority. I will not sacrifice faith for comfort. I will not exchange commitment for popularity. I will not abandon God to curry the favor of men. I will not serve the gods of materialism and self-indulgence or of personal preservation and convenience. So let it be known: as for me and my house, we will serve the Lord."

Suffering, Disobedience, and Gospel Amnesia

MILES V. VAN PELT

THE BOOK OF JUDGES represents the "Dark Ages" for God's Old Testament covenant people. It was a time of great spiritual, economic, and political oppression. It was also a time of tremendous confusion. God had kept all his promises to his people (Josh. 21:45), but they were still suffering and experiencing hostility from the surrounding nations. The sentiments of this time are well expressed by the judge Gideon: "Please, sir, if the LORD is with us, why then has all this happened to us?" (Judg. 6:13).

Gideon's question is important, and it is one that we have all asked amid our own suffering and hardship. Why us? Why me? Where is the Lord in all this suffering? If we listen carefully to the text, our questions may be answered.

First, God's people were suffering because of their own disobedience, which had fractured their covenantal relationship with God (2:2, 20). Second, Israel's disobedience was due to spiritual amnesia. They had forgotten the Lord their God and all the wonderful works he had done (v. 10). Third, God's people were suffering because God loved his people and desired to bring them to repentance and obedience (vv. 4–5, 22). This severe mercy was designed to restore the covenant relationship, not to obliterate it: "It is for discipline that you have to endure. God is treating you as sons. For what son is there whom his father does not discipline?" (Heb. 12:7).

The evidence of God's mercy came in the form of judges, who were raised up by God to deliver his people from oppression, to remind them of God's great saving works, and to promote covenant fidelity (Judg. 2:18). But when each judge died, Israel quickly returned to their disobedience and idolatry, and the cycle began all over. The good news is that Jesus has finally and forever broken this cycle of death and disobedience by experiencing death *for our* disobedience. He is now the ever-living Judge who sits at the right hand of the Father (Heb. 10:12; 1 Pet. 3:22), claiming our obedience and promoting our perseverance. Do you desire obedience? Then remember his gospel!

FEBRUARY 21 • JUDGES 4

The Strength of Weakness

MILES V. VAN PELT

THINGS HAVE BECOME so bad in Israel that Deborah, a woman, must lead and bring God's word. Barak appears to be a coward and refuses to enter into battle unless accompanied by Deborah. And then, finally, the enemy is defeated by the deception and trickery of yet another woman, Jael. Have the men wimped out? Have they abdicated their role as leaders? Is Israel suffering from a lack of male headship? No, but if you are thinking such thoughts, you may have missed the point of the story.

Israel is once again suffering because of their sin. Because they had done evil in the eyes of the Lord (Judg. 4:1), the Lord sold them into the hand of their oppressors (v. 2), which was designed to provoke their repentance, as indeed it did (v. 3). The lesson that the Lord was trying to teach is that he alone is God and thus worthy of our undivided worship. To teach this lesson, the Lord sets out to save his people from their oppression in a way that will instruct both their head and their heart.

Against the great chariot hoard of Jabin and Sisera, the Lord raises up two women and a man to free Israel from twenty years of oppression. The Lord delights to work in and through human weakness. He alone saves his people, and he alone is worthy of our worship. The Lord delivers (v. 14), and the Lord goes out to battle our foe (v. 15). These statements are not figurative; they represent reality. The problem, however, is that sin has blinded us to reality.

77

In order to save them from their spiritual blindness, God once again works to deliver his people in a remarkable way. The deathblow to the enemy is delivered by a housewife, Jael, who crushes the head of Sisera by driving a tent peg through his skull. This should remind us of Genesis 3:15, where God promised to similarly conquer our ultimate foe for us. Only he can save us from sin and Satan.

The strength to lead does not come from within us. No, it comes from resting in the power, strength, and authority that the Lord wields on our behalf. As it is written, "'My grace is sufficient for you, for my power is made perfect in weakness.' Therefore I will boast all the more gladly of my weaknesses, so that the power of Christ may rest upon me. For the sake of Christ, then, I am content with weaknesses, insults, hardships, persecutions, and calamities. For when I am weak, then I am strong" (2 Cor. 12:9–10).

Transforming Fear into Worship

MILES V. VAN PELT

"NOT TO US, O LORD, not to us, but to your name give glory" (Ps. 115:1). The Lord is jealous for the honor of his splendor, and he desires that his people be captivated and transformed by the wonder of it. In order to press this reality deep into our hearts, he uses three hundred men armed with torches, clay pots, and rams' horns for trumpets. The Midianites outnumbered this meager band of ill-equipped soldiers by over four hundred to one (Judg. 8:10), not including the innumerable camel cavalry (7:12). But Israel's victory was quick. At the sound of trumpets, smashing jars, and a great shout (v. 20), the Midianite soldiers were thrown into a frenzy and destroyed themselves (v. 22). God's people did not raise a sword but stood by as God taught them an old lesson: "Fear not, stand firm, and see the salvation of the LORD, which he will work for you today. . . . The LORD will fight for you, and you have only to be silent" (Ex. 14:13–14).

Why does God save in this way? Why does he place his people in difficult or even impossible situations only to save them in ways that are humanly impossible? The answer is, so that we might know, really know, and trust, deep down, that the only one who can save God's people, either in everyday life or from ultimate death, is God himself. There is no salvation apart from God alone, lest we boast, saying, "My own hand has saved me" (Judg. 7:2). Everything else is idolatry, a form of self-salvation.

When God saves, he leaves no doubt in the mind of his people that he has done for us what we could not do for ourselves. When we are weak, he is strong. And when we come to know in the core of our being that God alone is our refuge and strength, our fear is transformed into worship (7:10, 15), and our idols can finally be dislodged from our hearts. The suffering and hardships of this world are temporary but full of purpose. They discipline and instruct us, train us, and cause us to long for that day when they will vanish like the mist and vapor that they really are.

FEBRUARY 23 · JUDGES 16:23-31

Salvation in Death

MILES V. VAN PELT

HE WAS A NAZIRITE from birth and for life (Judg. 13:4–5; cf. Num. 6:1–21). He was empowered by the Spirit of the Lord to judge and save Israel in the darkest of days (Judg. 13:25; 14:6, 19; 15:14). He was misunderstood by his family, betrayed by women, and given over into the hands of the enemy. He was raised up by God, a savior of the people, but the people would not have him. Samson was born into this world to suffer and die in order to show God's people the cost of their salvation and the power of his grace. The text is clear. Samson's greatest victory came with his death (16:30).

Consider how the New Testament reflects upon Samson and some of his fellow judges. They were men "who through faith conquered kingdoms, enforced justice, obtained promises, stopped the mouths of lions, quenched the power of fire, escaped the edge of the sword, were made strong out of weakness, became mighty in war, put foreign armies to flight" (Heb. 11:33–34). And why would men like this endure hardship, mocking, imprisonment, and even death? "So that they might rise again to a better life" (Heb. 11:35). In other words, they recognized that they, like us, are aliens and strangers on this earth, citizens of an eternal kingdom yet to be revealed. The key to this life is found in the next life.

And so let us embrace the testimony of Samson and run the race now set before us. How, you ask? By "looking to Jesus, the founder and perfecter of our faith, who for the joy that was set before him endured the cross, despising the shame, and is seated at the right hand of the throne of God" (Heb. 12:2). Like Samson, Jesus suffered many things, was rejected by his people, and was handed over to the enemy (Mark 8:31). And like Samson again, Jesus's greatest victory came in death. But unlike Samson, Jesus rose from the grave in order that he might impart life to his people. If you long for the power of this resurrection life, then embrace the death of this ultimate Judge, who has "abolished death and brought life and immortality to light through the gospel" (2 Tim. 1:10).

FEBRUARY 24 · RUTH 1:1-18

Hesed Love

PAUL E. MILLER

THE "HIDDEN" WORD that ties the book of Ruth together is *hesed* (translated in 1:8 as "deal kindly"). *Hesed* means covenant love. When you "do *hesed* love" you commit yourself to the object of your love no matter how that person treats you. Why? Because your love is not based on that person's attitude toward you but on your commitment to him or her. So if your wife (or friend) is cranky, you don't retaliate by withdrawing or lashing out. Your response to your wife is not based on how she treats you. It is love without an exit strategy. It is a love like that which God showed us in Christ.

We can't look to the world around us and hope to find this sort of love in plentiful supply. *Hesed* love is a rare commodity today, and the only perfect expression of it is found in the love that led to the cross of Christ. This is why Paul told husbands to love their wives "as Christ loved the church and gave himself up for her" (Eph. 5:25).

Hesed love separates the men from the boys. Literally. Nothing defines a man more than his commitment to endure in love. When things don't work out for a boy, he takes his marbles and goes home. But a man stays. *Hesed* love bears the weight of integrity—our words and our life match. So if you commit to love a woman in marriage, you bear the cost of that no matter what. That's when you leave the boy behind and the man emerges.

The only way you can love this way—loving without the promise of love in return—is to be hidden in the shadow of God's wings. That's what Boaz noticed about Ruth: "Under [God's] wings you have come to take refuge" (Ruth 2:12). Boaz noticed Ruth's faith, her living dependence on the God of Israel. God's *hesed* love for us drove him to the cross—that is the power for our *hesed* love. Although this love is beyond the capacity of man by nature, the energizing presence and power of the Holy Spirit makes it possible.

FEBRUARY 25 · RUTH 1:19–2:18

The Cost of Love

PAUL E. MILLER

EVERYONE LOVES RUTH'S covenant of love to Naomi: "Where you go I will go . . ." (Ruth 1:16). Countless couples have used it for their wedding vows. All well and good, but what happens if the other person stops loving you? What happens when your love becomes only one-way?

After Ruth makes that stunning commitment, she immediately begins to bear the weight of love. For starters, how about a thank you from Naomi for one of the greatest, most beautiful commitments of love anyone has ever made? Nope. Just painful silence (1:18). What about being introduced as Naomi walks with you through the gates of Bethlehem? Nope. More silence, as the pain intensifies (1:19). What about thanks to God for this amazing commitment of Ruth's, so that Naomi is not alone? No. Nothing there, either. Naomi just rails against God even as Ruth stands there, right next to her (1:20–21). What about some help the next day when Ruth goes out to get some food? No, she just sits there (2:2). What about some guidance as to what field to go to, maybe even some background information on powerful relatives who might help? Nothing. Nada. You're on your own, Baby.

Ruth cheerfully and without bitterness bears the weight of living with a depressed and at times bitter old woman. She shows us how not to be ruled by our feelings, by our desire for comfort. There is something oddly attractive about not living for your feelings. It is actually freeing not to be buffeted by how other people treat you. No longer are you ruled by the other person's response, but by Christ.

If this sounds impossible and far beyond our reach as men, it is! But such weakness on our part need not lead to despair, for we have the promise of an indwelling Holy Spirit who is at work in us to equip us and empower us to love in ways that this world knows nothing of. In this way, the beloved is blessed, and all glory goes to God.

FEBRUARY 26 · RUTH 4:13-17

Goel or Golf

PAUL E. MILLER

THE WOMEN GATHER around Naomi as she holds her new grandson, Obed. They call him a *redeemer*. The birth of this baby means that Naomi's family line is restored. She is no longer cut off from Israel. Her life has meaning and purpose . . . not to mention that her great-grandson will sit on the throne of Israel! All because of this little redeemer!

The book of Ruth actually describes a chain of redeemers: Ruth redeems Naomi (by committing to her), Boaz redeems Ruth (by caring for her in the field), Naomi redeems Ruth (by helping her get married), Boaz redeems Ruth (by marrying her), and finally Obed redeems Naomi.

Every male Israelite was a potential redeemer or (in Hebrew) a *goel*. *Goels* personified God's law. They showed his love at a local level. So if a family member got into debt and was at risk for being enslaved, a *goel* could buy back that person. If someone lost his property, a *goel* could buy it back. The law just sits there. A *goel* doesn't. He moves out into problems and fixes them. Jesus, as he traveled around Galilee, was the ultimate *goel* for Israel, healing the sick, caring for the poor, and loving the unlovely.

Now Jesus calls us to continue his chain of love, to be *goels* for the world. Sure, golf is a great way to relax, and relaxation is a form of Sabbath rest, critical for a healthy life. But we can inhale the spirit of the age and build our free time around golf or boating or travel. You are not your own. You have been bought out, redeemed by the world's greatest *goel*, Jesus of Nazareth. The price he paid for you is literally out of this world. So building your life around golf (or the equivalent) is not an option for you. Others can. You can't. God is calling you, like Boaz, like Jesus, to seek and to save. So look for people in need: a disabled man without a job; a young couple with an old, broken-down car; a young family struggling to make ends meet. Take them to lunch. Listen. Pray. Soon an idea, a plan, will begin to form, and you'll begin the work of redeeming. Go, *goel*!

FEBRUARY 27 • 1 SAMUEL 1:1–2:11

Waiting on the Lord

RYAN KELLY

MANY PSALMS SPEAK of *waiting on the Lord* (e.g., Psalms 31; 37; 38; 39). That phrase isn't found in 1 Samuel 1:1–2:11, but the idea is scattered throughout. Hannah, of course, is waiting on the Lord for a son. But she is, in many ways, representative of all the godly in Israel amid troubled, spiritually barren days. The ending verse of Judges sums up both the sinful chaos of Israel at the time and the anticipation of what might be around the corner in God's redemptive plan: "In those days there was no king in Israel. Everyone did what was right in his own eyes" (Judg. 21:25). There was no righteous rule among the people; and yet, a righteous ruler was something God had promised long ago (Gen. 49:10; Deut. 17:14–20).

As 1 Samuel begins, we are just barely introduced to Israel's current leadership, Eli the priest and his two sons (1 Sam. 1:3). It is not until later, in chapter 2, that we learn of the sons' gross wickedness and their father's weak passivity (2:22–25). These are dark days. Thus, we also read of God's coming judgment on this "worthless" priesthood (2:27–36). God will tear down before he builds anew.

Back to Hannah and her son, Samuel. As 1 Samuel unfolds we find out that it isn't Samuel who will be the long-awaited, promised king of Israel. But he will be integral to these transitional days as God "brings low and . . . exalts [and] raises up the poor from the dust . . . to make them sit with princes" (2:7–8). This, from Hannah's prayer, seems unusually grand and far-reaching for the occasion. But even more than thanking God for a miraculous son or an end to barrenness, Hannah envisioned God's coming judgment and salvation. She foresaw that God "will give strength to his *king* and exalt the horn of his *anointed*" (2:10). Not coincidentally, that's almost identical to how 2 Samuel draws to an end. King David exults, "Great salvation he brings to his *king*, and shows steadfast love to his *anointed*, to David and his offspring forever" (2 Sam. 22:51).

Hannah waited on the Lord. In his timing and in his way, God began to bring his promises to pass. Of course, such grand promises awaited even further fulfillment almost a thousand years later in David's greater Son, Jesus. That's why Mary praised God in similarly grand and far-reaching ways when she received news of her miraculous child (Luke 1:46–56). And yet, still today, God's people must again "wait for the revealing of our Lord Jesus Christ" (1 Cor. 1:7), who will come again to bring all of God's promises to their full and final completion. Wait on the Lord!

FEBRUARY 28 • 1 SAMUEL 3

The Word of the Lord

RYAN KELLY

THE ONLY THING worse than God not speaking is when he speaks words of inescapable judgment. Let's begin with the first part: God not speaking. That is how 1 Samuel 3 begins: "the word of the LORD was rare in those days; there was no frequent vision" (1 Sam. 3:1). Like the four hundred years of prophetic silence before John the Baptist, this was an age when God was eerily silent but was about to speak.

When God did speak to Samuel, in 1 Samuel 3, it is understandable that the young boy would be unaware that it was the Lord who called for him. More problematic is that old Eli was rather slow to wonder whether the Lord could be speaking to Samuel. Eli was Israel's senior priest, and yet the word of the Lord was rare, in those days, even to him. Proverbs 29:18 says, "Where there is no prophetic vision the people cast off restraint." They do whatever is "right in [their] own eyes" (Judg. 21:25). If God doesn't speak, we stray; we perish.

But as God begins to speak once again in 1 Samuel 3, it is not good news but judgment. Eli's house (his family) will come to an end "because his sons were blaspheming God, and he did not restrain them" (1 Sam. 3:13). Eli is commendable for his persistence in learning what God spoke to Samuel (v. 17), but his response to the message of imminent judgment is one of sad acceptance, if not characteristic passivity: "It is the Lord. Let him do what seems good to him" (v. 18). And yet, the Lord will indeed do what seems good to him; the next chapter will record the devastating fulfillment of the prophecy (4:10–18). Make no mistake: God's word is sure, whether promising salvation or judgment.

But the judgment of Eli's house was not merely a judgment on Eli's sin. Remember, "The Lord kills *and brings to life*; . . . he brings low *and he exalts*" (2:6–7). He was doing more than one thing at once. He was tearing out the old and beginning something new. He was now proclaiming through Samuel not just a word of judgment on wayward priests but a fresh word of hope to all Israel. The Lord "revealed himself to Samuel at Shiloh by the word of the Lord. And the word of Samuel came to all Israel" (3:21–4:1).

How good it is when God speaks! How good it is that he *has* spoken to us so fully and clearly in his word. May we, like Samuel, daily say, "Speak, for your servant hears" (3:10).

The Problem of God's Presence

RYAN KELLY

DESPITE THE HOPEFUL return of "the word of the LORD" (1 Sam. 3:21–4:1), the rest of chapter 4 is beyond bleak. The Philistines trounce Israel in battle, wiping out her priests and taking away the ark (4:10–18). Israel had presumed that the mere presence of the ark ensured God's help and victory (4:5). But God was teaching them that his ark was far from a good luck charm. Indeed, he was teaching both the Philistines and the Israelites that there could actually be a *problem* when God's presence is in your midst (5:1–7:2).

The Philistines placed the captured ark in the temple of one of their gods, Dagon, as a trophy of the "defeat" of Israel's God. But the living God will not be mocked. Dagon was found face down before the ark the next morning and then headless the second morning (5:3–4). These were not coincidences but signs of God's judgment: "The hand of the LORD was heavy against the people . . . , and he terrified and afflicted them with tumors" (5:6). Thus, the Philistines asked themselves, "What shall we do with the ark . . . ?" Off to Gath with it, some suggested (5:8). Then, to Ekron (5:10). Finally, after multiplying havoc at each stop, back to Israel it went (5:11)—as though this were some sort of terrifying game of hot potato. In the end, God proved that "all the gods of the people are worthless idols" (Ps. 96:5). Further, *he* trounced the Philistines—in their land and without a single Israelite to help. Hannah had foretold it so well: "Not by might shall a man prevail. The adversaries of the LORD shall be broken to *pieces*; against them *he* will thunder" (1 Sam. 2:9–10).

The Israelites themselves learned similar lessons. The men of Beth-shemesh "rejoiced to see" the ark return (6:13). They celebrated, even memorialized, its return. But God "struck some of the men" when "they looked upon the ark" (6:19). Seventy men were killed. The people mourned and asked themselves questions reminiscent of the Philistines' questions: "Who is able to stand before the LORD, this holy God? And to whom shall *he* go up away from us?" (6:20). So they sent their God away for "some twenty years" (7:2).

The living God is no good luck charm, no victor's trophy. Nor will he be gazed upon with mere curiosity. He will not be trifled with. "Among those who are near me I will be sanctified, and before all the people I will be glorified" (Lev. 10:3). Without the blood of Christ, we too would wish to send God away before he destroyed us. His presence would be a huge problem. But Jesus has provided the way (Heb. 10:19–23). So draw near!

MARCH 2 • 1 SAMUEL 8

A King, but What Kind?

RYAN KELLY

WHAT WAS WRONG with Israel's cry for a king? After all, God had promised Abraham, "Kings shall come from you" (Gen. 17:6). The promise to Judah of a future ruler was even more specific (Gen. 49:10). Further, recall that the book of Judges ended with the summary statement that Israel's sinfulness was owing to a void of godly leadership: "In those days there was no king in Israel" (Judg. 21:25). Hannah's prayer, too, anticipated a *king*, an *anointed* one coming in God's strength (1 Sam. 2:10). The prophet Samuel temporarily filled a void of godly leadership in Israel (1 Samuel 3–7). But then we come to 1 Samuel 8 and read of a genuine problem: faithful Samuel is now old, and his sons (and successors) are not faithful (vv. 1–3). Once again, a sad vacuum of godly leadership looms on the horizon. So, from one angle, the elders' cry for a king is simply a desperate attempt to fix an all-too-common problem in the Old Testament: faithful men die, and their sons do not always walk with God.

Of course, that is far from the whole picture of 1 Samuel 8. God himself states explicitly that the people's demand for a king is a rejection of *him* as king (v. 7). They desire a king "like all the nations" (v. 5), a king who will "go out before us and fight our battles" (v. 20). This is in stark juxtaposition to the claim in the previous chapter that "till now *the* LORD has helped us" (7:12).

A king was indeed part of God's plan for Israel, but he would have to be one "whom the LORD your God will choose," one who did not acquire things for himself, who feared the Lord and kept his law (Deut. 17:15–20). In other words, he was to be a king *not* like the nations' kings. The kings of the nations *take* and *take* and *take* from the people. Did you notice that repeated theme in Samuel's warning (1 Sam. 8:11–17)? And yet Samuel's stern threat falls on deaf ears as the people continue to demand a king of their own making (vv. 18–19). In judgment, God will give them exactly what they've demanded (see chs. 9–10).

What Israel needs is *a man of God's own choosing*—one who will insist that "the Lord saves not with sword and spear. For the battle is the LORD's" (17:47). Or, even better, they need a king who will come "not to be served but to serve, and to give his life as a ransom for many" (Mark 10:45). Even today, God's people desperately need the reminder to trust *him* at all times—not princes, not chariots, not human strength, not human wisdom (see Pss. 20:7; 118:9; 146:3).

MARCH 3 · 1 SAMUEL 12

A People for Himself

RYAN KELLY

MUCH OF THE OLD TESTAMENT contrasts God's covenantal faithfulness with his people's unfaithfulness to him. First Samuel 12 is no exception.

This chapter is like a prophetic cosmic courtroom. Samuel simultaneously plays both defendant and attorney, calling on the people to "testify against" him if he has been unfaithful to them (12:3). With the Lord as witness, the people acknowledge that Samuel has indeed not been unfaithful (vv. 4–5). The prophet is vindicated. He is, therefore, fit to put the people on the stand before the Lord ("stand still" in v. 7 is literally "present yourselves").

Samuel builds his case against the people by recounting the key instances of God's faithfulness in history (vv. 7–8), similar to psalms like Psalm 78. Alongside the stories of God's faithfulness are laid those recurring cycles of the people's forgetfulness, God's chastisement, their eventual cry to God for help, and God's answer to prayer with deliverance (1 Sam.

12:9–11). Israel's most recent rejection of the Lord, in favor of "a king . . . like all the nations" (8:5), is one in a long sequence of periods when the people forgot their God and feared the wrong thing (this time it was the Ammonites they feared; 12:12).

Through the miraculous sign of an immediate, serious storm (during the dry months of harvest), God confirms Samuel's word to the people (vv. 16–18). To all this, the people respond seemingly well: they confess their sin and ask for prayer (v. 19). Yet, how many times in Israel's long past has a moment of spiritual sanity proved temporary? So there is an element of uncertainty regarding this new king and the people under him (notice the "if you" language in vv. 14–15, 25). What is not uncertain, however, is the Lord's commitment to his great name and, by extension, his unswerving commitment to his people: "the LORD will not forsake his people, for his great name's sake, because it has pleased the LORD to make you a people for himself" (v. 22).

As God's people today—millennia later, under a new and better covenant (see Hebrews 8–10)—how much more can we attest to God's astounding covenantal faithfulness! We, all the more, must "consider what great things he has done" (1 Sam. 12:24). Indeed, we must not forget who he is, what he has promised and performed, and to what he has called us as his people. We must not fear the wrong things—"Only fear the LORD and serve him faithfully" (v. 24). We must not "turn aside after empty things that cannot profit or deliver" (v. 21). Or as the apostle John simply put it, "Little children, keep yourselves from idols" (1 John 5:21).

MARCH 4 • 1 SAMUEL 14:1–23

The Lord Saved Israel That Day

RYAN KELLY

UPON FIRST READ, the first half of 1 Samuel 14 seems very encouraging for Israel. After all, Israel wins a rare victory against the Philistines (compare with ch. 4); Jonathan models tremendous faith; and in the end, God gets the glory (14:23). However, something is not right here.

Jonathan's confidence in God (14:6) stands in stark contrast to the severe lack of faith his father, Saul, showed in the previous chapter. Greatly outnumbered against the mustering Philistines (13:5–7), Saul grew fearful and impatient, taking the priestly duties into his own hands to expedite a blessing from God (13:8–13). Yet, this one act of disobedience meant that God had now placed an expiration date on Saul's kingdom (13:14). Chapter 13 ended with the still-looming threat of the Philistines, who not only still greatly outnumber Israel's army but also have an abundance of cutting-edge weaponry, while the Israelites have "neither sword nor spear" (13:19–22).

Such military economics are no problem for God, and hence no problem for Jonathan in chapter 14. But this contrast between father and son continues throughout the chapter. We see Saul staying put with his six hundred men (14:2) while Jonathan is engaging the Philistines with only a young armor-bearer at his side (v. 6). Why? "It may be that the LORD will work for us," Jonathan claims in unpresumptuous-yet-bold faith, "for nothing can hinder the LORD from saving *by many or by few*" (v. 6). The numbers matter not. So two men sneak up, and twenty Philistines fall (v. 14). God then shakes the ground and induces "a very great panic" (v. 15). Without any mention of how or why, "the tumult in the camp of the Philistines increased more and more" (v. 19). Even more mysterious, "every Philistine's *sword* was against *his fellow*, and there was very great confusion" (v. 20). We're not told how, but we surely know who's behind it. God turned the mass and might of the Philistine army against itself. Again it proves true: "Not by might shall a man prevail" (2:9).

Don't forget about Saul in all of this. He eventually joins Jonathan in battle, but only after he sees Philistines falling like dominoes. He's following, not leading. Even worse, he calls for the ark when he realizes Jonathan is missing (14:18) but quickly waves off the ark when he sees clear signs of a Philistine defeat (v. 19). He looks for the Lord when he's desperate, but waves him off when all seems well. Repeatedly, Saul proves to be a man who walks by sight, not by faith. May the opposite increasingly be true of us (2 Cor. 5:7).

A Man of God's Own Choosing

RYAN KELLY

THRICE NOW WE HAVE read of God's rejection of Saul's kingdom and of another who would eventually reign in his place (1 Sam. 13:13–14; 15:26–28; 16:1). Saul was "the people's choice," so to speak, a king of their own making. The Lord had told his people before they ever entered the land that their future king would be one "whom the LORD your God will choose" (Deut. 17:15). That's exactly what's happening in 1 Samuel 16. "I have provided *for myself* a king," God tells Samuel (16:1). But who will it be? What kind of king is this?

God's choice is one that surprises even Samuel. Surveying Jesse's sons, Eliab (the oldest and likely the tallest) clearly stands out. Samuel thinks, "Surely" this is "the LORD's anointed" (v. 6). But, no—not Eliab, nor any of the seven sons presented to Samuel. There is one more son, but Jesse didn't even think to mention him without some prodding from Samuel (v. 11). The son in question is the youngest, which can also mean "smallest" in Hebrew. When Saul was first introduced, his unparalleled stature was stressed: "From his shoulders upward he was taller than any of the people" (9:2; repeated in 10:23). He looked like a king who would "go out before us and fight our battles" (8:20).

David, by contrast, not only is the youngest/littlest of eight but also has the lowly task of keeping sheep. No doubt he still smells like sheep when he's introduced to the prophet. And yet, "this is he," God tells Samuel (16:12). And so David is anointed king-elect right there "in the midst of his brothers" (v. 13). As God had explained to Samuel earlier in the story, "the LORD sees not as man sees: man looks on the outward appearance, but the LORD looks on the heart" (v. 7). He wants "a man after his own heart" (13:14).

Applying these truths to ourselves, it is frightening to ponder all the ways we sinfully assess people and scenarios solely by outward appearances. Often we even assess ourselves based on the outward appearance that we think others see. Even more frightening is to ponder that the Lord looks on our hearts and sees it all perfectly. He knows us better than we know ourselves.

We would be absolutely hopeless were it not for another, even more momentous time when God worked in unexpected, seemingly upside-down ways. Almost no one looked at Jesus and thought, "This is it; this is the one." But he was *truly* "the man of God's own choosing." His cross looks weak and foolish to many, but to those being saved it is power and salvation (see 1 Cor. 1:18–31).

MARCH 6 • 1 SAMUEL 17

The Lord Saves Not with Sword and Spear

RYAN KELLY

REMEMBER WHAT GOD whispered to Samuel in the last chapter: "Do not look on his appearance or on the height of his stature" (1 Sam. 16:7). Those words should still ring in our ears as we're introduced to the giant Goliath (17:4–10). We're also reintroduced to David, and notice what's emphasized: he's the youngest (v. 14), a shepherd (v. 15), and a messenger to the battlefield—not a soldier (vv. 17–22). What a contrast!

Then there's another great contrast. Saul and his army "were dismayed and greatly afraid" of Goliath (v. 11). When the giant threw down his daily challenge, they "fled from him and were much afraid" (v. 24). David surely noticed the remarkable size, but it was Goliath's blasphemy against God that was David's concern: "Who is this uncircumcised Philistine, that he should defy the armies of the living God?" (v. 26). David is not only unafraid of the giant; he is undeterred in his resolve to do something about him. Yet, as great as David's faith is, the faithlessness and fear of the others is equally remarkable. Saul (the tallest Israelite) should be the one to fight Goliath. But he lets a young shepherd go in his stead (vv. 33–37). He even puts his kingly armor on David, a comical but telling scene (vv. 38–40).

With a slingshot and five stones, David went out to Goliath. His concern was not for his own safety but for God's honor. His confidence was not in himself but in God. David's speech (really, a mini-sermon) on the battlefield summarizes the whole scene: "You come to me with a sword and with a spear and with a javelin, but I come to you in the name of the LORD of hosts, . . . whom you have defied. This day the LORD will deliver you into my hand" (vv. 45–46). Then, notice, David hopes this will send a message up both sides of the valley, into both camps: ". . . that *all the earth* may know that there is a God in Israel, and that *all this assembly* may know that the LORD saves not with sword and spear. For the battle is the LORD's" (vv. 46–47).

This isn't so much a story about David's great faith, let alone about us conquering our own personal Goliaths in life. We're often like the other Israelites, cowering in fear before a seemingly insurmountable threat. We too need someone to rescue us. And that's what Jesus did. For God's honor and our salvation, he conquered Satan, sin, and death (Heb. 2:14–15). He didn't appear impressive or strong. His cross looked like hopeless defeat. But in the resurrection God proved otherwise. In light of those realities, ponder afresh what truly is weak and what truly is strong (see 2 Cor. 4:7–18; 12:7–10).

MARCH 7 · 1 SAMUEL 25

Who Is on the Lord's Side?

RYAN KELLY

DESPITE HIS GROWING rage against David, Saul recognizes that God's hand is upon David and that he will soon be king (1 Sam. 24:17–20). Saul will continue to simultaneously hunt David (26:1–2) and acknowledge his inevitable success (26:25). Saul gets barely a passing mention in 1 Samuel 25, but really the chapter is about two "kings"—one rejected by God, yet still technically the king (Saul); and one who isn't yet officially the king but certainly will be (David). More and more people in Israel are recognizing David as the inevitable king, even treating him as if he were already king.

But not everyone. Nabal and Abigail are a microcosm of that national tension: some siding with Saul, others with David.

That's the key to understanding Nabal's refusal of hospitality to David and his men. "Who is David? Who is the son of Jesse? There are many servants these days who are breaking away from their masters" (25:10). Nabal sees David as a rebel scheming a coup. He is unwilling to provide the basic hospitality expected in their culture, let alone honor David as God's man.

David *is* God's man, but he is not perfect, as his quick-tempered response to Nabal's rebuff indicates (v. 13). David plans a revenge that might remind us of an old western flick (vv. 21–22). It looks tough and dramatic, but it is not godly or kingly.

Unlike her husband, Abigail recognizes David as the rightful king. She also recognizes what is and is not kingly. So with great tact, she brings gifts fit for a king (vv. 18–20) and makes one of the longest, richest speeches of any woman in the Bible. She boldly asserts that God has sent her to intervene, to keep David from evil and regret (vv. 26, 31). She pleads for forgiveness on behalf of her foolish husband—that's what Nabal means: *fool* (v. 25). Yet, most of her speech recounts, with astounding detail, the great promises spoken by God about David's coming kingdom (reread vv. 28–31). Not only does she protect her household from David's sword and protect the Lord's anointed from senseless sin, but she also reminds David of God's sure promises and thereby strengthens David's faith.

Many people "set themselves . . . against the LORD and against his anointed" (Ps. 2:2). That's what Saul was doing. That's what Nabal was doing. And that's what the Romans and the Jewish leaders were doing when they crucified the Christ (see Acts 4:23–28). May we always side with the true King. May we leave vengeance to him (Rom. 12:19). May we thank him for those providential interventions that keep us from sin, and for those promise-recounting saints who strengthen us in our faith.

A King Who Gives

RYAN KELLY

WHAT A ROLLERCOASTER ride we're taken on in 1 Samuel 27–30! In chapter 27, David grew so weary of Saul's pursuit that he fled to Philistia for cover. Even worse, he and his men ran raids for Achish, king of Gath. It got Saul off the chase, but it wasn't David's finest hour. The scenario turned worse when, in chapter 29, the Philistines prepared to wage war with Israel again. Would David fight against his own people, the Israelites? Or would he acknowledge to Achish that he'd been playing him? Thankfully, neither had to happen, since the Philistine commanders vehemently opposed having David with them; thus, David and his men were sent back to Ziklag. Imagine the relief they must have felt, getting out of a pickle and heading back to their wives and kids.

But then we learn that the Amalekites had raided Ziklag, capturing every wife and child (30:1–4). Worse still, David's men blame him for the mess and consider stoning him (v. 6). What would you do next, if you were David?

We read on and see that "David strengthened himself in the Lord his God" (v. 6). He also inquired of the Lord (v. 8). God tells David to pursue the Amalekites and rescue the captured wives and children, and he assures him that he will succeed in this (v. 8). David and his men proceed and are indeed successful. They rescue wives, children—everything (vv. 18–19). They even plunder what the Amalekites had left behind (v. 20).

As they return home, however, a squabble arises over dividing the spoils. Some stingy fellows say, "Those too weak to chase down the bandits shouldn't get an even share with those who risked life and limb!" They speak of "the spoil that *we* have recovered" (v. 22). But David corrects them: it is "what *the* Lord has given us. *He* has preserved us and given [our enemies] into our hand" (v. 23). Thus, all shall share alike, even those too weak and weary to work for it (vv. 10, 24). This king *gives* rather than *takes* (see 8:11–18)!

Does all this remind you of anything? Jesus, too, faced death one dark night. Almost all had deserted or turned against him. And so he prayed. He "strengthened himself in the LORD." And then he went resolutely to the cross. Through the cross, "he disarmed the rulers and authorities and put them to open shame, by triumphing over them" (Col. 2:15). He entered the strong man's house and plundered his goods (Matt. 12:29). He led out captives and gave them gifts (Eph. 4:8). In fact, what do we have that we have not received (1 Cor. 4:7)? It's all of God's grace. He's a good king. So when we face our darkest days we, too, can strengthen ourselves in the Lord.

Building a Better House

RYAN KELLY

WITH THE ARK now safely in Jerusalem and David settled into his palace, the king has the idea to build a "house," a temple for the ark of God (2 Sam. 7:1–2). It seems like a good plan. The prophet Nathan certainly has no objection to it (v. 3). But God has a different plan—a better, bigger plan. God will build *David* a "house" (v. 11)—not a physical structure, but a household, a dynasty. Solomon, David's son, will in due course build a house/temple for the Lord (v. 13), but God will "build" something even more enduring and important.

God's promises to David have near and far implications. Some promises are limited to Solomon, such as, "When he commits iniquity, I will discipline him" (v. 14). Some stretch far beyond Solomon, into eternity: "I will establish the throne of his kingdom *forever*. . . . And your house and your kingdom shall be made sure *forever* before me. Your throne shall be established *forever*" (vv. 13, 16). Such grand promises could mean either that there will be an unending line of Davidic sons who will forever occupy the throne or that one will come who is eternal and will reign forever. Of course the rest of the Bible shows that it's the latter. Even hundreds of years before that true Son of David came, Isaiah wrote,

To us a child is born,
> to us a son is given. . . .

Of the increase of his government and of peace
> there will be *no end*,

on the throne of David and over his kingdom,
> to establish it and to uphold it

with justice and with righteousness
> from this time forth and *forevermore*. (Isa. 9:6–7)

It is because of passages like 2 Samuel 7 that the New Testament makes so much of the fact that Jesus was both the Son of David and the Son of God. As the angel told Mary, "He will be great and will be called the Son of the Most High. And the Lord God will give to him the throne of his father David, and he will reign over the house of Jacob forever, and of his kingdom there will be no end" (Luke 1:32–33; see also Heb. 1:5).

Surely David could not have imagined just how grand and far-reaching were those promises spoken through Nathan. But look again at David's exuberant response of praise (2 Sam. 7:18–29). He is utterly awestruck with God's glorious ways. How much more should we praise God for the great things he has done and continues to do? And let's also remember, God's plans are always better than ours (Rom. 11:33–36). Second Samuel 7 is powerful proof of that.

MARCH 10 · 2 SAMUEL 9

At the King's Table

RYAN KELLY

KINGS OF OLD often killed any who could lay claim to the throne, especially those attached to a previous, antagonistic regime (see 2 Kings 10). This is no doubt what's in the mind of Ziba (Saul's servant) and Mephibosheth (Saul's grandson) as they're summoned to David's palace. But each quickly finds out that David's sole intent is to show kindness, not harm, to Saul's family.

David is a man of his word. He had promised Jonathan and Saul that he would not cut off their house or destroy their name (1 Sam. 20:15, 42; 24:21–22). In fact, David loved Jonathan like a brother and planned to do him good. Of course, Jonathan died back in 1 Samuel 31. So now, after things have settled down a bit, David is eager to make good on his promises to the household of Saul. But who is left? Only one: Mephibosheth.

Almost every mention of Mephibosheth adds that he was lame or crippled (2 Sam. 4:4; 9:3, 13). His lame condition means that he's completely dependent on others; he has nothing with which to commend himself to the king. As Mephibosheth himself says, why would David "show regard for a dead dog such as I?" (9:8). It is only for Jonathan's sake that David does so (v. 1).

David shows Mephibosheth much regard indeed. All of Saul's fortune is bestowed on him (v. 9). And such wealth requires a staff, so Ziba, his sons, and his servants will work the land and serve Mephibosheth (v. 10). What's more, Mephibosheth will eat at the king's table, always (v. 10); he'll eat "like one of the king's sons" (v. 11). It's almost as if Hannah's prayer had this scene in mind: "He raises up the poor from the dust; he lifts the needy from the ash heap to make them sit with princes and inherit a seat of honor" (1 Sam. 2:8).

David showed "the kindness of God" to Mephibosheth (2 Sam. 9:3). If we know the Bible's story well, we see the fingerprints of 2 Samuel 9 in God's kindness to us. Jesus welcomes the weary (Matt. 11:28) and dines with repentant sinners (Luke 5:30–32). While "we were still weak, . . . Christ died for us" (Rom. 5:6–8). We may not be physically lame, but we were born spiritually lame. And Jesus not only welcomes the lame but heals them (Isa. 35:6; Matt. 11:5). We are unworthy, yet he treats us as sons. He dines with us, and one day we will dine with him in glory (Isa. 25:6; Rev. 19:9). Until then, let us commune with him through prayer, Scripture, corporate worship, and the Lord's Supper. And let us "welcome one another as Christ has welcomed" us (Rom. 15:7).

Confrontation, Confession, and Consequences

RYAN KELLY

IT IS DICEY to confront a king, even if you're a prophet. Nathan's confrontation, however, blends shrewdness, humility, and boldness in perfect measure. Confrontation isn't easy for anyone, even the most courageous saints. But it is absolutely essential in the community of faith. Just imagine the David story without a Nathan in it. Or imagine a Nathan who lacks the courage or conviction to speak. It could have been a very different story.

The prophet's parable of a rich man stealing from a poor man plays to the reality that we see sin in others far more easily than we see it in ourselves. We are often outraged at others' misdeeds and dismissive of our own. But David's outrage and demand for justice is on the table (2 Sam. 12:5–6) before he realizes the parable is about him. He bites the bait, and Nathan yanks the line: "You are the man!" (v. 7).

David receives the rebuke. His confession is short but not dismissive: "I have sinned against the LORD" (v. 13; cf. Psalm 51). Though he sinned against all kinds of people in the previous chapter, he recognizes that all sin is fundamentally against the Lord (see Ps. 51:4). We've seen in other parts of 1–2 Samuel that David isn't perfect, but we've also seen that, on the whole, he is "a man after [God's] own heart" (1 Sam. 13:14). While David's multiplied sins in 2 Samuel 11 prove the former, his confession here in chapter 12 proves the latter. This is a man very different from Saul. Twice the prophet Samuel confronted Saul, and twice Saul shifted blame and didn't repent (1 Sam. 13:11–13; 15:16–21). When Jonathan confronted him, Saul cursed him and hurled a spear at him (20:30–33). There is nothing of the sort in David's immediate, unqualified, and God-ward confession. May we take note!

With true confession there is forgiveness (see Ps. 32:3–5). Nathan tells David, "The LORD . . . has put away your sin" (2 Sam. 12:13). God's grace *is* greater than our sin—even if that great grace includes consequences.

David will feel the pain of this season of rebellion for the rest of his life. His household will be wracked with conflict (v. 10). One from his own home will rise against him and take his wives (v. 11)—only a few chapters later we see his son Absalom do this (chs. 15–16). Also, and most immediate of the consequences, the child born of David and Bathsheba will die (12:14–19).

After the child's death, David continues to model repentant, restored faith. He goes "into the house of the LORD" and worships (v. 20); he receives the Lord's chastisement (vv. 21–23); and he comforts his grieving wife (v. 24).

MARCH 12 · 2 SAMUEL 22

Looking Back, Looking Ahead

RYAN KELLY

DAVID'S LIFE HAS BEEN plagued by a steady stream of enemies, but in the end, the Lord has "delivered him from the hand of all his enemies" (2 Sam. 22:1). As David looks back in reflection on his life, he writes not a lament about how many enemies he's had to face but a praise song for how much deliverance and faithfulness the Lord has shown.

David's praise is far from mild or timid. He describes God's deliverances with extreme language: cracking open the earth, devouring with fire, riding on a cherub, shooting lightning like arrows, and so forth (vv. 8–20). Of course, David has in mind events that looked much less *apocalyptic* than this—like his getting out of Gath by acting crazy (1 Sam. 21:10–15; cf. Psalm 34). But he knows what kind of God it is who works in unseen ways. Thus, his praise for God is lively and lofty.

Let's pause here to ask ourselves some questions. When I reflect on my life, do I interpret things through a *God-lens*, seeing him as the central figure of it all? Do I think primarily in terms of trials, or of God's deliverance and faithfulness through dark days? When I talk of God and his work, do I do so in vanilla, stale ways? Or do I dare to praise God as David did, with extreme words and great passion? David is once again an instructive example for us (Rom. 15:4).

That said, David's song is far more than a personal reflection to be imitated. David is no ordinary guy; he is the Lord's "anointed" (2 Sam. 22:51). Therefore, it is important to step back and consider this within the grand plan of God. The books of Samuel begin and end with songs of praise: Hannah's in 1 Samuel 2:1–10 and David's in 2 Samuel 22. They have a number of similarities, and therefore should be thought of as bookends that help interpret what's in between. It is their similar endings that are particularly important: Hannah said, "He will give strength to his *king* and exalt the horn of his *anointed*" (1 Sam. 2:10); David wrote, "Great salvation he brings to his *king*, and shows steadfast love to his *anointed, to David and his offspring forever*" (2 Sam. 22:51). Do you see? What Hannah foreshadowed in her prayer had now come to pass—and more!

And yet, as much as 2 Samuel 22 is a high point in redemptive history, we read on just a bit more and find David doubting God, sinning, and steering the nation into near-judgment (2 Samuel 24). God's people need more than a David to shepherd them. Praise God, one greater than David *has* come (see Acts 2:29–36).

MARCH 13 · 1 KINGS 3

True Wisdom

GRAEME GOLDSWORTHY

SOLOMON IS A PUZZLE! The power struggles that led to his being anointed as king (1 Kings 1–2) seemed to fulfill God's promises to his father, David (2 Sam. 7:11–14). We have the assurance that "Solomon loved the LORD" (1 Kings 3:3). Solomon's dream, in which the Lord said, "Ask what I shall give you" (v. 6), evoked a request that was humble and discerning: "Give your servant therefore an understanding mind to govern your people, that I may discern between good and evil" (v. 9).

Solomon's judgment in the case of the two prostitutes followed (vv. 16–28). It could be claimed that Solomon merely used some astute applied psychology to discover the mother of the living child. In this context, however, the picture of true wisdom is being skillfully built up. Solomon foreshadowed Christ, and Solomon's role was defined by God's promises to David. He understood that he needed the help of God to know how to rule God's people. His shrewd judgment demonstrated that he had the wisdom of God in him (v. 28).

This wisdom was not only a matter of discernment in making judgments that affected real people and real problems. It came in the context of the messianic promises of God concerning the throne of David and his successors. The picture of Solomon's wisdom continued to develop alongside the splendor of the royal court. The high point came with the building of the temple in Jerusalem.

The promises to David focus the covenant blessings originally announced to Abraham (Gen. 12:1–3). Solomon's wisdom, then, operated within the framework of the covenant, the Davidic kingship, Jerusalem, and the temple. And yet, its influence was felt in the surrounding nations as people and rulers flocked to hear Solomon's wisdom (1 Kings 4:34). Finally, the queen of Sheba came to test Solomon and was astonished at his greatness and his wisdom, as well as the splendor of the temple and the prosperity of his court (10:6–9).

But now, "something greater than Solomon is here" (Matt. 12:42). If for Solomon "the fear of the LORD is the beginning of wisdom" (Prov. 9:10), for us it is faith in the One who is greater than Solomon. Christ is our wisdom (1 Cor. 1:30), and in him "are hidden all the treasures of wisdom and knowledge" (Col. 2:3). Our worldview must center on Christ and his gospel.

Preparing for the Final Temple

GRAEME GOLDSWORTHY

WE SHOULD NOT ignore the seemingly innocuous dating of when Solomon began to build the temple (1 Kings 6:1). In this way the writer links the temple with the exodus from Egypt. Solomon's temple was the climax of the process of redemption begun in the exodus. The temple signified the goal of redemption: the presence of God with his people. The sacrificial ministry of the temple expressed the reconciliation of sinners with a holy God. The temple became a central theme in the history of salvation and foreshadowed the dwelling of God among us in the new temple, which is the resurrection body of Jesus (John 2:19–22). This Old Testament expression of salvation shows that God saves his people in order to have fellowship with them.

Although Solomon did follow certain ritual prescriptions in building the temple (1 Kings 6:7), the presence of God and his blessing were never mere formalities tied to buildings and ritual. Solomon also had to live by the word and commandments of God (vv. 11–13). That he later failed in this (11:1–8), and that the glories of David and Solomon faded and were destroyed, did not mean that God was not faithful on his part. The amazing faithfulness of God is seen in the fact that the prophets foretold a renewed temple in the midst of a renewed people, and it is that new temple that Jesus claimed to be.

In the New Testament, the temple is where Jesus now is, at the right hand of the Father (Heb. 9:24–26; 12:22–24). But the temple is also wherever Jesus dwells by his Spirit. As the apostle Paul put it, Christ Jesus is himself "the cornerstone, in whom the whole structure, being joined together, grows into a holy temple in the Lord. In him you also are being built together into a dwelling place for God by the Spirit" (Eph. 2:20–22). Peter echoes this life-changing truth when he declares that we are nothing less than "living stones . . . being built up as a spiritual house, to be a holy priesthood, to offer spiritual sacrifices acceptable to God through Jesus Christ" (1 Pet. 2:5).

This glorious truth is what stirs us to "proclaim the excellencies of him who called you out of darkness into his marvelous light" (1 Pet. 2:9). It is difficult for us to understand the solemnity of holiness that filled the temple of Solomon. To stand in the presence of God who condescends to dwell among us should move us greatly to live by God's word and to worship him in spirit and in truth.

Anticipating David's Greater Son

GRAEME GOLDSWORTHY

SOLOMON, AND ALL ISRAEL, had to learn that the blessings of God did not flow automatically from the externals of covenant religion. This is a lesson we all need to learn. A formal adherence to the church and its ordinances counts for nothing without submission to God's word and his Christ.

There may appear to be a contradiction between God's putting his name permanently in the temple (1 Kings 9:3–5)—a way of signifying his presence among the people—and the ultimate destruction of the temple by the Babylonians. But when the earthly forms had been destroyed, the prophets spoke of an eventual renewal that would last forever.

Solomon and many of his successors did not heed the warning against turning away from following the Lord. In the end, nothing could prevent the destruction that came at the hands of the Babylonians. The logic of this passage is simple and brutal. There is always a conditional element to the covenant promises; we cannot claim the grace of God *for* us without living by the grace of God *within* us. The narrative goes on to foretell the destruction of the temple and of Jerusalem. Israel did become "a proverb and a byword among all peoples" (v. 7; Deut. 28:37). We learn later that good King Josiah's attempts to reform the practices of the people and avert judgment ultimately failed (2 Kings 23:26). There is a horror in the prospect of a people so blessed by redemption from slavery who yet have abandoned the Lord their God (1 Kings 9:8–9). The same horror attaches to those who, knowing the truth of the gospel of our salvation, nevertheless abandon our gracious God and his Christ.

The fact that Solomon failed only highlights our own failures to live by God's word. It also directs us to the greater Son of David who did everything according to his Father's will. Jesus was faithful in every way to do the will of his Father and so to fulfill the requirements of God for his people and their king. Our acceptance with God is grounded on the faithfulness of Jesus to be the true Son of David. Solomon's failures were not the end, for now we have a true and faithful Son of God (Heb. 3:6). Jesus was shown to be this faithful Son in his resurrection (Rom. 1:3–4), the resurrection that justifies us who believe (Rom. 4:25).

Divine Faithfulness amid Human Unfaithfulness

GRAEME GOLDSWORTHY

THIS IS ONE of the saddest chapters in the history of God's people. Solomon truly had it all. He was gifted with the wisdom of God, riches, and honor. He ruled over the most powerful and extensive Israelite kingdom ever to exist in ancient times. He was blessed to have the temple in the city of David, a sign of the presence of God with his people. His kingdom was, by God's design, the nearest thing to heaven on earth. And yet he turned from all this to the love of pagan women. He deliberately went against the Lord's prohibition of such mixed marriages, even though God had warned him that foreign women would turn his heart after other gods (1 Kings 11:2).

For us, this is not only a warning against forming such relationships with unbelievers; it is also a caution against broad-minded tolerance of religion. The spirit of our age insists that all gods are the same god, and that all religions lead to this god. This is rank unbelief and apostasy. It is an evil in the sight of the Lord that forfeits the right to the blessings of God's kingdom. Many Christians have made shipwreck of their spiritual lives by marrying unbelievers. Almost inevitably their hearts are turned away from God. Equally damaging is the failure to stand up for the uniqueness of Christ as the only Savior.

What is astonishing is the faithfulness of God to his covenant promises in the face of human infidelity (vv. 12–13, 32–36). Solomon did have his kingdom taken from him, yet God preserved his name in this chosen place (v. 36). While Solomon reverted to power politics in a vain attempt to stave off the effects of his folly (v. 40), the writer, perhaps with a touch of irony, reminds us of the good times and the wisdom of Solomon (v. 41–42).

How could a wise man be so foolish? Perhaps it is a warning to us all that sometimes it is very easy to move from godly wisdom to worldly wisdom. The Israelites coming out of Egypt under Moses turned from God and his word at the high point of their experience of God's grace. Solomon turned from God's word at the high point of his experience of God's grace. How much more vigilant we need to be so that we do not turn from the light of the gospel to a path of worldly wisdom (Heb. 2:1–4).

MARCH 17 • 1 KINGS 14:21–31

Awaiting Israel's True King

GRAEME GOLDSWORTHY

THE TRAGIC DECLINE in Judah's covenant faithfulness continued. Rehoboam, son of Solomon, should have exemplified the God-given role of the son of David. We are reminded that he reigned in the city where God had chosen to put his name (1 Kings 14:21). But he bore the name of God in vain (Ex. 20:7). Rehoboam should have been the focus of the covenant promises. Instead, he led Judah further into apostasy and sin. He forfeited every blessing that God had promised his people and that he had already demonstrated from the time Moses led Israel out of Egypt. When the current Egyptian king invaded and removed the treasures of the temple, Rehoboam resorted to shoddy bronze substitutes for the stolen shields of gold that had been a part of Solomon's riches and wisdom (1 Kings 14:25–27; cf. 10:17, 23–25).

The short valedictory for Rehoboam is tragic (14:31). The writer records the evil of his seventeen years as king but relates only the bare minimum concerning his personal existence. He would be remembered only for his apostasy. The evil of the king held sway over his people. Even though the Lord had driven nations out of the Promised Land before Israel, the people showed themselves to be no better than these idolaters (vv. 22–24). There can be no neutrality in our allegiances to the gods of this world.

The depressing assessment of the son of Solomon also characterized the history of some of his successors. The outcome was the violent end of the kingdom of Judah and all its glory. It is a history that would need rewriting and, indeed, that *was* rewritten by the One greater than Solomon who was to come.

The failures of Rehoboam and his people point us to our own failures and to the need we all have to be able to present a perfect life history, not our own, for our acceptance with God. Jesus, the true Son of David, has lived for us the perfect life we all have failed to live. He died to pay the penalty for the lives we *have* lived but shouldn't have. If there is any lesson to be learned from Rehoboam's example, it is that personal ambition can lead us to squander our inheritance in the knowledge of Israel's true King.

MARCH 18 • 1 KINGS 18

The Lord, He Is God

GRAEME GOLDSWORTHY

PROBABLY ONE OF the best-known stories of the Old Testament is Elijah's contest with the prophets of Baal. Elijah confronted the threat of total apostasy in the northern kingdom of Israel. King Ahab and his pagan wife Jezebel had turned the nation away from God to worship the Canaanite gods. Elijah announced that a drought would afflict the land (1 Kings 17:1). The blessings of the land flowing with milk and honey would be withdrawn.

The showdown came with the challenge for a contest on Mount Carmel between the Lord's prophet and the prophets of Baal. It would be easy to see this as nothing more than a show of supernatural strength, a contest to see which side could perform the most spectacular miracle. But much more was at stake here. Elijah challenged the people of Israel to decide whom they would follow, the Lord or Baal (18:21). Standing alone against the 450 prophets of Baal, he told them to prepare a sacrifice but light no fire, and then call on Baal to hear them. So it happened. All day long the pagan prophets called on Baal, but there was no response.

Now, note what Elijah did: he repaired the altar of the Lord according to God's original directions. The sacrifice was laid on the altar and saturated with water. Then, Elijah approached at the time prescribed for the offering, and he prayed to the God of Abraham, Isaac, and Israel to hear him. He was not simply banking on a spectacular miracle. He was following the word of the Lord concerning the sacrifice for sin. Fire came down from heaven to consume the sacrifice, just as it had done when Moses and Aaron inaugurated the burnt offering (Lev. 9:24) and when David offered the sacrifice (1 Chron. 21:26).

It is not the miracle as such but the return to God's way of reconciliation that turns the people to renewed faith: "The LORD, he is God" (1 Kings 18:39; cf. v. 37). Later, Paul was to write, "Jews demand signs and Greeks seek wisdom, but we preach Christ crucified, a stumbling block to Jews and folly to Gentiles" (1 Cor. 1:22–23). The way to God is not of our devising. Those who seek for spectacular signs and wonders need to come back to God's way and be reconciled to him through his Son.

MARCH 19 • 2 KINGS 2

A Foreshadowing of Our Own Resurrection

GRAEME GOLDSWORTHY

THESE VERSES TELL the remarkable story of the prophet Elijah being taken up to heaven without dying. Genesis 5:21–24 tells of Enoch's similar experience. Though outside normal human experience, both events anticipate the resurrection of Jesus and the coming resurrection to eternal life of all who trust in him. Why Enoch and Elijah were spared death is not stated, although we are told that Enoch "walked with God" and "pleased" him (Gen. 5:22; Heb. 11:5).

All resurrections are defined by the resurrection of Jesus, and so we can learn much from Elijah's extraordinary experience. First, ever since the sin of Adam, entry into heaven for anyone can be achieved only through the death of Christ. With our knowledge of the gospel, we can say that Enoch and Elijah, along with all of God's Old Testament saints, were saved by the cross. Likewise, Christians will be resurrected to eternal life because of Christ's death. All of these resurrections are the fruit of Jesus's suffering for us. Second, we are reminded that this present life, with all that occupies us, is not all there is. The militant atheists of our time feed skeptical minds with the idea that our only destiny is to leave something behind because, for us, at death, there is only oblivion. Enoch, Elijah, and our risen Savior teach us that there *is* a "beyond" that gives all creation and our present life their meaning.

Before Elijah ascended, Elisha requested an inheritance, not of land but of Elijah's prophetic spirit. So Elisha was left to continue the prophetic ministry in the spirit of Elijah. He began with a series of healing miracles related to the promises of God concerning the good land (2 Kings 3–8). But Bethel (2:2–3, 23) was at the heart of Israel's rebellion against such promises. The drastic judgment upon the mocking young lads (v. 24) must be seen as directed at the apostasy of a people who had scorned the grace of God. This is a serious thing indeed. We cannot ridicule God's gracious program of redemption and resurrection, and expect to escape unscathed (Heb. 2:3).

MARCH 20 • 2 KINGS 5:1–14

The Cleansing Power of Simple Obedience

GRAEME GOLDSWORTHY

NAAMAN, A GENTILE, was unaware that the Lord God of Israel had already acted sovereignly in his life (2 Kings 5:1). Nor did he anticipate God's sovereign action that would lead to his leprosy being healed.

A little Hebrew slave girl in Naaman's household exemplified the missionary spirit, even if she didn't understand that her recommendation of Elisha (v. 3) echoed God's promise to Abraham concerning the nations (Gen. 12:3). When Naaman relayed the girl's news to the king of Syria, the king's response revealed his failure to see beyond political and military issues (2 Kings 5:4–5). It suited his plans to have Naaman healed, but his letter to the king of Israel was misinterpreted (vv. 6–7). Nevertheless, Elisha urged Naaman to come to him (v. 8).

Elisha's gospel was simple: go and wash in the Jordan and be healed. Naaman's reaction was predictable: anger at the scandal of such simplicity. He was outraged to be told to wash in an insignificant muddy stream like the Jordan. Surely he should have been told to do something spectacular, notable, and recognizably important. That a great and victorious general should sit in a puddle was humiliating and unacceptable. When he finally calmed down and followed his servants' bidding, he washed in the Jordan and was cleansed. He later confirmed that he was now submitting to the God of Israel (vv. 17–18).

This was one of the whole cluster of miracles linked with God's covenant with Israel—miracles that foreshadowed the gospel. It speaks to us of the simplicity of faith: believing God's prophetic word. The scandal for so many is that the gospel requires that we forsake the grand rivers of our world of self-importance, the elaborate designs we would devise for our own salvation. It leaves us with nothing to bring, so that we can cling only to the cross of Jesus.

MARCH 21 • 2 KINGS 17:6-23

Resisting the Pressure of Worldly Conformity

GRAEME GOLDSWORTHY

THE CAPTURE OF ISRAEL'S capital city by the Assyrians was not merely another military defeat in a world of conflict. The removal of the Israelites from the Promised Land was a second exile, similar to their ancestors' sojourn in Egypt. It was a further undoing of the things promised to Israel as God's covenant people. It was a stripping away of the tangible evidence of God's blessings. And it happened because of their sin against the Lord, who had proven his love and saving power in the exodus (2 Kings 17:7).

Since God had already demonstrated his faithfulness so decisively, this rebellion was all the more blameworthy. It seems inconceivable that a people so blessed should turn to the worship of false gods. They were allowing the customs and cultures of other nations to mold them. We must never think that we are immune to such temptation or invulnerable to the appeal of conformity to the world. Although time has passed and cultures have changed, the susceptibility of the human heart to this sort of deception remains tragically intact. This is the very danger that Paul warns us of in Romans 12:2: "Do not be conformed to this world, but be transformed by the renewal of your mind."

Christians are always under pressure to conform to worldly culture, a culture that is godless and expressive of a non-Christian mindset. God mercifully warned Israel by the prophets (2 Kings 17:13), but they would not heed the warning (vv. 14–16). It is easy for us to rely on the culture of our Christian heritage: a Christian upbringing, a signed decision card, church membership, baptism, and confirmation. However good these things are in themselves, they cannot save us. Nor can our modern Western, secular-technological culture save us. We are called to stand firm against anything that compromises faith in God's Christ. Jesus said, "The one who endures to the end will be saved" (Matt. 10:22; 24:13).

MARCH 22 · 2 KINGS 18:1-12

God Honors His Covenant Promises

GRAEME GOLDSWORTHY

HAVE YOU NOTICED how often God's covenant promises to David (2 Samuel 7) are referred to in 1 and 2 Kings (e.g., 1 Kings 2:4; 3:6; 5:7; 6:11–13; 8:15, 25; 9:4–5; 2 Kings 8:19)? And when the narrator wants to assess the reigns of the various kings of Judah, he compares them with David's reign (1 Kings 3:3; 5:7; 11:4–6; 14:7–9; 15:3–5, 11; 2 Kings 14:3; 16:2–3; 18:3; 22:2). And, God's preservation of Judah was said to be "for the sake of David" (1 Kings 11:12, 32, 34, 36; 15:4; 2 Kings 8:19; 19:34; 20:6). Likewise, Jerusalem is often called "the city of David." These recurrent references highlight the centrality of David and the covenant to the messianic promises of the Old Testament.

Now, we read that Hezekiah was one of the good kings, who did "according to all that David his father had done" (2 Kings 18:3). His rule was marked by his removal of the high places and all the implements of idol worship. From the beginning, the greatest threat to God's people was their tendency to follow the worship of their pagan neighbors. But not only did Hezekiah remove the idolatrous worship places (v. 4); he also trusted the Lord and held fast to him, and he kept the commandments (vv. 5–6). Therefore, he was granted success in his wars against Assyria and the Philistines (vv. 7–8). Here we see the continued blessings of the Davidic covenant.

By contrast, Hoshea, the king of Israel, suffered a severe defeat at the hand of Assyria because of Israel's infidelity to the Lord and transgression of the covenant (vv. 9–12). Israel's compromise with the world led to its exile and removal from God's covenant blessings. As the inheritor of the Davidic covenant and dynasty, Judah would last more than a hundred years longer than apostate Israel with its many different royal families. Judah and David's line was messianic and led eventually to great David's greater son, Jesus of Nazareth. Meanwhile, the northern kingdom of Israel disappeared from history as a distinct nation. By the time of Jesus, those who had returned from exile were, along with the descendants of Judah, known merely as Jews, a name derived from "Judah."

From this history we are reminded of the gracious covenant of God as it focuses on David and his descendants. We are warned against trying to combine our worship of God with false religion or idolatry. And we are pointed to the messianic line that brings us to salvation in Jesus, the son of David. Like Hezekiah, let us live in the light of these covenant promises.

Why You Can't Trust in Your Father's Faith

GRAEME GOLDSWORTHY

THE BREAKUP OF ISRAEL into the northern kingdom of Israel and southern kingdom of Judah came about because of the apostasy of Solomon and his son Rehoboam. God remained faithful to his covenant with David, and there were some good kings in Judah, such as Asa and Jehoshaphat (1 Kings 15:11; 22:43), and Jehoash, Amaziah, and Azariah (2 Kings 12:2; 14:3; 15:3). They did what was right in the eyes of the Lord, but some of them did not complete the necessary reforms by taking away the "high places" of idol worship (1 Kings 22:43; 2 Kings 12:3; 14:4; 15:4).

The two notable reformers were Hezekiah, who removed these idolatrous places (2 Kings 18:4), and Josiah (ch. 22). But between Hezekiah and Josiah was Hezekiah's son Manasseh. He did what was evil and rebuilt the high places that his father had removed; he reintroduced idolatry, magic, and human sacrifice (21:2-7). His crowning evil was the profaning of the temple, the dwelling place of God's holy name (vv. 4-7). Now, through Christ, God has made his name to dwell in us as his temple (John 2:19-22; Eph. 2:19-22; 1 Pet. 2:4-12).

Christian history is littered with examples of children who forsook the faith of their fathers and turned their back on the blessings of the covenant. Kings like Manasseh, although in the messianic line, showed a particular depravity in their unbelief and evil practices. We cannot presume on the covenant promises made to our fathers. Judah had to learn that its sinful presumption meant that Jerusalem, the city of God and the city of David, the place where the Lord made his name to dwell, would be destroyed in judgment.

The sovereignty of God in bringing to pass his promised blessings exists alongside human responsibility. God's purposes cannot be thwarted, but his kingdom will come with or without us, depending on our response to his offer of salvation. The destruction of Jerusalem and the exile of its people had been long foretold by the prophets, but a faithful remnant shall be redeemed and shall come with rejoicing to Zion (Isa. 35:10). Through faith, we are part of that remnant.

Repentance without Compromise

GRAEME GOLDSWORTHY

AFTER MANASSEH'S DEATH his son, Amon, reigned and carried on the evil of his father. He was assassinated after just two years, and his son Josiah became king. We are not told how or when Josiah became a man of faith. He was only a child when his reign began, and his reforms didn't begin till eighteen years later (2 Kings 22:1–3). We know that he did what was right in the eyes of the Lord, following the ways of David (22:2).

When he was about twenty-six, Josiah initiated repairs to the temple. Meanwhile, the high priest found a copy of the Book of the Law in the temple (22:8–20); some suggest it was the entire Pentateuch, others that it was only Deuteronomy. It is referred to later as the Book of the Covenant (23:2, 21). The book was brought to Josiah and read to him. The result was electric! Josiah tore his clothes, a sign of grief-stricken repentance. He was overcome with the sense of God's wrath against the nation's breaking of his law. He read the book to the elders, the priests and prophets, and the general public (v. 2).

This passage details Josiah's systematic demolition of the entire idolatrous religion that Manasseh had established (vv. 4–14). He didn't stop with Judah but pursued his reforms in the northern kingdom as well (vv. 15–20). His aim was to reestablish God's law in all Israel. But, although Josiah turned to the Lord with all his heart (v. 25), he could not fully undo the effects of Manasseh's evil (vv. 26–27). He could not change people's hearts; only the sovereign work of the Holy Spirit of God can do that.

Josiah shows us that true reformation, institutional or personal, cannot involve compromise. Unlike Hezekiah and other reforming kings,

Josiah attempted a full reformation of the religious life and practices of his people. But it was too late to undo the effects of Manasseh's evil. Only a new creation could rectify that; the nation had to be destroyed before being reborn. Sinners must die with Christ before they can rise with him (Rom. 6:1–11). Josiah teaches us that true repentance involves a radical change of heart and mind.

MARCH 25 · 1 CHRONICLES 16:1–36

Songs of Grace

GARY MILLAR

IT HAS BEEN a very long wait, but for David in this chapter it has definitely been worth it. Not since the days of Eli at Shiloh has the ark of the covenant, the symbol that God lives with his chosen people, been at the center of national life (and the Israelites of Eli's day were hardly the high point of biblical religion; see 1 Samuel 4!). But now, finally, the ark is back where it should be. Carefully, David places it in a specially prepared tent (just as Moses had done; 1 Chron. 16:1), makes appropriate sacrifices (vv. 1–2), and pronounces a priestly blessing over God's people (v. 2) before inviting the whole nation to share in a feast that will remind them of God's covenantal determination to bless his people in his land. Then David lines up a team to pray, thank, praise, and play (vv. 4–7), and the celebration begins in earnest.

What follows in verses 8–36 is a blast of "greatest hits" from the Psalms:

Psalm 105:1–15	(1 Chron. 16:8–22)
Psalm 96:1–13	(1 Chron. 16:23–33)
Psalm 106:1	(1 Chron. 16:34)
Psalm 106:47–48	(1 Chron. 16:35–36)

And why are these particular Psalms chosen? Because they all celebrate God's *covenant commitment to his people*. God has chosen his people, rescued his people, stuck with his people, protected his people, and above all, blessed his people amid a hostile world. And he does all this for people who lose and then ignore the ark, the great symbol of his presence! In other words, these are songs of *grace*.

It doesn't come easily to us (and perhaps to men in particular) to face up to our failures and shortcomings, and then to rejoice (even boast!) in our weaknesses (see 2 Cor. 12:9–10). But that is what this chapter calls us to do. In the gospel, God responds to our flawed character, terrible choices, cold indifference, and blatant rebellion with *grace*. He calls us to the joy of repentance. He calls us to face the mess and run to Christ, the one who became flesh and lived with us—the one who even now lives in us by his Spirit, joining us to him forever.

Yes, the past is not what it could have been. Yes, we have said and done countless things we would like to erase. But in Christ we are set free to celebrate *now*, not because of who we are but because of the God who is the gospel.

MARCH 26 · 1 CHRONICLES 22:6–19

A Father-Son Conversation

GARY MILLAR

IT'S ONE OF THOSE "father-son" moments, where David sits Solomon down and talks to him about what really matters. Men are not always fantastic at this; sometimes these moments can be a bit awkward, as we struggle for the right words to express deep emotions and truths. But not for David. Not this time.

The Chronicler knows that we have read Samuel and Kings (or if we haven't, we can do it anytime), so he makes little effort to retell the "whole story" of David and Solomon. Instead, he focuses on one thing—one thing that really matters. He focuses on the whole issue of atonement (see 1 Chron. 6:49; 2 Chron. 13:10–11; 29:20–24). And that's where the *temple* comes in.

David tells Solomon that the one thing he had really wanted to do was to build a "house to the name of the LORD my God" (1 Chron. 22:7). However, God had forbidden him to do this because of the blood on his hands (v. 8). Now it is time for Solomon to pick up where his dad left off. Solomon will be uniquely qualified to build the temple, because he will be a "man of rest" (vv. 9–10). In his life and his reign, Solomon will model the "rest" that God has promised to give his people in the land. More than that, he is the one through whom God will bring the rescuing King who will live forever (v. 10), through whom God will provide the ultimate atonement.

In order that Solomon may stay on track, David prays for "discretion and understanding, that when he gives you charge over Israel you may keep the law of the LORD your God" (1 Chron. 22:12). This is a wise fatherly prayer. The Chronicler here is interested less in Solomon's struggles in living this out and more in the fact that God himself is at work, step by step, to provide the ultimate atonement that will supersede anything we have seen before, as well as anything Solomon might build.

Our God is a promise keeping God. In this narrative, the (flawed) personalities involved pale into insignificance beside the fact that God is at work to build his kingdom, showing his people both their need for forgiveness and his determination to provide forgiveness through one greater than Solomon. The challenge for us as men is to pray like this for those whom we love, and to live in the light of the forgiveness that God has given us through the Lord Jesus.

MARCH 27 · 1 CHRONICLES 29:1-22

Sustain This in Our Hearts, O God!

GARY MILLAR

THE TEMPLE PROJECT clearly captures the imagination of the community, and therefore it affects their pockets! Both David and the people of Judah clearly understand the joy of giving (1 Chron. 29:9). It's an important reminder that our attitude toward giving is an accurate measure of the state of our hearts. How we *spend* reflects what matters to us. We give freely when we care. The Chronicler carefully points out that, for David's generation, the provision of forgiveness really matters.

For the first readers of Chronicles, returning from the exile, this must have come as a huge relief. They knew that they had messed up spectacularly; were they now beyond redemption? Was forgiveness still a live option? Somehow, through God's gracious provision, forgiveness is still within reach—for God is the God who provides ultimate atonement.

No wonder that David's prayer in verses 10–19 is so exuberant. He begins by describing the supremacy of God as the one who both creates and rules (vv. 10–11). After acknowledging that Yahweh is the only real giver and reaffirming his sovereign ability to direct events on earth, David turns to praise. However, straightaway, David is freshly humbled by the kindness of God in allowing mortal human beings to participate in his great salvation project.

In verses 17–18, David prays that God will work in the people's hearts to maintain throughout their lives the wholeheartedness, joy, and integrity that mark their present celebration. Then he prays the same thing for Solomon. Like the first readers, we know that, tragically, David's prayer was not answered. Both Solomon and the people (and the kings and people who followed) quickly lost sight of the greatness of God and wandered away. So what hope is there for their descendants, making their way back home after the exile? The only hope is in a radically new intervention of God—a radically new covenant with a radically different sacrifice. God's people need to be forgiven and transformed. They need to be equipped by God to live for him in new ways on this side of judgment. Thank God that, in the Lord Jesus Christ, we have this new and living hope. Let's ask him to make us men who live wholeheartedly, joyfully, and consistently for him!

Perfect Forgiveness

GARY MILLAR

IT IS DIFFICULT to do justice to this rich and sweeping prayer of Solomon. Like his father before him (1 Chronicles 16; 22; 29), he celebrates as the ark is placed right at the heart of national life—now in its permanent home in the temple. But the most striking thing about this prayer is *how little it says about the temple itself.*

In the preface to the prayer (2 Chron. 6:1–11), Solomon draws together the promises that Yahweh made to Abraham and Moses and those he made to David, both to send a King who would rule forever and to come and live among us, his people. This covenantal atmosphere pervades all of Solomon's prayer, as he tackles the key problem of having a relationship with God: God is perfect, but we are not (6:18).

The prayer is built around the possibility of God forgiving his people: "then hear from heaven and forgive the sin of your people" is the repeated refrain (6:21, 25, 27, 30, 33, 35, 39). The massive, "concrete" presence of the temple in the middle of Jerusalem is not simply a place of sacrifice (note that there is no mention in this chapter of Israel making any sacrifices) but a place that points to the real possibility of forgiveness.

(It was not yet clear in the unfolding story of the Bible exactly how this forgiveness could actually be achieved, although we now know that, near this very spot, hundreds of years later, a perfect sacrifice would be provided *by* God and offered *to* God, which would achieve a perfect forgiveness for everyone who trusts in him.)

The footnote to this magnificent prayer in 7:1–3 underscores the fact that God is committed to forgiving his people. As happened at the commissioning of the tabernacle and the beginning of the sacrificial system (Lev. 9:24), fire comes down from heaven and consumes the sacrifice.

What did Israel need? What do we need as men? We need a godly king and a proper sacrifice. In these chapters, the Chronicler brings these two biblical strands together, powerfully pointing us to the gospel of Jesus. So, let's be quick to admit that we are not in charge, nor are we perfect, but we are men who are secure in Christ!

Wisdom Is Not Genetic

GARY MILLAR

"WHEN I WAS a boy of fourteen, my father was so ignorant I could hardly stand to have the old man around. But when I got to be twenty-one, I was astonished at how much he had learned in seven years." Apparently, Mark Twain didn't actually say this (his father died when Twain was eleven), but that doesn't mean this "urban myth" doesn't say something important. The story of Rehoboam reminds us that, as we reach adulthood, many of us feel the need to assert ourselves. And all too often, in asserting ourselves, we reject the wisdom of older generations. That isn't very smart, but it's depressingly common—and Rehoboam is a prime example.

Rehoboam's father, Solomon, may have been the wisest man in history, but it seems that he has failed to convince his own son to listen to his father's instruction (see Prov. 1:8). Rehoboam is neither a wise nor a godly leader. When the more popular Jeroboam tries to bring some relief to the people from Solomon's excessive use of forced labor, Rehoboam makes a tragic error: he compounds Solomon's harshness with his own, choosing to listen to his foolish contemporaries (2 Chron. 10:10–11) rather than his father's seasoned advisors. The result is disaster.

The Chronicler wants us to learn three key things from this sorry account. First, harshness in a leader, whether at home, in church, or in society, is never a good thing. Second, God is sovereign, and he can use even things like Rehoboam's stubborn stupidity to advance his plans (v. 15). Third, the key theological problem in the northern kingdom of Israel is their subsequent attitude toward the messianic family (v. 19); it is likewise our attitude toward Jesus himself that shapes everything else in our lives.

So are you being an idiot just now? Are you being headstrong? Are you trying to prove to yourself and others that you can handle life? If so, now would be a great time to stop, because it will end in disaster. The way of wisdom is to throw yourself on the mercy and power of the Lord Jesus Christ. As Paul says, "we preach Christ crucified, a stumbling block to Jews and folly to Gentiles, but to those who are called, both Jews and Greeks, Christ the power of God and the wisdom of God" (1 Cor. 1:23–24).

How to Pray Big, Gospel-Centered Prayers

GARY MILLAR

LIKE THE REST OF US, King Jehoshaphat was capable of both great wisdom and great folly. He married into the worst regime in the history of northern Israel (2 Chronicles 18), but he also sought to be godly and to organize national life around faithfulness to Yahweh (ch. 19; but see 20:33). And he prayed. Jehoshaphat's prayer in 2 Chronicles 20 is one of the high points of the Chronicles. It is a great example of how we as men should pray big, gospel-centered prayers, crying out to God to come through on his promises.

Jehoshaphat starts his prayer by affirming the sovereign power of God (v. 6), before moving straight on to the promise keeping record of the God of the Covenant (vv. 7–12). Jehoshaphat views what is happening to Judah in his own day as being linked to the journey from the wilderness into the Promised Land many years before. Back then, God wouldn't allow his new people to attack their "relatives" from Edom and Moab. Now, Jehoshaphat argues that this has come back to bite them. What is Judah to do?

They are to fix their eyes on Yahweh (v. 12), for God can be trusted to keep his promises. That's why Jahaziel can say, "Thus says the LORD to you, 'Do not be afraid and do not be dismayed at this great horde, for the battle is not yours but God's'" (v. 15). God has promised to bring his people into the land and give them rest. When Jehoshaphat prays, he simply asks God to do what he says. And God does. His name is honored among the nations, and "the realm of Jehoshaphat was quiet, for his God gave him rest all around" (v. 30). Once again, God has come through on his promises.

Sadly, however, this "rest" enjoyed under Jehoshaphat doesn't last. It can't last, for even this basically godly king leaves the "high places" of Canaanite false religion intact. Life in Judah is a disaster waiting to happen. God's people don't need a basically decent king to improve things—they need a perfect king who can transform things, and bring not just temporary respite but the real rest found only in God himself. They need the one who says, "Come to me, all who labor and are heavy laden, and I will give you rest" (Matt. 11:28). It takes courage for men like us to face our restlessness and run to the one who can give us that rest—but it really is the only action that makes sense.

MARCH 31 · 2 CHRONICLES 29

Knowing God Is What Matters

GARY MILLAR

HEZEKIAH GETS ONE very important thing right: he knows that the Levites are crucial to Judah's relationship with God. This tribe that has no land inheritance ("the LORD is [their] inheritance"; Deut. 10:9) is a reminder that all of God's work is designed to bring us into a relationship with him. The Levites' role in teaching the Scriptures is crucial in keeping God's people on track. But it is the Levites' role in running the temple that comes into focus here.

If God's people are to survive the wrath of God and the curses of the covenant that have been poured out on them in the exile, what will they have to do? They will have to seek God's forgiveness. Their sin will have to be atoned for. And how does that happen? To understand that, the people of Judah need a functioning temple: it is the temple liturgy that so graphically highlights both the seriousness of sin and the need for God himself to provide atonement. Of course, this ultimately points to the incarnate Christ, who is himself the temple of God in our midst (see John 1:14). He has come to be and do for us all that the old covenant temple typified.

Like the other kings of Judah, Hezekiah left a seriously mixed legacy. But he got this right: knowing God is what matters, and this can happen only through the atonement that God provides. And where do we find out about this atonement? In the Scriptures, which speak from beginning to end of the Lord Jesus Christ, the one whom God made to be sin for us, so that we might be reconciled to God.

This chapter, then, breathes the importance of seeking forgiveness in Christ, of knowing God through the gospel, and of building our lives on the truth of Jesus Christ as found in the Bible. In our families and in our churches, we need men to take on this "Levitical role" of keeping the gospel the main thing. May God grant us the grace to be men like this.

All Stirred Up

COLIN SMITH

THE BOOK OF EZRA begins with a fascinating glimpse into how God moves his purpose forward in the world. The Promised Land was desolate, ruined by the devastation of war, and God's people were in exile, strangers in a foreign land. It had been like that for years.

But God began a new work by stirring up the heart of a king who did not even know him (Ezra 1:1). In the mind of Cyrus, there were many gods, each with their own province and people. But God is sovereign even over unbelieving kings. God can stir the hearts of people who do not know him as well as those who do. He speaks of Cyrus as his "shepherd," as the one who will "fulfill all my purpose" and even as the Lord's "anointed" (Isa. 44:28; 45:1). Doors may be opened through unbelievers in places of influence whose hearts have been stirred by the Lord.

Cyrus authorized God's people to return to Jerusalem and rebuild the temple. But who would want to go? The older men had settled into Babylonian life, and the younger men had never known anything else. But God stirred the hearts of godly men, who committed themselves and led their families in this great venture (Ezra 1:5). We serve a God who puts it in the hearts of men to attempt and accomplish great things by his Spirit and for his glory.

The great work to which these men were called was to rebuild the temple in Jerusalem. Their calling was to worship God, to walk with him in faith and obedience, and to be a light to people from all nations.

Is your spirit stirred up over this great calling? If so, be encouraged and press on in all that you are doing for the Lord. If you are on the sidelines of ministry, don't stay there. Find a way to give yourself to what God is doing in the world.

God always takes the initiative. He can stir up the spirit of a man who does not know him as well as the spirits of people who do. Use this truth for encouragement in sharing the gospel with those who do not yet believe and to motivate prayer for yourself and other believers, that God will stir up our spirits to become the people he is calling us to be.

APRIL 2 · EZRA 3

The Priority of Worship

COLIN SMITH

IMAGINE FIFTY THOUSAND exiles returning to their homeland, many of them seeing the Promised Land for the first time. Their journey probably took about four months, and soon after their arrival they gathered in Jerusalem (Ezra 3:1).

Priority number one for these men and their families was to establish worship. In time they would rebuild the temple, and after that they would secure the city walls. But the first priority was to build "the altar of the God of Israel" (v. 2).

These men wanted to do a great work for God. But they knew they had to start by being right with God themselves. They had sins to confess. They needed to seek God's face in prayer. And the daily sacrifices offered at the altar reminded them of their constant need of the One to whom all these sacrifices were pointing.

Fear was clearly a motive in making a priority of worship (v. 3). Not the grandest of motives, perhaps, but a good one nonetheless. The brave pioneers knew that they faced a hostile culture, and in the face of so many enemies they needed to know that God was their friend. If something or someone you fear drives you to seek God and to walk with him, you will have made good use of your fear.

Worship remains a priority for godly men today. So take the lead in establishing a time in your home for reading the Bible and for praying. Use this time to confess sin, to offer praise and prayer, and to give thanks for all that is yours through the sacrifice of Jesus Christ. And make a priority of regularly bringing your family to join with others for worship.

Once the altar was established, it was time to lay the foundation for the temple (v. 10). This was a moment to celebrate, and it was marked by singing, praise, and thanksgiving (v. 11). But to some of the older men, who remembered the magnificence of Solomon's temple that had been destroyed years before, the new replacement seemed pitifully small. So while the young men were cheering, the older men were weeping (v. 12). Don't let your past experience of God's blessing drown your joy in what God is doing now. God may have done greater works in the past. If so, give thanks for them, but don't live there. Your calling is to participate in what God is doing now, and to help others do the same.

APRIL 3 • EZRA 7:1–10

Study, Do, and Teach!

COLIN SMITH

AFTER A HISTORICAL review of how the first exiles returned to Jerusalem and rebuilt the temple, Ezra himself steps into the story. Ezra was a scribe, directly descended from Aaron. He came to Jerusalem with a second group of returning exiles nearly sixty years after the completion of the new temple. Much had changed in those years, and when Ezra arrived, he found that many of God's people had grown cold and were no longer walking faithfully with the Lord.

Ezra's vision was that there should be a community of believing people who lived according to the law of God. He wanted to see a great reformation, a revival in which God's people would truly be his servants, bringing honor to his name on earth and fulfilling their great calling to be a light to the nations.

The ministry of Ezra shows that it is the word of God that changes lives and shapes communities. Those who would be useful in God's service must become servants of his word. This means immersing yourself in Scripture, putting God's word into practice in your own life, and then teaching that word to others. Thus Ezra "set his heart to study the Law of the LORD, and to do it and to teach [it]" (Ezra 7:10). The order is important. Before you can teach the word to others, you have to establish a pattern of obeying it in your own life; and before you can obey the word, you have to know what it says.

If you feel that teaching others is beyond you, remember that a man who knows, believes, and obeys two verses of Scripture is able to help a man who knows only one. Wherever you are in your walk with God, there are others you can lead, teach, help, and encourage through the Scriptures.

The good hand of God was on Ezra as he pursued this ministry (7:6, 9, 28; 8:18, 22, 31) and, as you will see in the coming chapters, a great work of God was done in the lives of many people as a result.

The church today desperately needs the leadership and ministries of men like Ezra, who will study the word of God, put it into practice, and then teach it to others. By God's grace, may you be among them.

APRIL 4 · NEHEMIAH 1

Pray First!

COLIN SMITH

NEHEMIAH IS REMEMBERED FOR rebuilding the walls of Jerusalem, a massive project that called for the skills of a fearless entrepreneur, a disciplined project manager, and a shrewd leader. So it is striking that the first thing we learn about this man of action is that he was a man of prayer. His intimacy with God came before his activity for God, and in this he is a model for men with a mission today.

The story begins with Nehemiah hearing bad news. God's people in Jerusalem were in great trouble and shame (Neh. 1:3). Seventy years after the rebuilding of the temple, which we read about in Ezra, God's people were a small, struggling, demoralized community living in a ruined city without walls for defense.

Our first instinct on hearing bad news from people we love may be to take the initiative and come up with a plan to resolve the problem, but Nehemiah's first instinct was to pray. He wept, mourned, prayed, and fasted—and kept doing this for days (v. 4). Nehemiah prayed because he cared, and he cared because he prayed.

Nehemiah's prayer is a model for our praying today. Notice how he leaned on the character of God: he is the great and awesome God, who keeps his promises (v. 5). So Nehemiah claimed God's promise (vv. 8–9). He used God's own words from the Scripture as the basis of his prayer, which has all the marks of a man making a case: "Lord, you are the God who keeps his promises. Now here's what you have promised . . ."

But there is no arrogance in this prayer. Nehemiah appeals to God on the basis not only of his promise but also of his mercy. He comes to God knowing his own sins (v. 6) and the sins of God's people (v. 7). Effective prayer always involves confidence in who God is and *humility* because of what *we* are. True prayer is always an act of both faith and repentance.

The reason Nehemiah cared so deeply about the trouble and shame of God's people was that these people bore God's name: "They are *your* servants, and *your* people, whom *you have* redeemed by *your* great power and by *your* strong hand" (v. 10). God's name and reputation were at stake, and Nehemiah's weeping, mourning, fasting, and praying reflected not only a burden for God's people but a passion for God's glory.

At the end of the prayer, Nehemiah tells us that he was cupbearer to the king (v. 11). This meant that he had the ear of the most powerful man on earth. But that hardly gets a mention. What mattered was that Nehemiah had the ear of almighty God in heaven.

Dealing with Discouragement

COLIN SMITH

THE ADVANCEMENT OF GOD'S work provoked a vicious response, and God's people suffered the anger, rage, and ridicule of God's enemies (Neh. 4:1). A man who sets out to serve the Lord will endure seasons of opposition. Satan has a special eye on godly leaders, and if God has given you a share in his work, you can expect to experience your share of trouble.

Nehemiah's response was to pray and press on (vv. 4, 6). The people "had a mind to work," and soon the wall was built to half its height (v. 6). But this rapid progress brought consternation to their enemies, who threatened direct action against God's people (v. 8).

Facing a credible threat, Nehemiah prayed and set a guard (v. 9). He trusted God but also took reasonable measures to ensure the safety of the people. There is no contradiction in Nehemiah's strategy.

The biggest challenge lay not in the threats of their enemies but in the discouragement of God's people. The people doing the work were tired, the size of the task seemed overwhelming, and the resources for getting the work done were limited (v. 10). The work was halfway to completion, but at the midpoint of the project, God's people were losing heart.

Some of the immediate and extended families of the builders felt that reconstructing the walls was provoking their enemies and that it would be better to live with broken walls than with enraged enemies. So they appealed to the builders to stop the work and come home (v. 12). The message was simple: "The work you are doing is putting your own people in danger."

The intensity of feeling among the families is evident from the fact that the appeal to come home was made no less than ten times (v. 12). At a time when the workers were tired and their morale was low, the pressure to quit the work for the sake of their families must have been great.

Nehemiah's response was vigorous. He called on the workers to remember God and to fight for their families (v. 14). Their families thought that building the wall exposed them to danger, but Nehemiah showed the workers that *not* building the wall would expose their families to even greater danger.

God's people came together, and God's work continued. If you are discouraged in the work God has called you to do, draw strength from Nehemiah and his builders. Stand firm in your faith. Press on with the work. Do not give way to fear.

APRIL 6 · NEHEMIAH 8

The Power of the Open Book

COLIN SMITH

IMAGINE A FOOTBALL stadium filled with people. In the middle of the field there is a platform. The Book of the Law of Moses is brought out and Ezra, the scribe, climbs the steps and begins to read. Hours later, he is still reading, and the people are still listening. They know that when God's word is opened, God's voice is heard.

Nehemiah notes that along with the men there were also women, and there were children old enough to understand (Neh. 8:3). Children who are able to read will benefit from being with their parents in worship, and it is the duty of husbands and fathers to make sure that their families hear God's word both in private and in public.

Notice the process by which God's word brings blessing to God's people. It begins with hearing: "the ears of all the people were attentive to the Book of the Law" (v. 3). Then there is understanding: Nehemiah lists the names of the Levites (v. 7) who "gave the sense" of the Scriptures "so that the people understood the reading" (v. 8). This is the work that God has given to preachers today. They are to read the word of God and explain its meaning, so that God's people can understand its application to their lives.

When the people heard and understood the word of God, they realized how far they were from obeying it: "All the people wept as they heard the words of the Law" (v. 9). Men who seek God often find that the first effect of God's word is to show us our own hearts and to humble us on account of our many failures. God will often bring us to such a place of conviction, but it is never his purpose to leave us there. The danger inherent in any confession of sin is that it can lead to despair, and that is why Nehemiah turned the attention of God's grieving people to the joy of the Lord (v. 10). It is God's joy to forgive. So let his grace and mercy soothe your repentant tears.

Hearing and understanding God's word led to confession and then to rejoicing, but the chapter ends with the joy of obedience. On discovering God's command about the Feast of Booths, the people put God's word into practice. The word heard and understood produced confession, rejoicing, and obedience. That's the power of the open Book!

APRIL 7 · NEHEMIAH 9

Spiritual Renewal

COLIN SMITH

THIS CHAPTER BEGINS the story of a marvelous spiritual renewal among God's people, which is the main theme of the remaining chapters of Nehemiah. Massive effort had gone into rebuilding the walls of the city, but with these structures completed (Neh. 6:15), the focus moved to the people who lived there. What kind of people should live in the city where God has put his name (1:9)?

The word of God was central to the renewal of God's people. They read from the Book of the Law for a quarter of a day (9:3), and it was this immersion in Scripture that led to confession (v. 3) and commitment (v. 38). God will accomplish his great purpose of making you increasingly like Jesus through his Spirit and by his word. Read the Scriptures with a repentant, believing heart, and over time your life will be transformed.

This long chapter gives a marvelous summary of the entire Old Testament story, from the creation to the return of God's people from exile. Notice that the main focus is always on God. God created the heavens and the earth (v. 6). He called Abraham and made a covenant with him (vv. 7–8). He brought his people out of slavery (vv. 9–11). He guided, guarded, and provided for them in the desert (vv. 12, 15). He came down on Mount Sinai and gave them his good commandments (vv. 13–14).

Despite all the presumption (v. 16), stubbornness (v. 17), idolatry (v. 18), and disobedience and rebellion (v. 26) of his people, God is ready to forgive (v. 17). He is merciful and faithful (v. 19). He gives his Spirit (v. 20), and he is sovereign over marvelous triumphs (v. 22) as well as disastrous defeats (v. 27). He and he alone is the Lord (v. 6).

Hearing all this must surely have given God's people a new sense of privilege and a fresh awareness that their lives were caught up in the great sweep of God's vast redeeming purpose. What was true for them is true for you as a believer in Jesus Christ.

Reformation and revival begin when God's people are gripped, in a new way, with the glory of who he is and what he has done. Knowing and serving him ceases to be ordinary and feels like the greatest privilege in this world. Seeing who God is also produces a new awareness of sin and a fresh desire for holiness. Ask God to show you more of his glory, and to ignite in you a passion to please him as you read his word.

APRIL 8 · ESTHER 2

The Hidden but Involved God

ALISTAIR BEGG

THE KING HAD "lost his head," and as a result the queen had lost her crown! Ahasuerus had broken the bounds of propriety by commanding the presence of his queen, Vashti, for the sole purpose that his friends might feast on her beauty. Josephus, the Jewish historian, tells us that strangers were not allowed to look at the beauty of Persian wives. A husband's love for his wife will cause him to protect her and certainly not to provide her as an object of lustful intent (Matt. 5:27–28).

Vashti refused her husband's perverse command, whereupon he became enraged and removed her from being his queen. His actions here illustrate the biblical truth that "the anger of man does not produce the righteousness of God" (James 1:20). In the cold light of dawn, when he remembered the events of that evening, he realized that he had backed himself into a lonely corner. There is a price to pay for ignoring James's exhortation to be "slow to speak, slow to anger" (James 1:19).

In the events that follow we are introduced to Mordecai, whose cousin Esther wins first prize in the "Miss Persia Pageant" and, without disclosing her true identity (in obedience to her cousin), ends up in the king's bed and on the queen's throne. The question we must ask of these everyday events is, what are the unspoken lessons here about the unseen God? We find ourselves on the wrong track by looking to Esther and Mordecai as the hero and the heroine. Instead we look beyond them to God, who delivers his people sometimes dramatically and visibly and sometimes silently and secretly but no less miraculously. As the story unfolds, it becomes increasingly apparent that God, whose name is never mentioned, is mysteriously and yet unmistakably involved in the details. When we find it hard to make sense of history and even of our own little personal histories, we must keep in mind that God is working everything out "according to his purpose, which he set forth in Christ" (Eph. 1:9).

Perhaps God seems hidden to you when you most need him to make his presence known. Perhaps he appears uninvolved when you are most desperate to see him at work in your life. Rest assured that he is there, actively orchestrating everything for your good and his glory (Rom. 8:28).

Resting in the Providence of God

ALISTAIR BEGG

HAMAN'S REACTION TO MORDECAI'S unwillingness to bow down or pay him homage was one of unmitigated fury. He urged the king to issue a decree that would have resulted not just in the death of Mordecai but also in the annihilation of the entire Jewish population of Persia. Behind this impending holocaust, as throughout all the evil events of history, we find the activity of the one who "was a murderer from the beginning" (John 8:44).

The response of Mordecai is the very opposite of passivity. He is acutely aware of the trouble confronting the Jews, and his intervention is as purposeful as it is dramatic. He is not about to take no for an answer from his cousin the queen. There is a time to keep silent and a time to speak (Eccles. 3:7), and in Esther's case, silence is not an option that he would recommend.

Deliverance of the Jews is not contingent upon Esther's response, however (Est. 4:14a), because the plans of God are far bigger than human obedience or disobedience.

Esther is faced with a dilemma. She can sit tight and hope for the best in the apparent security of the palace, or she can step up, resting in the sovereignty of God, and face the prospect of death. Since the providences of God are seldom immediately self-interpreting, "who knows" but that Esther is facing the defining moment of her life (4:14b). We all face times when, like Esther, we must decide where our allegiance lies and where we will place our faith (Josh. 24:15).

Esther recognizes that it is not necessary for her to live, but it is necessary for her to do her duty. "If I perish, I perish" (Est. 4:16). She determines that it is better to die being obedient than to live in disobedience. God had placed her in a unique place for a unique purpose. He has done the same for us. Our lives are not necessarily marked by such drama, but they are lived in the place of God's appointing in order that we might fulfill the plans he has for us (Eph. 2:10).

APRIL 10 · ESTHER 6–7

God Fulfills His Purposes

ALISTAIR BEGG

THERE IS NOTHING in Shakespeare to match the tragedy, comedy, and irony of these events in Esther. Haman is about to discover the truth of Solomon's words: "The hope of the righteous brings joy, but the expectation of the wicked will perish" (Prov. 10:28).

God is the creator and sustainer of everyone and everything, and nothing happens except through him and by his will. Here we find the "unseen

God" at work in apparently inconsequential events—in tiny details like sleeplessness and choice of reading material!

God's timing is perfect. If Mordecai had been immediately rewarded for his uncovering of the assassination plot (Est. 2:19–23), the events of this night would never have unfolded in this way. Perhaps we feel that we have been overlooked when we have deserved recognition. We must leave God to order all our ways and always to do what is right.

Consider all that transpired to change the course of events, and then ponder the fact that God's plan for the deliverance of his people was in place even before the prospect of their destruction! Read Acts 2:23 and rejoice in the loving wisdom of our God. We must learn to trust God in the matter of timing and delays. Let us not miss his hand of mercy in the routine and ordinary events of our lives.

Haman once again proves the wisdom of Solomon: "Whoever digs a pit will fall into it, and a stone will come back on him who starts it rolling" (Prov. 26:27). He is about to meet with darkness in the daytime and grope at noonday as in the night (Job 5:14). He has been exposed. His sins have found him out, and all his pride and presumption is replaced by terror. Is there a more chilling sentence than "So they hanged Haman on the gallows that he had prepared for Mordecai" (Est. 7:10)?

Let us learn to view the activities of the Hamans of the world from a biblical perspective (Ps. 73:18). Let us rejoice that King Jesus is not capricious and vengeful like Ahasuerus but is instead gentle and lowly in heart (Matt. 11:28–30). In him there is hope for the hopeless and rest for the weary. God is fulfilling his purposes through the preservation of his people and ultimately in the provision of his Son, in whom we have redemption through his blood and the forgiveness of our sins (Eph. 1:7).

When the Blessings Are Taken Away

CHRISTOPHER ASH

A HUSBAND, A FATHER, a businessman, a leader, above all a good man. It would be surprising if we Christian men do not want to be like Job—at the *beginning* of the story. What a fine example he seems to be! In his family life he is blessed with children, and he cares for their godliness as well as their food, clothing, and education. Even when they have left home, he offers sacrifices for them as the head of the family. In his public life he is a successful, trustworthy, and recognized leader ("the greatest of all the people of the east"; Job 1:3). Above all, he is "blameless" (has a clear conscience) and "upright" (treats other people right), and he "fears" (honors) God and turns away from evil in regular repentance (1:1, 8; 2:3). In our terms, he is a pillar of his church and a respectable member of Christian society.

But the test of the heart—for us as for him—comes when the blessings are taken away: the wealth, the success, the reputation, and the children. It is then that Job's heart is revealed and the devil's necessary question is answered: does he *really* honor and love God because God is God, or does he just give the outward appearance of loving God because it will bless him and make him look good to others? That question comes to us too. Do I love, honor, worship, and fear God because he is God and for that reason alone? When my marriage is tough, when parenting is difficult (or when I cannot have children), when I am reluctantly single, or when I am redundant, poor, or under pressure—will I love God then?

None of us comes out shining from that test. Thank God for the one man in history who does—great Job's even greater successor, the Lord Jesus, who loves the Father when there is nothing but nothing in it for him. And thank God that by his Spirit you and I can begin to walk in Job's footsteps because we walk in Jesus's footsteps.

When It Feels As If God Is against Us

CHRISTOPHER ASH

JOB'S SUFFERINGS reveal Job's heart. What he says in suffering opens a window into his soul. He is under intense pressure. He has lost his wealth, his position, his children, and his health. But the worst pressure is that his so-called comforters accuse him of unforgiven sin. They say that his accursed state proves he is under the curse of God; the fact that he is "shriveled ... up" is "a witness against" him (Job 16:8). There is something of Job's comforters in us all. We hear of someone's misfortune and we can hardly help but wonder if in some way they deserved it; in the same breath, the thought occurs to us that perhaps our own happy state shows we deserve that too. How wrong we can be!

In this speech there are two very remarkable attitudes of Job's heart. First, despite how badly they are treating him, Job longs to be able to comfort and bring solace to his friends (v. 5). Far from wanting to "get back at them," he would love to be a real comforter to them when *they* face trials. This is quite different from how we men instinctively feel.

The second remarkable attitude we see in Job is that, despite feeling that God is against him (vv. 6–15), he knows in his heart of hearts that he must and can appeal to God (vv. 16–19). Because he has not sought to repay evil with evil (Rom. 12:17) and there is "no violence" in his hands (Job 16:17), he can offer a "pure" prayer from a pure heart, calling on God to vindicate him (vv. 18–19). He can do this only because he has an absolutely pure conscience.

Only Jesus does perfectly what Job foreshadows. In the extremity of suffering on the cross he prays for his persecutors, "Father, forgive them" (Luke 23:34). Despite accusation and false witness, his heart is pure before the Father and he knows he can appeal to the Father for vindication and can commit his spirit to him (Luke 23:46).

It is a wonderful thing for us men when, by the Spirit of Jesus within us, we begin to meet evil with good, to pray for those who treat us badly—in a marriage, in family life, in the workplace. Then we have the confidence that springs from a clear conscience so that we can pray in our deepest distress, sure that our heavenly Father hears us.

Vindication from Above

CHRISTOPHER ASH

I SUPPOSE THERE IS not much we men hate more than being laughed at. That people might be snickering at us behind their hands really gets to us. And there is not much we men love more than being admired. How good it is when people look up to us, ask our advice, come to us for guidance or permission, and treat us as men of weight and substance. This is how we feel.

Job was a great man, a preeminent leader in his region (Job 1:3); people treated him with great respect (29:7–10). And yet in this agonized speech he cries that he is excluded, estranged, and abandoned by those he thought were his friends, despised by his former servants, and disgusting to his own wife and siblings (19:13–17).

How does he respond? In one of the high points of Job's faith, he says that, in the face of universal mockery and disgust he can, must, and will appeal to God his Redeemer: "For I know that my Redeemer lives, and at the last he will stand upon the earth" (v. 25). Because his heart is right with God, Job knows that in the end God himself will stand up for him. A redeemer in Old Testament times was a blood relative who would stand up for a man under all circumstances. Job knows he has this relationship with God his Creator. And so his heart's hope is no longer for the approval of people; suffering so shapes him that he longs primarily for the vindication of God his Redeemer. In this hope he foreshadows the Lord Jesus, who was despised by people but loved and vindicated by the Father, who stood by Jesus and "redeemed" him from death on the cross.

What a deep work this will be in our hearts, as Christian men, if we begin to care less for the admiration of people—our wives, children, work colleagues, and neighbors—and more for the vindication that comes from God to all who are in Christ.

In the Furnace of Affliction

CHRISTOPHER ASH

MEN RESPOND VERY DIFFERENTLY to suffering. Many of us get frustrated and angry. This is only natural. We are angry at those who have closed doors of opportunity to us at work, frustrating our careers; or a wife who has made life hard at home; or children who have not turned out as we had hoped, frustrating our desire for the perfect home. We are frustrated by the limitations of old age or the constraints of illness, so that there is sport or travel we can no longer enjoy. And so we get cross and crotchety and grumpy. And yet, paradoxically, some men are actually matured, purified, and dignified by suffering. On them, the mark of suffering is a strangely beautiful thing. How so?

Job has been suffering acutely, and this has made him frustrated and angry. Elihu speaks to this in chapters 32–37. He is like the warm-up act before God takes center stage. Unlike the so-called comforters, Elihu says true and important things for Job to hear. We will focus on 36:8–16. Elihu is talking about God's justice. In verses 8–10 he says that, when people suffer, God exposes the sin and pride that may be in their hearts; he uses their suffering to bring repentance. Some people respond submissively and will be blessed in the end; others just get angry, rather than turning their sufferings to prayer (v. 13).

Then in verse 15, Elihu explains that God "delivers the afflicted by their affliction and opens their ear by adversity." Job is not suffering because he sinned (as his "comforters" claim); however, he has sinned as a result of his suffering, saying things he ought not to have said (e.g., 9:22–24)—and God will later rebuke him for this (38:2; 40:2, 8).

Even the Lord Jesus, though he never sinned, learned obedience through what he suffered (Heb. 5:8). How good it will be if we proud men can learn to bow down in humble penitence when we suffer, responding not with angry frustration but with a calm submission to God, trusting that he has good purposes for us in the end.

Bowing before God

CHRISTOPHER ASH

I LOVE BEING IN CONTROL. It makes me very happy to know what I'm talking about. When the conversation turns to an area of my expertise, I smile inside. "Ah, yes," I say, "I'm the man who knows." When I was a schoolteacher, I loved it when a class did what I said; I hated not being in charge—that frightening feeling that the kids' behavior was out of control. We men so love being in control and being knowledgeable that we are very reluctant to admit to not knowing or not being in charge. We exaggerate both our knowledge and our power.

Even Job, for all his godliness and perseverance, exaggerated the areas of life over which he had both knowledge and control. There were times when he more or less lectured God about how to run the world better. In this chapter, the beginning of the first of God's two majestic speeches, God begins by rebuking Job for speaking "words without knowledge" (Job 38:2). Job is given a tour, not of his old farm that he controlled and understood, but of the wild extremities of the universe and animal life—the invisible moral foundations of the earth (vv. 4–7), the limits of evil represented by the chaotic sea (vv. 8–11), the rising and setting of the sun (vv. 12–15), and so on.

There are times for us men when the chaos and evil of the universe invades "the farm," the spheres over which we have had control and that we thought we understood—our business, our locality, our state, our family, or our own bodily health. How do we respond when chaos invades? The proper response is to bow before God, not just in his sovereignty and power but particularly in his wisdom—to trust that he, the Creator, not only controls the apparently chaotic edges of the world but knows how to bring good out of evil. "Do you know . . . ? Can you control . . . ?" the Lord asks. To which the humbled man replies, again and again, "Oh, no, I don't understand and I can't control. But I'm prepared to bow in worship and trust that you, my Creator and Redeemer—you know and control, and you will work out your purposes of love for all who are in Christ."

True Prosperity

CHRISTOPHER ASH

WE MEN OUGHT to believe in the prosperity gospel. No, not as it is preached all over the world—the so-called gospel that promises wealth, happiness, power, and health in this present world to all who trust in Christ. Nor as it is preached in wealthy countries, where it also becomes the therapeutic gospel—that if I am a Christian man, I will feel good about myself, my moods will be improved, my self-esteem will be boosted, and I will live in "the sweet spot" of life. No, no, no! Not that kind of prosperity gospel. For we must enter the kingdom of God through many tribulations (Acts 14:22), and it is only those who share in Jesus's sufferings who will share his glory in the end (Rom. 8:17).

And yet there *is* a prosperity gospel, and we ought to believe it and yearn for it. Job 42 foreshadows it for us. The Lord restored Job's fortunes. Once again Job enjoyed great wealth and a wonderful family with beautiful daughters and joyful feasting. Turning to the New Testament, we find the writer James encouraging us to remember "the steadfastness of Job" and God's great mercy to him as we ourselves endure suffering and patiently await our Lord's return (James 5:7–11). Putting Job and James together, we understand that such a restoration of good fortune will indeed be ours, not necessarily in this life but most certainly when Jesus returns.

The new heavens and new earth will be a physical place (albeit a transformed physicality) with real bodily pleasures and delights that will make the most intense delights of this life pale into insignificance. How stupid are we men when we set our desires on the delights of this life—wealth, success, comfort, sexual delight, or job satisfaction. The Christian man who looks forward to retirement as an opportunity to travel and have great holidays is missing the point; there will be far greater enjoyment in the age to come! How wise we will be to look forward to the real and physical delights of the age to come, to live for that, and to suffer for and serve Christ gladly in the light of that future. Let Job's restored fortunes inspire us to hope for better things!

The Blessed Man

DOUGLAS SEAN O'DONNELL

THE BOOK OF PSALMS ends with all creation blessing God. The first lines of Psalms 146, 147, 148, 149, and 150—"Praise the LORD!"—capture the theme well. However, the Psalms begin with a poem about the blessed *man* (Ps. 1:1) and the Lord's eternal rewards for that man's righteous life. That righteous life is set within the context of a world to be judged (vv. 5–6) and is contrasted with the lives of "the wicked" (vv. 1, 4, 5, 6), also called "scoffers" (v. 1) and "sinners" (vv. 1, 5). In contrast with the wicked, the blessed man avoids worldliness. He doesn't "walk . . . in the counsel of the wicked" or "stand in the way of sinners" or "sit in the seat of scoffers" (v. 1). Instead of walking, standing, or sitting with such people, "day and night" he prayerfully thinks ("meditates") about God's covenant history, instructions, and promises ("his law"; v. 2). He sits with his Bible open; he stands in awe of God's revelation; he walks in God's ways. And because of this he grows by God's grace and is "blessed" by God.

How do we escape the judgment of the wicked, walk in righteousness, and grow in God's grace? We men join the man of Psalm 1 by meditating on the Man, the Lord's "Anointed" Son (Ps. 2:2, 7, 12). Psalms 1 and 2 are often called the Gateway to the Psalms because they open to us the book's two main themes: namely, that as God's covenant people we are to (1) "take refuge" in God's coming king (Ps. 2:12) and (2) "delight . . . in the law of the LORD" (Ps. 1:2). In Jesus the Christ, we receive all the blessings of Psalm 1's blessed man. If we abide in him, we bear fruit and we stand strong on the day of judgment. We will not wither away. Because God knows us (v. 6) in Jesus, we have been granted eternal life!

Join the blessed man. Take up your Bible. Read it. Think about what it says. Pray about its plan and promises. Marvel at God's gracious plan of salvation in Jesus.

What Is Man That You Are Mindful of Him?

DOUGLAS SEAN O'DONNELL

PSALM 8 IS THE ANTIDOTE for infectious anthropologies, such as the view of mankind that is too high (man is the captain of his soul) or the view that is too low (we are just evolved cosmic dust, living on a minor planet in a less than extraordinary galaxy). With a poetic inclusio, this hymn of praise opens and closes with a high view of God: "O LORD, our Lord, how majestic is your name in all the earth!" (Ps. 8:1, 9). What follows verse 1 is an upward focus. We look up at God when we read this psalm. We look beyond "the moon and the stars" (v. 3) to see God's "glory," which is "above the heavens" (v. 1).

Then, from that great height, we descend to see "man" (v. 4) and all that is "under his feet" (v. 6). There is a pause in the middle of the poem. We gasp. We join the psalmist in asking, "What is man that you are mindful of him, and . . . that you care for him?" (v. 4). Put differently, what is so great about people that you even give a thought to us? The question is never completely answered in the verses that follow. The psalm simply goes on to recount our privileged place among God's creation ("crowned . . . with glory and honor"; v. 5), focusing on our "dominion" over the animals: sheep, oxen, beasts, birds, fish, and sea creatures (vv. 6–8).

The New Testament, in a sense, takes up the psalmist's question, answering that what is so great about mankind is the Man Jesus Christ. Psalm 8 is quoted three times in the New Testament. Following the lead of those inspired authors, we understand that Jesus is the ideal man, who was "crowned with glory and honor because of the suffering of death" (Heb. 2:9). Through that glorious death, he tasted "death for everyone" (Heb. 2:9). Now, although "everything" has been put "in subjection to him" (Heb. 2:8), we still await the day when "every rule and every authority and power" (1 Cor. 15:24) will be put under his feet and "the last enemy," death, will be destroyed (1 Cor. 15:26–27). On that day, we men will join the children who cried out on the streets of Jerusalem long ago, "Hosanna to the Son of David" (Matt. 21:15).

A Life of Integrity

DOUGLAS SEAN O'DONNELL

THIS PSALM BEGINS by addressing God with a question expressed in two ways:

> Who shall sojourn in your tent?
> Who shall dwell on your holy hill? (Ps. 15:1)

If you had read Psalm 14 before reading Psalm 15, you might expect the answer to these questions would be "no one," since we are all too sinful (Ps. 14:3). But that is not the answer that Psalm 15 gives to these all-important questions. Nor is the answer messianic, that only the coming Christ can dwell there. Instead, the psalm answers the question by listing nine marks of holiness.

The best way to make sense of this list is not as a kingdom entrance exam but rather as a kingdom ethics report card. Those who are part of God's kingdom—that is, those who have taken refuge in the Lord—understand well enough the opening decree of the *next* Psalm, "I have no good apart from you" (Ps. 16:2). However, as is plain here in Psalm 15 and elsewhere in Scripture, God's saints seek to imitate God.

As Christian men, we are to look "to Jesus, the founder and perfecter of our faith" as we "run with endurance the race that is set before us" (Heb. 12:1–2), knowing that, without holiness, "no one will see the Lord" (Heb. 12:14). And the way we run the race is by following "Jesus Christ the righteous" (1 John 2:1), trusting that "he is the propitiation for our sins" (1 John 2:2) and walking "in the same way in which he walked" (1 John 2:6).

Some of the steps of that walk are described in the attributes and actions listed in Psalm 15. Being in a right relationship with God (Ps. 15:1) shows itself in being in a righteous relationship with our neighbors (vv. 2–5). For example, how do we handle our tongue? Do we "speak truth" (v. 2), respect other believers (v. 4b), and keep our promises (v. 4c)? Or, do we slander our neighbor (v. 3a) and reproach even a friend (v. 3b)? And how do we handle money? Do we act with openhandedness and bigheartedness? Or are we greedy for gain, no matter the means (v. 5)? As Jesus would later teach, it is our tongue (e.g., Matt. 12:37) and our wallet (e.g., Luke 19:8–9) that best demonstrate the authenticity of our relationship with the Father. God's children love God by loving others. And such righteous living assures our hearts before the holy Lord who dwells in unapproachable light (1 Tim. 6:16).

APRIL 20 • PSALM 19

What's Wrong with the World Today?

DOUGLAS SEAN O'DONNELL

"What's wrong with the world today?"
"I am."
Sincerely, King David.

While these opening lines play off of G. K. Chesterton's famous reply to the *London Times*, they reflect well David's thoughts in Psalm 19:12–14. In those verses David speaks of both his unknown and his known sins ("hidden faults" [v. 12]; "presumptuous sins," "great transgression" [v. 13]), as well as his need for deliverance from the dominion of sin. He asks for *pardon* from sin and *power* to overcome sin. He prays that his outward actions ("the words of my mouth") and his inward thoughts ("the meditation of my heart"; v. 14) would be "acceptable" to God, his "rock" (refuge from sin) and "redeemer" (deliverer who will pay for his sin).

But how did David arrive at that conclusion? The same way we all do. He saw his need for the gospel of God by encountering the living God through his works in creation (vv. 1–6) and his words in Scripture (vv. 7–11). As David meditated upon the heat of the sun and the light of God's perfect law, he conceded that he was the problem and God's grace was the only solution.

How often we miss these truths! When was the last time we were so greatly enjoying the heat of the sun that we were brought to the feet of the Son? All creation testifies to Christ, the Creator who created "all things" and in whom "all things hold together" (Col. 1:16–17). And when is the last time that reading God's "law," his "testimony," and his "commandment" (Ps. 19:7–8) led us to revere our Redeemer? Let us celebrate that "Christ died for the ungodly" (Rom. 5:6). Moreover, let us rejoice that because "Christ was raised from the dead by the glory of the Father, we too might walk in newness of life" (Rom. 6:4).

We all know what is wrong with the world: we are! Who of us hasn't made errors in moral judgment? A rash word? A crude joke? Who of us hasn't openly rebelled against God? Glorying in our achievements? Viewing immoral images? But thanks be to God that, through faith in Christ, we are "no longer . . . enslaved to sin" (Rom. 6:6). We know that our Redeemer lives (Job 19:25), and we also know that we can "stand against the schemes of the devil" (Eph. 6:11) and the deceitfulness of sin because we are "strong in the Lord and in the strength of his might" (Eph. 6:10).

APRIL 21 • PSALM 22

He Was Forsaken That We Might Be Forgiven

DOUGLAS SEAN O'DONNELL

WHILE JESUS IS the ultimate sufferer to whom this psalm points, David was the original one. It is important, therefore, that we first understand this psalm as an honest expression of Israel's persecuted king. Whatever David experienced before he penned this poem, his writing is so vivid that it brings us down into the depths of his despair.

While people scorn David, God seems silent. However, the king remains steadfast. He thinks of the past as he looks toward the future. Note the conjunctions—the "yet" of verses 3 and 9 and the "but you" of verse 19. The God who delivered Israel's "fathers" (v. 4), cared for David at his "mother's breasts" (v. 9), and delivered him from "the mouth of the lion" (v. 21) will surely "come quickly to [his] aid" (v. 19). King David will be vindicated! Then he will join "the afflicted" in praising the Lord (v. 26). He will delight in "the nations" coming to celebrate what God has done (vv. 27–31).

Like David, but through the sacrifice of the Son of David, we must live and suffer the world's mockery because we trust in the Lord (v. 8), remembering, as Jesus taught, "Blessed are you when others revile you and persecute you and utter all kinds of evil against you falsely on my account. Rejoice and be glad, for your reward is great in heaven" (Matt. 5:11–12). However, if our entire focus in reading Psalm 22 was on David's sufferings or our own, we would miss the whole point of the psalm. For as we read this lamentation, we ought to dwell on the wondrous cross of Christ.

In Matthew's passion narrative we find four quotations from Psalm 22, the last being the first verse of this psalm: "My God, my God, why have you forsaken me?" (Matt. 27:46). While we know the end of the story, as we do the end of the psalm—Jesus is vindicated, and the nations worship him—still, the Christian man ought to ponder anew the atonement. Why did Jesus cry out the first sentence of Psalm 22? It was because the verb of Jesus's question reveals his theology of the cross: "forsaken." He was forsaken by the Jews, by his disciples, but also and most significantly by his heavenly Father. Matthew doesn't directly explain the nature of this God-forsakenness, but he does record the dark cry of dereliction. Thankfully, Paul summarizes the story in this way: God made sinless Jesus "to be sin" so that we might be forgiven of our sins (2 Cor. 5:18–21). For such self-sacrifice and loving mercy, let all the nations worship him!

APRIL 22 · PSALM 27

Beholding the Beauty of God

DOUGLAS SEAN O'DONNELL

IN VERSE 1 OF PSALM 27, David speaks of fear, asking, "whom shall I fear . . . of whom shall I be afraid?" In his life, David knows what it is like for "evildoers [to] assail" him (v. 2) and for "an army [to] encamp against" him (v. 3). His confidence is in the Lord, who is "the stronghold" (v. 1). That is how Psalm 27 begins. However, in verse 4 the theme seemingly shifts. David desires the beatific vision:

> One thing have I asked of the LORD,
>   that will I seek after:
> that I may dwell in the house of the LORD
>   all the days of my life,
> to gaze upon the beauty of the LORD.

The "seeking" motif won't stop. God has called David to seek his face ("Seek my face"), and so, "Your face, LORD, do I seek" (v. 8). This theme, however, is not removed from the question of being afraid amid enemies. David wants to be with God not because he is an escapist. Rather, it is because he is a realist. He waits (and calls us to wait; v. 14) because God is worth the wait. To "look upon the goodness of the LORD in the land of the living" (v. 13) sustains David in a world that breathes out violence (v. 12).

What sustains you in times of trouble? Is the Lord your "light and . . . salvation," your "stronghold" (v. 1)? The Psalms are mirrors to our souls as well as worshipful confessions of faith. They turn our hearts to Yahweh, the only God who speaks, acts, sees, hears, and answers. They turn us to Jesus. He is our Savior not only from our enemies but also from Satan, sin, and death. More than that, he is the one worth living for, because "to live is Christ, and to die is gain" (Phil. 1:21). Death is gain because Jesus has conquered the grave and because death is the means by which we come face to face with the light of our salvation, the Lord God himself.

Life is hard. The Psalms testify to that. The Psalms also testify that the presence of God is worth enduring all of life's troubles and tribulations. Imagine living in a perfect world. Imagine no more fear of death and hell. Imagine seeing God face to face.

The Joy of Daily Repentance

DOUGLAS SEAN O'DONNELL

HOW WOULD YOU describe unconfessed sin? In Psalm 32, David describes it like this:

> For when I kept silent, my bones wasted away
> through my groaning all day long.
> For day and night your hand was heavy upon me;
> my strength was dried up as by the heat of summer. (vv. 3–4)

We all know how David felt. Unconfessed sin eats away at us. It makes us frail and depressed. It removes the joy of our salvation.

Psalms 6, 32, 38, 51, 102, 130, and 143 are called the Penitential Psalms. They are prayers of repentance. But they are more than prayers of repentance; they are also praises of God's merciful forgiveness. When we "confess [our] transgressions to the LORD" (Ps. 32:5), our "transgression is forgiven" and our "sin is covered" (v. 1). We can join God's people in singing "shouts of deliverance" (v. 7). We can be "glad in the LORD, and rejoice" (v. 11).

Martin Luther called the Penitential Psalms "the Pauline psalms" because they reminded him of Paul's theology of justification. In fact, in Romans 4:6–8 Paul quotes Psalm 32:1–2a to demonstrate that God counts us righteous "apart from works." In other words, it is not our own righteousness that makes us acceptable in God's sight; rather, God justifies the ungodly through faith in Jesus Christ. It is "the blood of Jesus his Son [that] cleanses us from all sin" (1 John 1:7). Only Jesus can deliver us from our enemies (Col. 2:15; Rev. 20:11–21:8), from death (1 Cor. 15:12–16, 35–58), from divine judgment (John 3:36; Rom. 5:1), and from sin (Gal. 1:4).

The Christian life is one of daily repentance. As Christian men, we must lead the way in our homes and churches by acknowledging our sin, confessing it to God, and rejoicing in the forgiveness we have in Christ.

Tasting God

DOUGLAS SEAN O'DONNELL

PSALM 34 FOLLOWS an acrostic pattern, with each verse beginning with the next letter of the Hebrew alphabet. This poetic device is used for a number of the Psalms, and part of its value is to aid memory. What did David want God's people to remember? He wanted them to remember that God delivers the righteous, those who "boast in the LORD" (see Ps. 34:1–3) and who live according to his ways (vv. 11–14). We can "exalt his name together" (v. 3) because the Lord hears, answers, provides, and redeems. He will deliver the righteous "out of all their troubles" (v. 17).

When Peter reflected on this psalm, he used it as a call to holy living in an unholy world. In 1 Peter 2:1–3, he ends his admonition to "put away all malice and all deceit and hypocrisy and envy and all slander" (v. 1) and to "grow up into salvation" (v. 2) by saying, ". . . if indeed you have tasted that the Lord is good" (v. 3). There he alludes to Psalm 34:8: "Oh, taste and see that the LORD is good!" Later, in 1 Peter 3:12–14, Peter quotes from Psalm 34:15–16 and exhorts Christians to suffer for righteousness' sake. We can "suffer for doing good" (1 Pet. 3:17) because we know God will judge those who persecute us (they will be "put to shame"; 1 Pet. 3:16) and we "will be blessed" (1 Pet. 3:14), or in the language of the psalm, we will "see good" (Ps. 34:12).

So often we are surprised by suffering, especially when unbelievers ridicule us or oppress us because of our faith. We shouldn't be! The normal Christian life involves enduring misunderstanding, ridicule, ostracism, and at times physical persecution. As Paul put it, "Indeed, all who desire to live a godly life in Christ Jesus will be persecuted" (2 Tim. 3:12). We need to man up by picking up our cross and following the Man Jesus Christ. The next time your boss makes a crude joke, don't laugh—and see what happens. The next time your coworkers on the road venture off to the "Unholy Club," decline the invitation and live with the results. It isn't hard to set ourselves apart from the crowd. What is hard is to do it all the time and take what comes our way because of it. Let the fear of the Lord and the goodness of God sustain us!

Delight Yourself in the Lord!

DOUGLAS SEAN O'DONNELL

LIKE PSALM 1, PSALM 37 sets the future of the righteous against the dark backdrop of the "wicked," named fourteen times (Ps. 37:10, 12, 13, 14, 16, 17, 20, 21, 28, 32, 34, 35, 38, 40) and also called "evildoers" (vv. 1, 9), "wrongdoers" (v. 1), "enemies of the LORD" (v. 20), "ruthless" men (v. 35), and "transgressors" (v. 38). Echoing the opening psalm—"the way of the wicked will perish" (Ps. 1:6)—David vividly describes the doom of the ungodly. He writes, "They will soon fade like the grass and wither like the green herb" (Ps. 37:1) and "[They are] like the glory of the pastures; they vanish—like smoke they vanish away" (v. 20).

Psalm 37 is an acrostic poem that uses the Hebrew alphabet to aid in memorization and add artistry to its truth. It is also often described as a "wisdom" psalm because it shares themes found in the wisdom literature of the Bible. Similar to the book of Proverbs, it emphasizes the timeless worth of righteousness. While justice is coming to the wicked, the righteous who "trust in the LORD, and do good" (v. 3) have the sure promise of abundant and everlasting life (the meek "shall inherit the land"; vv. 9, 22; see Matt. 5:5).

While as men we might be tempted to envy the wicked (Ps. 37:1) or to violently take matters into our own hands (v. 8), this inspired psalm exhorts us to turn from evil (v. 27), wait patiently for God's justice (vv. 7, 34), and put God first. We are to commit our ways to him (v. 5), take refuge in him (v. 40), and delight ourselves in the Lord (v. 4). When the scoffers mock us for wanting to live holy lives and to wholly delight in Jesus Christ, let us "rejoice and be glad," knowing that our reward will be greater than anything we can imagine (Matt 5:12). In the all-joyous presence of our Savior, the new heavens and the new earth shall be ours!

Preaching to Your Own Soul

DOUGLAS SEAN O'DONNELL

BECAUSE PSALMS 42-43 share a refrain ("Why are you cast down, O my soul, and why are you in turmoil within me?"; Pss. 42:5, 11; 43:5), they are rightly viewed as a unified lament. And in this song the psalmist sings about his desire to return to the temple and be in God's presence (42:2; 43:3–4).

Grieved by his physical distance from access to the Almighty, and grieved by the reproaches of his enemies and their mockery (Pss. 42:9–10; 43:1–2), the psalmist cries out in desperation. Using the simile of a deer panting for water and the hyperbole of having tears for his physical nourishment, he cries out to God, *for God.* He desires God, whom he mentions thirty-seven times in these sixteen verses. This holy thirst should be ours. We should desire to drink of God! He alone satisfies the soul.

The threefold refrain of Psalms 42–43 also teaches an important lesson. The psalmist's question, "Why are you cast down, O my soul, and why are you in turmoil within me?" is answered by the psalmist himself: "Hope in God; for I shall again praise him, my salvation and my God" (Pss. 42:5, 11; 43:5). Here the author does not counsel himself with the tenets of popular psychology or with the modern doctrines of self-reliance. He does not remind himself to trust in himself or to pull himself up by his own bootstraps. Rather, he exhorts himself to be dependent on God to rescue him from despair. Relying on the proven character and promises of God, the psalmist encourages himself to continue to hope in God despite his present situation. So, while outwardly darkness surrounds him, inwardly he resolves to lean upon the hope of God bringing him a bright future.

In Psalms 42–43, we witness faith wrestling with fear and hope with sorrow. And in this wrestling match, worship wins! Worship sprouts against all odds, like a wildflower in parking lot pavement. The irony is that, as the author seeks to return to the place of worship (the temple in Jerusalem), his earnest desire to do so becomes *worship* itself. Whatever situation we face, wherever we are, and whatever has got us down, let us join the psalmist now in such true worship.

No Fear

DOUGLAS SEAN O'DONNELL

MARTIN LUTHER based his famous hymn "A Mighty Fortress Is Our God" on Psalm 46. Have you ever had the experience of singing that song in a room of hundreds of men? I have, many times. As the room shakes with the voices of soaring tenors and booming basses, hearts are lifted heavenward in celebration of our Great Protector! In Psalm 46 God is described as "the LORD of hosts" (hosts = armies), who "is our refuge and strength, a very present help in trouble" (Ps. 46:1), or put simply, "our fortress" (vv. 7, 11).

With that truth about God in place, it logically follows: "Therefore, we will not fear" (v. 2). Despite apocalyptic upheaval ("the earth gives way" and "waters roar" and "the mountains tremble"; vv. 2–3), we are secure because God is in control. And yet, when troubles come, disaster strikes, or temptations arise, we usually trust in our own strength. We look to ourselves. Psalm 46 turns our attention upward. It raises our eyes to "the city of God" (v. 4) and to "God . . . in the midst of her" (v. 5). We are called to "behold the works of the LORD" (v. 8). He rules the world. He is the mighty Warrior, winning all wars. He will be exalted in all the earth.

As Christian men, we have the victory in Jesus, who is with us always (Matt. 1:23; 28:20) and has overcome the world (John 16:33). Through faith in him, we too have overcome the world (1 John 5:4–5). There is nothing in this world that can separate us from Christ's protective love. Tribulations, distresses, persecutions, and dangers may come our way, but they will not be the end of us. The powers of earthly rulers, cosmic forces, and even death cannot knock down our mighty fortress. Our security is set. Our victory is certain. We need not fear. "We are more than conquerors through him who loved us" (Rom. 8:37).

Sexual Sin and the Mercy of God

DOUGLAS SEAN O'DONNELL

WHAT MAN DOESN'T struggle with sexual sin? Thankfully, the Bible gives us many realistic heroes—saints yet sinners—who fell into the muck of sin and were graciously cleaned up by God. The background of Psalm 51 is David's adultery with Bathsheba. Until David was confronted by the prophet Nathan, he was blind to his sin. It's amazing! He committed adultery, Bathsheba got pregnant, and then David had her husband Uriah killed. I don't know what sexual struggles you have had this week, but hopefully your sin—and your blindness to it—hasn't reached David's depths of darkness!

Whatever darkness we have in the area of sexual impurity, Psalm 51 guides us to the light. We can join David in acknowledging and confessing sin:

> I know my transgressions (v. 3)
> Against you . . . have I sinned (v. 4)

We can join him in pleading with God for forgiveness:

> Have mercy on me (v. 1)
> Cleanse me from my sin (v. 2)
> Wash me (v. 7)
> Hide your face from my sins (v. 9)
> Deliver me (v. 14)

We can join him in asking for restoration:

> Create in me a clean heart (v. 10)
> Cast me not away from your presence (v. 11)
> Restore to me the joy of your salvation (v. 12)

And we can take those three steps not only for the sake of the spread of the gospel ("then I will teach transgressors your ways, and sinners will return to you"; v. 13), but also for the glory of God ("my tongue will sing aloud of your righteousness . . . my mouth will declare your praise" (vv. 14–15).

Jesus came for sinners. Jesus died for sinners. Jesus lives to say to sinners, "Your sins are forgiven. . . . Go in peace" (Luke 7:48, 50). Jesus is God's authorized agent to pronounce forgiveness and to bring restoration. He is the Savior who cancels all our debts—past sins, awful sins, seemingly unforgiveable sins. He alone can "wash" and "cleanse" us from sin (Heb. 9:19–28). So call out to him today, "Have mercy on me. . . . Cleanse me from my sin!" (Ps. 51:1–2).

APRIL 29 · PSALM 63

Thirsting for God

DOUGLAS SEAN O'DONNELL

OUR SOULS RESEMBLE the dry grass of an Arizona August more often than they resemble the tropical rainforest of the Amazon River basin. However, such dryness is not bad *if* it makes us thirsty for the life-giving God. Such thirst reminds us that we are *spiritually* alive. We *could* be thirsting for money, possessions, fame, intelligence, or human esteem; instead, our thirst is for God.

Psalm 63 is set in the "wilderness of Judah," and considering David's dire circumstances, what he says is amazing. His mouth is dry. His enemies are hot on his trail. His kingdom hangs in the balance. Yet here, he doesn't say that he thirsts for water, for the blood of his enemies, or even for salvation from the situation. Instead, there in a desert, with danger all around, he desires God! As with most of the Psalms, God is the theme. David mentions God six times in the opening verse and twenty times throughout this short song. However, in this psalm, while David sings of God's power, glory, love, and judgment, he focuses on his personal need for the person of God, with lyrics such as, "you are my God; earnestly I seek you; . . . my flesh faints for you" (Ps. 63:1); "when I remember you upon my bed" (v. 6); and "you have been my help" (v. 7). David especially focuses on the depths of his inner self. He speaks of his soul: "my soul thirsts for you" (v. 1); "my soul will be satisfied" (v. 5); and "my soul clings to you" (v. 8).

As we look at David's devotions in the desert, a question from a line of the old hymn arises: Is it "well with your soul"? Does your soul resemble David's? Do you have a soul that thirsts after, finds satisfaction in, clings to, and finds joy in God? Put in a specifically Christian perspective, and in the language of Philippians 3:8, do you "count everything as loss because of the surpassing worth of knowing Christ Jesus"? And because "Christ Jesus has made [you] his own" (Phil. 3:12), do you count the "loss of all things . . . as rubbish, in order that [you] may gain Christ and be found in him" (Phil. 3:8–9)? Put simply but profoundly, do you desire Christ? We should! For in him we find a well that never runs dry. As our Lord proclaimed, "Whoever drinks of the water that I will give him will never be thirsty again" (John 4:14).

APRIL 30 • PSALM 73

What to Do when the Wicked Prosper

DOUGLAS SEAN O'DONNELL

WHILE ASAPH BEGINS this psalm with an affirmation of the goodness of God (Ps. 73:1), this thought emerged only after the darkness of doubt described in verses 2–15. Asaph's envy of the arrogant had eclipsed his view of God's goodness. As he witnessed earthly injustice—the wicked prospering and the righteous suffering—he almost slipped into apostasy ("my feet had almost stumbled"; v. 2).

It took a renewed vision to sustain him. A visit to the temple ("I went into the sanctuary of God"; v. 17) was the cure for his spiritual shortsightedness. There, with God's people and in God's presence, he saw what happens to those who oppose God and his people ("I discerned their end"; v. 17). Those who have thought of God as deaf, dumb, and blind will face the hearing, listening, and seeing Judge. Their oppressions have not gone unobserved, and they will not go unpunished. Their scoffing will soon be stopped. The wicked "shall perish" (v. 27). God has "set them in slippery places" (v. 18).

Without warning, without a chance to escape or hope of future restoration, God will cut the chain of their pride, and they will fall headlong into justice.

But it is more than divine justice that sustains the psalmist. It is God himself! In four of the most heartfelt, beautiful, and uplifting verses in Scripture, Asaph sings of God's personal sustaining presence (v. 23), his promise of guidance into heavenly glory (v. 24), and his supremacy over all that earth has to offer (v. 25). "God is the strength of my heart and my portion forever" (v. 26). Having once envied the prosperity of the wicked, now he confesses that nothing in heaven or on earth is more desirable than God. To be "near God" (v. 28) is to possess far more than the wicked have and more than all that the world can offer.

Psalm 73 comforts us with the knowledge that God is caringly in control. It assures us that, at the end of earthly history, all the riddles of this puzzling world will be solved, the scales of justice balanced, and the sorrows of the pure in heart mended. More than that, it reminds us of our Savior, who showed absolute trust in the Father's will despite all the difficulties he faced, despite his sufferings at the hands of evil men, even to the point of death on a cross. In fact, that very cross is the absolute assurance that God is absolutely just (evil was dealt with) and absolutely good (he saves all who have made him their refuge).

MAY 1 · PSALM 77

Pondering the Mighty Deeds of God

DOUGLAS SEAN O'DONNELL

ANY PSALM THAT BEGINS, "I cry aloud to God, aloud to God" gets our attention. Asaph is desperate. He speaks of sleepless nights of mourning: "my soul refuses to be comforted" (Ps. 77:2); "my spirit faints" (v. 3); "I am so troubled that I cannot speak" (v. 4). However, he is not undone, as the final words of verse 1 confirm: "he will hear me." He trusts that God will listen and help.

Such confidence arises out of Asaph's meditation on the attributes and actions of God. He remembers the "holy" and "great" God (v. 13) and his "wonders of old" (v. 11). Specifically, he recalls the mighty act of Israel's exodus from Egypt (vv. 16–20). The imagery is enthralling and intense, beginning with, "When the waters saw you . . . they were afraid; indeed, the deep trembled" (v. 16).

When you are troubled, do you meditate upon the Lord? Do you ponder "all" his "mighty deeds" (v. 12)? And do you realize that God has "redeemed" us (v. 15) "by the hand" (v. 20) of someone greater than Moses (Heb. 3:1–6)? In the Lord Jesus Christ, the psalmist's questions find their ultimate answer: "Will the Lord spurn forever, and never again be favorable?" (Ps. 77:7). No! In Christ he will show us his favor: "For while we were still weak, at the right time Christ died for the ungodly" (Rom. 5:6). "Has his steadfast love forever ceased? Are his promises at an end for all time?" (Ps. 77:8). No! "In this the love of God was made manifest among us, that God sent his only Son into the world, so that we might live through him" (1 John 4:9). "Has God forgotten to be gracious? Has he in anger shut up his compassion?" (Ps. 78:9). No! "For God so loved the world, that he gave his only Son, that whoever believes in him should not perish but have eternal life" (John 3:16). Because of God's salvation in the past, at Jesus's death and resurrection, we can be confident in the present that he will bring about our full and final salvation in the future, at Christ's return and judgment.

When God Seems Far Away

MIKE BULLMORE

PSALM 88 IS SURELY the darkest of all the Psalms. Almost every other psalm ends with, or at least includes, some note of hope or praise. Not this one. There appears to be no relief.

We all experience this at times. Even though, as men, we want to be perceived as strong, we are privately aware of our weakness and frailty. Any deep disappointment or loss, any deep hurt, any prolonged sickness, any betrayal—really, any number of things—can make us feel what this psalmist, Heman, was feeling—lack of strength (Ps. 88:4), helplessness (v. 15), even despair (vv. 5–6). The fact is, being in a saving relationship with God through Jesus Christ does not mean that we will escape deep discouragement and even darkness. We will experience hard things, sometimes in waves, and sometimes for prolonged seasons. God has promised that we won't walk through those times alone, but he also hasn't promised that we won't at times *feel* alone.

So it's a good thing that God has lovingly included this psalm in his word. Otherwise we'd be left to wonder if God's sovereign love extended all the way to even our darkest experiences.

But Psalm 88 doesn't just describe a common human experience; it also provides a "prompt" on what to do during such an experience. Three times the psalmist tells us that he "cries out to God" (see vv. 1, 9, 13). That repetition provides a bit of structure to the psalm, but far more importantly it tells us what this psalm is and what it's here for. Psalm 88 is a *turning* to God in the darkness, and it calls us to do the same. Psalm 88 is a *telling* to God of the darkness, and it calls us to do the same. And Psalm 88 is a *trusting* of God despite the darkness, and it calls us to do the same.

Right at the beginning of this psalm the writer declares, "O LORD, God of my salvation . . ." Isn't that a striking statement, given the darkness of this psalm? Yet this is where Heman has put his hope. This is where there is a stake deep down into solid rock, and he has anchored himself to that stake.

Let's not miss that this psalm is a prayer. God does not belittle the prayer of the deeply discouraged or even despairing man. He wants us to remember that there is both safety and salvation in coming to him.

The God Who Protects

MIKE BULLMORE

PSALM 91 HAS BEEN a source of comfort and strength for believers for many generations, but you don't have to be a skeptic to find yourself asking questions when you read it. Questions like, "Really?" "No evil shall be allowed to befall you" (Ps. 91:10). Really? "It will not come near you" (v. 7). Really? And the asking of that question can become even more pressing if we've just read a passage like Psalm 88, for instance.

The fact is, we do experience evil and trouble. The world is a fallen place, filled with injustice and evil, and as Christians we are not exempt from the effects. What protection, then, is Psalm 91 promising? Clearly that's what this psalm is doing. Twelve times the psalmist claims that God will act in some way to protect.

Answering two questions will help us greatly here. First, whom does the psalm say God will protect? Starting at verse 3 and continuing on through verse 13, the psalmist says, "you." So who is the "you"? It's the one who "dwells in the shelter of the Most High" (v. 1; cf. v. 9). It's the one who says to the Lord, "My refuge and my fortress, in whom I trust" (v. 2). It's the same person that God himself describes as "holding fast to me" (v. 14). That is the one whom God will "deliver" and "protect" (v. 14).

That raises the second question: from what will God protect him? Verse 8 is key here. God will protect those who dwell in him from his judgment. We need to see that Psalm 91 is not promising that God will protect us from every hardship or effect of evil in this life. It *is* promising that we will be kept from God's judgment. Sometimes that means we will be spared *from* some effects of evil in this life. Sometimes that means we will be protected *in* trouble and hardship. But always we will be kept safe from any ultimate harm.

Jesus said much the same thing to his disciples: "You will be delivered up even by parents and brothers and relatives and friends, and some of you they will put to death. You will be hated by all for my name's sake. But not a hair of your head will perish" (Luke 21:16–18). Unless we want to say that Jesus was irrational, what that means is that there is a safety greater than safety from suffering, and Psalm 91 is saying that greater safety is absolutely guaranteed for those who have taken refuge in God. Even in suffering, those who dwell in God are absolutely safe.

God Will Set Things Right

MIKE BULLMORE

THERE IS A LONGING in all of our hearts for things to get resolved. Whether it's on the smaller scale of our daily work and personal relationships, or on the larger scale of racial tension and international conflict, we don't like things to be left unresolved. Deep in us there is a God-placed desire for things to be set right. Psalm 96 tells us that this is exactly what God will do.

Psalm 96 begins with an extended call for us to give praise to God (vv. 1–9). God is said to be "great" (v. 4), and he does "marvelous" works (v. 3). Several other praiseworthy attributes are ascribed to him as well, but the only specific action of God that is named in these opening verses is his making of the heavens (v. 5).

However, in the last four verses of this psalm, three times the psalmist speaks of God's future action of coming to judge the earth (vv. 10, 13). When the psalmist speaks of God "judging" here, he is not speaking solely of God condemning. He is speaking of God bringing justice and righteousness to all things. He is speaking of God setting all things right, and it is this promised future action that leads the psalmist to call all heaven and earth to rejoice, "*for* he comes to judge the earth" (vv. 11–13). All of creation will rejoice precisely *because* the Lord will come to judge in perfect righteousness. One thinks of the words of the apostle Paul in his letter to the Romans, where he speaks of all creation longing for the day when all will be set right (Rom. 8:19–23).

We all know, and all too well, that things are not now as they should be. We also know that God calls his people to pursue peace and justice now. But Psalm 96 tells us there is cause for great hope and there *will be* cause for great rejoicing, for there will come a day when all *will be* set right. "The LORD reigns!" (v. 10), and he will judge with righteousness, bringing all things to perfect resolution.

MAY 5 • PSALM 103

God Knows, God Remembers

MIKE BULLMORE

PSALM 103 IS LIKE a Thanksgiving table laden with rich food. Right from the start the psalmist speaks of "all" the "benefits" we have received from God (v. 2), with a clear intention to point out the abundance. There are "mercy" benefits (mostly in vv. 3–12). There are "compassion" benefits (mostly in vv. 13–18). And throughout the psalm there are listed the benefits of God's "steadfast love" (vv. 4, 8, 11, 17). There is one blessing, however, that stands out in bold relief. It is the fact that God "knows our frame; he remembers that we are dust" (v. 14). There is great hope and great comfort to be found in that truth.

Two wonderful things flow from the fact that God knows my frame and remembers that I am dust. First, it means that I don't need to pretend. The One who is the most important audience in my life is fully aware of who and what I really am. What a relief!

Second, the fact that God knows my frame and remembers that I'm dust means he's not expecting flawless perfection from me. This is no excuse for laziness or self-indulgence. It simply means God knows the limits of my ability. And because of my weakness, he deals with me with tender compassion (v. 13).

We will regularly fail. We will still sin. The amazing thing is that, even though we still sin, if we are in Christ, God no longer deals with us *on the basis of* our sin (v. 10). It isn't that he doesn't deal with the sin in our lives. It's that now he deals with our sin not according to our sin but according to his steadfast love (vv. 11–12; see also Ps. 25:6–7). There is no "benefit" greater than this for sinners like us, and there is nothing so entirely undeserved. And it all flows from this wonderful truth—that God knows our frame, remembers that we are dust, and deals with us with corresponding compassion.

It probably should not go without noting that this psalm begins and ends with a call to "bless God"—that is, to praise him for his goodness to us. Certainly near the top of the list of reasons to do so is this simple but profound fact: God knows us for who we really are, and he deals with us according to that knowledge. That's a great reason for gratitude and praise. So, bless the Lord!

MAY 6 · PSALM 107

The Rescuing Love of God

MIKE BULLMORE

APART FROM GOD, man gets himself into all sorts of spiritually dangerous and eternity-threatening situations. Four such situations are described in Psalm 107. We might not immediately find ourselves relating to what we see here, but if we read carefully and with spiritually attuned eyes, we will find much that maps onto our lives.

In each of four successive vignettes the psalmist describes some dire situation (Ps. 107:4, 10, 17, 23). Then, in each one of those scenes, two refrains are repeated exactly word for word: first, "Then they cried to the LORD in their trouble, and he delivered them from their distress" (vv. 6, 13, 19, 28); second, after an account of God's deliverance, "Let them thank the LORD for his steadfast love, for his wondrous works to the children of man" (vv. 8, 15, 21, 31). This repeated pattern of distress and deliverance is striking. One cannot miss it. Clearly, God wants us to get something here.

We need to see that, even though four different scenes are described, they are each speaking of the same fundamental situation. Whether it's aimlessness and isolation (v. 4), or enslavement (v. 10), or condemnation (v. 17), or overwhelming fear (v. 26), the scenes all describe the state of man on his own, separated from God. The obvious message in each case is that there is a desperate need for rescue; and the wonderfully good news is that, in each and every case, God rescues. He saves! The fact that God is a God of salvation resonates and reverberates throughout the Psalms, and that theme is sounded with particular strength in this psalm.

God saves no matter how our spiritual distress manifests itself—whether as alienation, enslavement, condemnation, or fear. God's rescuing love reaches to all situations and in all directions (see vv. 2–3). There is no situation, no *one*, outside the reach of God's rescuing love.

It is no coincidence that the language used by the psalmist here corresponds so completely to the language used by Jesus and by the writers of the New Testament to describe Jesus's saving work. The language of satisfying the hungry (v. 9), delivering from bondage (v. 14), delivering from destruction (v. 20), and providing safety and peace (vv. 29–30) all points unerringly to the salvation Jesus brings.

In light of this amazingly good news, we should happily take the counsel of both the first and the last verses of this psalm and thank God for his steadfast love.

MAY 7 · PSALM 110

The Lord Jesus Is a Warrior

MIKE BULLMORE

PSALM 110 IS OFTEN celebrated for its unique statement by King David about one whom David calls "my Lord" (v. 1). Here is the royal king, addressing someone even more royal. The writers of the New Testament clearly make much of this, identifying this greater King as Jesus (see Mark 12:35–37 and Acts 2:33–36). We have it on the best authority, then, that this psalm is about Jesus, and what a strikingly powerful statement it makes about him! "He will shatter kings on the day of his wrath" (Ps. 110:5). "He will shatter chiefs over the wide earth" (v. 6).

What comes to your mind when you think of Jesus? It's hard for us not to think first of the man who walked the dusty roads of first-century Galilee and Judea, as presented to us in the Gospels; we need the book of Revelation to give us the fuller and ultimate picture. There we see him riding a white horse, sword drawn. He is named "King of kings," and he is making violent war against his enemies (Rev. 19:11–21).

Psalm 110 anticipates that part of the picture of Jesus. It does, famously, speak of Jesus in his priestly role (v. 4), but it far more emphatically pictures Jesus as a Warrior King. It shows us Jesus going forth in holiness, glory, and fearsome power.

We need a humble, suffering servant who was willing to be "pierced for our transgressions," even "crushed for our iniquities" (Isa. 53:5). Upon that our salvation absolutely depends. But we also need a warrior, a champion on the field of battle, who will pursue and defeat all those who continue in opposition to him and threaten harm to us, his people. (The picture in Psalm 110:7, by the way, is of a warrior in pursuit, pausing momentarily to refresh himself and renew his strength before he continues on to rout his enemy.) Our hearts long for and rise to such a hero.

Our Lord Jesus Christ is this Warrior King. This is the Jesus whom we love, worship, and follow.

MAY 8 · PSALM 116

Our Death, Precious to God?

MIKE BULLMORE

THERE IS A STATEMENT in Psalm 116 that may strike you as a bit surprising, maybe even a bit off-putting. Verse 15 says, "Precious in the sight of the LORD is the death of his saints." How can this thing that is so heartbreaking to us humans be "precious" to God? Even when a death isn't untimely, the sadness of losing a loved one is close to the deepest grief a human can experience. When it *is* untimely, the grief can be overwhelming. How can such a thing be "precious" to God?

Psalm 116:15 (actually, all of Psalm 116) helps us to remember what death actually is, for the believer. For those who are in Christ, death is no longer the final enemy, the transition into eternal separation from God. In his death and resurrection, Jesus Christ conquered death for those who believe in him. His death paid the price for our sin, removing the penalty of death from us, and his resurrection overpowered death itself, a victory he promises to share with all who believe. So, for all Christians, "death [has been] swallowed up in victory" (1 Cor. 15:54). So now we can say, "O death, where is your victory? O death, where is your sting?" (1 Cor. 15:55). For those who are in Christ, for God's "saints" (Rom. 1:6–7), death is a transition into the presence of the Lord (2 Cor. 5:8), and it positions us for a glorious resurrection into everlasting life in heaven, where "death shall be no more" (Rev. 21:4).

All of this is grounded in the finished work of Jesus on our behalf, in which God the Father takes particular delight. Every Christian's death provides another occasion for God to rejoice over what Jesus his Son accomplished for us. The death of a Christian is the time when Christ's victory over death begins to be made personally effective. Jesus himself said, "I am the resurrection and the life. Whoever believes in me, though he die, yet shall he live" (John 11:25). Is it any wonder that God would say, "This moment of death, when I see my Son's victory over death now being made effective for another one of our redeemed people, is very precious to me"!

As we consider the deaths of dear fellow believers, as we consider the prospect of our own death, let us not lose sight of how God is viewing things. And let us let our way of seeing the death of believers become more and more like God's.

MAY 9 · PSALM 119:33–40

Give Me Life!

MIKE BULLMORE

GOD'S WORD REGULARLY celebrates its own power in the life of the believer. See, for instance, Isaiah 55:10–11 and Hebrews 4:12. Psalm 119 is in itself an extended catalog highlighting the power and effectiveness of God's word. Nearly every verse in this longest of the Psalms speaks of something God's word can do in the life of the believer.

One of the most consistent refrains in Psalm 119 is that God's word gives life. The psalmist repeatedly implores God, "Give me life according to your word!" (vv. 25, 37, 40, 50, 88, 93, 154, 156, 159). Two of those requests show up in this particular stanza (vv. 33–40).

What is this "life" that the psalmist so desires? It is the fullness of what we were made to experience in relationship with God. The human soul is hungry for that fullness. The problem is that, in our fallen state, we are inclined to seek satisfaction elsewhere (see vv. 36, 37). But there is no "life" in those other places. As Augustine so famously said to God, "You have made us for yourself, and our hearts are restless until they find their rest in you."[4] True life is found only in God, and God gives us that life through his word (see Deut. 8:3).

I think of the time when Jesus was teaching a crowd about his being the bread of life. That message was hard for people to understand, and many of them began to depart. Jesus turned to his disciples and asked, "Will you go away too?" Peter, in a moment of Spirit-inspired brilliance, said, "Lord, where else would we go? You have the words of eternal life" (see John 6:66–68). Peter did not mean that Jesus simply spoke *about* life. Peter had come to understand that Jesus was God, and that in him *was* life, and that this life had been mediated to him and the other disciples through Jesus's words.

The primary theme of Psalm 119 is that the believer feels devotion for God's word because he understands what God's word is and what it can do in his life. Verses 33–40 show, in particular, God's desire to give us life through his word. Every verse in this stanza is a request, a prayer. May these prayers become our prayers as we open God's word: "Give me life!"

Firmly Fixed and Exceedingly Broad

MIKE BULLMORE

AS WITH ALL the other stanzas of Psalm 119, in this stanza the psalmist praises particular qualities of God's word that call for our attention and then our glad-hearted and undying devotion (vv. 92–93). Two qualities stand out with unusual strength here, one in the first verse of this stanza and the second in the last verse.

First, in verse 89, the psalmist speaks of God's word being "firmly fixed" in heaven. God's word will stand unchanged through all time. It will maintain its authority in each and every generation here on earth (see v. 90). It will endure "forever." One need only think of the fixity of the countless stars in countless galaxies throughout the universe to gain a sense for what we are being told. Although stars may explode and morph, God's word remains stable and established and is therefore worthy of our undying trust.

Then, in verse 96, the psalmist says that God's word, specifically his "commandment," is "exceedingly broad." He contrasts this quality to the "limits" he sees in other "perfection" around him. One wonders what kind of "perfection" the psalmist has in mind. Was he thinking of certain experiences of natural beauty? Was it some perfection of human artistry or architecture? Whatever it was, he saw the limits. A view of majestic mountains, for example, could not at the same time hold the exquisite beauty of a desert flower. As impressive as the Jerusalem temple might be, it didn't possess the simple elegance of a beautifully woven robe or a particularly well-crafted tool. But God's word has no such limits. It speaks with authority to every situation. There is nothing it is not capable of addressing. It reaches out and encompasses all of life.

Together, these two qualities speak of the unlimited power and authority of God's word. It is indestructible through time. It is inexhaustible in its reach. Something like that calls for our full attention, and then our fully engaged devotion.

Firmly fixed. Exceedingly broad. What a sure foundation God's word is for our lives, no matter what we face!

God Our Helper and Keeper

MIKE BULLMORE

PSALM 121 SAYS two great things about God. The first is that God is a helper (vv. 1–2). Every one of us stands in daily need of God's help, and over and over again the Bible tells us that God is ready and eager to help us. It isn't just *our* eyes that look around for help (v. 1): "The eyes of the LORD run to and fro throughout the whole earth" to give help to those in need (2 Chron. 16:9). "Fear not, for I am with you; be not dismayed, for I am your God; I will strengthen you, I will help you" (Isa. 41:10). "Behold, God is my helper, the Lord is the upholder of my life" (Ps. 54:4). "The Lord is my helper; I will not fear" (Heb. 13:6). We will not always be aware of exactly how and exactly how much God is helping us. We walk by faith, not by sight. That's why God repeatedly tells us that he is helping us. Even in those loving reminders, he is helping us to believe and trust.

The second thing Psalm 121 tells us about God is that he is a "keeper" (vv. 3–8). That word "keeper" is wonderfully full of meaning. As it is used here, it basically means "protector." But as the psalmist reaches his triumphant conclusion, he speaks of the fact that God will maintain this protection "forevermore" (v. 8). In other words, he will "keep keeping" you. God will "keep" us in all our comings and goings in this lifetime and through all eternity. It is on this basis that Jesus says, "My sheep hear my voice, and I know them, and they follow me. I give them eternal life, and they will never perish, and no one will snatch them out of my hand" (John 10:27–28). Standing on the same ground, the apostle Paul tells us that nothing—either in life or in death—can really harm us and nothing can separate us from the love of God in Jesus Christ (Rom. 8:35–39). The Lord is a keeper, and he will be so forever.

When I think about what I really need from God, for this life and the next, it is hard for me to imagine anything greater than these two things that God happily *is* for me: my helper and my keeper.

In Quietness Is Your Strength

MIKE BULLMORE

HERE IS A PSALM that men in particular would do well to hear. Reading verse 2, however, we might not find ourselves immediately relating to the imagery. In fact, we might be tempted to pass over this psalm as something not entirely relevant to our masculinity. That would be a huge mistake, of course, and we would do well to see it as a mistake before we make it. Yes, God has made us to act and to get things done, not to just sit around. Still, there is a profound truth for us in this psalm that we, as men, really need to get.

It would be good to remember what the Psalms are for. The Psalms especially address our inner being—our mind, heart, and soul. They speak to what's going on with our fears, doubts, thoughts, discouragements, heartaches, and hopes. This psalm is addressed to a very particular inner reality, namely, when life feels overwhelming and we can be tempted to ask, "Is anyone really overseeing things? Is God really in charge and paying attention to how things are going in my world?"

David, the author of this psalm, would have had much opportunity to raise questions like this. After he was anointed as king, he went through a challenging ten years waiting for what God had promised would happen. During all that time there would have been a strong temptation for him to ask, "God, what is going on here?" Nonetheless, David decided not to lift up his heart in complaint, as if he knew better than God (Ps. 131:1). Instead, David purposed to rest himself in God (v. 2).

What does it look like to rest oneself in God? Like this weaned child is doing with its mother (v. 2), resting in God means simply trusting in his presence, his protection, and his care. This child is no longer fretting for something *from* his mother. He is simply resting *in* his mother. And just like this mother, God is present, and he is strong on our behalf. "The eternal God is your dwelling place, and underneath are the everlasting arms" (Deut. 33:27). Amazingly, even if we don't stop fretting, God won't stop being like that. But the fact is, we *can* rest.

Isaiah 30:15 says it so clearly: "In quietness and in trust shall be your strength." Men, that applies to us as much as to anyone.

MAY 13 • PSALM 135

The Deadening Effect of False Worship

MIKE BULLMORE

THE OLD TESTAMENT writers regularly compare the false gods of the various false religions to the one true God, and when they do so, they almost always point out the impotence of idols as compared to the powerful ability of our God. Isaiah, for example, makes much of this (see Isa. 44:12–20 and 46:1–7), and here in Psalm 135 we see the same theme. The psalmist announces, "For I know that the LORD is great, and that our Lord is above all gods" (v. 5), and then he proceeds to say, "Whatever the LORD pleases, he does, in heaven and on earth" (v. 6). Both in his control over nature (v. 7) and in his sovereign rule over human history (vv. 8–14), our God shows that he is powerfully able to do whatever he wills. And God is good (v. 3) in all that he does! On the other hand, the idols "have mouths, but do not speak; they have eyes, but do not see; they have ears, but do not hear, nor is there any breath in their mouths" (vv. 16–17). In short, they have no life or power.

Particularly sobering in this description of false gods is what the psalmist says in verse 18: "Those who make them become like them, so do all who trust in them." When the psalmist says that the worshipers of these idols "become like them," he's speaking of the characteristics he's just named: these idolaters can't speak, they can't see, they can't hear, and they can't breathe. In other words, there is a deadening effect that comes from worshiping and trusting in something other than God. There is a sapping of spiritual vitality that, unless reversed, will ultimately lead to total spiritual deadness.

We can see this same dynamic in our own culture, even though our "idols" are different. In fact, we can experience this dynamic in our own individual lives as well. To the degree that we are worshiping and trusting something other than God, we will experience a spiritual numbing that saps our spiritual senses and sensitivities.

That is not how God intends us to live. Jesus said it best: "I came that [you] may have life and have it abundantly" (John 10:10). Let us trust in the Lord with all our hearts and enjoy the vitality of life that God created us to enjoy in relationship with him.

MAY 14 · PSALM 139

Search My Heart, O God

MIKE BULLMORE

THE PROPHET JEREMIAH had much to say about what God is like. At one point he tells us that, even though the human heart is capable of great deceitfulness, God is nonetheless able to "search" our hearts, and he knows exactly what is going on in them (Jer. 17:9–10).

There are two ways to respond to a God who has that kind of power. You can do your best to avoid him, trying to hide, trying somehow to shield your heart from his sight, trying to convince yourself that God can't *really* know your heart, and that even if he does know, it isn't really that big of a deal.

That's one possibility.

The other option is to open wide your heart to this heart-searching God and say,

Search me, O God, and know my heart!
Try me and know my thoughts!

And see if there be any grievous way in me,

and lead me in the way everlasting!" (Ps. 139:23–24)

This is the way David chooses.

After meticulously and methodically cataloging the omniscience and omnipresence of God (vv. 1–6 and 7–18), instead of being threatened or put off by what might be taken as God's intrusiveness, David praises God, marveling at his greatness (vv. 17–18). And then David entrusts himself completely to God, imploring him to search his heart and to lead him away from any deceitfulness and into the ancient way of righteousness.

We might ask, how exactly does God search our hearts? Certainly one of the major ways is by his word. Hebrews 4:12 tells us, "The word of God is living and active . . . discerning the thoughts and intentions of the heart."

If I know that God searches my heart, and if I know that he uses his word to get that done, then I will regularly place myself humbly before his word. And when I do so my prayer will be, "O Lord, as I read your word, search me, O God, and lead me in the everlasting way!"

MAY 15 · PSALM 145

Exuberant Praise

MIKE BULLMORE

THERE IS IN US HUMANS the capacity for exuberance. God put that in us. We typically think of uninhibited exuberance as something belonging to childhood and youth, but thankfully, it is not limited to those periods of life.

Here in Psalm 145 David overflows with exuberant praise to God. He cannot contain himself, and it is clear that he isn't trying to. He is not afraid to use absolute terms (vv. 1–2). He is not reluctant to repeat himself (v. 3). He does not hesitate to pile up adjectives (v. 5). He gladly uses superlative language (v. 6). And he can't keep any of this to himself (v. 7). As you read these opening verses of Psalm 145 you cannot help but be aware of David's unrestrained exuberance.

So, how does this show up in my life and yours? Yes, we're all wired a little differently, and so our expressions of praise might not look exactly like David's. But this God whom David extols is our God too, and his greatness is absolutely undiminished. In fact, this psalm calls us to *join* in the exuberant praise (vv. 10–12). So what might this look like?

Certainly there is opportunity for this as we gather for worship with other believers. Regularly, the Bible calls us, when we worship together, to lift ourselves up to God. "Lift your hearts," we are told. "Lift your faces." "Lift your voices." You don't *have* to lift your hands, but lift something, especially your heart and voice, when you worship together with God's people.

But there ought to be private exuberance as well. As we read a psalm like this one in the privacy of our own devotional reading, there is wonderful opportunity to give expression to any impulse of exuberance in our hearts, maybe even finding a way to let body and voice loose in praise. I know there is in me a desire for this regularly, and surely I'm not alone. There is often strong desire in us to let something out and direct it up to God. He made us, at least in part, for this exuberant worship, and we find great fulfillment in doing what we were made for.

Let's join with David, saying along with him, "My mouth will speak the praise of the LORD, and let all flesh bless his holy name forever and ever" (v. 21). And then let Psalm 146 help you do it again tomorrow!

MAY 16 · PSALM 147

The Goodness of Knowing God's Rules

MIKE BULLMORE

AFTER READING OF the remarkable tenderness of God's love for his people and the almost unfathomable greatness of his power over the created world, the last two verses of this psalm (vv. 19–20) can seem more than a little anticlimactic.

Without any hesitation, the psalmist praises God, and calls us to praise God, for his tender and compassionate love for his people. The Lord "gathers the outcasts" (Ps. 147:2). He "heals the brokenhearted" and "binds up their wounds" (v. 3). He "lifts up the humble" (v. 6). He protects (v. 13), he blesses (v. 13), he brings peace (v. 14), and he provides for our daily needs (v. 14). He does this for all those who look to him and have put their hope in his steadfast love (v. 11). This, the psalmist says, is great reason to praise the Lord.

But even more striking in this psalm is the presentation of God's sovereign control of the created universe. He "determines the number of the stars" (v. 4). He "covers the heavens with clouds" and "prepares rain for the earth," making the "grass grow" (v. 8). He provides food for all living creatures (v. 9). He brings the changing seasons, each in their turn (vv. 16–18). All this makes the psalmist say, "Great is our Lord, and abundant in power" (v. 5). This too is reason for praise.

In light of these two great demonstrations of God's greatness, what gets said in verses 19 and 20 seems pale and small. But it isn't. What we need to understand is the incredible goodness of knowing God's "rules." Coming, as they do, from the perfection of God's own character, and given, as they are, out of his great love for us, these "rules" provide the foundation and direction for optimal human existence. As our Maker, God does indeed know best. Obedience to him is fundamentally a matter of trust in the goodness of his intentions and ways. It is, in fact, a great privilege to have and to know God's rules.

God has not left us adrift on a sea of uncertainty. He has made known to us his rules. And there is goodness for us here, a goodness on a par with God's compassionate love for us and his sovereign control of the world. Rejoice in the fact that God has made known his word to you. This, too, is great reason for praise.

The Pursuit of Wisdom

DAVE KRAFT

WHAT LOFTIER SEARCH could we embark on than the search for wisdom? What more valuable jewel in our crown of character could there be than that of the wisdom given to us by the very source of wisdom himself?

James reminds us, in his practical and helpful epistle, to ask for wisdom: "If any of you lacks wisdom, let him ask God, who gives generously to all without reproach, and it will be given him" (James 1:5).

In my early twenties I worked as a bank teller for a while, and each day multiple thousands of dollars passed through my hands. I felt a desperate need for wisdom beyond my years and experience. This was the first time I can remember asking for God's wisdom. I vividly recall memorizing (and I still regularly review) 1 Kings 3:9, 12, and 1 Kings 4:29, praying for the kind of wisdom Solomon asked for and received.

In the second chapter of Proverbs, this same Solomon who received wisdom is now encouraging us to go hard after it. He describes wisdom for us and shares some benefits of possessing it.

In verse 4 he describes this wisdom treasure hunt with two comparisons: (1) seek for it like silver, and (2) search for it as for hidden treasure.

In verses 5–11 he associates wisdom with knowledge, understanding, a shield, righteousness, justice, equity, every good path, and discretion. What a multifaceted jewel this wisdom is that we all so desperately need and for which we should earnestly seek.

What man following Jesus as Savior, Lord, friend, and teacher would not want to have such a wonderful gift as a companion through life as he faces difficult circumstances, financial stress, family challenges, and great temptations?

In verses 10–19 Solomon tells us that when this wisdom comes into our hearts, it will be pleasant and will protect us from evil men and women.

Heed Solomon's counsel and join in this magnificent search for the crown jewel of wisdom, which the Lord wants to lavish on all of us!

The Allure of Sexual Sin

DAVE KRAFT

AS OLD AS IS the subject of sexual sin, nothing could be more up-to-date and relevant. The statistics on those calling themselves evangelical Christians who struggle intensely in this area—often succumbing—are not very encouraging.

Christian men struggle enormously with issues of pornography and lust. As Paul Tripp has said, "We live in a world that has gone sexually insane." And this insane world is doing everything it can to drag us along in its wake. It's a lethal combination of a deceitful heart inside us (Jer. 17:9) and an evil adversary, the devil, on the prowl all around us (1 Pet. 5:8).

Solomon has both wisdom and warnings to share with us. In Proverbs 6:20–22, he points out the value of good teaching that can come from both mothers and fathers. We are to keep such teaching close to our hearts and let it be our guide in all facets of life. What he says is reminiscent of Deuteronomy 6:6–7.

Verses 23–35 of Proverbs 6 deal with the snare or trap that a seductive woman can lure us into, resulting in sexual sin. She is smooth-tongued; she hunts us down, using her eyes and her beauty to set the hook. There are devastating consequences from stepping into that trap. The man who goes down this road is lacking sense; he will destroy himself, incur wounds and dishonor, and be disgraced. That's quite a price tag for a few moments of illicit pleasure. Many a Christian man can testify to the price he has paid.

Verses 27–28 address the power of association. Two questions are asked: Can you carry fire next to your chest and not get burned? Can you walk on hot coals and not get scorched? The answer is obviously no!

This is where solid gospel accountability and community offer protection from bad associations. We need other men around us to ask the tough questions:

1. How might we be setting ourselves up for failure because of the movies, books, and music to which we expose ourselves?

2. How might we be making poor choices concerning the places we visit and the friends we hang out with?
3. In what way might we be deceiving ourselves, trying to convince ourselves we are doing okay when in fact we are not?

We need Solomon's counsel today more than ever!

True Wisdom Is Found in Christ

DAVE KRAFT

HERE WE HAVE another awesome and profoundly insightful passage on the critical topic of wisdom. It is noteworthy that wisdom is presented here as a person. We are admonished to seek her diligently (Prov. 8:17), to listen to her (v. 32), and to watch daily at her gates (v. 34). We are told in Colossians 2:3 that "all the treasures of wisdom and knowledge" are found in Jesus. He is the one we seek. The "she" of Proverbs 8 is now the "he" of Colossians 2, the second person of the Trinity.

Oh, to be encouraged that in him we have all the wisdom we need, seek, and long for. Speaking once again of Jesus, the apostle Peter says, "His divine power has granted to us all things that pertain to life and godliness" (2 Pet. 1:3). All that we need to lead lives pleasing and honoring to him is ours in Jesus. Not *some* things, not *many* things, but (did you see it?) *all* things! Jesus is our wisdom treasure trove, as we follow him all the days of our lives.

Solomon tells us that wisdom calls us, raises her voice, takes her stand, and cries aloud, trying to get our attention. But it's a two-way street: wisdom pursues us, and we, in turn, are to pursue the wisdom that is ours in Jesus.

This wisdom, found ultimately in Jesus, utters truth; it is not twisted or crooked but straight, right, insightful, and strong. This wisdom is better than silver, gold, or jewels. This wisdom has many brothers and sisters: prudence, knowledge, discretion, sense, counsel, strength, justice, wealth, and righteousness.

There are great advantages in having wisdom: through it we are blessed, we find life, and we obtain God's favor (Prov. 8:32–35). On the other side of the ledger, there is great peril in *not* having this wisdom. Lack of wisdom will cause personal injury and will actually lead us to *love* death: "all who hate me love death" (v. 36).

I love the song "All That I Need," by Twila Paris, where she speaks to Jesus, our true wisdom: "All that is good, all that is right, all that is truth, justice and light, all that is pure, holy indeed, all that is you is all that I need."

My brothers, all the wisdom we need—for all the times we need it and for all the areas in which we need it—is ours in Jesus!

MAY 20 • PROVERBS 11:9-13

Guarding Our Tongue Brings Great Gain

DAVE KRAFT

THE TONGUE CAN BE a source of great blessing or of great harm. One chapter in the New Testament, James 3, focuses especially on the bane and blessing of our tongue. We are told in verse 2, "if anyone does not stumble in what he says, he is a perfect [mature] man, able also to bridle his whole body." If we as men, through the grace of God, can gain control of our tongues, we are able to exert mastery over virtually every other area of our lives.

In Proverbs 11:9–13 we are told that

- we can destroy our neighbors with our *mouth* (v. 9);
- a city can be overthrown by the *mouth* of the wicked (v. 11);
- a slanderous *tongue* demonstrates untrustworthiness (v. 13).

In Proverbs 13:3 we read, "Whoever guards his mouth preserves his life; he who opens wide his lips comes to ruin." Did you catch that? Opening your mouth at the wrong time and saying the wrong thing can ruin your life! How many politicians, business leaders, or church leaders have you read or heard about who ruined their careers or family relationships by a significant slip of the tongue? Once the toothpaste is out of the tube, it's impossible to put it back in! The same is true of what we say. The toothpaste analogy has served me well through the years. It has taught me to guard my tongue and be prudent and careful in what I say, when I say it, and to whom I say it.

We all love to express our opinions and even our feelings, but as Proverbs reminds us, there are many times in life when "a man of understanding remains silent" (11:12). As the old saying goes, "Better to keep silent and be thought a fool, than to open your mouth and remove all doubt."

Silence can be golden!

MAY 21 · PROVERBS 15:25–33

Avoiding the Poison of Pride

DAVE KRAFT

WHAT MAKES THE DIFFERENCE between pride and humility? Here we have yet another amazingly insightful passage in Proverbs dealing with a character tension that is as old as the hills but as relevant as today's newspaper.

In Proverbs 15:25, Solomon tells us, "The LORD tears down the house of the proud." In verse 33 he says, "The fear of the LORD is instruction in wisdom, and humility comes before honor."

In between *pride* (v. 25) and *humility* (v. 33) we read, "The ear that listens to life-giving reproof will dwell among the wise" (v. 31), and, "Whoever ignores instruction despises himself, but he who listens to reproof gains intelligence" (v. 32).

How does a potentially proud man become a humble man? He does so by listening to those who would reprove him and by not ignoring the opportunities for instruction that the Lord sends his way.

Throughout the book of Proverbs we find the comparison between a fool and a wise man, and one of the distinguishing features of the wise man is the willingness to listen well and to grow by receiving reproof from others. Meanwhile, the fool in his old age will bemoan, "How I hated discipline, and my heart despised reproof! I did not listen to the voice of my teachers or incline my ear to my instructors" (Prov. 5:12–13).

The fool is the man who thinks he knows it all and who is not open to what others may offer by way of correction or instruction. In the words of the apostle Paul, "If anyone imagines that he knows something, he does not yet know as he ought to know" (1 Cor. 8:2). The last thing we should want to become is the man who thinks he knows it all and thereby demonstrates that he actually knows very little. It was John Wooden who said, "It's what you learn after you know it all that counts."

Do you have a teachable spirit? It should be at the top of your list of "most desired character qualities." We need to hear from God, our wives, our children, our friends, and our spiritual leaders. If you're not teachable, over time you will become the proud man whom God opposes (1 Pet. 5:5–6).

MAY 22 · PROVERBS 19:16-23

Dealing with Anger

DAVE KRAFT

IN PROVERBS 19:16-23, we encounter issues such as generosity, disciplining of children, anger, listening, plans, God's purpose, love, and fearing God. Here we will focus on anger.

We are told that "a man of great wrath will pay the penalty" (v. 19). Earlier in this chapter we read, "Good sense makes one slow to anger, and it is his glory to overlook an offense" (v. 11).

It is safe to say that many men have an anger issue. In some cases, they may even be required to attend an "anger management class" because authorities fear that they pose harm to family or friends. Years ago I heard a speaker say that the greatest cause of burnout for men between ages eighteen and thirty-five is bitterness, which is a close cousin to anger.

Bitterness can be the result of deep-seated anger that is left unaddressed for a long time. It is a poison in the soul that can take an enormous toll on our lives emotionally, spiritually, and relationally. Otherwise successful leaders have often struggled with significant anger and bitterness, and have made shipwreck of their lives and careers.

Many of us are slaves to anger. We are sleeping volcanoes, ready to erupt at any moment, and our families and friends are living in dread of what we may do.

What angers us?

- A family of origin that never understood or appreciated us (a father in particular)?
- Feeling we have been treated unfairly by an authority figure (a teacher, coach, or employer)?
- Having been sexually or physically abused?
- Having been teased, bullied, or made fun of while growing up?

Angry men have a long memory, and they keep score. Only by the power of the Holy Spirit and through the good news of the gospel can we recover our lives and enjoy the peace of God. Only by his grace can we be enabled to "overlook an offense." Where are you in all of this? If it's a recurring problem, seek accountability and wise counsel without delay.

MAY 23 · PROVERBS 24:10-12

Taking Responsibility

DAVE KRAFT

IF THERE IS ONE thing that separates the men from the boys, it's taking responsibility for our choices, our attitudes, and our behavior.

Mature men say things like "It was my fault." "I take full responsibility." "The buck stops with me." "I'm sorry; please forgive me."

Immature men play the blame game: "I'm the victim; it was *his* fault."

Proverbs 24:10–12 describes the man who grows "faint" when the pressure is on. He simply quits or throws in the towel when the going gets tough.

This is followed by a strong admonition to take responsibility for those in our immediate world who are being harmed or hurt. It is easy to play dumb, saying, "I didn't know," or, "I didn't have a clue." But God knows our hearts, and he knows what we absolutely did know but chose to ignore.

This tendency to blame others and not take responsibility when the heat is on is as old as the garden of Eden and as current as today's newspaper. When God confronted Adam about his sin, Adam immediately pointed to Eve and blamed her. Eve, in turn, blamed the serpent. Such a response to being held accountable continues to this day in every facet of life, church, and business. People deflect responsibility for their own sin by either excusing it or blaming others.

It has been noted that many men today are living in a season of extended adolescence. Men in their twenties and thirties are acting like collegians and not taking responsibility for their lives. The apostle Paul exhorts us all to "Be watchful, stand firm in the faith, act like men, be strong" (1 Cor. 16:13). To "act like a man" is to behave responsibly. It means standing firm, standing tall, and coming to the aid of those who cannot stand up for themselves. It means first taking responsibility for our own lives—to make our lives count for something beyond merely surviving. Then it means making unique and lasting contributions to those whom God places in our lives—our family, our friends, and those who don't yet know Jesus. Suffice it to say, when the going gets tough, the tough get going. They step out. They step up. They assume responsibility as they lean into the promise that "I can do all things through him who strengthens me" (Phil. 4:13).

MAY 24 • PROVERBS 31:10-31

Cherishing the Gift of a Godly Wife

DAVE KRAFT

AFTER ALL THE ADVICE, wisdom, and insight Solomon has given to young men, he concludes by considering the qualities of character in the most important person in a man's life: the woman to whom he will be married. Getting married and staying married to the right woman must assuredly be at the top of the list of those things that will help us stay on "the path of the righteous" (Prov. 4:18).

Someone has joked that behind every successful man is a surprised mother-in-law! But behind every God-fearing married man should *not* be a surprised wife but a supportive wife—a wife who can be the helper whom God has in mind for him (Gen. 2:18).

Whether you are married or not, Solomon's counsel is good. These twenty-two verses are filled with wonderful, admirable qualities of the godly woman. Here are a few that stand out:

- She does her husband good and not harm all the days of his life.
- She is hardworking and industrious.
- She is respected and well thought of by her children.
- She is generous.
- She is the kind of woman her husband can trust.

Paul makes it clear in 1 Timothy 3:2 that God's desire for married leaders (and for all married men) is that they be a "one-woman man." By this he means men whose eyes do not wander, men whose minds and hearts are faithful and devoted to their wives.

He desires men who are faithful to one woman all of their lives; men who are emotionally, mentally, and physically devoted to their wives. The Bible thinks so highly of the one-man–one-woman relationship that it equates it with Christ and his church (Eph. 5:22–33). It doesn't get any more valuable than that!

Those of you who are not yet married but want to be: pray over these verses and ask God to lead you in the selection of a lifelong partner.

Men who are married: pray over these verses, asking the Holy Spirit to use you in helping your wife as she seeks to be this kind of woman.

Work: Both God's and Yours

ZACK ESWINE

GOD GAVE US LOVE, play, rest, and worship. He also gave us work (Gen. 2:15). Solomon is right that each of us is a "worker" (Eccles. 3:9).

Notice how kind and relevant the Bible is. God gives language for our deepest questions. He knows what it means that we now have to work, not in Eden or in heaven, but in this in-between, "under the sun." God understands why a frustrated man cries out for significance. He knows that we have longings for "eternity" in our hearts (v. 11). He knows that, all too often, our work does not satisfy us. He knows we want to know that our work has purpose (v. 9). So, he gives voice to our questions in the pages of his Bible.

Notice too that God speaks of our work in light of his being the master worker who has "made everything" (v. 11), and Jesus affirms this as well (John 5:17). God works purpose and beauty into every season of your life, and he sets a longing for himself in your heart (Eccles. 3:10–11); he possesses a working knowledge of creation that dwarfs your own (v. 11); and his work is made with materials that endure and last, no matter what (v. 14). He's also actively involved in your daily work (v. 15). When you put on your shoes or boots this morning, he's already up and at the job site. He values your work. When you do your work today, you won't be working alone.

This is because work has a gift within it. That gift is the pleasure and enjoyment of God. What is more, God prizes the sweetness of Eden-like things after a hard day's work. The gift of food, drink, and rest in the company of those we love within the integrity of having worked hard and well is saturated with the pleasures of God (v. 13). God's gift is the gain you were made for.

This is why Jesus, a wiser man than Solomon ever was (Luke 11:31), calls out to you, "What does a man gain if he invests and receives return of the whole world but goes bankrupt when it comes to those treasures that were made by God to fulfill his soul?" (see Matt. 16:26).

Few people at work today will talk like this. But Jesus does. You were made for gain of a different kind, not what your work will get you in this world but what *his* work will give you day by day within it. A man with such daily treasure isn't missing out on anything. By grace, he can truly learn to say, "There is nothing better" (Eccles. 3:12).

MAY 26 • ECCLESIASTES 9:11–18

Godly Competition

ZACK ESWINE

WE COMPETE. We "race" each other and "battle it out." We try to prove who can provide the best "bread," gain the most "riches," and accrue the most "favor." We prize the one who is more "swift" or "strong," or "wise" or "intelligent" (Eccles. 9:11).

Jockeying for position like this all day, every day, in order to prove to persons imaginary or real that we are worthy of respect is no kind of life. People get hurt. So do we. Solomon tells us why.

First, we try to win the wrong battle. If we compare ourselves not to others but to the strength, speed, intelligence, and favor of evil, it turns out that we are nothing more than minor players in this world. No trophy we achieve can defeat evil or the death that evil brings upon us (v. 12).

Second, we rely on the wrong kinds of power. We see ourselves as kings, loud with ability. But one small whisper of God's wisdom, demonstrated in the quiet by a man we'd think weak, can overthrow us (vv. 14–17).

What good is it to win a trophy for being faster or smarter than one another when evil outpaces and defeats all of us anyway? Defeating evil is the true competition of your life. Only a power fit for that kind of battle will do.

Jesus is the poor wise man, with the kind of power we need. He comes to us like a humbled servant. We look upon his weakness and overlook him. But we do not realize that he is faster, stronger, smarter, and more favored than we are, more than anyone or any power that we esteem. His power is of a different kind, and so is the battle he will win.

Under the sun, this kind of talk about a competitor and a power of a different kind sounds ridiculous. After all, if we looked at the epitaph of the poor wise man, it might read, "Here lies a poor wise man. He rescued those who forgot him." "But I say that wisdom is better than might, though the poor man's wisdom is despised and his words are not heard" (v. 16).

We are invited now to confess our folly, aren't we? We've tried to win a race that we cannot win, by relying on useless powers. When we do, it is like forgetting the one who rescued us. But the true poor wise man teaches us graciously to pray, "Deliver us from evil" (Matt. 6:13). He then fulfills this prayer. Evil did its worst, and lost. The cross fell. The tomb emptied. True power rose. The real battle was won!

MAY 27 · SONG OF SOLOMON 2:8-17

True Love's Ways

ZACK ESWINE

MEN WHO USE words to sexually conquer, boyishly invite mothering, or powerfully control merely show their immaturity. By contrast, these verses show the blessing a good man's words are meant to be to a woman's heart.

First, we can learn how to bless our wives by reading God's inspired poetry. To suggest that love poetry isn't manly is foreign to God.

Second, a wife cherishes her husband's voice (Song 2:8) and lingers over it in her memory. Notice the quotation marks in these verses. She recounts to her friends what he has spoken of his love for her (vv. 10–15).

Third, she cherishes his view of her beauty. She is to him a "beautiful one," whose "voice is sweet," and whose "face is lovely" (vv. 10, 14). She cherishes his initiative ("Arise, my love"; vv. 10, 13). She delights to know that he wants to spend time with her ("come away"; vv. 10, 13). In fact, he wants his whole world to merge with hers. She is no sideline to his work or play or dreams. If he is a gazelle, he wants her out in the world with him, "in the clefts of the rock, in the crannies of the cliff" (v. 14). He wants nothing to come between them. He asks her to watch out for any little fox that might sneak in to damage or destroy the love they create and inhabit (v. 15).

The result? She knows that he is hers and she is his. He has forsaken all other women. She is his true delight. Therefore, feeling safe, cherished, honored, and protected, she passionately invites him freely to know her body and soul. "Turn, my beloved, be like a gazelle or a young stag on cleft mountains," she says. Come and graze among the lilies I have to offer you. Her body and soul is the pasture in which she longs for him to graze (v. 16). Their lovemaking is unhindered, with mutual delight.

If we haven't known this kind of love, God gives us hope. His grace points us to his design through these words. Many in the ancient church saw these words spiritually, too. We (even men) are like a bride longing in our souls for Jesus. We esteem him. We cherish his invitation, his spoken words of love. We memorize them and recount them to others. We invite him into the most intimate part of our life because to dwell with him is to know that we are lovely. And, more than that, to dwell with Jesus is to know, finally, what true loveliness is.

MAY 28 · SONG OF SOLOMON 4

A Steamy Scene of Sexual Wonder

ZACK ESWINE

THIS CHAPTER IN the Bible gives hot language to the passionate sexual experience that most of us dream about. Reread that sentence: for all of our talk and desire, screen histories and hook-ups, we are a sexually impoverished people.

Don't let this ancient poetry veil the steamy scene of sexual wonder that is portrayed for you here. God intends to teach you. First, notice that this husband meditates upon his beloved's eyes, hair, teeth, lips, mouth, cheeks, neck, breasts, and tongue, along with the varying fragrances of her body, and he notices the details of what she is wearing, including her jewelry. Elsewhere he will speak of her feet, her skin, her navel, her belly, her nose, and her head (Song 7:1–10). She experiences a man fully immersed in every part of her body.

Second, notice that he is therefore in no hurry. He does not rush, but slows into her wholeness. He takes intentional time to admire, to linger with, to delight over, and to bear witness to every inch of what is beautiful about her. He takes in her entirety with his eyes and paints the captivating beauty set before him with words. She experiences a man taking extended time with focused attention upon her. He has not touched her yet. Self-control is his to handle, not hers to relieve. He has enjoyed her presence and has spoken. There is no flaw in her, not because there isn't, but because he sees her as a whole woman, and she is altogether lovely to him (4:7).

Third, as a person who loves God, he is not afraid to speak with the most wholesome seductiveness of a good man's enjoyment. "You have captivated my heart with one glance of your eyes" (v. 9). "Your lips drip nectar, my bride; honey and milk are under your tongue" (v. 11). Let us "be drunk with love" (5:1)! She experiences his unveiled delight in her.

In response to his delight that guards and honors rather than consumes her, she invites him passionately and wholeheartedly to her. She is his garden. She calls boldly and happily to him: "Let my beloved come to his garden, and eat its choicest fruits" (4:16).

All of this vibrant lovemaking flows out of true love ("your love is better than wine"; 1:2), deep spiritual companionship ("my sister"; 5:1), and the covenant commitment of marriage vows ("my bride"; 5:1). Porn pales in comparison to the ravishing sexual love that God envisions for us. One-night stands can't captivate a heart the way genuine love can. Enjoying your spiritual sister, bride, and lover is not sinful to God. On the contrary, such married sexual love is God's gracious gift!

Religious Wickedness

DANE C. ORTLUND

GOD'S PEOPLE HAVE forsaken him. But not entirely the way we might expect. The people of Judah have not left behind religious observance and merely taken up explicit idol worship, sexual promiscuity, murder, or other outward sins. On the contrary, they continue to offer the appropriate sacrifices and perform the required rituals. There is much good activity in the temple at Jerusalem.

And yet the Lord calls Judah "a people laden with iniquity" and the "offspring of evildoers" (Isa. 1:4). He even likens Judah to Sodom and Gomorrah (v. 10). What has happened? The outward actions no longer reflect the state of the heart of the people of Judah. The work of their hands does not show the true state of their heart. The outside contradicts the inside. They do not care about the widow or the fatherless (v. 17). Why? Self-concern has gradually replaced other-concern. Love has left. This is sin.

For this reason, God says, he is fed up with their offerings (v. 11). He "cannot endure iniquity and solemn assembly" (v. 13). What a remarkable thing to say. God cannot endure the way sin has taken root in the sacred space of the temple and the ceremonies that take place there. This is religious wickedness.

All this might seem quite remote and removed from our own existence as men of God in the twenty-first century. But is not the heart-temptation the same? We too can easily slide into a way of life that retains the outward form of faithfulness while the heart wanders—as the apostle Paul would put it, "having the appearance of godliness, but denying its power" (2 Tim. 3:5).

What, then, is the way forward? How do we avoid such hypocrisy? Or, if we sense we are already in it, how do we get out? This passage that opens the book of Isaiah already points us in the right direction: "Come now, let us reason together, says the LORD: though your sins are like scarlet, they shall be as white as snow" (Isa. 1:18). God's answer to a heart resisting his grace is: more grace. The way out is not self-atonement or renewed moral fervor, but repentance (v. 27). Calming down and opening up, once more, to the Lord of compassion. He sent his Son, himself white as snow, to die on a cross and pay for our scarlet sins, to make us sinners white as snow by sheer mercy. All wickedness, irreligious or religious, is rinsed clean in this fountain of grace.

The Worth of Godly Leadership

DANE C. ORTLUND

GOD PUT ADAM in the garden of Eden "to work it and keep it" (Gen. 2:15), and in this way he was to "subdue" and "have dominion over" the earth (Gen. 1:28). In other words, God put man on the earth to lead. Every man is called to lead, at the very least in the context of his family, if he has one, and in the workplace. In the heart of every man is the healthy impulse to rule—however large or small the extent of such rule might be, whether the tasks at one's work cubicle or the oversight of a nation.

One manifestation of sin in Isaiah's day was the rejection and even inversion of this healthy impulse. Not only are the leaders among God's people (the prophets and priests) not following the Lord faithfully, but the people of Judah are glad to make *anyone* a leader (Isa. 3:6), regardless of their level of maturity and godliness, so long as they themselves don't have to lead. They say things like, "You shall not make me leader of the people" (v. 7).

And why are God's people resisting the call to fulfill the mandate of Genesis 1 and 2? They have wandered away from the Lord, "defying his glorious presence" (Isa. 3:8). When we leave or forget the presence of the Lord, fears arise. We forsake our high calling as men.

Leadership is scary. Risky. It will bring scars. Leading as God would have us lead—in our homes, our families, our neighborhoods, our offices, our churches—opens us up to criticisms of all kinds, to pain we could otherwise avoid. Such is life in a fallen world. But the Lord has said, "I will never leave you nor forsake you" (Heb. 13:5). Whatever happens in our attempts to lead, the Lord is with us. We have "his glorious presence" (Isa. 3:8).

Indeed, it is precisely in the pain and criticism we endure as godly leaders that we are most wonderfully aligned with Christ himself, the coming "branch of the Lord" (4:2), who shows us God's glorious presence in flesh and blood (John 1:14). Adversity-ridden leadership was the path for him. It is the glad path of discipleship for God's men today (1 Pet. 5:1, 10). He is present with us—gloriously present.

His Holiness, Our Messiness

DANE C. ORTLUND

WHAT IS THE "holiness" of God? It is the very God-ness of God. It is who he is, what makes him God—his transcendent beauty, his eternal dignity, his supreme worth, his unspeakable loveliness, his spotless purity, his resplendent glory.

When Isaiah sees the Lord in the temple, his holiness is the theme of the song of the seraphim (Isa. 6:3). Why? Because they are rejoicing in who God *is*. One reason men today are often tepid in their experience of church is that they are presented with a domesticated God, a junior varsity God, not the God Isaiah beheld in the temple. The real God summons men by grace into adventure. We see both of these—grace and adventure—in Isaiah's experience.

First, it is God's holiness that exposes Isaiah's own messiness. He is suddenly face to face with the holy God, and therefore he is suddenly face to face with his own non-holiness. "I am a man of unclean lips" (v. 5). Does this disqualify Isaiah? Not at all. Those unclean lips are touched, cleansed, purified. "Your guilt is taken away," he is told (v. 7). This is the summons of grace. The holy God makes unholy sinners holy. The unclean are rinsed clean.

Second, God sweeps us into adventure—a holy adventure, not of rescuing a princess from a tower but of rescuing other unclean sinners from the wrath of God. Isaiah answers God's summons to speak truth to other people (v. 8). This is what the grace of God does. It nestles our hearts into calmness, but it spurs on our hands and lips into action.

Who is your God? To whom do you pray? This is the true God, supremely holy but supremely gracious. In Jesus Christ, we see this come together in one man. He too cleansed sinners by touching them, and he too summoned them into adventure, the adventure of discipleship, the greatest thrill of life under the sun.

Hitting Rewind on Injustice

DANE C. ORTLUND

EVERY MAN, SOONER OR LATER, knows the pain of injustice. Favoritism at work, unfairness in a relationship, betrayal by a wife, ingratitude from a child, mistreatment at church—and a hundred other weekly injustices, small in themselves but cumulatively disheartening. And of course we ourselves are often guilty of treating others unfairly.

The unfairness of so much of life in this fallen world quickly generates discouragement and, eventually, cynicism. Why try to do good? Why bother to make a difference, when injustice and inequality are so rampant?

On the one hand, the unfairness of life is one reason the book of Ecclesiastes exists. Ecclesiastes is preventive medicine against cynicism. We must be realistic, not naive. But here in Isaiah 9 we are given a glimpse into the ultimate reason for hope and stability. God has committed himself to one day hit Rewind on all this world's crooked injustices and restore justice in every nook and cranny of life. Every wrong will be righted, every sin exposed, every mistreatment abundantly compensated. This is the meaning of Isaiah 9:7: "Of the increase of his government and of peace there will be no end, on the throne of David and over his kingdom, to establish it and uphold it with justice" (v. 7).

Whose government? Whose kingdom?

This is the government and kingdom of the one man who on this earth deserved fairness but got unfairness, who deserved justice but got

192

injustice. Thus the promise of Isaiah 9 has already dawned in the world in the middle of history. This is why Isaiah 9:6–7 is more than a warm inspirational thought for Christmas. This is our lifeline to sanity in an unjust world. God gave his own Son, the Prince of Peace, to be treated unjustly, so that we who trust in him can be guaranteed that one day every injustice against us will be rewound and straightened out. This is a peace, a justice, of which "there will be no end."

Our True Trust

DANE C. ORTLUND

WHEN MICHAEL JORDAN entered the NBA Hall of Fame, he concluded his speech by saying, "In closing, the game of basketball has been everything to me. My refuge. The place I've always gone when I needed to find comfort and peace." The way in which Michael Jordan sought refuge—professional basketball stardom—is unique to him; but the impulse to find his "refuge" and "comfort and peace" in the things of this world is not. That is every man's battle. In Isaiah 12 we are given the only real refuge and the only stable comfort and peace:

> Behold, God is my salvation;
>> I will trust, and will not be afraid. (Isa. 12:2)

What does it mean that God is a man's "salvation"? Certainly, it means we are delivered from our sins and assured of eternal life. But for the biblical writers it means far more than this. It means our heart is being drawn away from every fraudulent refuge in this world, those that promise so much but deliver so little: human approval, a certain salary, sensual pleasure, weekend comfort, spiritual achievement, career advancement, educational excellence, church involvement, physical prowess, and a thousand other things. All of these are in themselves morally neutral, but the fallen human heart is hardwired to pursue these created things as the supreme good and to sacrifice everything else to obtain it.

But notice what Isaiah says: *God* is his salvation. Therefore he will trust and not be afraid. Why do we fear? Why are we anxious? Because we are afraid that our functional refuges will collapse on us. We are fearful of not succeeding in a job, or not impressing someone we respect, or failing the test, or botching the sales pitch. We fantasize about succeeding in those real-life situations but have nightmares about failing. Feeling inadequate, we set up our career, our relationships, our studies, and many other good things as functional gods to which we look for significance and salvation.

But it is an insecure security, because it rests on performance. What if we could go into the interview, the conversation, the classroom, the pulpit, the game, already saved? What if we took God at his word in Isaiah 12? "God is my salvation!" We would be invincible, because we would be fearless.

JUNE 3 • ISAIAH 19:16–25

Mercy to Every Corner of the World

DANE C. ORTLUND

WHY DID GOD call Abraham? Why did he set Israel apart for himself? It wasn't ultimately for their own sake but so that they would be a blessing to the nations. This was the point from the beginning of God's chosen people: that Abraham's descendants "will be a blessing," so that "all the families of the earth shall be blessed" (Gen. 12:2–3).

As the history of God's people unfolded, however, certain foreign nations proved to be especially hostile toward them. Chief among these were Egypt, where Israel was in bondage for four centuries, and Assyria, who would lay waste to Israel and carry God's people off into exile. It would be especially surprising, therefore, for the people of God to be told through Isaiah in no uncertain terms that Egypt and Assyria would be preeminent among those blessed by God, along with Israel.

At first, one wonders how God could be so scandalously merciful to such wicked nations. But then we remember the sordid history of the Israelites themselves, who not only failed to bring other nations into loyalty to God but also invariably failed in their own allegiance to God. And then we begin to see what is perhaps the lesson of all of human history: no one is righteous. Paul delves into this reality throughout Romans 11 and concludes, "For God has consigned all to disobedience, that he may have mercy on all" (Rom. 11:32). God's people themselves need the grace they were mandated to channel out to the world.

When you invite your next-door neighbor to church, you are participating in the point of all of human history—the welcome of the nations into the mercy of God. The final act in the great drama is this: that by his own blood, Jesus Christ "ransomed people for God from every tribe and language and people and nation" to be "priests to our God, and they shall reign on the earth" (Rev. 5:9–10)—priests to God from Assyria and Egypt, from Brazil and Iran, from India and China, and from your own little corner of the world.

JUNE 4 · ISAIAH 25:6–12

The Death of Death

DANE C. ORTLUND

THERE IS ONE thing that all people everywhere agree is certain: we will all die.

We mentally postpone it and avoid it. We don't talk about it and generally don't think about it. It is awkward to discuss and painful to ponder. But it is unavoidable. The most healthy and longest-lived people on earth are, from about age thirty on, dying. Metabolism slows. The risk of various diseases gradually increases. Quickness on the basketball court inevitably wanes. No vitamin, no nutritional supplement, can stop the process of aging. We have become experts in hiding the appearance of aging, but aging itself is our master, not our servant. And one day, perhaps far off or perhaps very soon, the heart will stop beating and we will exhale one last time. We will be swallowed up by death.

According to the Bible, however, this is not the way it is supposed to be. Death is an intrusion. It is unnatural. Although death is certain in this current age, it is a foreign invader. Consider the three pictures the Bible gives us of human life without sin: Adam and Eve before the fall, Jesus, and the new heavens and new earth. Death is present in none of these: Adam and Eve died only after they sinned (Gen. 2:17); Jesus died but rose again, conquering death (Acts 2:24); and death will no longer afflict us in our final state (Rev. 21:4).

Here in Isaiah 25 we glimpse the great promise of what God will one day do for his people. "He will swallow up death forever" (v. 8). Death will die. Death will not have the last word. To die feels so unnatural to us because we were made to live forever. And for those who trust in Christ, we *will* live forever—in transformed but fully physical bodies, on this globe, reigning with him.

We know this to be true because we have been united to a Savior who entered into death and came out the other side, taking us with him. Indeed, though we will die physically one day soon, we who are in Christ have already been raised spiritually (Rom. 6:4; 1 Cor. 15:20–23). Resurrection life has broken in on our messy little lives. One day soon we will be the resplendent, radiant men God made us to be.

JUNE 5 • ISAIAH 28:14-22

Not in Haste

DANE C. ORTLUND

IN THIS STRANGE and wonderful passage, God declares that the inscription on the cornerstone of the future temple will be, "Whoever believes will not be in haste" (Isa. 28:16).

Have you tasted that?

The unanswered questions of a man's heart in haste are, Am I okay? Do I matter? How do I measure up? Am I significant? What's the judgment over my life?

But when Jesus came, he didn't require us to provide self-generated answers to such questions. He came to ease our burden (Matt. 11:28–30). He came to stop the haste. Paul even referred to Isaiah 28 and said that

Jesus himself is that cornerstone, so that whoever believes in Christ will not be in haste (Rom. 9:33; 10:11). If you are united to Christ, the courtroom verdict over your life is a past reality rather than a future dread. It's behind you, not before you. It's a period, not a question mark. You are justified. The sigh of the soul that you so desperately desire is yours, freely, abundantly, as you trust in Christ, the radiant Friend of Sinners. United to him, you are co-justified with him. For you to be un-okayed, Jesus himself would have to be un-okayed. His verdict is in, and therefore yours is in.

That's hard, strangely hard, to remember. As men we are wired to achieve, produce, and accomplish. That's good. But how easily this good impulse becomes our source of ultimate significance in a way that displaces the gospel. The pressures of life will force you into either greater rest or greater haste. One thing will determine which way you go: regular heart-bathing in the gospel of a secured, irreversible verdict won by the now un-condemnable Christ.

His imperturbable hug, his undeniable favor, are impervious to your mediocre work performance, fickle human approval, up-and-down marriage, poor leadership in family devotions, or reputation in the neighborhood.

How do you make it through another day, another week, without becoming cynical? Above all else, defibrillate your heart daily with the invincible favor of God shining down on you because of the love and sacrifice of another.

Only the doctrine of justification by faith alone will enable you to experience life as a joyful, relaxed gift, rather than a frantic, fretful attempt to impress.

Who God Really Is

DANE C. ORTLUND

GOD'S GREAT GLORY is his grace. "He exalts himself to show mercy to you" (Isa. 30:18). Perhaps our natural intuitions have us convinced that for God truly to glorify himself requires that he be aloof, standoffish, arms crossed. *Sin is serious,* we think. We are idolaters, after all (v. 22). Surely the glory of God is seen in his separation from sinners.

But notice what we find in this passage. "You shall weep no more. He will surely be gracious to you at the sound of your cry. As soon as he hears it, he answers you" (v. 19). What does a father or mother feel when the sound of the crying newborn wafts into the room? That irrepressible urge to comfort is an echo of what the heavenly Father feels when he hears us in our distress as we endure "the bread of adversity and the water of affliction" (v. 20).

We don't have to take this only as theoretical truth, for this truth of divine grace took on flesh. Isaiah says that one day "your Teacher will not hide himself anymore, but your eyes shall see your Teacher" (v. 20). This is precisely what happened in Jesus Christ. And what do we see in Jesus? Did God Incarnate keep himself distant from sinners, arms crossed and lips pursed? On the contrary; watch him, sweeping the children up into his arms, sitting down to eat with outsiders, reaching out and touching lepers. "We have seen his *glory*," writes John, "full of *grace* and truth" (John 1:14). His glory is seen in his grace. As the Puritan Thomas Goodwin put it, "Christ is love covered over with flesh."[5]

Who do you think God is? One reason the book of Isaiah is in the Bible is to nestle sinners into the calming truth that God not only loves us; he *enjoys* loving us. We are his. His heart is full to overflowing with compassion. He is not who we might think he is.

The Stability of Your Times

DANE C. ORTLUND

WE MEN SEEK stability in any number of things. It may be financial security, such as a retirement plan or having the mortgage paid off. It may be relational capital, such as one's reputation at church or respect in the workplace. Perhaps we're trusting in some kind of intellectual competence, such as passing the bar exam or demonstrating competence in theology.

None of these are bad. They are good things, worthy pursuits. We should seek them. But *how* do we seek them? This is the key question. Do we seek financial well-being, respect, and knowledge *in place of* or *in light of* God as our stability? The temptation is to seek the good things of the world as a substitute for divine stability rather than in light of it. Look at what Isaiah says:

> The LORD is exalted, for he dwells on high;
>> he will fill Zion with justice and righteousness,
> and he will be the stability of your times,
>> abundance of salvation, wisdom, and knowledge;
>> the fear of the LORD is Zion's treasure. (Isa. 33:5–6)

Of course, who of us as Christian men would disagree that God should be our source of stability? And yet, who of us is not tempted every day to funnel our existential confidence into one or more of the good things of earth? What, then, is the way forward?

On the one hand, it would be simplistic to prescribe a mechanical routine to generate trust in the Lord. Still, I ask you: Are you drawing daily strength from the promises of God that come to us in concrete form in Scripture? Are you breathing out your anxieties to God in prayer (Phil. 4:6–7)? Are you rising each day mindful of Jesus as the great Friend of Sinners who delights to walk with you through the sunshine and also through the darkness? Do you have a trusted brother or two who really know what is going on in your life and where sin is strongest in you these days? In such ways we grow into the deep safety of Isaiah 33:6. "He will be the stability of your times."

Eden Restored

DANE C. ORTLUND

THREE CENTURIES AGO the New England pastor Jonathan Edwards wrote, "Every atom in the universe is managed by Christ so as to be most to the advantage of the Christian, every particle of air or every ray of the sun; so that he in the other world, when he comes to see it, shall sit and enjoy all this vast inheritance with surprising, amazing joy."[6] That surprising, amazing joy awaiting us is the whole point of Isaiah 35.

This passage is depicting Eden 2.0, creation restored. This dry, barren, mourning world will be rinsed clean. Ponder the imagery used throughout this chapter: a desert flourishing, the blind seeing, the wilderness bursting with streams, and so on.

The question for a twenty-first-century man upon engaging Isaiah 35 is not, How do I apply this to my life? That would be a trivialization of this text. When a sufferer of terminal cancer is told a cure has been found, they do not say, "Great—now, how do I apply this to my life?" *They are going to live again.* They are going to be restored. They immediately order their entire existence around that great anticipation.

With Isaiah 35 open before us, the question for us is, Are we swimming in the mental and emotional universe of what God has told us our future is?

Here is what God is saying to us through this text: If you are in Christ, one day you will find yourself on this earth, minus sin and disease and hospitals and medicine and alarm clocks and apologies and tears and resentment and dashed hopes and relational friction and unexplainable sadness and shame and boredom and mustered-up happiness. And you'll find yourself in a transformed but fully physical body, unable to sin, at *rest;* feeling better physically than you ever could, even in your earthly prime;

enjoying this earth as it was meant to be enjoyed—the food, the flowers, the mountains, the sunsets, the friendships, the uproarious laughter, the games, the songs, the smells, the basketball, the fishing, the knitting, the running, the learning, the conversations. And, shot through everything and over everything and giving meaning to everything: the "everlasting joy" (v. 10), in God, that we were created for.

What would you say to a billionaire's eight-year-old son who complains that he doesn't have enough toys? You would say, "Don't you know what's coming?"

JUNE 9 • ISAIAH 40:1-8

Final Comfort

DANE C. ORTLUND

ISAIAH CONTRASTS HUMAN "flesh" with the divine "word." Flesh falters; the word abides. It is an absolute antithesis. Our human existence comes and goes—as James says, we are "a mist that appears for a little time and then vanishes" (James 4:14). Just the opposite is the word of the Lord, which abides forever. Utterances from heaven are immovable, invincible. In this stark contrast, "the glory of the LORD shall be revealed," as all flesh sees what comes from the mouth of the Lord (Isa. 40:5).

And what is it that comes from the mouth of the Lord? What is the word he speaks, that reveals his glory and is beheld by all flesh? Pardon of iniquity (v. 2). Comfort from heaven (v. 1). Divine provision for all our sins (v. 2).

This is who God is, and the message of the entire Bible. But we do not need to take Isaiah's word for it, for in opening his Gospel account, the apostle John picks up all the same language to tell us who Jesus Christ is. John says that "The *Word* became *flesh* and dwelt among us, and we have seen his *glory*" (John 1:14). Here we see the same triad of God's Word, human flesh, and divine glory. But whereas in Isaiah 40 God's Word and human flesh are utter opposites, in John 1 *the two are overlaid*. The Word took on flesh. God's ultimate Word of comfort to the world was the incarnation, the "enfleshing" of God's own Son—as C. S. Lewis called it, "the humiliation of myth into fact, of God into Man."[7]

In that mystery is where true and final comfort for God's people is found. In this man, himself also God, we not only hear that our "warfare is ended" (Isa. 40:2); we see that warfare tangibly get ended on a little hill outside Jerusalem. The Word of God, which stands forever, was crucified. Why? So that withering grass and fading flowers—men like you and me—can stand, forever, by grace.

JUNE 10 · ISAIAH 43:1-7

A Perfect Ransom

DANE C. ORTLUND

THE OPENING VERSES of Isaiah 43 are deep roots for storm-tossed trees. All through Isaiah 40–55, the Lord forbids fear. And here, as chapter 43 opens, he establishes this exhortation in the firmest of all foundations: his redemptive work on our behalf. In between two commands not to fear (Isa. 43:1, 5), he roots this courage in the fact that he has redeemed us (v. 1). We are precious to him (v. 4). He loves us (v. 4). He is with us (v. 5). He will bring us home to himself (v. 5).

But how do we know? How can we be sure of these things? As we roll out of bed each morning, a hundred failures from the past week may come to mind. We tend so strongly toward waywardness, toward fickleness. Our own hearts deceive us, and our motives are seemingly never wholly pure. How can we *know* of God's certain care in our lives?

Because of verse 3: "I give Egypt as your *ransom.*" The word used here for ransom is *kopher,* one of the most theologically loaded words in the Old Testament. It means the price paid to buy back a life. It's used all through the Pentateuch to describe how sin is atoned for in the Israelite sacrificial system. And the entire sacrificial system is fulfilled, epitomized, finalized, consummated once and for all in the great Sacrifice, the great Atonement, the Ransom of all ransoms. Jesus Christ is himself the true priest, the true sacrifice, and the true temple all integrated into one human being.

How can we be sure of Isaiah 43:1–7? Jesus died. God said he would gladly give Egypt as a ransom. He did far more than that. He gave his own Son as a ransom. Jesus passed through the waters and was overwhelmed so that, when we pass through the waters, we aren't.

Well did the hymnist, drawing on Isaiah 43:2, write,

> When through the deep waters I call thee to go,
> The rivers of sorrow shall not overflow;
> For I shall be with thee thy troubles to bless,
> And sanctify to thee thy deepest distress.[8]

JUNE 11 · ISAIAH 45:22–25

Turn to God and Be Saved

DANE C. ORTLUND

"TURN TO ME and be saved, all the ends of the earth! For I am God, and there is no other" (Isa. 45:22). No other verse in Isaiah sums up the entire book so well as this: salvation for sinners everywhere who take refuge in the one true God. That is the message of Isaiah.

Throughout Isaiah 40–48 we see the utter supremacy of God more clearly than perhaps in any other portion of Scripture of comparable length. The futility of idols, the omniscience and mighty power of God, and the folly of our self-salvation projects are the themes of these chapters.

And how does God save? By his own initiative and action. He does not meet us halfway. He undertakes all that is necessary. "Only in the LORD, it shall be said of me, are righteousness and strength" (45:24). Even those who refuse this salvation will one day bow the knee and confess with their tongue that he is God (v. 23).

Is this real to you? Or does it bore you? Do these truths seem ethereal, abstract? If so, repent! One day we will stand in the presence of the one who spoke these words, and *this* life will be the vague and shadowy one. What will that day be like? We will glory in the Lord, this passage says (v. 25)—exult, boast, rejoice, in him and him alone. It will pour out of us, unprompted, for we will see him as he is, there in the presence of Christ. The New Testament takes the words of Isaiah 45:23 and ascribes them to *Christ*: "Therefore God has highly exalted him and bestowed on him the name that is above every name, so that at the name of Jesus every knee should bow, in heaven and on earth and under the earth, and every tongue confess that Jesus Christ is Lord, to the glory of God the Father" (Phil. 2:9–11).

Turn to him. Be saved. Glory in him. Be at peace.

JUNE 12 · ISAIAH 50:7–11

Walking in Darkness

DANE C. ORTLUND

"LET HIM WHO WALKS in darkness . . ." (Isa. 50:10). What darkness are you walking in today?

Pain is not, for most of us, the islands of our experience but the ocean. Darkness is a constant companion. Troubled relationships. Physical malady. Financial adversity. Marital strife. Vocational discouragement. The ache of regret. Such realities are not anomalous. This is normal life under the sun. What washes into your consciousness as you awake in the morning, making you cringe? Our Sunday morning smiles often do not reflect what is happening in the soul.

"Let him who walks in darkness and has no light . . ." It would be one thing to walk in darkness with a flashlight, or at least a candle. But what if we have no light at all? Not only do we walk in darkness, but we often feel totally alone, without help, hopeless. We have no light.

"Let him who walks in darkness and has no light trust in the name of the Lord and rely on his God." This is where the Bible takes us, and this is our true lifeline. The answer of Scripture to our darkness is not the elimination of darkness but the presence of God. Our mighty Friend walks with us. He cares for us, tending to us and gently overseeing us—as Psalm 23, among other texts, expresses so beautifully.

After all, he has shown us the length to which he is willing to go to assure us of his care. "He who did not spare his own Son but gave him up for us all, how will he not also with him graciously give us all things?" (Rom. 8:32). In a dirty room in an obscure town twenty centuries ago, the light of heaven entered into this dark, exhausted world. Born of Mary, this one identified himself as the "light of the world" (John 8:12). Our ever-present Savior walks with us, weeps with us, calms us in the darkness. The disaster we tend to make of our lives will one day be sorted out, made new, and cleansed. The clock is ticking on the darkness of our lives. A new day will dawn.

> And the city has no need of sun or moon to shine on it, for the glory of God gives it light, and its lamp is the Lamb. (Rev. 21:23)

The Scandal of Substitution

DANE C. ORTLUND

BRITISH PASTOR JOHN STOTT once wrote that the essence of sin is man substituting himself for God and that the essence of salvation is God substituting himself for man. In our fallenness, we try to go up and displace God from his throne and rule in his place. In his mercy, he has come down and borne our punishment in our place. This is the reality Isaiah 53 is unfolding before our eyes.

The message of Christianity is that every human being is fallen—"all we like sheep have gone astray" (Isa. 53:6)—but that in Jesus God became one of us, one more sheep. But he was not a sinful sheep; he was "a lamb that is led to the slaughter" (v. 7). And the slaughter he underwent on the cross is the slaughter I deserve because of my trenchant heart-rebellion against my Maker. "He was pierced for our transgressions" (v. 5). I owed the bill, but he wrote the check.

This scandal of substitution is the only thing in this sin-sick universe that brings rest, wholeness, flourishing, *shalom*—that existential calm which for brief, gospel-sane moments settles over you and lets you see for a moment that in Christ you truly are invincible. The verdict really is in. Nothing can touch us. He was pierced, crushed, wounded; we are healed. We try to switch places with God. Instead, God in Christ switched places with us.

Preaching on Isaiah 53, the French reformer John Calvin said,

> We should come to our Lord Jesus Christ, who was willing to be disfigured from the crown of his head to the soles of his feet, covered in wounds, whipped time and again, who bore the crown of thorns, who was nailed up on the cross, whose side was pierced. This is how we are healed; this is our true medicine with which we must be content and to which we must lend our affection, knowing that never in any other way can we find rest, but that we would be tormented and tortured to hell if Jesus Christ did not console us and appease the wrath of God toward us.

JUNE 14 · ISAIAH 55

He Will Abundantly Pardon

DANE C. ORTLUND

"MY THOUGHTS ARE NOT your thoughts," God says (Isa. 55:8). "As the heavens are higher than the earth, so are my ways higher than your ways" (v. 9). What is the Lord talking about?

These statements are often taken to communicate the great mystery in what God does. Life takes a strange turn circumstantially, and we tell each other, "His ways are not our ways!"

But note what the text actually says. In the immediately preceding verses, the sinner is told to seek God and call upon him, so that the Lord "may have compassion on him." We should return to God, "for he will abundantly pardon" (v. 7). And then, "*For* my thoughts are not your thoughts . . ."

Isaiah 55 is inviting us to believe the unbelievable, to refute our natural, intuitive ways of thinking, so enmeshed in scorekeeping and law-ishness. Isaiah 55 is inviting us to calm down and let God love us. Have compassion on us. Abundantly pardon us. This is not a denial of our sinfulness.

It is looking our sinfulness square in the face and receiving a love that gets underneath it all. The radiant sun of divine favor is shining down on us, and while the clouds of our sin and failure may darken our feelings of that favor, the favor cannot be lessened any more than a tiny, wispy cloud can threaten the existence of the sun. The sun is shining. It cannot stop. Clouds or no clouds—sin or no sin—the sun is shining on us. The Lord looks on his children with utterly unflappable affection. In Christ, every reason for God not to abundantly pardon has been swept away.

His ways are not our ways. We sin. But he loves sinners. We fail. But he loves failures. And as I step out into my day in soul-calm because of that free gift of cleansing, I find that actually, strangely, startlingly I begin to live out practically what I already am positionally. I delight to love others. It takes effort and requires the sobering of suffering. But love cannot help but be kindled by such love.

How can we possibly stiff-arm this? Repent of your small thoughts of God's love, your resistance to the compassion and abundant pardon of the Lord. Repent and let him love you.

JUNE 15 · ISAIAH 57:14–21

Where God Lives

DANE C. ORTLUND

WHERE DOES GOD DWELL? Some might say, in a temple. Others, in heaven. What does this text say? "I dwell in the high and holy place, and also with him who is of a contrite and lowly spirit" (Isa. 57:15). A few chapters later, God will reiterate that the one to whom he looks is "he who is humble and contrite in spirit" (66:2).

In this frantic world of futile attention-seeking, Isaiah calms us into quiet significance. Voters seek the attention of their political leaders. Sports fans seek the attention of their hometown heroes. Employees seek the attention of their bosses. Men seek the attention and respect of their wives. Intellectuals seek the attention of publishers. We men long to matter. We long for significance.

And the Lord of heaven tells us he lives in two places. His attention rests on two locations. One, "the high and holy place." He is, as Isaiah says twenty-nine times, "the Holy One of Israel." He is sacred, we are profane; he is holy, we are sinful. He is infinite purity and ineffable beauty. He is other. But there's another place he lives. He also lives with the man "who is of a contrite and lowly spirit." The heartbroken, the humbled, the saddened, the one who walks in darkness, the man who feels the weight of his own sin. The Lord does not live with the cocky, those posing and preening, the manipulators for the sake of self-advancement, the slick.

What's the point? *God delights to refresh discouraged sinners.* This is not a bonus or extra credit to who God is. This is the very heart of God, who in Jesus said that he is "gentle and lowly in heart" (Matt. 11:29). He fills the empty and revives the distraught. Many reasons for distress wash into our lives—illness, betrayal, weariness, aging, and above all our own sin and folly. And it is the man who opens up to the Lord, drawing near in honesty, the man who refuses to make excuses and cover up, to whom the Lord is irresistibly drawn. He loves to revive frail sinners. They have his full and undivided attention.

JUNE 16 • ISAIAH 61:1-7

God's Upside-Down Economy

DANE C. ORTLUND

WHEN JESUS SHOWED UP two thousand years ago, he spent most of his time with precisely the kinds of people we would expect him to avoid: outsiders, tax collectors, prostitutes, sinners. Yet perhaps it is what we should have expected, in light of passages like Isaiah 61.

Here we read that good news from heaven is not sent to those who grace the cover of *Men's Health* or receive the largest professional athletic contracts or have made it in Hollywood. Good news from heaven is for the "brokenhearted," the "captives," "all who mourn," and those suffering from a "faint spirit" (Isa. 61:1–3).

Why? Because these are the blessed ones among us who are no longer playing the world's games. They have died to themselves. They have been brought to painful honesty about the fallenness of the world and the fallenness that infects even them. They are the losers of the world. And God says that those who refuse to amass a personal empire of significance and instead abandon themselves to the Lord alone "shall eat the wealth of the nations, and in their glory you shall boast" (v. 6).

This is how God has set up the world. Indeed, it is how he himself, in the person of his own Son, lived in the world—rejected by the admired leaders, embraced by the outsiders. And why? So that through his death and resurrection the low might be exalted, the condemned might be accepted, those rejected by the world might be embraced by heaven—so that all who forsake the prison of personal ambition and praise might have liberty proclaimed to them. This is the divine economy.

Have you experienced this release? It feels like death. But it is the only way to life. The result? "Instead of your shame there shall be a double portion; instead of dishonor they shall rejoice in their lot; . . . they shall have everlasting joy" (v. 7).

JUNE 17 • ISAIAH 65:17-25

Coming Home

DANE C. ORTLUND

ALL OF US KNOW, deep down, the pain of alienation. We know we are foreigners, exiles, strangers in this fallen world. When we return to our home nation after traveling abroad, we taste the joy of coming home; but even then, we know we are not experiencing fully what the soul longs for. Even in our own living room we can feel estranged.

The message of the Bible is that we were, at one time, truly *home*. In Eden we had not yet been estranged. But with the fall into sin, we became alienated—not only from Eden but also from God, from one another, and even from ourselves. The story of redemption is God's work throughout history to restore us to him, to one another, and to ourselves. In Isaiah 65 we are given a glimpse into what this final restoration in a "new heavens and a new earth" (v. 17) will look like. In short, it means Eden will be regained—this time invincibly. We will be home. No more death, no more futility in our work, no more building a home only to leave it to another (vv. 21–22).

In C. S. Lewis's *The Last Battle,* the final book in the Chronicles of Narnia, Jewel the unicorn expresses everyone's thoughts as Aslan's people enter the restored Narnia: "I have come home at last! This is my real country! I belong here. This is the land I have been looking for all my life, though I never knew it till now."[9] That is exactly what we will feel one day as the sun sets on this hellish world and the new world dawns. The horrors of the old age will die away. We will pass through the wardrobe into Narnia. We will be home at last. "I will bring them home," God says (Zech. 10:10). We will weep with relief. We will see him face to face (Rev. 22:4).

How can this be? Here's how: God in Christ refused the glory he rightly deserved to enter the hell and mud of our world to grab us and drag us, kicking and screaming if need be, into the new order, the new world of *shalom* and flourishing and sun and wine and calmness and nonfrivolous laughs. All of sheer grace. All to be simply received. Available to anyone who refuses to pay for it.

JUNE 18 · JEREMIAH 1

God's Call and God's Presence

PAUL R. HOUSE

JEREMIAH AND HIS FRIEND Baruch (Jeremiah 36) produced one of the Bible's most significant books. This opening chapter introduces Jeremiah's difficult times (Jer. 1:1–3), strenuous calling (vv. 4–16), and determined enemies (vv. 17–19). Most importantly, it stresses that God will be with Jeremiah (v. 19). God's presence is always the believer's reason for courage and faithfulness (Matt. 28:16–20).

God's call came during hopeful times, the days of Josiah (c. 640–609 BC), who reformed Israel's worship (Jer. 1:2; cf. 2 Kings 22–23). But most of Jeremiah's ministry occurred during hard times (Jer. 1:3), days when Judah sank into moral and political chaos under the self-serving leadership of Jehoiakim (609–598 BC) and Zedekiah (597–587 BC). Despite Jeremiah's ministry, the people did not repent, so Jerusalem fell (1:3; cf. Deut. 28:15–68). Like Jeremiah, we do not get to pick the times we live in or our ministry's results. Our job is to follow God regardless of circumstances.

God's message through Jeremiah addressed these spiritually corrupt times. Before Jeremiah's birth, God chose him to carry his message to Judah and other nations (Jer. 1:4–5). Despite Jeremiah's youth, God chose him as his ambassador (vv. 6–7). To calm Jeremiah's fears, God promises to be with him and to put the right words in his mouth (vv. 8–9). Jeremiah will declare destruction, rebuilding, and renewal. He must warn of coming judgment because the nations have rejected God and worshiped idols (vv. 10–16). God's servants must share *his* words, not their own. Like Jeremiah, our task is to be God's messengers, even when the words are hard to share.

Speaking God's words will make Jeremiah many enemies (vv. 17–18). Indeed, the whole land will oppose him. But his enemies will not prevail, for God will be with him (vv. 8, 19). God's promised presence will protect his word and his servant until the work is done. This presence must be enough for Jeremiah. It must be his most cherished reward, for the results he desires will not happen in his lifetime.

God's presence must be enough for us now, as we minister in our own difficult times. We may suffer as Jeremiah did. So we must be satisfied with God's presence. Having him is success. Nothing matters more than having him as we follow his call.

JUNE 19 · JEREMIAH 3:6–4:4

The Results of Repentance

PAUL R. HOUSE

JEREMIAH 1:11-16 AND 2:1-3:5 state plainly that God's people have sinned against him. They have worshiped idols, the works of their hands. They have strayed from God, though he redeemed them from slavery (see Hosea 1–3). By Josiah's time (640–609 BC), Israel and Judah had been reduced in size and significance (Jer. 3:6–10). Assyria had conquered Israel in 722 BC because of her sins (3:6–10; see 2 Kings 17). But Judah learned nothing from Israel's destruction (Jer. 3:6–10). Both Israel and Judah needed to repent, to turn from their sin and back to God. Through repenting they could receive promises of forgiveness, a new home, and healed hearts. These promises are still available to us today.

Despite Israel and Judah's spiritual failures, God offers hope. Despite past rebellion, they may return to him, for he is merciful and patient (3:11–12; Ex. 34:6–7). God will receive those who repent. He will not turn them away. God still promises to forgive those who confess their sins (Jer. 3:13; 1 John 1:9–10), trusting Christ's death to atone for them (1 John 2:2).

God also offers a *home* to those who repent. Israel's people were scattered around the world in the Assyrian Empire, but God pledges to bring them back to Jerusalem for worship, by ones and twos if necessary (Jer. 3:14). He will give them faithful, godly leaders (v. 15), and the greatest of these will be the Messiah (23:1–8). Many nations will join Israel in worship (3:17). Judah and Israel will reunite (v. 18), live together, and serve God; Isaiah 65:17–25 and Revelation 21:1–8 share this vision of home.

With these promises made, God addresses his people's hearts. There will be no hope or home unless their hearts change (Jer. 4:1–4), unless they desire God rather than idols. A changed heart will lead to confession of sin and to obeying God again (3:25); it will embrace truth, justice, and righteousness (4:2). A changed heart wants God, returns to God, receives God, and is healed (3:22).

God never changes. He still loves to give us hope, to bring us home, and to heal us. Unlike *our* hearts, God's heart is always merciful and patient (3:12). So pray now. Tell him your sins. Ask him to forgive you because you trust in Christ. Receive his healing forgiveness.

A Profile of Faulty Religion

PAUL R. HOUSE

GOD APPOINTS JEREMIAH as the tester of Judah's spiritual "metal" (6:27-30), and Jeremiah takes up this task (7:1-8:3). He proclaims a searing sermon that exposes Judah's sinful thoughts and behavior. While doing so he draws a telling profile of faulty religion that echoes true today.

Faulty religion trusts in external observances and institutions, rather than in the realities they represent. Judah trusted in the temple's existence, in the services held there, and in the sacrifices they offered there (Jer. 7:1-4, 21). They forgot that these outward things represented God's presence, God's worship, and God's forgiveness. They replaced God with symbols of God.

Faulty religion exhibits ungodly behavior. The people saw no contradiction in attending worship services and then going out and breaking all of God's commands (7:8-10). Thus, they made God's temple a hideout for thieves and robbers (7:11; cf. Matt. 21:12-13 and parallels).

Faulty religion rejects God's instructions (Jer. 7:13). Instead, Judah followed the evil ways of their wicked hearts (7:24; 3:19-25). They had ignored God's previous prophets, and now they ignored Jeremiah (7:25-27). Because of their sin, truth perished, and righteousness died with it (7:28-31). Judgment became certain (7:32-8:3).

Despite this embrace of faulty religion, however, hope remained. They could obey God's command to change by seeking justice for the helpless, seeking God instead of idols, and seeking God's word again; they could once again act like God's people (7:3, 5-6, 18-20, 23). They would then find him blessing them instead of disciplining them yet again (7:23; Lev. 26:1-13).

It is easy to twist biblical faith into faulty religion, especially when our hearts have strayed from God. Incredibly, even when we choose faulty religion for a season, the Lord stands ready to forgive and restore (Revelation 2-3). Only our reluctance to repent keeps us from restored fellowship with God and continued usefulness in his service.

Our Incomparable God

PAUL R. HOUSE

HUMAN HISTORY CHRONICLES worship of a vast array of false gods, including the gods of money, sex, and power. In Jeremiah's day, Israel worshiped the true God but also the Canaanite god Baal and several Egyptian deities (Jer. 7:9–10, 16–20). As prophet to Judah and the nations, Jeremiah presents the only God, the *incomparable* God (10:1–16). Only this God merits worship.

The incomparable God differs completely from the deities worshiped by the nations. Israel need not worry about these gods (vv. 1–3). Their worshipers look for signs in the heavens and make well-crafted images of what they think the gods are like (vv. 2–4). They do so because these gods cannot speak (v. 5). Such gods cannot help their followers; their worshipers must carry them, not the other way around (v. 5). These gods are man-made. They cannot save, teach, or support us. We must not trust in or fear them.

The incomparable God is the King of kings. Jeremiah lived when the great Assyrian and Babylonian kings ruled the world. He knew all about power. So it is significant that he asserts that God is greater, stronger, and wiser than any ruler or any god (vv. 6–7). The Lord is the living, true, and everlasting One. He never dies; all nations must bow before him; so it is foolish to bow instead before idols (vv. 8–10). Isaiah and Paul agree that every knee will bow before God the Father and God the Son (Isa. 45:23; Phil. 2:9–11). As Christians, we gladly do so.

The incomparable God created the heavens and the earth, and maintains creation through his wisdom (Jer. 10:12–13). This separates him from all other gods (vv. 14–16). These gods have no breath, no life, and no power. They are not real. Their followers face death alone (v. 11). Only the Creator will endure, always saving his people.

Bowing before the incomparable God is the way of salvation for all people and all nations (John 14:6). It is also the way to meaningful, wise living. In a world filled with powerful political figures, claims about other

214

gods, and fears of all sorts, it is vital to know that the Lord rules all creation. If we have him, we have all we need.

JUNE 22 • JEREMIAH 15:10-21

Even God's Best Servants Must Repent

PAUL R. HOUSE

JEREMIAH WAS one of God's best servants, but he was not sinless. Like all believers, he walked a long road with God that had many high and low points (Jer. 1:1–3). These verses mark one of the lowest points. Sometimes even God's best need to repent.

Jeremiah had become filled with self-pity and fear. He resented the constant opposition he had to face. He wondered why everyone was against him—as if he owed them money or they owed him (15:10)! He doubted that his ministry did the people any good (vv. 11–12). He wondered what God's promise of protection (1:17–19; 15:11–12) was worth, when he and his nation were headed for poverty and exile (vv. 13–14). Jeremiah felt abandoned by both God and the people.

Jeremiah accused God of lying to him even though he had done all that God had asked of him. He had endured persecution (15:15), studied and spoken God's word (v. 16), avoided the wicked (v. 17a), and accepted loneliness as part of his job (v. 17b). In return, he said, he had gotten only ceaseless pain and trouble (v. 18a). Where was God when he needed him? He compares God to a "deceitful brook," a water source that ran dry (v. 18b). Jeremiah blamed God for his hard life. He expected so much more; he felt that God had promised more.

God had heard enough. He told Jeremiah, "If you return [repent], I will restore you" (v. 19a). Jeremiah had to turn from self-pity, fear, and accusing God. He needed to return to speaking "what is precious, and not what is worthless" if he wished to remain God's prophet (v. 19b). God reminded Jeremiah that, in reality, he had never lied to him: he promised opposition

(1:17–19), and it had come (11:18–23; 15:10). He promised to protect his life (1:19), and he had. Now God repeated these promises (15:20–21). Did Jeremiah want to keep standing with God? If so, he had to repent.

Happily, Jeremiah did repent. His willingness to hear God's word and change his ways set an example for all God's servants, including his best, such as Peter (John 21:15–19) and John (1 John 1:9–10). Daily repentance is part of walking with God. It provides a bridge from self-service to renewed service of the living God (Jer. 10:1–16).

JUNE 23 • JEREMIAH 17:1-13

God Knows Our Hearts

PAUL R. HOUSE

LIKE MOSES (see Deut. 6:4–9; 7:17; 8:11–20), Jeremiah takes great interest in the human heart. Jeremiah 4:1–4 stressed that the heart is where repentance begins, and Jeremiah 11:18–20 gave a real-life example of how devious the heart can be. Now Jeremiah declares that the heart may trust in many wrong things and can hide its true nature from others, but God knows our heart.

God knows what, or whom, we trust. Some hearts trust and treasure idols. Indeed, these idols are "engraved" on their hearts (17:1). Idols represent gods that humans make. The "Asherim" mentioned in verse 2 were images of fertility and sexuality. Fertility in ancient agricultural economies led to wealth (vv. 3, 11), so hearts that worshiped sexuality simultaneously bowed to money. Sex and money are routinely linked today in advertising and media of all sorts. What is not routinely shown is the bondage that worshiping them creates both now and later (v. 4). The heart that treasures idols will soon find itself in chains.

Some hearts trust in human strength (v. 5). They believe intelligence, planning, and diplomacy can solve any problem. Such people do not think they need the Lord; their hearts turn from him (17:5). They forget that human resources are limited; those who trust them eventually dry up "like a shrub in the desert" (v. 6; Ps. 1:4). Human strength is good, but it is not infinite like God's strength.

Gratefully, some hearts trust in the Lord (Jer. 17:7). Their only boast is that they know him (see 9:23–24; 1 Cor. 1:30–31; 2 Cor. 10:17). Their hearts have deep roots in God's sustaining power (Jer. 17:8a; Ps. 1:3). They are not anxious in hard times, for their hearts rest in God (Jer. 17:8b; Phil. 4:4–8), the "fountain of living water" (Jer. 17:13). God is their king and their hope (vv. 12–13).

What does God see in your heart? Do you know, love, trust, and serve God no matter what the cost? Do you want him more than approval, money, sex, power, and ease? Jeremiah did. Do you want forgiveness in Christ and a useful place in his service? Faithful followers of Jesus do. Your heart is either watered by God's endless springs, or planted in a desert wasteland. It is either sick and beyond healing, or healed by the Lord (v. 9). God knows your heart. Do you?

JUNE 24 · JEREMIAH 23:1-8

The Messiah, David's Righteous Branch

PAUL R. HOUSE

GOD PROMISED TO establish David's throne "forever" (2 Sam. 7:16). Four centuries later, Jeremiah took comfort in this promise. After Josiah died (609 BC), the next four kings were rotten branches of David's family tree (Jeremiah 21–22). They were bad "shepherds," whose mismanagement of Israel and Judah—their "flock" (23:2)—led to defeat and exile. In this depressing situation Jeremiah took comfort by looking to the future, when David's righteous Branch, the Messiah, would save the flock once and for all. God's greatest promise gave Jeremiah hope in dark days.

Bad shepherds have led the people into sin, and thus to being scattered (23:1–2a), but better days lie ahead. God promises to punish the wicked shepherds, gather the people again, and give them good shepherds (vv. 2b–4). By Jesus's time, God had kept this promise. Israelites filled the land. The flock was home, and the faithful ones waited for their true Shepherd (Luke 2:22–38).

God promises to send a righteous Branch from David's family. Unlike the bad kings, he will rule justly, wisely, and righteously. Unlike the bad kings, he will save Judah and Israel and make them secure (Jer. 23:5–6). Jeremiah uses a pun to make this point. The Babylonian conquerors of Judah gave King Zedekiah his name, which means "Yahweh is my righteousness." In other words, they gave him a pious-sounding name that had no basis in reality—a name he did not deserve. By contrast, the Messiah will be named Zedekenu, "Yahweh is our righteousness." He will provide righteousness for the people. He will merit his name.

God promises a greater day when this king comes. The exodus was incredible (Jer. 23:7); returning home to live in the Messiah's kingdom will be greater still (v. 8), exceeding all of God's amazing past deeds. The flock that followed Jesus, the Great Shepherd (Heb. 13:20; 1 Pet. 5:4; John 10:11), found him to be all that Jeremiah had promised, and much more.

The New Testament teaches that the promised righteous Branch has come, and will come again to rule forever in justice and righteousness (2 Pet. 3:1–13). Today, many believers live under oppressive governments. Others have better circumstances, yet long for final peace, security, and justice. We can all take comfort in the promise of the second coming of King Jesus. He is our righteousness, salvation, security, and hope.

JUNE 25 · JEREMIAH 26

Faithful, Dangerous Ministry

PAUL R. HOUSE

GOD CALLS ALL BELIEVERS to use the gifts he gives us for faithful, fruitful ministry (1 Cor. 12:4–11). Ministry basically means "serving God by serving others." Some Christians are paid for their full- or part-time ministry, while others share God's word with family, friends, and strangers (or enemies!) in other ways.

Jeremiah's life shows how dangerous faithful ministry can be. By this point in the book he has encountered the enemies and needed the protection God promised in Jeremiah 1:17–19. Having survived one threat on his life (11:18–23), he now faces another, which reinforces the fact that faithfulness, not popularity or safety, is our goal in ministry.

Faithful ministry requires loving, honest sharing of God's word in ever-changing circumstances. Good King Josiah has died and has been replaced by Jehoiakim, who becomes Jeremiah's worst enemy (see Jeremiah 36). Being God's prophet has gotten more dangerous. Nonetheless, Jeremiah shares the same old message of repentance (26:1–6). As before, he does so in the hope that the people will be spared (vv. 3, 13). Faithful ministry requires love, especially when it includes a tough message.

Faithful ministry accepts the risks involved with sharing unpopular words from God. The people do not think Jeremiah has their best interests at heart. They think him unpatriotic and blasphemous (vv. 7–11). When they call for his death, all Jeremiah can do is state his innocence and claim that his message comes from God (vv. 12–15). He does not change his message to pacify his hearers.

Faithful ministry depends on God's protection. Some brave souls rise to Jeremiah's defense. They recall Micah's words in Hezekiah's day. It seems that they believe Jeremiah and repent (vv. 16–19, 24). God's word has been heard, and God's servant has been spared. Other prophets were not so fortunate. Jehoiakim killed a prophet named Uriah (vv. 20–23), but God kept his promise to protect Jeremiah. His life was a special gift in days when other faithful persons perished. Jeremiah was not necessarily more faithful than Uriah; God simply had different purposes for each man.

Faithful believers face persecution in several nations today. They are told to stop speaking God's word or face loss of job, family, home, or life. Yet they stand firm, trusting that faithfulness matters most. Those of us living in safer places need their boldness. We must not let minor threats alter our consistent, loving, biblical witness to our family, friends—and, yes, our enemies!

God's Good Plans for His Exiled People

PAUL R. HOUSE

FROM MOSES'S TIME to Jeremiah's, more than seven hundred years, God warned Israel that unchecked sin would bring exile (Lev. 26:14–39; Deut. 28:15–68). Now this threat has become reality. In 597 BC Babylon took Judah's king, several officials, and many craftsmen captive (Jer. 29:1–2). A worse defeat and more general deportation occurred in 586 (39:1–10; ch. 52). Yet God did not reject his people, for he had promised that renewal would follow exile (Lev. 26:40–45; Deut. 30:1–10). Jeremiah knew God had good plans for his exiled people. His trust in God's promises helped him see beyond the horizon of divine discipline.

God's good plans required submission to God's discipline. False prophets tell the people the exile will last only two years (Jer. 28:1–4; 29:8–9). Jeremiah tells them to plant gardens, have families, and prepare for a seventy-year stay (29:4–6, 10). They must not rebel against Babylon. Rather, they are to "seek the welfare of the city" where they have been sent, for the exiles' and the city's fortunes are linked (v. 7). Often used today in support of urban missions, this verse is actually more radical than that. It tells exiles to minister to their oppressors for seven decades. Daniel provides the best example of someone who accepted this call (see Dan. 9:1–19). Only those who trust God's purposes can submit to his will in this manner.

God's good plans include a future based on hope and seeking God. God promised to sustain the people in Babylon and bring them back to Judah after seventy years (Jer. 29:10). The people were to "seek" God through prayer as they waited on him to keep his promises (vv. 11–13). Such prayer must come from the heart (v. 13; see 4:1–4; 11:20; 17:1–13). The exiles must trust God in the very core of their being. Happily, those who seek God from the heart will find him (29:14).

God's good plans include us. He forgives forever all who trust in Christ, all who seek him with all their heart. Sometimes believers face God's discipline for stubborn sinning. Even then God has good plans. He disciplines us to turn us back to him so that we can share in his work again (Heb. 12:3–17; Revelation 2–3). God's plans are always good, whether we are at home or in exile.

Days of Healing and Songs of Thanksgiving

PAUL R. HOUSE

JEREMIAH 30-33 REVELS in the bright future God promised his faithful ones in 29:1–14. The weary prophet's spirits soar as he looks to days of healing and thanksgiving, when the Lord will be Israel's God and they shall be his people (30:22; 31:33; see Lev. 26:12), when the Messiah (Jer. 30:9; 33:14–26) and the new covenant (31:31–40) will be in place. These promises are so certain that God instructs Jeremiah to write them in a scroll as a permanent record (30:1–3). Thus, they became as real as looming judgment. They became a source of present hope.

Days of healing will follow days of terrible spiritual and physical sickness (vv. 4–17). Israel and Judah experienced God's judgment during Jeremiah's time. They suffered distress, fear and captivity, loss of allies, and loss of land (vv. 4–16). God inflicted these gaping wounds due to their flagrant sins (v. 15). Yet the God who disciplines is the God who uses that discipline to heal (v. 17). He pledges to return them to their land and send the Messiah (vv. 3, 8–9).

Songs of thanksgiving will accompany this healing homecoming (vv. 18–24). Cities will be rebuilt, Israel's children will come back, and worship services will occur again (vv. 18, 20). Their rulers will be native born, not foreign adversaries (v. 21). Beyond exile lies home and family. Most of all, reconciliation with God awaits them (v. 22). Healing, restoration, and reunion make joyous singing impossible to resist.

Jeremiah never experienced the fulfillment of these future promises. That did not matter. The promises comforted him because he understood that no work for the Lord is ever in vain. When God's promised hope becomes as real as our circumstances, healing and thanksgiving result. God's bright future breaks into our present gloom, comforting us. And we can sing for joy.

New Covenant, New People, New Home

PAUL R. HOUSE

THE NIGHT BEFORE his death, Jesus ate a last Passover supper with his disciples. Raising a cup, he declared it "the new covenant in my blood" (Luke 22:20; 1 Cor. 11:25). He quoted Jeremiah 31:31, the only place "new covenant" appears in the Old Testament. Therefore, understanding this verse is crucial for understanding our Lord's death, the Lord's Supper, and the Lord's promises. Linked by three uses of the phrase "Behold, the days are coming," verses 27–40 envision a new covenant, a new people, and a new home for God's people. When Jesus offered the cup to his disciples, he offered them all these things. When we share the Lord's Supper, we proclaim our acceptance of these promises.

First, God promises that, after giving them a new start in the land (31:27–30), he will make a new covenant with Judah and Israel (v. 31). God's covenants with Noah, Abraham, Moses, and David marked new points in redemptive history. Each of these covenants included and exceeded its predecessors. This new covenant of Jeremiah 31 is the final one. It keeps all God's prior promises and makes even greater ones.

Second, God promises a new people. Unlike the exodus generation, the new covenant people will be faithful, because God will place his law in their hearts (vv. 32–33). He will be their God, and they will be his people (v. 33; see 7:23; 24:7; 30:22; 31:1; 32:38; Gen. 17:7; Lev. 26:12). They will all know him (Jer. 31:34). Jesus's disciples represented this new people, and so do believers today.

Third, God promises that this new covenant will never end (vv. 35–37). Echoing God's covenant with Noah in Genesis 8:20–9:17, this covenant

222

will last as long as the earth does (31:35–37). It will be as final as the fixed order of day and night.

Fourth, God promises the people a new home. Like Isaiah, Ezekiel, and John, Jeremiah portrays perfected Jerusalem as the covenant people's final, safe home (Jer. 31:38–40; cf. Isa. 4:2–6; 65:17–66:24; Ezekiel 40–48; Rev. 21:1–8). Inhabitants of the new Jerusalem will never be exiles again.

When we share the Lord's Supper we remember his death. We also claim God's promise that we are new people headed for a new home because the new covenant in Jesus's blood is permanent and glorious. As Jesus promised, someday we will dine with him in our new home (Luke 22:28–30) that Jeremiah envisioned.

JUNE 29 · JEREMIAH 33:14–26

God's Unbreakable Promises

PAUL R. HOUSE

AS THE BABYLONIAN army attacked Jerusalem, Jeremiah languished in a makeshift jail (Jer. 33:1). All around him desperate, depressed people were coming to terms with the end of all they had ever known. The land lay desolate (vv. 12–13). Many believed that God had forsaken his people (vv. 23–24). In this seemingly hopeless situation, the Lord reminds Jeremiah that his covenant promises and his mercy never fail. There is always hope. More specifically, the Davidic Messiah is the key to hope, for all covenant promises merge in him.

Because the Messiah was coming, there was hope for Jerusalem (vv. 14–16). The capital city was collapsing under the weight of injustice and unrighteousness. Yet when the Messiah comes the city will bear the Messiah's character and name; it will be called "The LORD is our righteousness" (33:16; see 23:5–6; Isa. 1:27–31). He will execute justice and righteousness.

Because the Messiah was coming, there was hope for the priesthood. Babylon destroyed the temple and scattered the priests (Jer. 52:12–30). Yet the Messiah's righteous rule will include an enduring priesthood (33:17–18).

Because the Messiah was coming, there was hope for the monarchy and the people. David's lineage must always have a member on the throne (vv. 19–22). God's people cannot disappear; he will always have mercy on them and preserve them (vv. 23–26). As we saw in 31:35–37, these promises are as sure as the fixed order of night and day.

Christians believe Jesus of Nazareth is the promised Davidic Messiah (Matt. 1:1–17; Rom. 1:3–4, e.g.). We believe that all of God's covenant promises are kept through Jesus's life, death, and resurrection. Yet Jerusalem fell again after Jesus came, and even today, many centuries later, God's people are in danger in many places. How will God keep these promises?

The New Testament writers are unanimous in their answer: Jesus will come again. He will judge all wickedness when he comes. He will rule forever in a new Jerusalem, in a new heaven and earth (2 Pet. 3:13; Rev. 21:1–8). His death on our behalf already makes him our sacrifice and chief priest (Heb. 4:14–5:10), and he has called us to be his kingdom of priests, ministering to others in this world (1 Pet. 2:9–10; Ex. 19:5–6). When he comes again, nothing will interrupt our worship; nothing will harm us ever again.

So we take hope in what heartened Jeremiah centuries ago. The Messiah is coming. He will resolve all terrible situations. Until then, we do not just wait: we wait with confident hope.

JUNE 30 • JEREMIAH 39

God's Promises to a Brave Gentile Believer

PAUL R. HOUSE

GOD CALLED JEREMIAH to be a prophet to the nations, not just to Judah (Jer. 1:5, 9–10). Sadly, he had little success with either Jew or Gentile. Baruch was a notable Jewish exception (see 32:1–15; chs. 36; 45). The most prominent Gentile exception was Ebed-melech, an African official in Judah's royal court (38:7–13). Ebed-melech, whose name means "Servant of the King," was probably sold to Zedekiah. When Jeremiah was imprisoned in a muddy cistern, Ebed-melech confronted the king and rescued the prophet. He believed Jeremiah's words when Jeremiah's kinsmen did not. As Jerusalem disintegrated, God gave Ebed-melech the same promises he offered Jeremiah and Baruch.

God promised Ebed-melech that he would endure the fall of Jerusalem and all the related terrors (39:1–10, 16–18), although he would have to suffer just as Jeremiah and Baruch did. The Bible clearly teaches that God does not spare his people from life's pains. Rather, he asks them to minister to others in even the worst of circumstances.

God promised to deliver Ebed-melech and give him his life as a gift when death seemed inevitable (39:17). God promised the same to Jeremiah and Baruch (1:17–19; 45:1–5). This was a special promise, since other faithful people died at the hands of the wicked (26:20–24). Life is always a gift from God; it is not a right.

God made these promises because Ebed-melech put his trust in (39:18). His faith led to action, for he helped Jeremiah when doing so was unpopular. By faith he identified with God's people, and by faith he became one of them.

God created the heavens and the earth (Jer. 10:1–16; 33:2) and all peoples. He loves every person he created (John 3:16), regardless of ethnicity, and desires each one's salvation. Old Testament non-Israelite believers like Ebed-melech, Rahab, and Ruth prove this point, as do the Gentile converts in the New Testament. All those who trust in God by believing in Jesus Christ (John 14:1–7) receive all of God's promises. They, like Ebed-melech, find comfort even as their world falls apart.

Brutal Babylon Will Fall

PAUL HOUSE

WORLD EVENTS OFTEN discourage us. Mighty nations and big corporations seemingly rule the world, crushing lowly persons and lands. We can feel helpless, unsure of what God is doing. Such feelings are not new. In Jeremiah's day, Babylon's armies brutalized many kingdoms (Jeremiah 46–49), conquered Judah, and burned the temple (52:1–23). Jeremiah 50 comforted Judah by announcing Babylon's coming fall and God's redemption of his seemingly insignificant people. It offers us the same comfort in our corrupt and dangerous world.

God rules the world, not Babylon's idols (50:2). Like most ancient nations, Babylon believed that many gods exist (v. 2; Isa. 46:1–2). They thought these gods ruled particular territories and peoples. When these gods got mad at their people, they turned them over to their enemies (Jer. 50:7). Thus, the Babylonians believed that Jeremiah spoke for Judah's deity, yet they failed to share Jeremiah's belief in the only God, the creator and ruler of the heavens and the earth (10:1–16; 33:2). Today, militant religious groups of all sorts make claims for their gods. Since their gods do not rule the world, however, the world's peoples can find hope in Christ, who brings peace (John 14:27; Isaiah 11).

God judges arrogance and brutality. Eventually, all man-made gods amount to nothing more than the worship of money, sexuality, and power. Empires never expand without the brutality needed to gain these idols. Jeremiah accuses Babylon of gnawing Israel's bones, like a lion tearing a sheep (Jer. 50:17). Babylon did not treat fallen foes as people, but merely as impediments to slaking their political desire. Thus Babylon arrogantly defied God (v. 29). All greedy and vicious conquerors face God's righteous judgment. Therefore, like Jeremiah we can work and wait for justice, knowing God's justice will prevail.

God redeems his people, however far they have wandered from him. God's people have become lost sheep (vv. 6–7), but they will return to him (v. 4). They will seek an everlasting covenant with him (v. 5; see chs. 30–31). They will return home (50:19), but Babylon will be turned into a wasteland (vv. 39–43). Exiled in Babylon for decades, Daniel longed for this redemption (Dan. 9:1–19). Now we know its reality in Jesus Christ, and we await its fulfillment when he comes again (2 Thess. 1:5–12).

Whatever happens, however discouraging, do not despair, for God alone rules and redeems. What we do faithfully for the Lord is not in vain. Surely the book of Jeremiah has taught us this!

Taking Comfort in God's Character

PAUL R. HOUSE

LAMENTATIONS RELATES the confessions and prayers of people in the middle of suffering for their sins. These people are the very ones Jeremiah warned. Having suffered the loss of their land, temple, and capital, they now ask God for forgiveness and restoration. Since their actions caused their pain, how can they hope for such outrageous grace? The speaker in this passage invites his people and us to know that we can do so only because of God's character.

God's character gives us hope. God punished the speaker so thoroughly that he lost hope (Lam. 3:1–20). Then he recalled that God's steadfast covenant love never ends (v. 22a). God keeps his promises. Among the greatest of these promises is that he forgives all who confess their sins. His compassionate mercy for repenting people never ends (v. 22b). God's loving mercy is renewed every morning, every day that we live, every time we repent (v. 23a). God's faithfulness to his promises is greater than our sin (v. 23). Hope returns when we remember that God is our portion in life (v. 24). If we have God we have all we need, even if nation and temple are gone.

God's character gives us endurance. God "is good to those who wait for him" (v. 25). Thus, we can wait for his salvation from our well-deserved punishment (v. 26), from the bondage we chose. We can accept the troubles we have brought on ourselves (vv. 28–30) when we know that God does "not cast off forever" (v. 31). We can persevere in hope because God "does not afflict from his heart" (v. 33). He does not enjoy punishing us. He does so to bring us to repentance (vv. 37–39).

God's character gives us the boldness to pray. Since God loves, forgives, shows mercy, and afflicts to heal from sin, we can bring anything to him. We can even ask him to help us in the situations he has brought about to punish our sins (vv. 40–66). God has redeemed us from our enemies in the past, and he will do so again (vv. 58–60).

Lamentations expresses good news for fallen believers. God disciplines those he loves (Heb. 12:3–17; Revelation 2–3). When we awaken amid the disasters we have caused, we find God ready to forgive. The same God who forgave Moses, Jeremiah, and Peter remains faithfully forgiving now. Trust his character as you repent today.

Help Wanted, Full Time: Must Sit on Scorpions

GREG GILBERT

CHAPTERS 2-3 RECORD EZEKIEL'S call by God to be a prophet to the people of Israel. Right on the heels of the amazing vision of God's sovereignty and power in chapter 1, God tells Ezekiel that his job will be to speak God's word to Israel (Ezek. 2:4). And that won't be an easy task. The people are "impudent and stubborn" (2:4), a "rebellious house" (2:5–8). Ezekiel's job, God says, will be like sitting on scorpions (2:6)!

Ezekiel is to speak the words of God, even though the people aren't going to listen. Throughout these two chapters, two big ideas alternate back and forth. First, Ezekiel is a "bound" man and must speak only what God tells him to speak (2:8–3:3; 3:16–27). When he eats the scroll (3:3), he is internalizing God's word, making it his own. As a "watchman" (3:17), his responsibility is to sound a warning to the people. Most of all, God tells Ezekiel to bind himself with cords, and then God takes away his power of speech *except when God has given him a message* (3:24–27)!

The second big idea of chapters 2–3 is that God knows full well how the people are going to respond to Ezekiel's message: they will reject it (2:1–7; 3:4–11). Even a foreign nation, God says, would listen to Ezekiel's message, but Israel will not.

God "has his people's number." They probably think they are really putting one over on him, but he knows their hearts, and he knows how they are going to respond to his message through Ezekiel. That takes the force out of their rebellion, doesn't it? I've noticed the same thing in my children when they decide to disobey or even throw fits. They may be hot with anger, but they're too small to do much about it. They're all will and no power! That's us, too, when we rebel against God. Even when we think we're punishing God in some way, in his eyes, our rebellion is very small and manageable.

But notice one last thing. Despite the people's rebellion, God sends his word to them anyway (2:7; 3:11). Have you ever realized that God's very act of speaking to us, of revealing himself to us, is an act of grace? Faced with our rebellion and sin, God could have spoken just once—in judgment—and then gone silent. But wonderfully, he didn't! He showed amazing grace and mercy to us by speaking again through Jesus Christ—and this time it was a word of forgiveness!

JULY 4 · EZEKIEL 11:14-25

Determined to Save

GREG GILBERT

MOST ACCOMPLISHMENTS in our lives require determination. If you're going to succeed at your job, or complete a project, or stay in shape, you've got to stick with it in the face of obstacles. But have you ever realized how determined God himself is to carry out his purpose of salvation? Despite all the obstacles of our continued sin and rebellion, he *will* forgive. He *will* save.

Chapters 4–11 contain one oracle of judgment after another against the people of Israel, and throughout, God is making it clear that his judgment of them is utterly and completely right. It isn't just that the people have made a few mistakes or fallen a bit short of a high standard. It's that they have abandoned God to worship other gods and have insulted him in the process—even turning their backs on him and, in essence, pushing a sharp stick up his nose: see the ESV textual footnote on Ezekiel 8:16–18! As a result, God mounts his royal chariot and departs from the temple (See 10:18–19; then 11:22–25).

By the time God has finished promising and describing the destruction that is about to befall Jerusalem, Ezekiel is overwhelmed. "Ah, Lord GOD!"

he cries. "Will you make a full end of the remnant of Israel?" (11:13). Then, over the next few verses, God answers: "No, I will not." Yes, they will be scattered among the nations in exile, God says. But even there, God will be a sanctuary to them (v. 16); he will protect them; and one day he will gather them together again in the land (v. 17). Moreover, he will remove their hard heart of stone and give them a new heart and a new spirit, so that they will no longer disobey his law but rather obey it and live in peace (vv. 19–20).

Those were sweet words amid the cataclysm Ezekiel had been prophesying. God wasn't abandoning his people forever, sinners though they were. He would return one day and save them (see 43:1–5). And the glorious thing is that, despite our sin, God has not abandoned us, either! Sometimes people look at their lives and say, "Surely God won't forgive *this*!" But he will. He is a God of dogged determination—determination to save!

JULY 5 · EZEKIEL 18

I Don't Deserve This!

GREG GILBERT

"DO YOU THINK you deserved that discipline?" That's what my dad would always ask me after justice was meted out in our home. Most of the time, I'd just answer, "Yes, sir," because I didn't want to talk about it anymore. But many times, in my childish reasoning, I was thinking, "No way. I didn't deserve *that!*"

By Ezekiel 17, you can feel the tension rising dramatically. God is about to execute judgment, and Israel's last move is to retreat into a self-deceived assurance that *surely* it isn't really going to happen. So in chapters 17, 18, 19, and 20, the Israelites invent four big reasons why God's judgment cannot possibly take place: there's no need to worry, because their allies will save them from Babylon (ch. 17); they don't deserve judgment (ch. 18); God would never destroy the Davidic dynasty (ch. 19); and God surely wouldn't bring their glorious history to *this* kind of end (ch. 20).

Let's take a closer look at the self-deceiving reason they give in chapter 18, because it's a delusion that is all too common for us: "We don't deserve this!" You can see their argument in 18:2: "The fathers have eaten sour grapes, and the children's teeth are set on edge!" In other words, "We didn't sin! It was our ancestors, and now we're having to take the punishment for it!" In fact, they actually say, in verse 25: "The way of the Lord is not just!"

The whole of chapter 18, then, is God's forceful (and detailed) rejection of that idea. Over and over, he says, "It's not true that people are punished for sins they didn't commit." If a man is righteous, God says, he'll live (vv. 5–9). If not, he'll die; his sin will be on his own head (vv. 10–13). But if a wicked person *repents* of his sin, he will live and not die (vv. 21–23). God's message to his people is clear: "It isn't just your fathers who sinned; it's *you. You* have sinned, and *you* will die."

Like Israel, we all have a tendency to falsely assure ourselves that God doesn't take our sin seriously. We tell ourselves that there's no need to worry about it, or that God won't finally do anything about it, or that we don't deserve his judgment. But of course we do deserve judgment, and he will execute it—either on us, or on Jesus Christ in our place! As you walk through your day today, make sure your heart isn't taking God's grace to you for granted. Be glad that even though you *do* deserve judgment, you won't get it—because Jesus took it in your place.

JULY 6 · EZEKIEL 34

God Is Great, God Is Good

GREG GILBERT

WHEN YOU THINK of God, what comes to mind? A powerful king? A righteous judge? The omnipotent creator? What emotions do those thoughts create in your heart? For many of us, when we think of God, we're not filled with joy and happiness but rather with feelings like dread, guilt, and fear. But is that really how thinking about God should affect us? Or does the Bible tell us something different?

Beginning in the middle of chapter 33, the tenor of Ezekiel's book changes dramatically. Where all had been judgment and destruction, this is the moment of the Great Reversal, where death and despair give way to shouts of joy. Chapter 34 is where the light really begins to shine brightly, and God tells his people that he himself is going to comfort them, care for them, and love them.

The chapter begins with God's condemnation of the "shepherds" of Israel—its leaders (34:1–10). Instead of caring for the people, God says, they have been exploiting them. So God takes matters into his own hands: "If you won't care for my people, I will do so myself" (see v. 11). Over the next few verses, God describes how he is going to care for his people (vv. 11–16), making it clear that his care will involve justice for those among them who are oppressed and judgment for the oppressors (vv. 17–22). Finally, in verses 23–31, God promises that the Davidic throne will be restored (vv. 23–24). What's more, back in verse 15 God had promised that he himself would be their Shepherd, their King. What God is saying is amazing: the future King will be a descendant of David who *is God himself*!

In all of this, God is giving his people a beautiful vision of safety and security, promising that he himself—their Great Shepherd—will care for them. Do you often think of God like that—eager to care, full of compassion, angry at exploitation and abuse? Sometimes we think of God as the ultimate Game Master, forever setting up situations to test us and see how we'll respond. But that's not how the Bible presents God. God's heart is *for* us. He passionately wants our good, and that's what the gospel of Jesus Christ is all about. It's not the bad news that you should just live better, or the bad news that God wants to put you under a new set of rules, or the bad news that he wants to drain all the fun out of your life. It's the *good* news that there are pleasures forevermore in God's hand, and he desires to give them to us!

Lay Your Trophies at His Feet

GREG GILBERT

GOLD MEDALS. The Lombardi Trophy. The Stanley Cup. MVP. Highlight reels. Heisman. Cy Young. World Series. Super Bowl. World Cup. The Finals. It's all about the glory, isn't it?

Ezekiel 36 falls in the middle of a long passage where God is describing not only how he will ultimately rescue his people from the coming destruction, but also the amazing and varied ways he's going to do good to them. He will give them care in the face of abuse, life in the face of death, and triumph in the face of defeat. But in the midst of it all, he also wants them to know—and wants the watching world to know—that the glory for their salvation belongs not to them but to *him*, and him alone.

In verses 16–20, God reminds the Israelites why he had sent them into exile in the first place. It was because they had defiled the land with their ways and deeds, especially their idolatry. But then, even after he poured out his wrath against them and scattered them among the nations, even there they profaned him (v. 20). By rights, God should have destroyed them, wiping them off the face of the earth. But he didn't. Why not? He tells them in verse 21, and it's a deeply surprising reason. He doesn't say it was because he liked them, or because their sin wasn't as bad as it seemed. It was because "I had concern for my holy name."

God continues to explain this to them through the next few verses. He is acting to save Israel, not for Israel's sake, he says, but "for the sake of my holy name" (vv. 22, 32). He will rescue them, to be sure—gathering them back to their land, rebuilding their cities, even giving them new hearts. But the reason will be so that "the nations will know that I am the LORD . . . when through you I vindicate my holiness before their eyes" (v. 23). The glory—all of it—would be his.

Do you ever feel tempted to be proud about the fact that you're a Christian? Paul tells us that, just like Israel's rescue from exile, our own salvation is not for our own glory but "to the praise of his glorious grace"

(Eph. 1:6). The crowns we receive will not be to make *us* look good, like some kind of heavenly trophy; the crowns will be for us to throw at Jesus's feet, so that all the glory goes to him.

Life Out of Death

GREG GILBERT

OF ALL THE GREAT blessings of salvation that Jesus won for his people, perhaps the greatest is *life*. In the gospel, death-deserving rebels against God are promised that they will live eternally. This section of Ezekiel's prophecy is a beautiful portrait of how God will rescue his people from their sin and its horrific consequences. Instead of destruction, they will now have salvation; instead of defeat, triumph. And as God shows Ezekiel in this valley of dry bones, their spiritual death will be turned to spiritual life.

God took Ezekiel, in a vision, to a valley filled with dry bones. The whole valley was filled with death, and there was no life anywhere to be found. Asked by God if the bones could ever live, Ezekiel answered wisely—and with great trust—"O Lord GOD, you know" (37:3). Then God told Ezekiel to do something extraordinary; he told him to prophesy to the bones, that is, to preach to them (v. 4). As Ezekiel did so, the bones began to rattle, came together, and soon were covered with flesh! Ezekiel prophesied again, and the breath of life blew into them; they stood and became a mighty army.

The point of the vision was not so much to show that God had power to bring *physical life*, but to show that he could bring *spiritual life* out of spiritual death. God makes that point clear in verses 11–14; Israel was spiritually dead, but here was God, promising dramatically that he would give them life. Essentially, God was promising the impossible—to bring joy out of his people's despair, life out of their death—and he would do it ultimately through the life, death, and resurrection of Jesus Christ.

At its heart, this is what Christianity is all about—the miracle of life when there is only death. It's not merely ethical teaching or social engagement or moral reformation. It's about God miraculously bringing life where death once reigned. Do you think of your faith in Jesus that way? Do you understand and rejoice in the amazing thing that has happened in you? God has the power to bring life out of death. He makes lives scorched by sin come alive again. He makes hearts fossilized by rebellion beat again and *live*. He takes dry bones and gives them life. Where in your life is there death? Hold those areas out to the God who gives life. Let his word wash over them. Repent and believe in him, and let them live again!

JULY 9 · DANIEL 1

God's Gracious Hand of Providence

BRYAN CHAPELL

DANIEL AND HIS FRIENDS must have wondered if there would ever be any purpose for their lives in Babylonian captivity. But then these young Israelites were taken to live in the Babylonian palace, probably so that their captors could learn how to govern these Israelite exiles. In the palace, death was the instant consequence for any word or action that displeased the king. Despite the risks, however, these young Israelite men determined to honor their Lord.

The account of Daniel and his friends reminds us that there are risks to holiness. We cannot presume that serving God will get us a pass on life's difficulties. In fact, both Jesus and his followers promise persecution for the faithful (e.g., Matt. 24:9; 2 Tim. 3:12).

Since their training in the king's court led to remarkable privileges, you might assume that these young Israelites' trials were all over: Daniel and his friends needed only to go along with the program, accept the privileges offered, and keep their heads down. But they did not.

For reasons that are unclear (probably related to the king's fine food being either devoted to idols or denied to their families), the young men believed they would defile themselves if they ate the food that the king provided. So Daniel asked the chief of the eunuchs (his jailer/trainer) to allow him and his friends to subsist on what was essentially a vegan diet.

The chief assumed that the king's food was healthier and feared punishment if he did not keep these prize captives in tip-top shape. But Daniel persuaded him to experiment for ten days. The result: Daniel and his friends looked healthier than their peers.

We may be tempted simply to admire Daniel for standing for his values. But Daniel's focus was different. This account, as well as all that follows in the book of Daniel, makes it clear that Daniel and his people's preservation was due to the providential hand of a gracious God. The Lord was working a grand plan of redemption for his wayward people (see Dan. 1:2, 9, 17, 21). Daniel showed great valor and took great risks, but all was because of his confidence in, and his response to, the grace of a greater God.

Daniel's challenges remind us always to examine the ways in which we are being tempted to compromise our values. The grace Daniel experienced reminds us to trust and obey our God of timeless providence and provision, no matter what the earthly consequences may seem to be.

JULY 10 · DANIEL 2

When the Bottom Falls Out

BRYAN CHAPELL

KING NEBUCHADNEZZAR wanted his wise men to interpret a dream whose details he refused to reveal to them; he was testing them, to see whether they really had supernatural insight. When the wise men made excuses for not being able to interpret the unknown dream, the cruel king ordered all of them killed.

Daniel was a wise man, too, and was about to become collateral damage (Dan. 2:13). In an instant, he had plunged from the heights of a privileged palace life to being the victim of a murderous king's ire. Even if we haven't lived in a palace, most of us know what it is like to have circumstances abruptly change—to be on the top of the world one day and limping through a crisis the next.

When our world turns ugly, we may cry in grief, yell in anger, try to exploit our resources, or simply collapse. All such responses are understandable, but Daniel's was different. He turned to the God he trusted—a God who was about to teach the king about who *really* controlled the past, the present, and the future (vv. 31–45).

Asked to interpret the pagan king's dream, Daniel first asked for additional time. But his request was not designed to provide opportunity for human ingenuity or an escape plan. Daniel used the time to inform his friends of the need for prayer—and to pray (vv. 17–18).

When the bottom fell out, Daniel fell to his knees. Other options were available to him. He was a smart guy. He could have called in some favors, tried to negotiate a settlement, or planned a rebellion. In a crisis, other options are usually available to us, too (write the memo; call in the experts; send the check). Still, Daniel's priority was on turning to the God who had rescued his people in the past and had promised to preserve their future with a coming Messiah (vv. 44–45).

When God revealed the mystery of the king's dream, Daniel could have claimed personal credit, but instead he gave praise to God (vv. 28–30, 45). Daniel's example reminds us that, in times of great stress, there is no greater priority than turning to the God of grace to deliver us—in the way and at the time that he knows is best.

Our rescue may not be in a timing or turn of events that we immediately understand—after all, the ultimate rescue of Daniel's people was still many generations in the future—but it is always from the hand of the God who preserved his covenant people and provided Jesus.

JULY 11 · DANIEL 3

Into the Furnace

BRYAN CHAPELL

THE SPOTLIGHT temporarily shifts from Daniel to his three friends, who have also learned to trust the grace of Israel's God.

Jealous of the privileges of Daniel's friends, enemies plotted against them. Fast talk tricked the vain king into enforcing idolatrous practices, which set up Shadrach, Meshach, and Abednego for the accusation that they were remaining faithful to Israel's God (Dan. 3:10–12). When Shadrach, Meshach, and Abednego refused to bow to the king's golden image, he ordered them thrown into a death furnace. Here, again, we learn that faithfulness does not guarantee an "easy street" life.

The example of Daniel's friends also shows us that God wants us to acknowledge that his provision is sufficient, loving, and good, even if it does not line up with our own immediate desires. If we are to withstand the trials of this world, we must be able to affirm, "I may not understand this challenge, but I trust that God knows best, and I will honor him regardless of what comes."

Shadrach, Meshach, and Abednego did not go into the fiery furnace assuming they would be saved. They said, "Our God whom we serve is able to deliver us. . . . But if not, be it known to you, O king, that we will not serve your gods" (vv. 17–18). The three believed that their God was capable of rescuing them immediately, and would ultimately rescue them—even if only by their passage from this life to eternity—but they did not pretend that they could predict or demand particular actions from God.

They simply trusted that the God who had delivered them in the past—and had promised to deliver his people eternally—would do what was best, even if they could not discern the particulars of his plan. They trusted God's providence more than their predictions, his wisdom more than their desires, and his grace more than any grand scheme that they could devise.

God miraculously delivered them, and yet their faithful words teach us that we should not always expect such immediate miracles. Tragedy does not mean that God has vanished. Faith is often refined in the furnaces of life, making God's presence and grace all the more powerful and precious.

Never Give Up

BRYAN CHAPELL

THIRTY-TWO YEARS had passed since Daniel's first interpretation of Nebuchadnezzar's dreams had burst the king's illusions about his own greatness (Dan. 2:36–47). Now Nebuchadnezzar needed a reminder about the limits of his greatness and glory. One day, as he walked atop his palace, surveying his kingdom, he said, "Is not this great Babylon, which I have built by my mighty power as a royal residence and for the glory of my majesty?" (4:30). He was just asking for trouble. And that's what he got.

Months earlier, Nebuchadnezzar had dreamed of a majestic tree growing to wondrous heights. In the dream, the tree was cut down and stripped of its greatness at the command of a heavenly messenger (vv. 13–14). The dream had terrified the king, and once again he had called for Daniel to interpret the vision.

The interpretation was as simple as it was scary: King Nebuchadnezzar was going to have a great fall. He would lose his mind and live in the fields like an animal until he acknowledged that God alone is sovereign over all things.

This poignant account of a man's ruin and restoration dramatically reveals a gospel story of God's mercy toward those who have stood against him. It is a timeless reminder that God shows his grace to those who honor him now, even if they have failed to do so in the past.

With the severe mercies of his grace, our God can break the will and win the heart of those most resistant to him. So we must pray for the salvation of those whom God places in our care, with the confidence that he is able to break the hardest heart. The battle may be long before it is won. Daniel's testimony of God in Nebuchadnezzar's life began decades before the details of this chapter. But the king finally did acknowledge Daniel's God.

We must not cease working and praying for a brother, father, wife, or friend. Never give up. Never give up. Never give up. It does not matter how hard the heart. God can reach it.

Grace, Greater Than All Our Sin

STEPHEN T. UM

THE LIFE OF the prophet Hosea still holds great intrigue for modern readers. He appears to be the model of a noble, devout man. He is committed to his God and committed to his marriage. God had commanded Hosea to marry a woman named Gomer, even though she was going to be unfaithful to him (Hos. 1:2). Despite that forbidding foreknowledge, Hosea did his best to build a family with Gomer (v. 3). When she ran away, Hosea pursued her (3:1–2). There was no amount of adulterous behavior that could dissuade him from expressing and maintaining his deep love for her.

Perhaps it is natural to compare ourselves to Hosea. We desire to be steady, constant, and uncompromisingly gracious. And yet, to measure ourselves against Hosea is to miss the point of his book. The point is that *we are Gomer*. We are God's adulterous wife. Rather than being valiant people who never abandon ship, we are adulterous people who look for satisfaction and fulfillment in other lovers. We go back on our promises all too easily and frequently.

What is the result of our rebellion? In the book of Hosea, Gomer bears three children, each of whom is symbolically named to represent God's judgment on Israel. For example, Hosea and Gomer's second child is named "No Mercy" because God will no longer show mercy (1:6). Their third child is named "Not My People" because God can no longer call Israel his own (v. 9). It is a bleak picture.

What, then, is the hope for God's modern-day adulterous people? In verses 10–11, Hosea told his readers of a day when things would be set right—a day when they would be embraced again by a recklessly gracious God. "Not My People" would be renamed "Children of the living God" (v. 10). The New Testament tells us that this new reality has come to pass through Jesus. The apostle Peter makes this connection explicit: "Once you were not a people, but now you are God's people; once you had not received mercy, but now you have received mercy" (1 Pet. 2:10). In Christ,

we are the children of the living God (Rom. 8:16). And when we come
to see that we have been embraced despite our adultery, our hearts are
moved to faithfulness. When we recognize that we are adopted despite
our rebellion, we are moved to obedience.

JULY 14 • HOSEA 6-7

The God Who Heals and Binds Up

STEPHEN T. UM

AS WE CONTINUE to read Hosea, the picture that emerges is grim. We have
just finished an extensive section in which the Lord's promise to punish
his people is front and center (Hosea 5), and he will shortly bombard the
reader with examples of their widespread unrepentance (6:4–7:16). And
yet, sandwiched in between these two sections is a brief responsive prayer
of repentance (6:1–3). It is as though Hosea knows that his readers need
some reprieve; we need an opportunity to offer the kind of repentance
that his harsh prophetic words are intended to evoke. Hosea's prophecy is
punctuated by repentance.

Consider 6:1: "Come, let us return to the LORD; for he has torn us, that
he may heal us; he has struck us down, and he will bind us up." Here we
learn the purposes of the Lord in judgment and punishment. He tears that
he may heal; he strikes down that he may bind up. Everything that Hosea
is writing is intended to make us say, "Let us return to the Lord!" Do you
see the dynamic at work here? When you are so intent on pursuing other
idols that you are willing to sever your ties with God, God is so intent on
pursuing *you* that he is willing to sever your ties to your idols—even if
that means that you must endure some momentary trial or pain. In this
way, trial is intended to drive us *toward* God rather than *away* from him.

And how do we know that God ultimately uses trials for our good?
Because he underwent the ultimate trial in our place! In Jesus Christ, God
himself was struck down in order that he might bind us up; he was torn
in order that he might heal us. He received the judgment and punishment
we deserved so that we might receive the acceptance and reward that he

deserved. And when Hosea 6:2 promises resurrection, it is ultimately pointing to the resurrection of Christ (Luke 24:46; 1 Cor. 15:4), which is the assurance of our own future resurrection (1 Cor. 15:20–23). This astounding grace gives us the assurance that we will be embraced when we "return to the Lord." May this self-giving love of God lead you to "cry to [him] from the heart" (Hos. 7:14), to "seek him" (7:10), and to offer the "steadfast love" he desires (6:6).

The Tender Heart of God

STEPHEN T. UM

HOSEA ENVISIONS ISRAEL as a rebellious, stubborn, idolatrous child (11:2), oblivious to the provision and care of its father (11:3). It is no surprise at this point that Israel has wandered far from the Lord. What is surprising, however, is the unstoppable tenderness of God toward his people. While they are "bent on turning away from [him]" (11:7), he is bent on showing them compassion (11:8).

In one of the more moving sections of the book, we are given a look into the inner dialogue of God as he wrestles with the waywardness of his child. Only a moment after threatening to turn a deaf ear to their cries (11:7), he finds himself unable to do so (11:8). His heart recoils from the idea of abandoning his people. Instead, he will roar like a lion to call his children home to him (11:10–11).

This is the tender heart of our God. Though we constantly turn away from him, he cannot even stomach the idea of turning away from us. Even when we think we are pulling it off on our own—completely oblivious to his fatherly care—he refuses to leave us to our own devices. And when we wander from home, he raises his lionhearted voice so that we can hear again his compelling call.

Make no mistake; this is God's approach to us even when we are at our worst. How can we be sure? God was so intent on embracing his people that he sent Jesus to be all that we could never be. The New Testament sees

Jesus as the "son" of Hosea 11:1 (Matt. 2:15). In other words, he came to do all that Israel had repeatedly failed to do. He fulfilled all of the covenant responsibilities and bore all of the covenant curses so that God's covenant breaking people could receive all of his covenant blessings. It is in Jesus that the justice (Hos. 11:5–7) and mercy (vv. 8–9) of God perfectly meet and kiss. And in him our identity and standing as children of God is secure (John 1:12). May his soft and gentle heart touch your hard heart, leading you to walk in faithfulness with God (Hos. 11:12).

JULY 16 · HOSEA 14

Returning to God

STEPHEN T. UM

WHEN WE WANDER, God is so desirous for us to return to him that he even helps us by giving us the words to say ("take with you words"; Hos. 14:2). In much the same way as when Jesus gave his disciples the Lord's Prayer (Luke 11:1–4), Hosea gives Israel a guide to repentance (Hos. 14:2–3). At the end of a lengthy series of prophecies, Hosea wants it to be eminently clear that his goal throughout has been to see God's people return to him (v. 1).

What does it look like to return to the Lord? In the Old Testament, it took three things: (1) a request for mercy ("take away all iniquity"; v. 2); (2) a sacrificial offering ("accept what is good"; v. 2); and (3) the forsaking of other gods (i.e., surrendering allegiances and idols; v. 3).

What is the result of following this God-given script of repentance? Hosea 14:4–8 offers one of the most beautiful pictures of holistic restoration in all of Scripture. God promises his people that he will "love them freely." Nothing will hinder his love because he will heal their faithless hearts (v. 4), and he will be the sole source of their flourishing (v. 5). The prophet almost reaches his poetic limits in attempting to describe the beauty of the restored relationship.

How does this connect to us today? While the altogether perfect and sufficient substitutionary death of Jesus on our behalf has forever removed from the script any need on our part to offer yet another sacrifice (Hebrews 9–10), repentance today remains much the same. When we wander, we are called to turn toward God for mercy and turn away from the idols that enslave us. Remarkably, repentance means that, even in this life, we will enjoy this promised flourishing! And this flourishing is far greater than anything on offer anywhere else in the world. When we turn to God, our "evergreen cypress," he becomes the constant source of our fruit and sustenance (Hos. 14:8). He is what our hearts have been searching for all along. "Whoever is wise, let him understand these things" (v. 9).

JULY 17 · JOEL 2

God's Wake-Up Call

STEPHEN T. UM

JOEL'S PROPHECY WAS handcrafted to awaken his hearers from a fatal slumber. He calls for blaring alarms to shake up a people who had been lulled into the sleep of sin and rebellion (Joel 2:1). As always, the result of sin is the erasure of the beauty of Eden and the arrival of destruction (v. 3). The forecasted judgment is terrifying in its scope: it will be cosmic (vv. 2, 10), communal (vv. 6, 9a), and personal (v. 9b). On top of this, the judgment will be meted out by the Lord himself (v. 11), ensuring that it will be swift and thorough.

We typically approach a passage like this from one of two angles—either fear or detachment. On our first reading, we tremble with Joel's original hearers (v. 1). But this response is unsustainable—it is impossible to live in a perpetual state of fear. So, we try to remove ourselves from the picture. Perhaps we begin to think about our historical distance from the time of Joel, or maybe we're aware of some apparent interpretive difficulties regarding Joel's prophecy. And thus we try to absolve ourselves from applying Joel's words to our own lives.

Responding to Joel's prophecy with a feeling of detachment doesn't work either. It is impossible to exclude ourselves from the judgment promised in this passage. Both responses ignore the reality that our sin has cosmic (Rom. 8:19–23), communal (1 Cor. 5:6–7), and personal impact (Isa. 59:2).

What, then, is the proper response to the warning alarm of Joel 2? Ironically, it is to turn toward the one who has promised judgment ("return to me with all your heart"; Joel 2:12–13). When we hear the warning trumpet of verse 1 rightly, we hear it as a call to repentance and return (v. 15). And on what basis do we turn back to this God? On the basis of his character. He is "gracious," "merciful," "slow to anger," and "abounding in steadfast love" (v. 13). More than that, he is a restorer and renewer (vv. 19–27).

The promises of Joel 2—including the promise of the outpouring of the Holy Spirit (vv. 28–29)—are accomplished in the death and resurrection of Jesus (Acts 2:14–24). He endured the judgment of God that no one else could endure (Joel 2:11). In his death he dealt with sin in all of its cosmic, communal, and personal aspects. In his resurrection he secured ultimate restoration and renewal. As a result, the last trumpet will not be one of warning but of resurrection celebration (1 Cor. 15:52). Knowing this, let us gladly return to our God with "all our heart."

JULY 18 • AMOS 3

Relationship Involves Responsibility

JULIUS J. KIM

THIS MESSAGE OF JUDGMENT was unexpected, but God had had enough. He needed to discipline his people for their forgetfulness and faithlessness. They had forgotten that their special relationship with God also involved a responsibility to think and live faithfully and righteously. They had taken God and each other for granted.

When all is going well, it is easy to forget that God is the source and sustainer of all things. It's easy to think that the blessings we have are due to our own energy and efforts. It's easy to live our lives as practical atheists—as if God didn't exist. This is what had happened to Israel.

Israel had it all. Compared to other nations, they had a unique and intimate relationship with the Creator and Redeemer. They were rescued from the bondage of Egypt. They were adopted into the family of God. They were given the Promised Land. These experiences of election and exodus formed the very core of their identity. But Israel forgot that these blessings did not guarantee God's overlooking of their sin of ingratitude and irresponsibility. Quite the opposite! Indeed, when we forget to be thankful, we lose sight of who we are and how we are to live.

Israel was oppressing those who needed care and support (Amos 3:9; cf. 4:1). They were involved with hoarding and looting (3:10). Though *shown* mercy, they did not *show* mercy. Though granted blessings, they showed no grace. "He has told you, O man, what is good; and what does the LORD require of you but to do justice, and to love kindness, and to walk humbly with your God?" (Mic. 6:8) Was there any hope for Israel? Is there any hope for us?

Thanks be to God! When we are faithless, he is faithful. When we forget, he remembers. When we show no mercy or grace, God is rich in mercy and grace. He will save a remnant for his own glory (Amos 3:12), and he will save us. He did this ultimately through Jesus on the cross, where judgment and mercy meet. On the cross, Jesus, the perfect Son of God, received the punishment we deserve for our lack of justice, mercy, and kindness. On the cross, Jesus revealed the grace that we so desperately need. This justice and mercy now compels us to remember anew the special relationship we have with our gracious Father, through the Son, in the Spirit. This relationship involves a responsibility to repent and believe the gospel, to walk humbly and thankfully, and to reveal justice, kindness, and mercy to those whom God has placed in our lives.

Living from the Inside Out

JULIUS J. KIM

"WOE TO YOU, scribes and Pharisees, hypocrites! For you are like white-washed tombs, which outwardly appear beautiful, but within are full of dead people's bones and all uncleanness. So you also outwardly appear righteous to others, but within you are full of hypocrisy and lawlessness" (Matt. 23:27–28). Jesus doesn't mince his words. For all of their outward obedience, these Pharisees were rotting on the inside. Israel, during the time of Amos, was no different—they were living "outside in."

Here in our passage, Amos indicts Israel for their sin of pretension—for thinking that their external ceremonies would somehow please God (Amos 5:21–25). Did they think God could not see their hypocrisy and idolatry (vv. 6–7), their injustice and greed (vv. 10–12)? Did they think God could not see their hearts?

Are we any different? Do we sometimes go through the motions while our hearts are not seeking the Lord and his will? What the Pharisees during Jesus's day, the Israelites during Amos's day, and sometimes we today fail to see is that God looks at our hearts and our lives: "For the LORD sees not as man sees: man looks on the outward appearance, but the LORD looks on the heart" (1 Sam. 16:7). God wants us to live *from the inside out*: "I the LORD search the heart and test the mind, to give every man according to his ways, according to the fruit of his deeds" (Jer. 17:10).

Here in Amos 5, God calls on us three times to "seek" him, emphasizing that God must change our hearts before we can truly "live" or "do good" (see Amos 5:4, 6, 14). We can escape the judgment of our hypocrisy and idolatry only through God's grace alone. Through his death and resurrection, Jesus offers us new life, changing our dead hearts into new ones as we place our faith in him alone. Relying solely on Jesus, we now have Spirit-filled power to live from the inside out.

Jesus promises us, "I am the vine; you are the branches. Whoever abides in me and I in him, he it is that bears much fruit, for apart from me you can do nothing" (John 15:5). What then is our calling? The apostle Paul states it well: "Therefore, as you received Christ Jesus the Lord, so walk in him, rooted and built up in him and established in the faith, just as you were taught, abounding in thanksgiving" (Col. 2:6–7). Let's live from the inside out!

Discipleship through Discipline

JULIUS J. KIM

THOUGH DIFFICULT, divine discipline is purposeful, bringing glory to God and good to us his people. The Bible teaches that God uses all things—even the tough times—for our growth and maturity. The author of Hebrews reminds us that, as children of God, we will sometimes undergo discipline in order that we might become more like Jesus. After quoting from the book of Job, he uses earthly fathers as an analogy for God: "For they disciplined us for a short time as it seemed best to them, but he disciplines us for our good, that we may share his holiness" (Heb. 12:10). Though it may hurt, divine discipline ultimately benefits us as we grow in holiness.

Amos highlights two truths to teach this: (1) God must discipline his people for their sin (Amos 9:1–10); and (2) God will *disciple* his people through promises of grace and restoration (vv. 11–15). God disciples us through discipline, sovereignly using all our circumstances for our good.

We can see this in what God states about himself in this chapter. He is holy and righteous and will judge sin (vv. 1–4, 9–10). He is also sovereign, in control of everything everywhere (vv. 5–6). And amazingly, he is full of grace and mercy (vv. 7–8). He reminds Israel and us that he delivered them from their bondage in Egypt for the purposes of blessing, and he will do it again. Then, providing unimaginable hope, God states unequivocally that he will "raise up," "repair," and "rebuild" (v. 11). He is a promise keeper, faithfully restoring his sinful people in ways that they do not deserve. Using images from farming and winemaking, God promises to thoroughly restore and reclaim them from bondage to blessing.

These blessings will even trickle over to other nations (v. 12). The apostle James in Acts 15:16–17 quotes these verses from Amos to reveal how God's promises of restoration and blessing are fulfilled through Jesus Christ. With his life-transforming death and resurrection, Jesus provides ultimate blessing. How? He does this through his own suffering. On the cross, Christ received the penalty for our sin, so that all who trust in him receive the blessing of forgiveness and righteousness (2 Cor. 5:21).

Knowing this changes us—knowing that we are more sinful than we can even imagine and yet more loved than we can ever dare hope. We can face life's difficulties with renewed hope, strength, and patience, knowing that God is discipling us. Divine discipline is purposeful, bringing glory to God as we grow ever more like Christ our Lord.

JULY 21 · OBADIAH

Trust and Obey the King

JULIUS J. KIM

WHY DO THE WICKED prosper and the good suffer? Asked by poets and prophets alike, this is an honest question spurred on by the often difficult realities of life. Both the poet Asaph and the prophet Jeremiah asked this of God in their trials (Ps. 73:2–12; Jer. 12:1). In similar circumstances, we too can doubt God's presence in our lives. The prophet Obadiah tackles this issue head-on, providing both understanding and encouragement to help us keep trusting and obeying our King.

In brief but powerful words, Obadiah first proclaims judgment on Edom and then pronounces hope for Israel, revealing that God is sovereign and his will is powerful and purposeful.

First, as God proclaims judgment against Israel's neighbor Edom, we see that nothing and no one stands outside of God's reign and rule. He is King over all, not just Israel. God denounces Edom for siding with Israel's enemies, shunning Israel in their time of need, stealing their goods, and selling their sons as slaves (Obad. 10–14). Edom is treating Israel just like Esau treated Jacob. God will thus punish Edom as he punished the father of their nation, Esau. God is in control of the past and the present, of brothers and of nations. This should give us comfort and courage to wait patiently and prayerfully on the Lord when our days are filled with more questions than answers. God is powerful and purposeful in all his ways. We can trust and obey him.

Second, in pronouncing hope for Israel, God reminds us that his promises are true and good. His presence and provision is a promise that he will keep to the very end. Obadiah reminds us to maintain our faith and hope in our King, even amid hardship. Why? Because our enemies will be defeated in the "day of the LORD," when they "shall drink" (vv. 15–16). Both of these phrases refer to God's consuming and vindicating justice. In addition, we have access into the Land of Promise, where God's peace reigns forever. Obadiah describes the lands to the north, south, east, and west to picture the vast extent of our King's reign of peace.

These promises provide breathtaking hope through the life, death, and resurrection of Jesus, our Messiah King (Mark 1:14–15). In Jesus, death is defeated and eternal life is our blessing. At his first coming, Jesus "drank the cup" of God's wrath for us, bearing the sword of judgment for our sins. At his second coming, on the "day of the LORD," Jesus will bring the sword of justice to usher in a future filled with peace. United to King Jesus, we can trust and obey.

JULY 22 · JONAH 1

When God Says Go and You Say No

SAM STORMS

TRY TO ENVISION JONAH relaxing after dinner one evening, perhaps reflecting on the day's events. Quite suddenly, and without warning, he hears the voice of God! Realizing what he must do, he asks his wife to hurriedly pack his bags; he's going on a trip. He walks out of his house in Palestine, looks to the east, down that long road that leads around the great Arabian desert to the valleys of the Tigris and Euphrates rivers, toward Nineveh; he pauses momentarily to catch his breath, and with the voice of God still echoing in his head, he does a 180 and heads west, in the opposite direction.

Jonah's attempt to flee "from the presence of the LORD" (Jonah 1:3) was futile, of course, as David reminds us in Psalm 139:7–10. Even more shocking is that this prophet didn't merely hesitate or ask God for some explanation but deliberately defied the command from on high. How different this is from the response of Isaiah (Isa. 6:8) and Paul (Acts 26:19), to mention just two examples. Amos once asked, "The lion has roared; who will not fear? The Lord GOD has spoken; who can but prophesy?" (Amos 3:8). Well, Jonah, evidently!

The subsequent story of Jonah's efforts to skip town and hide out in Tarshish (on the far west coast of Spain, beyond Gibraltar) is well known. What concerns us here is the price one must pay for disobedience. In order to make an important spiritual point, Donald Grey Barnhouse capitalizes on the words in Jonah 1:3, "he paid the fare": Jonah, of course, never made it to Tarshish, having been thrown overboard by his fellow passengers. But he didn't get a refund on his ticket! The end result of his disobedience was that he paid the full fare but failed to reach his destination. According to Barnhouse, it's always that way: when you flee from the Lord you never get to where you're going, and you always pay your own fare; when you go God's way, on the other hand, you always get to where you're going and he picks up the tab!

Disobedience is both frustrating and costly. It may be satisfying in the short term, but in the long run you will never ultimately succeed. God lovingly guarantees your defeat. And it comes at a high price. It will cost you more than you would ever want to pay, whether it be peace of mind, joy, contentment, your spiritual health, or sometimes even your life.

God will accomplish his purposes, with or without our participation. Jonah learned this lesson the hard way (see Jonah 4). What he failed to experience was the incomparable joy of obedience, the deep delight, in spite of all costs, that comes when we say yes to the call and commands of God.

The Danger of Getting Used to Grace

SAM STORMS

JONAH HAD EVERY reason to be happy. He was called of God to be a prophet, a high honor indeed. Though he was disobedient, God didn't abandon him. Though he was cast overboard, God preserved his life. Through Jonah's encounter with the sailors, God saved them. Through Jonah's preaching to the Ninevites, the greatest revival in history broke out. But in this final chapter Jonah, much to our dismay, is in a royal blue funk!

The explanation isn't difficult to discern: Jonah hated the people of Nineveh! He didn't want them to experience God's saving grace. He would rather die than help extend God's redemptive work beyond the borders of Israel. He reflected on God's mercy to this pagan people and said, in effect, "Over my dead body!"

Are you afraid to let God be God? Jonah wasn't confused about God's merciful character (Jonah 4:1–3). He knew that his proclamation to Nineveh of impending judgment would likely elicit their repentance, in response to which God would save them. But he preferred that Israel alone be the recipients of such divine kindness. He evidently wanted God to suppress his natural inclination to show mercy. He wanted God to act out of character. Perhaps it isn't just that Jonah didn't like the Ninevites; he appears not to like God either, at least when God is inclined to save Gentiles!

Jonah's problem, among others, was that he had a very short memory. He was only days removed from having been delivered by God from the belly of the fish. Though he deserved to die, God preserved him alive. Yet, no sooner had he set foot on dry ground than he appeared to forget God's undeserved kindness toward him. When grace is unending, we tend to forget that it is undeserved. We become accustomed to its blessings and take it for granted.

But before we too quickly condemn Jonah, we need to ask ourselves some pointed questions: Do we secretly resent God's saving intentions toward Islamic fundamentalists? Do we begrudge his kindness and favor among people of a rival political party? Are there times when we are embittered at the success of professing Christians from a different denomination? Let us never forget that, in a manner of speaking, we were all at one time Ninevites. Praise God that he was merciful to us! And may we, unlike Jonah, be the willing instruments of his mercy to others.

What Does the Lord Require of You?

JOE THORN

GOD HAS REDEEMED a people for himself. In the Old Testament we see him rescuing his people out of bondage to slavery and idolatry, though they always drifted back to worshiping God in false ways or worshiping false gods. And now, though we have been redeemed from slavery to sin, we too drift. We drift by forgetting God's rightful place in our lives and becoming preoccupied with ourselves. We can also drift in the midst of following God by overcomplicating the life of faith, adding to his word and burdening ourselves with things that he neither prescribes nor permits.

So what does the life of faith look like? What does God really want from us? In Micah 6:8 he is very clear. What is good and what God requires of us is to do justice, to love kindness, and to walk humbly with God.

He calls us to do justice, not just talk about it. This means we must care not only about what is right but also about people who are impacted by right and wrong. It's a calling to protect the innocent and speak up for those whose voices are not heard. It's one thing to be *for* justice, but to *do* it is something else. God wants us to be active in the lives of our neighbors as we seek to love them.

But the Lord also calls us to *love* kindness and mercy, not just do it. We may sometimes show mercy to someone out of a sense of duty, but God wants our hearts to be fully engaged: to show compassion for the weak and weary, to help the troubled and the wayward out of brotherly love for people made in God's image. We must never think that our affections do not matter to our obedience. Duty discharged without delight ultimately dishonors

God. May God enable us to enjoy and find abiding pleasure in the display of kindness to others, much as he rejoiced in his kindness to us in Christ Jesus.

And in all of this, God calls us to walk humbly with him. The life of faith is one of ongoing communion with God through Jesus Christ our Lord. We walk with the Lord by faith in constant dependence on his grace for life, forgiveness, and all things. Such faith is sure to create humility and kill hubris, and keep us from wandering beyond the will of God.

JULY 25 · MICAH 7:18-20

When God Cast Our Sins into the Depths of the Sea

JOE THORN

SIN HAS BEEN WRECKING and wreaking havoc in the world since Genesis 3. Its dominance in the world and its continued impact in our personal lives can cause us to lose hope. But when facing the suffocating presence of sin, we find life in the gracious character and work of God.

There is no god like the Lord—forgiving sins and pardoning the guilty. He does not demand religious penance; rather, he calls us to honest repentance and is ready to forgive all who come to him by faith. His love for sinners is shocking, not only in that the Holy One loves unholy people, but also in that his love is unchanging and unending (Rom. 8:35–39). It was his love that moved him to send his Son, Jesus, to die for unworthy sinners like us (Rom. 5:8). And through Jesus he has cast our sins into the ocean and buried them there forever. Our sins are taken away, as far as the east is from the west (Ps. 103:12), and we now know God as our God. We are his people, and his steadfast love and faithfulness is our security.

We must never forget that God "delights" (Mic. 7:18) in pouring out upon us his "steadfast love." This is not something that must be extracted from God by force. Nor is it a display of kindness that he begrudges. God loves nothing more than to set aside his anger against us and shower us with "compassion" (v. 19). So great is his love that he will "cast our sins into the depths of the sea" (v. 19), far from his sight and forever removed from his mind. He has dealt with our sins in Jesus so that they might never be recovered or ever be used against us.

Though sin remains with us, it no longer condemns us. Though sin continues to frustrate us, the Lord finds no fault in his people who have been forgiven, cleansed, and declared to be righteous by the mercy and merits of Jesus. We must not allow sin to capture our hearts by enticing us to love it or leading us to despair over it. Sin is a great evil, but our God's grace is much greater.

JULY 26 · NAHUM 1

The Reality of Wrath

JOE THORN

OUR HOLY AND JUST GOD is a terrifying reality for the wicked, for he will punish all sin and take vengeance on his enemies. In Nahum we find this threat of judgment as well as the promise of victory and deliverance for God's people. These two truths become the foundation of hope for an oppressed people.

Evil men plot against the righteous, and for a time evil seems to have the upper hand in this world. But God has promised to make things right in the end. His promise to crush the head of the devil (Gen. 3:15) is his guarantee that Jesus Christ will one day overthrow the devil and bring perfect judgment to the world. Wickedness must be punished; indeed, it will be punished, and God's people will be set free.

But we must not lose sight of the grace of God in his Son, Jesus Christ, for all have sinned and fallen short of God's glory (Rom. 3:23). Even Christians were at one time the enemies of God and children of wrath (Eph. 2:1–5). Our sin must be answered as well. And it was Jesus who took the wrath of the Father against our sins (1 John 2:2). Through his death he satisfied the wrath of God on our behalf, so that we could be forgiven and accepted by God. It is only because of the love of God, the sacrifice of his Son, and the powerful work of the Holy Spirit that we have been rescued from wrath and will be received into glory.

Whereas some might prefer a God in whom there is no wrath, would he be holy and righteous and worthy of praise if he were not angered by sin and evil? Do we want our God to be unaffected and unmoved by the presence of wickedness in our world? God's wrath is actually an expression of his love for justice and purity. For him to remain indifferent toward sin would not enhance his character but cast a shadow upon it.

The wrath of God will be perfectly carried out against all ungodliness, either through judgment on the cross for all who believe, or through the judgment of sinners in hell. And he invites all who are willing, and accepts all who come.

What to Do When God Seems Absent

JOE THORN

SOMETIMES GOD SEEMS slow or even silent. When our days are filled with pressing needs and trouble and we do not see the Lord's provision or protection, we sometimes find ourselves asking, "Why do you . . . remain silent?" (Hab. 1:13). It may almost seem as though God doesn't care. Our cry is that of the psalmist: "How long, O LORD? Will you forget me forever?" (Ps. 13:1). But the truth is, while God sometimes delays the answer we seek, he is never silent. He has spoken to us in his word, and his promises to us remain true.

Like Habakkuk, you may be watching as your plans, hopes, or even your entire world is in jeopardy. The wicked may be winning, and God's people may be suffering. The temptation we all face in such circumstances is to take matters into our own hands and act as though *we* were God. But remember that your situation and affliction are not unique. Throughout the history of redemption we have been bringing our fears and frustrations to God, especially when we cannot see him (Psalm 73). And God continues to patiently remind us of his justice, faithfulness, and salvation.

All evil and sin will one day be answered and overcome by God's justice (Ex. 34:6–7), and the wicked will one day stand before God in judgment. The Lord is trustworthy and faithful to do what he has said. He will judge and redeem. He will rescue and save. One day the whole earth will be filled with his glory. Until then we must rest in the surety of his word.

In our days of uncertain outcomes and certain pain, we must choose to wait with eager anticipation for the fulfillment of God's promises. Be patient. Do not lose hope. Remember the Lord, who said, "Be still, and know that I am God" (Ps. 46:10). We can trust him in all things because he has already given us his Son, and if he has given us his Son, "how will he not also with him graciously give us all things" (Rom. 8:32)?

Rejoicing in the God of Our Salvation

JOE THORN

EVER SINCE THE FALL of mankind in the garden of Eden, life has been marked by struggle and suffering. At times, our struggles can appear so large that they seem to eclipse the God who stands above all of it and can be found *in* all of it. For many, our difficulties become the lens through which we evaluate our life. And when all we see is the darkness, life quickly becomes an exercise in vanity.

But even when our world is falling apart, we must look to the God who is there. He is present and active in every part of our lives (Psalm 139). We cannot make sense of our circumstances until we see and embrace the Lord who saves us. Only then do we find purpose in pain, strength to persevere, and joy that leads to song.

This does not mean we should ignore our affliction, or pretend that life isn't hard. There is no value in simply putting on a happy face. God does not call us to "grin and bear it" when we are scared or hurting. It is true that life is often more than we can handle. And that reality must be met with the presence and purpose of God, who uses our trials to strengthen our faith (James 1:2–4) and causes all things to work together for the good of those who love him (Rom. 8:28).

Habakkuk had finally come to the place where he was content to suffer loss without falling into despair. The crops (or our business ventures) may fail. Profit may turn to loss. Prosperity may give way to devastation. But the resolve in Habakkuk's heart—and, by God's grace, in ours as well—is that he (and we) "will rejoice in the LORD" (Hab. 3:18). When the God of our salvation is our "joy" (v. 18), instead of wealth and fame and power, we can face the most adverse of circumstances. When our confidence is in God's "strength" (v. 19) and not our own, no threat or danger or loss can undermine our commitment to his purposes.

In our fear, pain, loss, and confusion God remains steadfast in his promises, presence, and purpose. This is the truth that lifts our countenance and leads us to proclaim his excellencies even in the day of trouble.

JULY 29 · ZEPHANIAH 3

Waiting . . . for a Change

MICHAEL LUMPKIN

TIMES WERE BAD. There was no escape. The circumstances just seemed impossible to endure. A voice came from God, and the message was overwhelming. The call to action? Wait.

What?! Wait?!

The people had not waited on God but rather had sought their own wisdom (Zeph. 3:1–7). Isn't that what we try to do as men? Don't we default to trying to fix whatever's broken? Trying to find a way out? We want to fix ourselves because, in the end, we want credit for the fix. The truth, however, is that what most needs fixing in us—our unrighteousness—is something we cannot fix on our own.

Zephaniah tells the people that, from God's perspective, their present difficulty doesn't compare to the future despair of his judgment. But despair leads to hope. With the message of future judgment, Zephaniah also brings a message of mercy. There will be a day ("that day"; vv. 11, 16) when there will be judgment for many and mercy for others. When God is present—and he is—those who reject him will see what a vile thing it is to do so (v. 8). Those who have received mercy will rejoice at the cleansing they have received through God's sovereign act of grace (vv. 9–13, 17).

First Peter 3:18 states, "For Christ also suffered once for sins, the righteous for the unrighteous, that he might bring us to God, being put to death in the flesh but made alive in the spirit." God's promise of Christ is the only way his people are gathered to him.

Second Corinthians 5:10 states clearly that Jesus Christ, the righteous one, is also the Judge. He will judge those who have not waited on God's salvation through Christ. Everyone will have to give an account to Christ. He will be either their merciful Savior or their righteous Judge.

God reminds us of future judgment so that we may deal rightly with our present circumstances. It's a matter of perspective. Are you trying to "fix" yourself? God alone saves. Do you feel shame? Christ has removed your shame. Do you feel that your suffering is judgment? Christ, your Judge, bore your judgment on the cross. Rejoice! For God has removed his judgment of you through Christ. Therefore, wait.

JULY 30 · HAGGAI 2:1–9

People Are God's Place

MICHAEL LUMPKIN

HAGGAI WAS A PROPHET sent by God to command the people to rebuild the temple, after their return to Jerusalem from exile in Babylon. The people had spent most of their efforts setting up their own homes rather than building the temple, which represented God's presence with his people. The people responded to Haggai's message, and got to work.

About a month into construction, Haggai was given another message from God (Hag. 2:1–9). God was calling the people to take notice of their work, remember the temple's purpose, and continue. To bolster their courage and strength, Haggai encouraged the people with a simple statement from God: "I am with you" (v. 4).

The temple was God's dwelling place among his people, yet he says he is with them now, even before the new temple has been completed. God

259

desires to dwell, not in buildings, but in the midst of his people. He says that his presence will lead to their security, their joy, and his praise. And all of this will lead to peace.

Men want to build. We want to build something that lasts. We want to fortify and protect. Essentially, we want peace, both for our homes and for ourselves. However, we also fear failure. Haggai makes clear that peace will be ours when we find joy in those things that bring God praise. And, one thing that surely gives God praise is the obedience and delight of his people. And it comes full circle: as we rest in obedience to God's commands, we are strengthened and become fearless.

Ephesians 2:19–22 says,

> So then you are no longer strangers and aliens, but you are fellow citizens with the saints and members of the household of God, built on the foundation of the apostles and prophets, Christ Jesus himself being the cornerstone, in whom the whole structure, being joined together, grows into a holy temple in the Lord. In him you also are being built together into a dwelling place for God by the Spirit.

The temple in the Old Testament shows that God's dwelling is with his people. In Ephesians 2 we see that the church (the gathering of redeemed people) is God's temple. God is making a "temple" for himself in the church, through Jesus Christ and by the work of the Spirit. We must build up the people of God in the joy and strength of the Lord, through his word. While buildings may help give us a place, it's the people that give God praise.

God Remembers

MICHAEL LUMPKIN

REBUILDING THE TEMPLE alone wasn't enough. God wants to reside in the hearts of men, and this requires repentance, a change of heart from selfish, sinful pursuits to God-ward affections. Zechariah was tasked to bring the message of continual repentance to the people of Israel, so that they would not grow weary waiting on God to give them peace.

"God helps those who help themselves." We have probably all heard this folksy phrase, and if we're not careful we may read verse 3 in just that way: "Return to me, . . . and I will return to you." What we have to remember is that God had already sovereignly and graciously delivered his people out of Babylon and brought them back home. Now, he demanded the appropriate response to his gracious initiative: repentance. And repentance would lead to praise.

Zechariah's first charge to the people was that they should remember what had befallen the previous generation: They ignored God's word to them. They listened to themselves and did not trust God. However, God's word accomplished its end eventually, overtaking them even amid Babylonian captivity (it takes that, sometimes!).

To magnify Zechariah's message of repentance, God sent him visions. These visions revealed that, while other nations seemed to be at peace, God's people were not. The visions were given to encourage the people to continue their repentance—because God had not forgotten them. They were in danger of disbelieving again, because their faithfulness didn't seem to be paying off. God, however, was reminding them of his faithfulness by promising judgment on his enemies and a merciful remembrance of his promise to preserve his people.

Are you dangerously close to giving up? God has not forgotten you. The apostle Paul assures us that the good work of salvation that God has already begun in our hearts will be brought to its consummation at the day of Christ (Phil. 1:6). Knowing this to be true is the greatest motivation to the passionate pursuit of God in all things. Simply put, whatever God starts, he completes. He is preparing you to be with him forever (Heb. 10:14). That is why his promise can be trusted: "I will never leave you nor forsake you" (Heb. 13:5b). In the meantime, remember that we have a sympathetic priest in Christ, whom we can call upon for mercy . . . again and again and again (Heb. 4:14–16).

AUGUST 1 · ZECHARIAH 9

None Other

MICHAEL LUMPKIN

AT THE TIME OF ZECHARIAH'S writing, God's people are embroiled in hostility from the surrounding nations (9:1–8). Life is frantic. Oppression is ever present. We today know what this is like—not because of literal military enemies, usually, but simply because of the fallen circumstances of life.

How does God comfort his people, then, and how does he comfort us today?

In the same way—by speaking peace (9:10). The calming message from heaven is: peace. But how do we actually see this message of peace take shape? Isn't this abstract and unhelpful?

Not at all. The peace of which God speaks in verse 10 takes concrete shape in the coming King promised in verse 9. Zechariah 9:9–17, from which two of the Gospels quote (Matt. 21:5; John 12:15), prophesies about the true and future King who will bring peace. When Jesus was born, the angels announced "peace" on earth (Luke 2:14). Zechariah 9:9 spells out the glorious entrance of this peace-bringing king. He will be a humble king, who fulfills all of Scripture. He will be a ruling king, whom no enemy can oppose (v. 10). He will be a protecting king, empowering his people's victory (vv. 14–15). He will be a saving king who rescues his people, treasuring them above all other treasures (vv. 16–17). This king is Jesus Christ, and you can trust him.

But how can we, who fail so often, know that this peace is ours? The answer is that the day came when Jesus entered Jerusalem, laying down

262

his life for sinners like us—in Jerusalem, the very place where Zechariah had called the people to repentance! The Lord appeals to the blood of his covenant with Israel (9:11). How true indeed that God would remain merciful to his people on account of the blood of the covenant—the blood of his own Son (Luke 22:20; Heb. 12:24).

For those who believe in Jesus, blood-bought peace has washed over them. Even when we are embroiled in stormy circumstances at work, in our family, with our physical health—Jesus Christ "shall speak peace" (Zech. 9:10). The external state of our lives need not dictate the internal state of our souls. Walk with Christ. Be at rest.

AUGUST 2 · ZECHARIAH 12:1–13:1

Look upon the Pierced One

MICHAEL LUMPKIN

AS WE NEAR the end of the Old Testament record, it is as if there's a crescendo to the music played throughout the Minor Prophets. Every note seems to increase in pace and volume and beauty, resounding with the song that redemptive history in the Old Testament will find its culmination, its fulfillment, in the Christ who is to come . . . but not yet.

It is this singular hope that resonates through Zechariah in this passage. He starts at the beginning, with God as Creator, where Scripture begins (Genesis 1) and where an awareness of our need for God also begins (Romans 1). Remembering that God is the God of all creation is essential to our faith (Hebrews 11), especially when all the world seems to be against us.

God speaks of "that day" as a culmination of Israel's hopes for a king, a kingdom, and peace. This day will come, however, through much difficulty, time, and pain. Specifically, there will be "mourning" over "him whom they have pierced" (Zech. 12:10). John 19:34–37 quotes Zechariah 12:10 as Christ's side is pierced by the soldier's spear, fulfilling this passage. His pierced side proved his actual physical death, causing despair among those who looked upon Christ as the David-like king.

Zechariah goes on to speak of the house of Levi in mourning as well. The Levites were the priestly tribe of Israel. Hebrews 4:14–16 says that Jesus is the great sympathetic priest to whom we can run for mercy and grace when we need it. He intercedes because he is alive and enthroned.

Zechariah 13:1 then says there will be a fountain that will bring cleansing from all sin and uncleanness. God will, through the "pierced one," bring to himself a people of his own, holy and pure, cleansed by his atoning death on the cross.

As men, we want to measure up to what is expected of us. We want to do the job and do it well. We want results and the satisfaction that what we do matters. Let's stop for a moment and look upon the "pierced one." We can rest in the fact that, as Christ pleases God in our place, so he is pleased with us (2 Cor. 5:21). He did "the job" we could never do. With this in mind, we can labor well until he comes for his own, knowing that he has already accepted us.

AUGUST 3 • MALACHI 3:6–12

The Heart's Delight

MICHAEL LUMPKIN

WHAT IS YOUR heart's deepest delight?

In Malachi's day, the people had listened to Haggai's and Zechariah's pleas to rebuild the temple and repent of disbelief. Over time, though, the people grew weary of waiting on God to bring a Messiah King into that rebuilt temple to lead, and perhaps even to conquer. In their weariness, they grew lazy in their duty before God and cold in their delight toward him. They had thought their hard work would usher in their deliverance.

They ceased being careful to obey God. They stopped bringing in the tithes of food that God commanded be given to help care for his people ("Will man rob God?"; Mal. 3:8). Without a leader in sight, the people became selfish with their goods, protecting their own interests.

God commands his people to repent and replenish the storehouse with their tithes. He promises his provision and protection if they will obey him in this way. He wants to bless his people, so that the nations will acknowledge God in their midst. Their delight in God will be a witness to the nations, and what they do with their goods will show their delight in him.

Is that our testimony? Does the way we handle our possessions show that we delight in God? What we delight in is what matters most to us. The way to recover our delight in God is not just to start giving. First, remember why you ceased (or never started) giving to God's work in the local church. The principal reason in this passage is a lack of patience with God's promises being fulfilled—a failure to believe that God will come through.

Christ has come. Christ will return. God will come through. In the meantime, like the early church (Acts 4:32–37), we must be generous in the household of faith because we are unified in our delight in him (Acts 4:23–31). In this way, our corporate witness to the world will be that God alone is our all-satisfying treasure.

God with Us

DAN DORIANI

MATTHEW'S ACCOUNT of Jesus's birth (Matt. 1:18–25) logically follows the genealogy (vv. 1–17). The emphasis lies on Jesus's identity more than on the birth itself, which is mentioned only briefly (v. 25). In that day, a person's identity was established by parentage, livelihood, and hometown. So the Gospels label Jesus the son of Joseph, the carpenter, from Nazareth. This passage goes deeper. Jesus was born of a virgin: Mary was "betrothed to Joseph, [and] before they came together she was found to be with child from the Holy Spirit" (v. 18). No *human* fathered Jesus; the Spirit of God did. Jesus was not born of a sinful liaison. He was begotten of the Spirit, sinless, God Incarnate. In all religions, mankind reaches up to God; in the Bible, God descends to us.

Jesus normally reveals his identity by his actions (forgiving sins, rising from death). Here Matthew states the titles that declare his identity. He is *Jesus,* which means "God saves," because "he will save his people from their sins" (v. 21). He is *Christ,* the anointed one (v. 18), for the Father anointed him with the Spirit (3:16) to fulfill the roles of Prophet (21:11), King (27:37), and Priest (Heb. 4:14). Jesus is Immanuel, "God with us" (Matt. 1:23). This title is also a promise, and the wonderful truth it expresses, "I am with you," appears three times in Matthew—here, to explain the incarnation; as Jesus teaches the apostles (18:20); and as strength for the Great Commission (28:20). Jesus is "God with us" in every moment, great and small. Regardless of our circumstances and no matter how great the trial or temptation, we can know with heart-calming assurance that our God is with us.

We also see the Father's wisdom in placing Jesus with Mary and Joseph. Both of them were chaste (1:18), and Joseph's reaction to Mary's pregnancy shows both his sense of justice and his kindness, for he refused to shame her when she seemed to have been unfaithful (v. 19). After the angel told Joseph the truth, we see his faith in action (vv. 24–25). So our passage shows God's gentle care for Jesus his Son, and his sovereign power in inaugurating his redemption of us, his children.

AUGUST 5 · MATTHEW 3:1–12

What Is True Repentance?

DAN DORIANI

IN MATTHEW 3, John the Baptist prepares the way for Jesus's ministry by calling the people of Israel to repent. John, Israel's first prophet in four hundred years, proclaimed repentance not in Jerusalem or its temple, but in the desert wilderness. The desert reminds us of the wilderness where God purged Israel of sin after the exodus. John's place was remote—a day's journey from Jerusalem—but people came from everywhere to hear him cry out, "Repent, for the kingdom of heaven is at hand" (Matt. 3:2).

Lest anyone miss John's importance, Isaiah had foretold that his "voice" would cry, "Prepare the way of the LORD" (Isa. 40:3). John's food and clothing verified his austere message. Great crowds came to John and confessed their sins.

Some were sincere in their repentance, and some were not (Matt. 3:7–12). So, what *is* true repentance? Some think repentance is a *feeling* of sorrow for misdeeds. Others say the Greek term for "repent" means "to change the *mind*." But repentance shapes the whole person—mind, heart, and hands. To repent is to turn to God in faith, covenant loyalty, and obedience.

Repentance is more than remorse that we hurt someone or a pang of guilt after getting caught. Judas felt remorse—what Paul called worldly sorrow—and killed himself. In worldly sorrow, the sinner looks inward to his pain, shame, grief, or self-condemnation. Godly sorrow looks upward, to God's grace in Christ. The sinner hopes for restoration to God and man. The Westminster Larger Catechism calls repentance "a saving grace, wrought in the heart of a sinner by the Spirit." The sinner senses that his sin is repugnant, but that God is merciful. He "hates his sins [and] turns from them all to God." We repent when we know that the Father forgives our sins for the sake of Christ, and plan to walk with God in new obedience. This is surely a great reason to run *to* God when we sin rather than *from* him.

AUGUST 6 · MATTHEW 5:17-20

Jesus, Our Law-Keeper

DAN DORIANI

JESUS WAS PERFECTLY RIGHTEOUS, but he baffled his contemporaries. He acted like a rabbi, gathering and teaching disciples, but he violated sacred Jewish traditions that they (wrongly) considered part of God's law: he touched lepers, healed on the Sabbath, and welcomed sinners. He also seemed to teach against the law, restricting the freedom of men to divorce (Matt. 19:3–9) and repeatedly saying, "You have heard that it was said . . . But I say to you . . ." (5:21–44). But Jesus's teachings and actions complete the law. He did not "come to abolish the law" but to fulfill it. He declared by his own authority (for there is none higher) that no part of the law can fail.

Jesus says that not even an "iota" or a "dot" of the law will fail (v. 18). "Iota" refers in this case to a marking the size of a comma in written Hebrew that can be omitted without loss of meaning, like the silent *e* in spoken English. The Hebrew "dot" is also very small, really just a shift of the pen that differentiates similar letters, like *h* and *k*. Scripture is secure, without error. God's law—his instruction—like all his word, is imperishable.

Jesus fulfills the law in two ways. He both *keeps* it and *teaches* it perfectly. He obeys every requirement of the law, and he does so with inward love. He teaches the law by instructing his disciples (us!) to do the right things for the right reasons, not from fear of punishment or calculation of gain, but from love of God and neighbor.

The law has no trifling commands. Each command expresses God's character, truth, and righteousness. Years ago, so-called believers dismissed belief in miracles as an impediment to faith. Today, they say biblical sexual ethics are an affront to modern sensibilities. One religion professor said it is "important to state clearly that we . . . reject the straightforward commands of Scripture." This man, if a believer, ranks last in the kingdom. "Did God actually say" (Gen. 3:1) introduces the oldest temptation.

When Jesus says, "unless your righteousness exceeds . . . you will never enter the kingdom" (Matt. 5:20), he doesn't teach salvation by works. Jesus demands righteousness, but he also *supplies* it for us by his death and resurrection (Matthew 26–28). Matthew 5:20 outlines his coming teachings. Disciples surpass scribes by grasping the heart, not just the "manageable" external code of the law (vv. 21–48). Disciples surpass Pharisees by living for the divine audience, not the human, and by seeking God's kingdom and righteousness (ch. 6).

When Worry Is Sinful and When It Isn't

DAN DORIANI

THE HIGH POINT of the Sermon on the Mount may be Matthew 6:33: "Seek first the kingdom of God and his righteousness, and all these things will be added to you." But first, Jesus engages the gods that keep us from seeking the kingdom: reputation (vv. 1–4, 16–18), wealth (vv. 19–24), and security (vv. 25–32).

The section on wealth concludes not with a command, "Don't serve money," but with a choice: "No one can serve two masters. . . . You cannot serve God and money" (v. 24). Jesus speaks to disciples who *have* chosen God: having taken that step of faith, they need not be anxious about material things like food or clothing (v. 25).

The command "Do not be anxious" (or "Don't worry") appears in the beginning, middle, and end of this passage (vv. 25, 31, 34). Jesus explains *why* disciples shouldn't worry. First, we shouldn't worry because, "is not life more than food?" (v. 25). Since God cares for all parts of life, he surely cares for our material needs. Second, since God cares for his lesser creatures, such as birds, he surely cares for us, his children (v. 26). Third, worry accomplishes nothing. It can't lengthen life and may shorten it (v. 27). Fourth, God adorns flowers with unmatched beauty, and he clothes grass faithfully. Flowers and grass are symbols of the brevity and fragility of life (Isa. 40:7). Life *is* fragile, but if God cares for plants, he will protect us, despite our little faith.

Jesus's disciples have faith, but their worry proves the weakness of their faith. Great faith comes not by looking inward, to the believing self, but by looking upward, to God. By faith we stop thinking like pagans, filled with anxiety about food and clothing. Pagans, thinking like orphans, worry. Disciples, thinking like children, relax.

Anxiety may not always be sinful. It's wrong to tally our worries or let them congeal into one mass of anxiety (1 Pet. 5:7), but Paul had a proper anxiety (same Greek word) for all his churches (2 Cor. 11:28). Paul felt concerned, but he apparently saw his anxiety as a *problem,* not as a *sin.* There is a form of concern that is not sinful, as we take that concern to God.

Then, as faith quiets our fears, we find God's will and follow it. We may plan for tomorrow's food, but we don't worry, knowing the Father supplies every need. Liberated from worry, we seek his kingdom and righteousness.

AUGUST 8 · MATTHEW 7:24-29

Building Your Life on the Rock

DAN DORIANI

THE CONCLUSION OF the Sermon on the Mount summons disciples to listen and obey. That is what wise men do (Matt. 7:24). We don't truly understand God's word until we obey it (John 7:17). As the saying goes, "Do, and you will know."

When we hear Jesus's words, we hear *him.* When ordinary people talk, there are gaps between our words and ourselves. We speak imprecisely and misrepresent ourselves. We change our mind; what we said yesterday may not be what we think today. But there is no gap with Jesus. He is who he says, and he does what he says. Therefore his words are "the rock" (Matt. 7:24), the sure foundation for life.

Notice: Jesus says "the rock," not "a rock." What might "the rock" be? Matthew 16 tells us. When Peter confesses that Jesus is "the Christ, the Son of the Living God," Jesus says he will build his church "on this rock"—that is, on the true confession of Christ (16:16, 18).

Builders construct houses on various kinds of foundations (7:24–27). In dry weather, every house looks sound, but the storm reveals the quality of the work. When catastrophe strikes a solid house, it stands. The house built on sand, the wrong foundation, will collapse. Every creed or philosophy seems to work when life is easy. But when storms batter us, those who build on Christ remain strong. An agnostic may say, "I've faced storms and stayed strong." But what of the last storm, when life ends?

Let us ask, "What is my rock? Is my foundation sure?" God is a rock, a refuge for his people (Ps. 27:5). And Jesus is the rock. If anyone refuses him and his instruction, his house will collapse with a great crash (Matt. 7:26–27). Although Jesus is addressing his disciples, he ends his sermon with a warning. He says it is not enough to *study* his teaching. We must do what Jesus says. Anything less is self-deception.

Unlike the scribes, Jesus spoke with confidence (vv. 28–29). Rabbis quoted prior rabbis to corroborate their instruction. Today, we footnote experts. But Jesus was a legislator, not a commentator. He declared, "Truly *I* say to you." Notice again that Jesus does not issue a command; he demands a choice. How will you build? What foundation will you choose? The wise man builds on the rock—Jesus, our Savior and Lord.

AUGUST 9 · MATTHEW 9:9-13

He Came to Call Sinners

DAN DORIANI

THE CALL OF MATTHEW follows a series of miracles that demonstrate Jesus's power over disease, nature, demons, and sin (Matt. 8:1–9:8). The miracles draw *crowds,* but Jesus wants *disciples.* Previously, Jesus said it's *hard* to be a disciple (8:18–22). Here he says *anyone* can be a disciple, and there is joy in it.

In Jesus's day, religious men offered themselves to rabbis as followers. Jesus reverses that. He summons an irreligious, unrighteous man to follow him. Tax stations were located on roads near cities like Capernaum, where Jesus lived and Matthew worked (4:13; 8:5). Matthew (the author of this Gospel) had to have known about Jesus, so the command, "Follow me," is not as abrupt as it might seem. When Jesus sees Matthew at his tax booth, he sovereignly summons and Matthew obeys. Matthew shows his faith by his deeds. He leaves everything, gets up, follows Jesus, and hosts a banquet for Jesus and his friends.

Matthew's actions are exemplary, but some observers thought it odd. Tax collectors, to them, were sinners, traitors, Roman collaborators. They didn't realize that Jesus had come into the world specifically to call sinners (Luke 19:10). (Of course, we're all sinners, so there was no one else for

Jesus to call!) Jesus sealed his choice of Matthew by sharing a meal with Matthew's sinful friends. This stunned the Pharisees. Why did Jesus do this? What lay behind his policy? Sharing a formal meal signified friendship and acceptance. Did Jesus accept these sinners?

Indeed he did. He called them, ate with them, ran toward them, and threw his arms around them—because he loved them. They were worse than they thought, but he was better than they could hope for. Perhaps the Pharisees envied the attention Jesus gave sinners, but Jesus, as the true physician, goes to the sick, not to the "healthy" Pharisees. Their version of righteousness led them away from God. God desires mercy, not sacrifice (Matt. 9:13). "Sacrifice" here means strict obedience to God's law. Obedience is good, but in a world of sinners, mercy is greater. Jesus wants to transform Matthew and all disciples, but his *accepting* love precedes his *transforming* love, then and now.

AUGUST 10 · MATTHEW 10:16-33

Suffering with Jesus

DAN DORIANI

IN MATTHEW 10, Jesus teaches the twelve apostles, whom he has just called, how to conduct themselves in their mission. Matthew 10:16–33 describes the dangers of discipleship and Jesus's strategies for facing those dangers.

The first principle is found in the middle: A disciple should "be like his teacher" (vv. 24–25). So the apostles must go to the people of Israel, proclaim the kingdom, heal the sick, and do so without money, trusting God's provision. It is a great privilege to be like Jesus, the Master, but privilege brings danger, since great leaders attract great foes. They "called the master . . . Beelzebul," that is, Satan or an ally of Satan, so they will malign and attack his followers too (v. 25). "Beware of men," Jesus says (v. 17). Floggings and trials await. How then shall disciples conduct themselves, as Jesus sends them out as sheep among wolves (v. 16)?

First, disciples are "wise as serpents"—shrewd enough to hide themselves to avoid their enemies. Yet they are "innocent as doves." That is, they embrace a heedlessness that allows bold speech without concern for the results. Beyond persecution by the state, disciples can expect betrayal by family. Being forewarned, we are ready to endure to the end (vv. 21–22). Endurance is active; it can include flight. If one town is hostile to the gospel, we should simply run to another town, for wherever we go, we'll find people needing to hear the gospel (v. 23).

Jesus foretold and Acts shows that the apostles did suffer beatings and trials. Yet each trial gave an opportunity to testify. While we always prepare when we know we will speak, the Lord promises to give us words in dangerous situations when preparation is impossible and fear assails us.

Jesus tells us to choose our fears wisely (vv. 26–31; 1 Pet. 3:14). People fear wild animals, cancer, heights, tornadoes, war—that is, they fear death. But Jesus says, "Do not fear those who kill the body." Rather, we must fear God, "who can destroy both soul and body in hell." Proper fear of God includes awe, respect, even love. If we love God, we also confess that he is our Father and Lord. If we do, he will confess that he knows us on the last day (Matt. 10:32–33).

AUGUST 11 • MATTHEW 13:1-23

Take Care How You Hear

DAN DORIANI

JESUS STARTED TO teach in parables on the "same day" that his family demonstrated that they didn't understand him (Matt. 12:46–50), which was also the same day that certain Pharisees saw Jesus's signs and decided he was Satan's ally (12:24).

The parable of the sower is the archetypal parable of the kingdom, the foundation for other parables. When Jesus interprets it, he sets the pattern. When he says that he is the sower (13:37), he makes himself the lead in his own stories. The parable reflects common farming practices of the day. Farmers scattered seed, then plowed and waited. The disciples heard the parable but didn't understand it.

Why did Jesus stop speaking plainly and start teaching through veiled stories? Jesus said his parables both give and take away. They take away from "them" because, to quote Isaiah, "seeing they do not see" (v. 13). Parables punish people like the Pharisees. The more Jesus revealed, the more hostile they became. For them, parables are obscure and remove the light. But parables *give* to disciples, because the stories are graphic yet mysterious. They tease the mind into thought, so that we love the truth when we hear it. The disciples already know, but Jesus gives them more because they seek more. Jesus blesses his disciples, because we embrace God's reign and hear his message (v. 16).

Jesus is the Son of Man. As the sower, he scatters the seed of his truth everywhere. The varied soils represent the ways people respond to Jesus's message of the kingdom. Some people are no more receptive than a hard dirt pathway. Some initially show great enthusiasm for spiritual things. They love the idea of a free gift of eternal life, but when they discover the cost of discipleship, they fall away. Others appear to believe but bear no fruit, because the gods of this age choke it out. The final group hears, understands, and bears an astonishing harvest.

The parable asks us to assess ourselves. Do we genuinely hear Jesus's instruction? Are we shallow or deep? Fruitless or fruitful? Above all, we must see that Jesus is sowing his seed even today. Will we listen, endure, and bear fruit?

AUGUST 12 · MATTHEW 16:21-28

Confessing Christ

DAN DORIANI

IN MATTHEW 14-17, Jesus trains his disciples. A high point arrives when Peter declares that Jesus is "the Christ, the son of the living God" (Matt. 16:16). He confesses sincerely, but doesn't fully grasp his own words (did you understand your first "I love you"?). Because the disciples held false notions regarding the Messiah, Jesus "strictly charged" them to "tell no one that he was the Christ" (v. 20). Jesus must define himself as the suffering

Messiah. He begins to show them "that he must go to Jerusalem and suffer
. . . and be killed" (v. 22). This is the first in a set of four stark predictions
of the crucifixion (see also 17:12, 22–23; 20:18–19).

Peter, who has just called Jesus the Son of God, now rebukes him!
When Peter confesses the truth about Jesus, he becomes foundational to the
church—with Jesus as the cornerstone (16:18; Eph. 2:20). But when Peter
rebukes Jesus, insisting he must not be crucified, Jesus calls him "Satan."
Satan means adversary, and here Peter acts like one. He is a different rock,
one that makes men stumble.

Jesus presents a choice. Will Peter—will we—set our minds on the
things of God or the things of men? Men love power, peace, and prosperity. God knows that love leads to suffering, and suffering leads to glory. If
anyone would follow Jesus, he must take up his cross.

The church has tamed the word "cross." The polished crosses around
our necks and in our churches blind us. We describe modest griefs and
call them "the cross I bear." We expect the church to supply excellent
programs and appealing worship; the idea of suffering for Christ is only
an occasional notion, something we avoid. Let us never shun the place of
suffering—at home, at work, or in the church. True disciples will lose this
life, if necessary, to gain eternal life with Christ. We follow Christ, through
suffering, to glory.

What to Do When Someone Sins against You

DAN DORIANI

MATTHEW 18:15–20 presents Jesus's plan for reconciliation whenever one
disciple sins against another. The offended party does not withdraw or
gossip; he *goes to* the sinner. He tells the sinner his fault. The Greek word
implies a logical element. The speaker makes his case and brings evidence.
The meeting is private. Privacy fosters dialogue and makes repentance
easier (the exception is when a public person commits a public sin, and

thus a public rebuke may be appropriate; Gal. 2:11–14). The goal is to "gain" or win the brother by leading him to repent. To rebuke sin is an act of love (Lev. 19:17–18). To listen to words of correction is an act of wisdom (Prov. 9:9).

There are two dangers that this teaching counteracts. The timid rebuke no one, fearing confrontation and resistance. Zealots rebuke everything, but the reference to "two witnesses" slows the zealot by implying that the sin must be public enough for several people to see it.

This plan, when executed in love, often works. If it fails, but there are willing witnesses, the offended party takes them along for a second rebuke. This principle, from Deuteronomy 19:15, prevents false accusations and frivolous charges. If the sinner still fails to respond, the church addresses the matter. If the sinner is obstinate, the church treats him "as a Gentile and a tax collector." Jesus does not here say the church *should treat tax collectors poorly;* he welcomed them. But Jesus's hearers treated tax collectors as men standing outside the community. So the impenitent sinner stands outside the body, excommunicated. Yet even this extreme action aims at reconciliation (2 Thess. 3:14–15).

The church cannot, on its own initiative, open the gates of heaven or consign anyone to hell. God sets the standards, but the church restates them. When church leaders "bind" (Matt. 18:18), they warn that heaven is closed to sinners who refuse repentance. Church leaders "loose" when they declare that heaven is open to every sinner who repents, whatever their sin.

The last two verses of our passage (vv. 19–20) comfort the church in this process. Church discipline is painful. Jesus assures leaders that if they agree on a matter ("anything") before them, the Father grants his special presence and action. We may apply these verses to godly prayer in general, but they apply especially to prayer for the holiness of the church and its people.

Joining the Children in the Praise of Jesus

DAN DORIANI

WE CALL JESUS'S FINAL entrance into Jerusalem "triumphal" for a reason, but misunderstanding, conflict, and tears filled the day. Most of the crowds that praised him as "Son of David" could not see that he was a king but more, and a prophet but more (Matt. 21:5, 9, 11).

As kings sometimes did, Jesus inspected the temple to see if all was in order. It was not. God had ordained the temple as a place of "prayer"— which meant sacrifice, worship, and instruction for both Jews and Gentiles (vv. 12–13). Around this time, the outer courts, reserved for the Gentiles, had become a place for commerce in animals and currencies. Whatever their business practices, the merchants robbed the Gentiles of peace for worship. As king, prophet, and priest, Jesus cast them out, so that the temple might again be a place of prayer for the nations.

To call this the "cleansing of the temple" understates things. As king, Jesus judged its current overseers and reasserted his authority over Israel's faith and identity. By banishing the money-changers, he condemned corruption and the priests who allowed it. Then he opened the temple to the blind and the lame, who may have been banished from it (v. 14; cf. Lev. 21:18), and he healed them. Thus Jesus expelled the commerce that the authorities permitted, and permitted pariahs whom the authorities expelled. Jesus graciously welcomed outsiders, and he still does today.

The high priests protested "the wonderful things" Jesus did, but their indignation focused on the children who cried, "Hosanna ["May God save us"] to the Son of David!" (Matt. 21:15). Jesus replied, "Have you never read"—that is, "Don't you understand"—that God "prepared praise" from the mouths of babies (v. 16)? This line comes from Psalm 8, which opens, "O LORD, our Lord, how majestic is your name," and continues, "Out of the mouth of babies and infants, you have established strength" (or "praise"). In essence, Jesus says, "Don't you see that God ordains that *children* praise God? That is why they praise me." The priests should have joined the children; we should too. Jesus is Lord and God. He deserves our praise, in houses of worship and in all of life.

We Love Because He First Loved Us

DAN DORIANI

JEWISH LEADERS OFTEN tried to trap Jesus, and although that must have grieved him, their trick questions provided occasions for vital teaching. The leaders couldn't agree on what the greatest commandment was, but Jesus knew that God himself had summarized the law in Deuteronomy 6, shortly after he delivered it.

The greatest commandment is also the most daunting: "You shall love the Lord your God with all your heart and with all your soul and with all your mind" (Matt. 22:37). Mark 12:30 adds, "and with all your strength." That is, we love God with every power, faculty, and talent—even our sense of humor.

We love God with heart and soul when we give him our affections and when he comes first in our convictions and commitments. We love God with the mind when we learn his truth, see the world as he sees it, and dedicate our past, present, and future to him. We love God with our strength when we devote the body, with all its skill and energy, to him. We love God when we train our will to follow him, whatever the price.

In all of this, we simply answer the love that God has freely bestowed on us. "Be imitators of God" (Eph. 5:1) is a great theme of Scripture. We forgive because Jesus forgave (Eph. 4:32). We serve because Jesus served (Matt. 20:26–28). Above all, we "walk in love, as Christ loved us and gave himself up for us" (Eph. 5:2).

"We love because he first loved us" (1 John 4:19). When God pours his love into us, that leads us to love our neighbors as ourselves. Our love for God precedes and empowers our love for neighbors.

We don't always love ourselves properly, but we should love our neighbor as we *ought* to love ourselves. Love organizes, unites, and protects every virtue, every command. We love parents when we honor them. We love our wives with our faithfulness. We love neighbors by telling the truth *to* them and *about* them, and by promoting their good instead of coveting their goods. So the life of the redeemed flows from God's prior, covenantal, and gracious love.

AUGUST 16 · MATTHEW 26

The Extravagance of Worship

DAN DORIANI

MATTHEW'S PASSION NARRATIVE shows how people interacted with Jesus in his last hours. The chief priests and elders determined to arrest and kill Jesus (Matt. 26:3–5). Judas supported their plot by betraying Jesus to them for thirty pieces of silver (vv. 14–16). But between these scenes, we meet a woman who anoints Jesus with costly perfume (vv. 6–13). While the priests will do anything to kill Jesus, and Judas will take money to betray him, she pours perfume worth a year's wages to honor him before his death. John says the woman is Mary, sister of Lazarus, whom Jesus raised from the dead. She understood that Jesus had to die and wanted to honor him for it.

Mary's costly perfume came from an alabaster jar. Breaking the jar's tapered neck, she poured all the perfume on Jesus's head. The aroma filled the room. Then, the disciples began to complain: "Why this waste? For this could have been sold for a large sum and given to the poor" (vv. 8–9). We learn elsewhere that Judas led the protest, motivated by his habit of stealing from the disciples' common purse (John 12:6). The disciples didn't realize that Jesus's atoning death was near; to them, one day looked like another.

Jesus and Mary knew better. As Jesus defended her, he instructed the disciples: "You always have the poor with you, but you will not always have me" (Matt. 26:11). Jesus was not saying that people can never be rescued from poverty; he was paraphrasing Deuteronomy 15:11, which says the poor are always present, so that God's people should always be generous to them. Jesus himself was generous. By his miracles, he fed and healed the poor. The incarnation was God's supreme gift to the spiritually poor. Clearly, we should honor and care for the poor.

Yet at the hour of Jesus's death, it was right to defer all other duties and focus on him. Mary poured perfume on his body to prepare him for burial (Matt. 26:12). This was a unique moment. We can always care for the poor; this was the one hour to care for Jesus. Mary was right to give her extravagant gift. Custom demanded anointing before burial, so Mary gave her wealth to prepare Jesus for it. Jesus deserved this honor. Mary thanked Jesus in advance for giving his life for her, and Jesus promised that her (and our) devotion to him would always be remembered.

AUGUST 17 · MATTHEW 28:16–20

Make Disciples: Our Great Commission

DAN DORIANI

WE CALL THIS PASSAGE the Great Commission, and rightly so. Jesus commissions his disciples to do something great: to disciple the nations.

After the resurrection, the angels told the women at the tomb that Jesus would meet them in Galilee (Matt. 28:7). Now the disciples went to the mountain that Jesus specified. They worshiped Jesus, "but some doubted" (v. 17). "Doubt" could also be translated "hesitated." It might mean that some of the disciples just couldn't take it all in. The journey toward mature faith is hard. Not even the sight of the risen Christ resolved everything. It takes time to become mature. Yet the disciples had grown enough to receive Jesus's charge to them. Jesus had taught them; now they had to teach others and take the gospel to the world.

Verses 18–20 have a sandwich structure, opening and closing with reasons to obey with confidence the command of verse 19. The first reason to obey the call to mission is that the Father has given Jesus all authority (v. 18). He already had authority; now it is clearer and has a wider scope: authority over heaven and earth. Second, he will always be present to guide and empower the apostles on their mission (v. 20).

The central command (and sole imperative in the Greek) is "make disciples" (v. 19). Three participles surround this command, explaining *how* the disciples are to make disciples: by going, baptizing, and teaching. In the past, the nations were welcome to come to Israel; now Jesus's apostles will *go* to the world. Then, they are to *baptize*. Baptism is the sign of entry into the covenant people. The apostles disciple the nations by asking for a visible commitment. The apostles are also to *teach* everything that Jesus commanded. As Christ's disciples today, commissioned by him, we read the Gospels not just for beloved words or for verses we have memorized or underlined but to take to heart everything he commanded.

Jesus calls us not merely to "share our faith" but to make disciples and lead them to maturity, so that they in turn can lead the next generation to him. So then, because Jesus has *all* authority, he commissions us to disciple *all* the nations, teaching *all* that he commanded, assured that he is with us *always*, to the end of the age.

AUGUST 18 · MARK 1:21-34

The Gospel Is a Savior

SCOTTY WARD SMITH

JESUS'S IDENTITY AND WORK should be the primary focus and passion of every man's life. At the beginning of Mark's Gospel, God's *Spirit* comes upon Jesus, preparing readers for the central question addressed in the first eight chapters of Mark: Who is Jesus? Jesus is the Son of God, the long-promised Messiah, the one through whom the much anticipated kingdom of God has arrived. And at the end of Mark's Gospel, God's *wrath* comes upon Jesus, putting an exclamation mark on the central question addressed in the last eight chapters of Mark: What has Jesus come to do? Jesus has come to take our place on the cross, bearing the judgment we deserve.

Four of Jesus's first disciples—Simon, Andrew, John, and James—were given a crash course in kingdom discipleship, right out of the gate. They quickly discovered that Jesus's gospel is equally disruptive and redemptive. Jesus called these men from their fishermen's nets to himself—a calling that has more in common with a subpoena than an invitation. They would eventually return to their nets, but first they needed to learn to be with Jesus. The same is true for us. The gospel is a Savior to know and love, before it is anything else.

Consider the early education Jesus gave these men.

They saw Jesus teach in the synagogue with authority. Mark doesn't emphasize the content of Jesus's teaching as much as its impact: everyone was astonished. But astonishment in this synagogue would soon become contempt in Israel's temple, for Jesus reveals the depth of our need and the offense of God's provision—the cross. This is a process that continues throughout the Christian life.

They saw Jesus heal the demonized with power. The kingdom of darkness was served notice early in Jesus's ministry. The head of the serpent would soon be crushed (Gen. 3:15). But Jesus was preparing his disciples not just for ministry in evil places but also for their own battles with darkness and brokenness. When, like Paul, we learn to boast in our weaknesses, the treasure of the gospel is released for the benefit of others.

They saw Jesus heal the sick with compassion. Jesus is a wonderful, merciful Savior. When Simon's mother-in-law was healed, she got up and began serving all of them. Was this a providential parable, a demonstration that recipients of God's grace become conduits of God's grace? Yes, for the indicatives of grace always lead to the imperatives of love. The gospel runs *to* us so that it might run *through* us. As Jesus loves and serves us, so we love and serve others. This love marks us as Jesus's disciples (John 13:34–35).

AUGUST 19 • MARK 4:26–29

Your Labor Will Never Be in Vain

SCOTTY WARD SMITH

CHAPTER 4 IS ONE of the few concentrated sections of teaching in Mark's Gospel, and the emphasis in this section is on the counterintuitive nature of life in the kingdom. Things are not as they appear. Resistance to the kingdom is fully expected, and the growth of the kingdom will be pervasive but gradual. God is building for eternity, not for next week. Indeed, we must learn to "walk by faith, not by sight" (2 Cor. 5:7).

As opposition to Jesus quickly intensified, our Savior carefully nourished the disciples' understanding of life in the kingdom of God—an education *we* ourselves constantly need. Four elements stand out in this particular parable: sower and seed; sickle and harvest. As the Messiah, Jesus came to announce the arrival of the promised kingdom. He is the quintessential Sower. The seed is the gospel of the kingdom, with its irrepressible, inexhaustible germinating power. Though the journey from sprout to harvest is a slow-grow, the harvest is surely guaranteed. God's timing is better than Swiss. The sickle of the gospel will harvest ripe grain wherever it is scattered among the nations.

As those who know and love Jesus, we should find great encouragement in this parable. Our labors in the Lord will *never* be in vain. Like Paul, as those called to share the gospel we too will be able to say, "I planted, Apollos watered, but God gave the growth" (1 Cor. 3:6). All of history is bound up with God's commitment to redeem his people from "every nation, from all tribes and peoples and languages" (Rev. 7:9). The gospel will continue to bear fruit throughout the world (Col. 1:6).

But neither will Jesus's labor *in us* be in vain. God will bring to completion the good work he began in us (Phil. 1:6). As brothers and friends, we need to encourage one another with this good news, and cultivate friendships that facilitate our growth in grace.

In the Scriptures, however, the sickle symbolizes not only full granaries but also completed judgment (Joel 3:13; Rev. 14:14–19). Much later, Jesus's disciples would understand that the Sower also had to become the Reaped. The giver of eternal life *to* us first became the giver of *his* life *for* us. On the cross, Jesus became sin for us, "so that in him we might become the righteousness of God" (2 Cor. 5:21). He took the judgment of our sin so that we might receive the gift of his righteousness. We simply cannot be too familiar with this good news. Jesus is our substitute to trust before he is our example to follow.

When People Take Offense

SCOTTY WARD SMITH

SO MUCH FOR A hometown hero's welcome. Even in his childhood home of Nazareth, the opposition to Jesus grew ugly. Though the members of the synagogue were astonished at his wisdom, and no one disputed his "mighty works" of healing and deliverance, "they took offense at him." The reference to Jesus's vocation as a "carpenter" was offered to marginalize him, not compliment him. This becomes more obvious when we realize that a son was identified by his father's name, not his mother's. To refer to Jesus as "the son of Mary" was to cast doubt on his paternity.

Open ridicule, however, didn't catch Jesus by surprise. As Isaiah had proclaimed centuries earlier, the Messiah would be "despised and rejected by men" (Isa. 53:3). As the disciples discovered, this would include members of Jesus's own family as well. Earlier in his Gospel, Mark chronicled an episode when Jesus's mother and brothers tried to "seize him," because they thought he was "out of his mind" (Mark 3:21). These experiences were invaluable preparation for Jesus's disciples, who were about to begin their first missionary journey (6:7–13).

As men living on this side of the life, death, and resurrection of Jesus, we too must be prepared for the offense the gospel generates, beginning in our own hearts. Why is the message of the cross so offensive, even considered foolishness (1 Cor. 1:18–25)? The gospel simultaneously declares the depth of our need (a perfect righteousness) and the singularity of our hope (the person and work of Jesus)—an education that continues throughout the Christian life. Thus, the gospel is for nonbelievers and believers alike; for we, who by nature are allergic to God's grace, are called to grow in God's grace until the day when Jesus returns to finish making all things new.

Why was Jesus unable to perform any "mighty works" in Nazareth (Mark 6:5)? This editorial comment isn't stressing the inability of Jesus but the devastating power of unbelief. The only thing in Mark's Gospel that

Jesus is said to marvel at is the unbelief he encountered in his hometown (v. 6). "He came to his own, and his own people did not receive him" (John 1:11).

Jesus isn't a miracle-on-demand Savior. Faith isn't great because it motivates a reluctant Christ to action. Great faith is connected to an active Christ—Jesus the Messiah—whose mighty acts announced the breaking in of the kingdom of God. We don't claim God's promises for private amusement; God's promises claim *us* for his kingdom advancement. The gospel shows us that faith isn't a muscle to flex as much as it is a Savior to trust.

AUGUST 21 · MARK 7:1-23

Rich Relationship or Empty Ritual?

SCOTTY WARD SMITH

THIS ENCOUNTER BETWEEN JESUS and a group of Israel's leaders provides an invaluable set of contrasts that demonstrate the essential difference between a religion of man's tradition and the gospel of God's grace. As we grow in Christ, the difference should become increasingly obvious—and odious—to us.

The traditions of men versus the commandments of God. The Pharisees were offended when the disciples ate with "defiled hands," showing contempt for the ceremonial washings prescribed by the elders. In an effort to safeguard obedience to God's law, the Pharisees built a "fence" around the law by creating traditions not required in the word of God.

On the surface, this practice appeared honorable; but to Jesus, it was blatant hypocrisy, worthy of the same judgment God leveled against his people centuries earlier through the prophet Isaiah (Mark 7:7). To replace God's commands with our traditions is to replace God's worship with our vanity. In essence, it is self-worship.

External compliance with form, versus the internal reality of faith; lip service versus heart worship. God wants our hearts. He wants our hearts to be *near* him. He is passionately jealous for our love. All of the commands of God can be summarized in one great command: we are to *love* the Lord our God with all of our heart, soul, and mind—with *everything* we have and are (Matt. 22:37–38). When God has our hearts, he has everything else.

From Genesis through Revelation, God is pursuing a people for rich relationship, not for empty ritual. But as the Pharisees and scribes demonstrated, it is quite possible to be scrupulously committed to the details of one's religion and utterly miss the riches of biblical salvation.

The obedience of pride and fear, versus the obedience of faith and love. The truth is, the Pharisees were not obedient enough—not as God desires us to be. God wants us to obey him by the motivation of faith and love, not out of pride and fear. All forms of performance-based spirituality and legalism represent a "dumbing down," a lowering of the demands of God's law. The traditions of man are far more "doable" than the commands of God.

The demands of the law drive us to the delights of the gospel. Indeed, God's law demands a perfect righteousness that can be found only in the gospel. Jesus underscored the greatness of our need by stressing that our defilement comes from within, not from without. It isn't what we eat, but who we are, that's the real issue. The only washing that will suffice is the one we freely receive through the blood of Christ.

AUGUST 22 · MARK 10:35–45

Dealing with Our Desire for Glory and Honor

SCOTTY WARD SMITH

JAMES AND JOHN'S request arose from the same yearning in the heart of every man: as image bearers of God, we long for glory—to live commendable and significant lives. We want to matter, and for good reason. Having placed Adam in the garden of Eden, God commissioned his first human son to nurture it and cause it to flourish. Like Adam, we too were designed to do substantive and enduring things with our lives. God "has put eternity into man's heart" (Eccles. 3:11), a design for relationship and impact that will outlast this life.

So we shouldn't be shocked that Jesus did not rebuke James and John when they asked for positions of glory. The Bible commends the quest "for glory and honor" (Rom. 2:7)—as long as it isn't "self-seeking" (v. 8). James and John thought glory came through ruling, through elevation—sitting on either side of an enthroned Jesus. Their perspective was riddled with their fallenness, and Jesus seized the moment to teach the "Sons of Thunder" (Mark 3:17) about the true meaning of glory and how it can be attained. Glory isn't gained through ruling but through serving—by taking the lowest place, not the highest.

Like all God's sons, James and John would eventually experience glory, in the life to come (Col. 3:1–4). But their most pressing need in *this* life wasn't for glory but for mercy. Mark underscores this truth by placing the story of blind Bartimaeus right after Jesus's encounter with James and John. Consider the contrast between the two stories: James and John, physically seeing, were spiritually blind, as revealed by their quest for greatness. Bartimaeus, physically blind, was spiritually seeing, as revealed by his cry for mercy.

But how could James and John in all their blindness, or Bartimaeus for that matter, or *any* of us, be granted mercy?

We receive mercy and attain true greatness, ultimately, because Jesus, who had eternal greatness, took the place of consummate lowness, becoming a servant to all (Mark 10:45). Jesus, who is eternally free, was bound to a cross, so that we who are systemically bound might be free forever. We were spiritually dead, in need of life; Jesus, the Creator of life, died the death that gives *us* life. We were blind, but Jesus opened our eyes, both to our *need* for mercy and to the *means* of mercy—Jesus himself. His finished work on the cross guarantees that our present work in this world—and in the world to come—will matter forever.

As the servant love of Jesus captures us, we delight to pursue true greatness through servanthood.

Greatness Veiled in Weakness

SCOTTY WARD SMITH

THE HUMILITY JESUS commended in Mark 10 takes on a profound meaning in chapter 11. Jesus didn't come into the world simply to model meekness and servanthood but to fulfill his calling as the Servant of the Lord—to offer his life as a sacrifice of atonement and propitiation for our sins (Isa. 52:13–53:12; John 1:29). Yet the people of God could not imagine that the Messiah of God would be offered as the Lamb of God. Jesus's disciples were equally incredulous. Mark 10:32–34 records the third time Jesus was overtly clear with his disciples about not only the painful betrayal and cruel death but also the certain resurrection that awaited him in Jerusalem. They were "slow of heart" to understand the gospel, just as we are slow (Luke 24:25).

If, as many have reasoned, Mark's Gospel voices the apostle Peter's memory of these events, it would explain why Mark devotes such a large percentage of his Gospel to the last week of Jesus's life—and his death, in particular. Peter, who had tried to dissuade Jesus from the cross, learned to delight in Jesus's cross (Mark 8:31–33; 1 Pet. 1:3–12). A notion unthinkable gave way to joy unspeakable (1 Pet. 1:8). As we grow in grace, may we too learn to boast in the cross and grow in joy (Gal. 6:14).

Mark's account of Jesus's entrance into Jerusalem, riding on the colt of a donkey, anchors the story in the prophecy of Zechariah 9:9, for all the promises of God find their emphatic "Yes!" in Jesus (2 Cor. 1:20; 1 Pet. 1:10–12). The paradox of greatness veiled and revealed in weakness permeates the whole story. In advance of the day when wolves and lambs will be friends (Isa. 11:6), Jesus calms an unbroken colt as he rides it through busy streets and loud cries of "Hosanna!"

The price of peace would be costly for the Prince of Peace; Jesus rode his colt to the cross. But he will return on a warhorse (Rev. 19:11–16). Defeated evil will become eradicated evil. Until that day, we are to live and love as "prisoners of hope" (Zech. 9:12), for Jesus is coming back to finish making all things new (Rev. 21:1–5).

Great Grace Begets Radical Generosity

SCOTTY WARD SMITH

MARK 12 IS A COLLAGE of stories that record various attempts to undermine Jesus's authority and integrity. Chief priests, teachers of the law, elders, Pharisees, Herodians, and Sadducees alike all try to "trap him in his talk" (Mark 12:13). But it is *they* who are trapped in the emptiness of their religion and the fullness of their unbelief.

In sharp contrast to those who "devour widows' houses"—preying upon their vulnerability (v. 40)—Jesus celebrated a poor widow as the one most worthy to be in his Father's house. What a paradox! Her two copper coins were of greater worth than all the riches the people put into the temple treasury that day. Why? True worship is born from the right treasure. It is no coincidence that Jesus's teaching on the great commandment (vv. 28–30) preceded this story. We will love God with all our heart, soul, mind, and strength, with everything we have and are, as we realize the measure of God's great generosity toward us in creation and redemption.

She, who was rich in God, gave from the poverty of her possessions. They, who were rich in possessions, gave from the poverty of their religion. Our monetary gifts don't finance God's kingdom; God's kingdom enriches us, reminding us that we are stewards, not owners. "What do you have that you did not receive?" (1 Cor. 4:7). We often sing, "Praise God from whom all blessings flow," and yet more often we assume that we acquire our wealth "the good old-fashioned way—we *earned* it."

As men, we must remember that it is God who gives us the power to create wealth (Deut. 8:18). This will keep us humble. We should also take to heart that the only sin that the New Testament actually equates with idolatry is greed (Col. 3:5). This realization should keep us sober, for as Jesus taught us, we cannot serve both God and money (Matt. 6:24). Yet the gospel liberates us to serve God *with* our money. It makes us both grateful and generous.

The apostle Paul pointed to the church of Macedonia as an example of what can happen when grace invades the hearts of God's people—even whole churches: "We want you to know, brothers, about the grace of God that has been given among the churches of Macedonia, for in a severe test of affliction, their abundance of joy and their extreme poverty have overflowed in a wealth of generosity on their part" (2 Cor. 8:1–2).

Great grace begets radical generosity. Cheerful givers are humble receivers and "miners" of the unsearchable riches of Christ (2 Cor. 9:8–9; Eph. 3:8).

Becoming a Member of a Gospel Posse

SCOTTY WARD SMITH

HAVING ALREADY WARNED the disciples that all of them would "fall away" (Mark 14:27), Jesus now revealed the price of keeping them forever. For Peter, James, and John, the wonder of the Mount of Transfiguration (9:2–13) gave way to the slumber in the garden of Gethsemane. But we're not to look for a moral to this story; rather, we must see the Savior *in* the story. The point of this text is not, "Don't go to sleep on Jesus"; rather it is that "Jesus died for weak apostles and sinners"—just like you and me. Jesus remains faithful when we are not. He, who bids us watch and pray, never ceases to watch and pray for us.

Gethsemane isn't a model for us to follow; rather, it's a gift for us to receive. An old hymn asks the question, "Must Jesus bear the cross alone?" to which we must reply with a resounding "Yes!" Before we even *think* about taking up our cross (Matt. 16:24–26), we must understand the cross that Jesus took up for us. *Only* Jesus could drink the cup of God's wrath (Jer. 25:15; Isa. 51:17; John 18:11); and he did so, so that he might deliver us from being judged for our sins (2 Cor. 5:21; 1 Thess. 1:10; 5:9–10; Rev. 14:9–10).

Isaiah described the coming Messiah as "a man of sorrows, and acquainted with grief" (Isa. 53:3). As we consider Jesus's preparation for his death on the cross, this might be one of the greatest understatements of all time. The joy set before Jesus (Heb. 12:2) did not negate the pain required before the joy. Indeed, the certainty of his resurrection could not diminish the agony of his separation from his Father. When Jesus uttered his desperate plea (Mark 14:36), he wasn't having second thoughts about going to the cross; but perhaps this was his first full realization of what being totally cut off from his Father's presence would mean.

As men, we need to own how much we have in common with Peter, James, and John. We will boast in Christ (1 Cor. 1:31) to the extent that we are willing to boast in our weaknesses (2 Cor. 12:9)—to be honest about how much we really need Jesus. Hypothetical sinners experience only hypothetical grace. It is a beautiful thing when men relate to one another as a "gospel posse"—a band of brothers groaning and growing in grace together.

AUGUST 26 · LUKE 1:39-56

Living for God's Glory

JARED C. WILSON

"AM I STRONG ENOUGH? Do I have what it takes?"

"Will I be able to get ahead in the world and provide for my family?"

"Will I be remembered? Does what I do matter in the long run?"

Most men think about these things often, both explicitly in their worries and implicitly in their actions. And these are not, in themselves, wrong things to think about. But because sin is real and our flesh is always at war against the spirit, too often these areas of concern become areas of *self*-concern. We have in mind with these questions our own name and renown, our own glory.

In Luke 1:39–56 we find these very issues in play, and what can be humbling for the Christian man is to see that we learn their proper context and proportion from a teenage girl!

Mary has been blessed with the greatest blessing anyone could ever receive—to bear the Messiah, King Jesus, in her virgin womb. She knows that she will, from this moment on, be considered blessed by future generations.

And yet, her song of praise is not to or about herself—it is about the glory of God.

Her soul is not full of itself; it is magnifying the Lord (v. 46). When she examines herself, she sees only lowliness, poverty, weakness. But when she sees herself in the light of God's grace, she sees his glory, his riches, his strength working through her. We learn a valuable lesson from her song of praise: "His mercy is for those who fear him from generation to generation" (v. 50).

So if we are concerned—as all men ought to be—about living in power, taking care of our loved ones, and establishing a generational legacy of honor, we must take care to remember that our lives are centered on God's glory, not our own. The alternative is the way of worldliness that leads to destruction. Mary says that God "scatters the proud in the thoughts of their hearts" (v. 51). What a dangerous thing this is. And so easy to succumb to. When Mary uses the word "scattered," I think of the story of Babel, where they are building the tower to heaven to "make a name" for themselves (Gen. 11:4). What happens? God knocks it down and disperses them. "God opposes the proud" (James 4:6).

If you come in pride, claiming your own strength, you have made God your enemy. But if you come in faith—the acknowledged littleness of faith—what then? James 4:6 says, "[He] gives grace to the humble." Which is exactly what Mary says in verse 52: "he has . . . exalted those of humble estate."

AUGUST 27 · LUKE 2:22-38

Unexpected Revolution

JARED C. WILSON

OFTEN OUR JOY comes in ways we do not expect. In the days of Jesus, the people of Israel were very much awaiting the arrival of the Messiah. They looked forward with eager expectation and zealous hope for the day when the promised one would jump onto the scene, overthrow the Roman oppressors, and reestablish God's tangible kingdom on earth. The dominant vision for this deliverance involved stallions and swords. But then the King finally did come. And he was riding on a donkey! There were no swords in the air, but rather palm branches. Yet the kingdom of God was coming nonetheless, in this peaceable rebellion.

When the blind Simeon finally saw the salvation of Israel, he was not beholding some muscular warrior armed for battle. He was holding up a baby. And yet the salvation this baby carried was no less powerful, no less vindicating, no less revolutionary. In fact, by coming as a baby, by coming in humility and low "estate" (Luke 1:48, 52), by coming to serve and to teach and eventually to die, Jesus brought an even more dramatic rebellion than if he had come with the zealot's armed force.

Simeon declares the child Jesus a "glory to your people Israel," but also "a light for revelation to the Gentiles" (2:32). He brings a salvation that God has prepared "in the presence of all peoples" (v. 31). This was no Plan B. This was not some unexpected twist in God's covenant story. What Paul calls the "grafting in" of the Gentiles (Rom. 11:17–24) was forecast as part of God's redemptive purposes throughout the Old Testament prophecies. And now that Christ has come, he is putting the plan into effect.

Christ's work, then, frustrates the Gentiles' search for glory apart from the God of Israel and unravels the Jews' search for glory apart from the inclusion of the Gentiles. Christ has not come to overthrow physical kingdoms—at least, not yet—but to overthrow spiritual ones, the toughest ones to overthrow. Simeon promises Mary that "a sword will pierce through your own soul" (Luke 2:35).

What's in your soul that the gospel ought to run a sword through? Are you searching for pleasure and meaning in ways contrary to God's plan? Are you trying to write the story of your own glory with your life? Are there areas of stubborn sin that you have yet to attack with the power of Christ's grace?

We try and try and try. We think the best answer to our bad behavior is trying to look good. We're allergic to looking un-tough. But hope and joy come in unexpected ways. It's leaning on the finished work of Christ that finally undoes our desires for fulfillment apart from him. As Simeon could tell you, not even religion can do that.

Resisting Temptation

JARED C. WILSON

THE TEMPTATION OF JESUS works backwards and forward. It works backwards because we see, in the ways that Satan tempts Jesus, the exact same ways he tempted Adam and Eve. If you remember, the serpent led Eve to believe that the forbidden fruit was good for food. This parallels Satan tempting the hungry Jesus to turn the stones to bread. Then Eve saw that the fruit was "a delight to the eyes" (Gen. 3:6). This is similar to Satan showing Jesus the dazzling cityscape of all the promised kingdoms. Finally, the serpent promised Eve that, by taking of the fruit, she could become like God—indeed, that she would become a kind of god herself. We see Satan tempting Jesus to exploit his own deity in Luke 4:9–11.

At each step of the way, the Accuser echoes the temptation of Adam and Eve in his temptation of Jesus. But whereas Adam and Eve succumbed to temptation, rebelling against God's will and bringing death into the world, Jesus withstands the temptation, holding to the Father's will. He thereby brings life into the world for all who will trust in him.

This is where you and I stand each day as men. Like Adam, we are passive. With Adam, we suffer from indwelling sin. Temptation rises up to meet us each day, in these same three ways. We are tempted to fulfill our appetites with money, with sex, with all kinds of fleeting pleasures, as if they are what will really satisfy the "rumbling tummies" of our flesh. We are tempted by the things we see, by what dazzles us—we want to look good, powerful, successful, put-together. And we are always tempted to put ourselves at the center of our lives, to exalt ourselves and live like little self-worshiping gods. This is all our fault, but it began thanks to Adam.

But Christ's victory over temptation works forward. We see in Adam's fall our own sinfulness, but we see in Jesus's obedience our righteousness. We are forgiven by his grace. We are filled by his grace. And we can withstand temptation by his grace (1 Cor. 10:13). Through faith, we even receive Christ's perfect submission to the Father's will as if it were our own! And at each point of temptation, when we set our minds to the perfect work of Christ, we find the strength to say no to the Tempter and yes to God's glory. Unlike Eve, we don't have to run out of *It is writtens*.

When we go our own way, we prove we've still got Adam in us. But when our Accuser comes calling, we can plead Christ's obedience. Sin is all our fault, but it ends, thanks to Jesus.

AUGUST 29 · LUKE 7:36-50

The New Math of the Gospel

JARED C. WILSON

THE PURITAN PREACHER Thomas Watson once said, "Until sin be bitter, Christ will not be sweet."[10] What he meant was, until we see ourselves for who we truly are apart from Christ—the depth of our need, the extent of our brokenness, the totality of our depravity, and the condemnation we deserve—we will not see Christ for all that he truly is.

The woman in this story whom the Pharisees have declared a sinner understands the great divorce between herself and Jesus. It is for this reason that she has determined to serve him and bless him. The Pharisees, on the other hand, think themselves to be Jesus's peers at least, so of course they probably think they are doing him a favor letting him come and eat with them.

The dinner host, Simon, grumbles inwardly, not just because he doubts Christ's holiness in allowing this scandalous scene, but because he considers himself to have higher standards than Jesus. He knows what this woman is up to. He knows this woman's sin. If Jesus knew the woman like he knows her, he reasons, he wouldn't allow her to touch him.

But the gospel turns our religious math inside out. There are not "good people" and "bad people" in the mathematics of the gospel. There are bad people and Jesus. So the story Jesus tells about the man with two debtors serves a dual purpose. It reminds us that we all stand indebted to Christ. Religious and irreligious, people far off and people nearby, "prodigal sons" and "older brothers"—we are all debtors to grace. But the parable also shows us that the more mindful we are of our indebtedness, the more of

God's grace we will know. We are in big trouble if we think that we need only a little bit of God!

When we are on spiritual autopilot, trusting in our own wisdom and relying on our own strength, it is fundamentally because we don't think we need God all that much. This is functional self-righteousness. But the more in tune with our inner inability and spiritual poverty we become, the more of Christ we will experience and the more honor we will give him.

AUGUST 30 · LUKE 8:40-56

Little Faith, Big God

JARED C. WILSON

THERE IS AN important truth embedded in this story of two healings. Obviously, we see the power of Jesus Christ to heal the sick and raise the dead. That's a very important truth. We see his mercy and his tenderness, too. That's also very important. But there's something else, something so helpful to our hearts, in the comparison and the contrast between Jairus and the woman with the bloody discharge.

Jairus, we see, is a ruler of the synagogue. He is a man with power. He is educated, credible, a man of authority and probably of wealth. The woman, for all intents and purposes, is his exact opposite. She is a woman, first of all; but also, because of her condition, she is considered unclean. She's an untouchable. She is also poor and of little regard socially.

If Jesus had come to play the religious game or the political game or the worldly game, he would have ignored the woman. She does not even have the courtesy (the courage?) to approach him directly. She knows a man of his stature would likely not stoop to consider a woman of hers. So, in effect, she tries to "steal" the blessing (Luke 8:44). Jairus, on the other hand, approaches Jesus directly. He is humbly imploring, of course, but he fully expects that Jesus can and will heal his daughter.

Jairus believes Jesus can heal his daughter, and in a way, he believes Jesus will. The woman, however, believes Jesus can heal her, but in a way, believes he wouldn't if she asked. And yet, Jesus provides the healing they both desire.

Here is the important truth to consider: It is not just that Jesus's salvation is available to both high and low, rich and poor, powerful and weak. Jesus's salvation is equally available to both big faith and little faith. Jairus exercised a bold faith, the woman a timid faith. And yet both got the fullness of healing needed. We learn from this something crucial for the Christian life: it is not a strong faith that saves us, but a strong Christ. One doesn't need to be a spiritual behemoth to receive Christ's blessings, just the meekness to say, "I need you. Heal me!"

Even a mustard seed of faith—if it is true faith—receives all the eternal riches of the glory of the omnipotent Christ. You need never fear your "littleness." God's grace is enough.

AUGUST 31 · LUKE 9:28-36

Christ Alone

JARED C. WILSON

IN THIS MIRACULOUS event called the transfiguration, Jesus peels back the curtain, as it were, to show Peter, James, and John a glimpse of his full glory. It is as if Jesus has opened the door into heaven, just for a bit, in order to confirm his deity to his followers and to encourage them for what lies ahead in his ministry—namely, his crucifixion.

The appearance of Moses and Elijah beside the Lord Jesus in this revelatory moment is not incidental. Moses represents the Law, with all its depictions and demands of righteousness. Elijah represents the Prophets, with all their forecasts and expectations of righteousness. There stands Christ Jesus alongside the Law and the Prophets.

Peter's inclination is a lot like ours. He is thinking with a compartmentalized spirituality. He wants to put up three tents, one for each of them. If we imagine our own life—with all of its demands and responsibilities and expectations—we tend to have the same approach. We imagine our life like a calendar or a to-do list. Jesus gets a position in the charts of our schedule. He gets the "spiritual" slot; he fills the "religion" box.

A friend of mine gives a great illustration about how we think of our lives like a big conference table. Around the table sit the representatives of each aspect of our lives. There's a seat for our Career self, a seat for our Sexual self, a seat for our Hobbies and Interests, a seat for our Family, etc. Then we "accept" Jesus into our life. We give him a seat at the table. Jesus fills our Religious self, we imagine.

But this is not how Jesus operates. He is the fulfillment and satisfaction of every part of our self, and so he deserves the ruling seat over all of our selves! Jesus requires, not just a part of our life, but our whole life. So, my friend says, Jesus comes in salvation and effectively fires everyone at the table. Now we've really accepted him.

When the glorious smoke clears in the transfiguration event, Moses and Elijah are gone. "Jesus was found alone" (Luke 9:36). This is because the demands of the Law and the expectations of the Prophets are all fulfilled in him. He is the summation of every obligation and the satisfaction of every need.

SEPTEMBER 1 · LUKE 12:13-21

Rich toward God

JARED C. WILSON

JESUS ONCE SAID that it is very difficult for a rich man to enter the kingdom of heaven. Not impossible (for all things are possible with God), but very difficult. Why?

I think we see the answer in this parable, where we find an example of a man so caught up in the pursuit of *stuff* that he has forgotten what really matters. He's taken good things—wise investment, providing for his family, providing employment for others, good stewardship in general—and made them ultimate things. The pursuit of more, bigger, better has effectively become his god.

In fact, we see that his very security and his very happiness are tied up in what he can attain and what he can build to hold what he has attained. He is storing up goodies for himself, but he's not rich toward God.

The warning is clear: "Fool! This night your soul is required of you, and the things you have prepared, whose will they be?" (Luke 12:20). As Jesus asks elsewhere, "For what does it profit a man to gain the whole world and forfeit his soul?" (Mark 8:36).

We must not become earth-rich and God-poor. When the day of accounting comes, when the kingdom's currency is requested for entrance into paradise, all the wealthy, fun-loving, permanent-vacation-taking souls will come up totally empty-handed.

Now, some may read this parable of the foolish rich man and think to themselves, "Ah, he should have cared more for others. If he had given more money away, he'd have the treasure of having done good." And it *is* imperative that we do good to others, but that kind of giving is a poverty all its own. When we reach the gates of Paradise and are asked for the currency of the kingdom to prove our right to enter, we best not try to hand in our own righteousness. The Bible says, "All our righteous deeds are like a polluted garment" (Isa. 64:6).

No, when the opportunity comes to present our justification for entry into everlasting rest, we need only present an empty hand, saying, "I have nothing of my own to offer. But I am clothed in the righteousness of Christ that I have received through faith, which makes me totally vested in his unsearchable riches. My Savior, in the great grace of God, has purchased my entrance for me."

Or in the words of the beloved hymn, "Nothing in my hand I bring, simply to the cross I cling." *That* is how to be rich toward God.

SEPTEMBER 2 • LUKE 15:11–32

Cheap and Costly Grace

JARED C. WILSON

MOST CHRISTIANS UNDERSTAND the parable of the prodigal son as a chronicle of the dangers of wild living and the loving acceptance by God of repentant sinners. Yet the parable goes much deeper and is more applicable than we might first imagine.

First, the parable is as much about the older brother as it is about the "prodigal." We tend to forget that there are plenty of verses in Luke 15 dedicated to the grumbling of the prodigal's older brother. It is easy to mistake those latter verses for a kind of coda, or "afterword," but really they are the "end stress" of the story. The father's entreating of his firstborn, who was upset that his wayward kid bro would be so ceremoniously received, is how Jesus is bringing the story home.

Thus, this parable really should be called "the parable of the self-righteous son," or at least, the "parable of the two self-centered sons." By depicting the central sins of both the younger and the older brother, Jesus is showing that these boys are not so different, at least not at heart. Each in his own way was making presumptions about his standing with the father.

Second, the parable is as much about legalism as it is about license. In Luke 15:1–2, we see that these Pharisees and scribes were grumbling about the way Jesus both attracted and welcomed "tax collectors and sinners." So when Jesus gets to this story about the lost son, the reckless hedonism depicted is more the background of his larger point, not the point itself.

The Pharisees and scribes did not need a cautionary tale on the dangers of wild living. They already believed such lifestyles were sinful. What they needed was to have their tidy moral universe disrupted. Jesus is puncturing the puffed-up balloon of self-righteousness. We even see this natural human impulse in the prodigal's repentance. When he comes to his senses, he doesn't presume to return to his father's good graces; he assumes that he will become one of his dad's workmen. But Jesus doesn't call us servants; he calls us friends (John 15:15).

Third, the parable is more about grace's welcome than it is about sin's danger. Jesus is definitely showing that sin is destructive and a squandering of God's grace. But Jesus is also showing that the older brother's pride in his own obedience was just as distancing between himself and the father. What Christ has done, then, by dying to forgive all our sins and to put an end to our self-reliant attempts at obeying our way into God's approval, is to show us how costly grace is, how much it covers, and just how great the welcome of the Father can be for those who repent of both their bad deeds *and their good ones.*

God's Everything for Your Nothing

JARED C. WILSON

BY ALL EXTERNAL MEASUREMENTS, the Pharisee and the tax collector could not be more different. The Pharisee was well regarded by his Jewish countrymen. He had all the religious merit badges. He was well educated and well behaved. The tax collector, on the other hand, was despised by his culture, seen as a traitor to his very people. He was identified most blatantly as a "sinner," the lowest of the low, a greedy, unholy scoundrel.

And yet something remarkable happens when two men from any walk of life, even if vastly different, enter into the presence of God. They become spiritual equals. The ground is level, as they say, at the foot of the cross. So the Pharisee and the tax collector in Jesus's parable are more alike than they realize, certainly more than the Pharisee realizes. They both carry in their hearts a spiritual wasteland. Apart from God, all they possess is nothing—nothing, that is, but need. The Pharisee's merit badges credit him nothing. The tax collector's money earns him nothing.

But there is a difference between the two men. Jesus says the tax collector went home from the temple justified. The Pharisee did not. How can that be?

The difference is that the tax collector *owned* his spiritual poverty. He was ready and willing to admit to the holy God that he was a miserable sinner, that he had absolutely nothing to offer God but his own emptiness. The Pharisee, on the other hand, was trying to trade in his righteous living for the approval of God. But no amount of our obedience can earn us the perfect righteousness we need to be justified. That comes only by God's grace received through faith.

And that's what the tax collector had: the empty hand of faith. You and I must follow his example. If you think of the great exchange announced in the good news—Christ's righteousness traded for our sin—picture yourself coming to that "bargaining table" with God, entering that temple to be considered in the blazing light of his infinite perfection. When you come to this bargaining table, bring nothing with you. If you try to trade in any amount of obedience for God's approval, you will go home empty-handed. Instead, own up to your emptiness. Trust in Christ. And when you do, he will trade his everything for your nothing. That is the essence of the gospel: justified by faith alone.

SEPTEMBER 4 · LUKE 19:1-10

Chosen to Receive and Obey

JARED C. WILSON

IF YOU LOOK CAREFULLY, you will see the outline of the Christian life in this story of the wee little man named Zacchaeus. It begins, as our spiritual journeys with Christ often do, with Zacchaeus considering Jesus. He has gone to "take a look" at this man whom many are worshiping and following. Before we are saved, we tend to do the same. We "take a look" at Jesus. What did he say? What did he do? Are the things Christians believe about him true? If we're really interested, we will get as close a look as we can, climbing our own sycamore trees by going to church, reading books, talking with Christian friends, and so on.

But salvation begins not when we "take a look" at Jesus but when Jesus takes hold of us. Jesus spots Zacchaeus and says, "I see you, little man. Come on down; I'm going to come to your house." If Jesus had not done this, would Zacchaeus have "received him joyfully" (Luke 19:6)? Maybe. Maybe not. In any event, we see here that the life of discipleship begins not when we choose Jesus but when Jesus chooses us (John 15:16). But this doesn't mean we have no part to play—oh, no!

When Christ calls us, the call has great effect. We worship Christ when we finally see him for who he truly is. We're no longer just "considering" Jesus; we have gotten some glimpse of his glory, and it has changed us (2 Cor. 3:18). We hear the good news, and it strikes us for the first time as good news! It strikes us as good news that is *for* us. So, like Zacchaeus, we receive Jesus gladly. He is coming to receive us, and so we receive him. He is entering our heart, so we rejoice at the bigness of his own heart, that the very God of the Universe would choose a man of such small stature to be his friend, to be his brother! What a great joy.

But we do not stop there. No, the disciple of Jesus, seeing the great satisfying joy there is to be had in him alone, is willing to give up whatever is required. Having Christ, we have all. So we can consider everything else a loss (Phil. 3:7). Zacchaeus immediately begins giving back what he has sinfully taken, and more besides.

When Jesus saves a man, he saves him into a life of joy and obedience, *of joyful obedience.*

SEPTEMBER 5 · LUKE 22:24-30

The Way to Greatness

JARED C. WILSON

LIKE THE DISCIPLES, we seem to be always jockeying for position. We are driven to succeed, to prosper, to win. So when someone else gets the promotion at work, someone else gets the recognition at church, someone else gets the trophy at play, we battle resentment. It happens in a million ways, big and small. For some of us, it takes merely losing a parking space or the big piece of chicken at dinner to feel slighted.

At work or at church or at home we may feel like we aren't properly respected. And maybe we aren't. But when the disciples are trying to figure out which one of them should be declared the greatest, Jesus does not allow it for a second. Instead, he identifies such concern for what it really is: worldliness.

"This is the way those who do not know God think," he is saying. He contrasts this concern for one's position—for respect, for renown, for power—with the kingdom of God.

It was a jockeying for position, remember, that first brought sin and death into the world. Adam and Eve wanted to be greater than God had already declared them to be. This is pride, and it will rot us out from the inside. If you think back to the great blueprint of the kingdom of God, the Sermon on the Mount, remember how Jesus begins with those Beatitudes, announcing that God's kingdom has come to set things right side up. In the kingdom, then, the blessings come not to those who trust in riches or power or earthly happiness, but to the poor, the downtrodden, the grieving.

Jesus himself has come not to lord his deity over sinners but to dwell alongside them; to identify as one of them, despite being sinless himself; and to serve and to suffer and to die. This is the way of the kingdom. It is the opposite of pride.

And yet—there is glory in it. Jesus commands humility from us but he does not leave the humble man hanging! It is the meek, remember, who will inherit the earth.

Jesus here tells his followers not to worry about their position, their power, their respect and renown. God will take care of that. If we will humble ourselves, God will exalt us at the proper time (1 Pet. 5:6; James 4:10). Vindication will come. So he promises them thrones (Luke 22:30). The way to true greatness, in the meantime, is to get low.

SEPTEMBER 6 • LUKE 23:26-49

In Christ Alone

JARED C. WILSON

IT WAS THE DARKEST moment in history, darker even than the original fall of mankind in the garden of Eden. For here came Jesus Christ, the sinless King of the Jews, serving and sacrificing, loving and leading, all to forgive us and redeem us—and, facing his flawless mercy and abundant love, we killed him! This was humanity's collective dark night of the soul.

But because God's sovereign grace is greater than all sin and darkness, he takes what we mean for evil and uses it for good. There is no moment where this is more real than in the crucifixion of his Son. There at the cross, wrath and pardon intersect. The cross, which is silliness to those who are dying in their unbelief, is the glory of everlasting freedom to those who repentantly trust in Jesus Christ. This clash of darkness and light is evident throughout Luke's crucifixion account.

In Luke 23:29–31, Jesus warns the weeping women about the judgment to come on Jerusalem. In verse 34, Jesus intercedes for those callously gambling over his clothes, ignorant of the redemption at hand. In verse 40, the repentant thief rebukes his condemned companion, warning him about the dangers of his mockery of Christ. Each of these moments is a portent of the wrath deserved by sinners.

But then, in contrast, we have Jesus's reception of that repentant thief in verse 43. We have the dawning realization of the centurion in verse 47.

In verse 45, the sun's light failed, but the curtain of the temple was torn in two. This is another vivid picture of what is happening on the cross. Christ's death, for the Christian, means life. His day of darkness becomes our everlasting light, especially as we follow his atoning work from death to glorious resurrection.

We must remember that God does not cut corners when it comes to his holiness. His law must be fulfilled. He will punish sin—no ifs, ands, or buts. The question we face, then, is, What will the cross be to us? Will it be our shame, or our glory? Will Christ's work be of no importance to us—just a historical curiosity or religious sentimentality? Or will it be our only boast? Because our sin will be punished. And if we refuse to trust in Christ's taking of the punishment, we will have to take it ourselves. Only one way leads to everlasting life.

True depth of satisfaction, power, and joy comes from truly seeing the depth of Christ's work on the cross, seeing the light of hope in the darkness of his death. In Christ alone will we find forgiveness of sin, freedom from guilt, and affectionate reconciliation with God the Father.

SEPTEMBER 7 · LUKE 24:13-35

It's All about Jesus

JARED C. WILSON

THE MODERN CONCEPTION of Jesus as a "live and let live" kind of guy bears almost no resemblance to the actual Jesus of the Bible. Jesus often invades personal space. He refuses to tolerate ambivalence, far less being ignored. He is constantly forcing the issue *of himself.* The things Jesus says and does place himself at the center of human life, at the center of the universe, even.

People must reckon with this man and his message, sooner or later. And there is such a thing as reckoning with him "too late."

In Luke 24, we see Jesus after his resurrection sort of sidling up alongside the disciples on the road to Emmaus. He inserts himself both into their conversation and into their sense of history, of spirituality. This is not out of place. Jesus is "the radiance of the glory of God and the exact imprint of his nature" (Heb. 1:3), through whom all things were created. And one day "all things" will be subjected to Jesus (1 Cor. 15:27–28), so that he might in fact "fill all things" (Eph. 4:10).

So when Jesus tells these men that the entire Bible is about him (Luke 24:27), he's not blowing smoke. He's actually clearing the air!

From beginning to end, the Bible is about Jesus. We see his footprints there in the garden grass and in the exodus desert. We see his shadow in the sacrifices and the temple rites. We hear of his glory in the Israelite warfare, his suffering in the Israelite lament, his kingship in the Israelite prophecy. Every page of the old covenant Scriptures is whispering his name. And of course this whisper becomes a shout—a joyful, exultant declaration—in the New Testament, where he finally comes in the flesh to inaugurate God's kingdom and set his people free through his death and resurrection.

Our place in the story God is telling with the universe, then, is the same as these disciples' place. We must have our eyes open to him (v. 31), to recognize Christ's presence in the fabric of history and in our daily routines. His presence fills our lives and, as always, forces the issue. Will our lives be all about us? Or all about him? Cleopas and his companions enjoyed a good kind of "heartburn" (v. 32) with the realization that Jesus Christ had invaded their very existence, centering their souls on him and sending them out to proclaim his greatness and love.

This is our mandate: to see Jesus, to *fixate* on him, recognizing that all our life is all about him. And to share Jesus. Because his glory is the greatest joy in all the universe. And one day, his glory will be all that the universe will know (Hab. 2:14).

There Was a Man Sent from God

JON BLOOM

RIGHT IN THE MIDDLE of one of the most beautiful, breathtaking, magisterial descriptions of the eternal Son of God ever penned, the apostle John, abruptly it seems, writes these words: "There was a man sent from God, whose name was John" (John 1:6). They almost feel like an interruption, a distraction.

Is the apostle directing our eyes away from God the Son, the Word, the Life, the Light, in order to look at a man? No. The apostle is directing us to see the Son *through* a man. This seemingly odd insertion about John the Baptist reveals something else profound and mysterious: God has chosen to make human witnesses the windows through which we see Jesus.

For fallen humans, witnesses are windows to the truth. That's why, whenever we must judge whether someone is telling us the truth or not, we almost always look for a witness. There is something uniquely powerful about an objective person who confirms the truth of another's testimony, someone who has nothing worldly to gain from verifying what he or she believes to be true. If that witness is willing to suffer loss by his verification, it is even more powerful. And if many witnesses are willing to suffer loss, even of their own lives, to confirm the truth of a person's testimony, it is exponentially powerful.

John the Baptist "came as a witness . . . that all might believe through him" (John 1:7). He was the first in what has become a great "cloud of witnesses" (Heb. 12:1) to the truth of Jesus's testimony. This cloud has swelled to millions and millions, each witness having seen Jesus through the witness of another. Thousands more join this cloud every day. And many in the cloud have lost, or soon will lose, their lives because of their witness. And because of their loss, all the more will see Jesus and believe in him—through the window of their witness.

When we hear the call of Jesus and follow him, Jesus says to us, "You will be my witnesses" (Acts 1:8). Our faith is not a private matter. It is a public window through which God wants to reveal Jesus to others. That is our primary call on earth, no matter what other tasks God has given us to accomplish. We are not our own (1 Cor. 6:19). We, like John, are men sent from God.

Jesus Will Provide the Wine You Need

JON BLOOM

WHY DID THE WINE run out at the Cana wedding? Did the hosts plan unwisely? Did uninvited guests turn up and exceed their capacity? Did the hosts run short of funds to provide enough wine? The Bible doesn't tell us, but whether it was a failure of human wisdom, strength, or resources—all familiar failures to us—there was a need that the human hosts could not meet.

Unknown to the hosts, the Lord of hosts, veiled in flesh, was a guest at this wedding. Mary knew, though, and she knew that he was able to meet their every need. So she informed Jesus about the situation, and glorious grace flowed freely.

But the glory that Jesus manifested at this wedding was more than his omnipotent authority over nature. For those who could see it that day, a deeper, brighter glory of the triune God's abounding, all-sufficient love for foolish, weak, sin-impoverished people blazed forth. Out of Jesus's fullness, the wedding guests received "grace upon grace" (John 1:16). They drank the very best earthly wine ever created, made by the Creator of grapes himself. But more than that, the wine they drank freely was a foretaste of the gospel. Jesus knew the time for making the real gospel wine of Calvary had not yet come (2:4). But this wedding wine, poured out of vessels of purification, foreshadowed that best of all wines, which would be served after humans had done their sinful, insufficient best to meet their need and failed. This wine would flow freely, with infinite abundance, from the purest Vessel of all time for the greatest wedding of all time.

That's why, when you run out of "wine" today, when you fail in wisdom, power, or resources, or fail to meet the righteous requirement of God's law, or fail to love the Lord with all your heart, you need not fear. Jesus, your

Lord, your Groom, the Master of the Great Wedding Feast, has infinite power and infinite love and is "able to make all grace abound to you, so that having all sufficiency in all things at all times, you may abound in every good work" (2 Cor. 9:8). Trust him. Jesus will provide the wine you need. Just "do whatever he tells you" (John 2:5).

SEPTEMBER 10 · JOHN 3:16-21

Come to the Light, and Really Live

JON BLOOM

WE MEN IMAGINE ourselves as light-seekers, brave souls on the noble quest for the naked truth. But Jesus, the Truth (John 14:6), gives us a hard dose of the naked truth to wake us from our fantasies: "And this is the judgment: the light has come into the world, and people loved the darkness rather than the light because their works were evil" (3:19).

Our noble quest is put to the test when the Truth seeks us out. It turns out that we do not seek true light. What we seek is glory, pleasure, and worship for ourselves (John 5:44; 2 Tim. 3:4). Created as moons, we seek to be suns, and our foolish minds are darkened (Rom. 1:21). And if the light that is in us is darkness, how great is our darkness (Matt. 6:23)! As the real Light shines, the naked truth about us is exposed and we flee to the darkness to conceal our evil.

But here is the astounding, wonderful news for us dark-dwellers: the Light is love (1 John 4:8)! The Light is shining to *save* us, not *condemn* us (John 3:17)! Jesus, the Light of the world, does not want us to remain in darkness but to have the light of life (John 8:12). He came to deliver us from the domain of darkness and transfer us to his kingdom of undying light (Col. 1:13). He came to become the darkness of our sin for us so that in him we might become the light of God's perfect righteousness (2 Cor. 5:21). He came so that we might live unashamed in the light.

Are there things you are concealing in the darkness, afraid to expose to the light? Do you fear God's condemnation? Do you fear the collapse of the reputation you have crafted?

Do not be afraid. Let Jesus's perfect love for you cast out your fear (1 John 4:18). His word to you is this: "I have come into the world as light, so that whoever believes in me may not remain in darkness" (John 12:46). Jesus offers you complete forgiveness and cleansing (1 John 1:9) and eternal life (John 3:16). All darkness offers you is destruction.

Come to the Light, and really live.

SEPTEMBER 11 · JOHN 4:1–45

Lift Up Your Eyes in Your Unexpected Field

JON BLOOM

ARE YOU LOOKING for a harvest where God has you right now?

On this dry, dusty day, God planned a harvest for the disciples where they least expected it. To them, Samaria was a "fly-over" region that had to be passed through to get from Judea to Galilee. It was populated by half-breeds and heretics, not the gospel target group the disciples saw as their calling. They were not looking for a harvest of the kingdom of God in Sychar. It was just a rest stop for them.

But Jesus saw white fields in Sychar. And he saw in the least likely resident of Sychar the ripest heart. She was a worldly, world-weary sinner who had come to the well in the heat of midday, most likely to avoid meeting anyone else. And there she met the Person she least expected: her Creator. And to her, Jesus declared in clearer words than he had yet spoken to anyone else, "I who speak to you am [the Messiah]" (John 4:26). And in talking with her he both reaped and sowed, for through her many Samaritans from the town came to Jesus and believed in him (v. 39).

The disciples were puzzled by what they saw Jesus doing, until he told them to lift up their eyes (v. 35). Then they saw a crowd of Sycharians making their way to the well, and suddenly they found themselves in a harvest—of Samaritans!—and they had the unexpected joy of reaping where they had not sown or even thought to look for a field. They had thought they were just passing through on their way to their real calling, and here they were reaping a greater harvest at the rest stop than they had yet seen in Judea or Galilee.

Often, the harvest Jesus has for you is where you least expected it, *in whom* you least expected it. You find yourself in a place that you assume you're just passing through, perhaps a place where you don't really want to be. But lift up your eyes: you may be in a field where God has been sowing gospel seeds unseen by you, and he's inviting you to reap what you did not sow, in a field where you never thought you would find a harvest.

Why Jesus Made Things Worse

JON BLOOM

YOU FEEL THE tension mounting as you read this chapter. Things were getting very serious. The Jewish leaders were now discussing Jesus's execution (John 5:18). But that's not the most shocking thing we read.

Jesus had purposefully and provocatively healed a man on the Sabbath. And in response to the leaders' objections he had consciously and clearly declared that he not only had a unique relationship with God the Father, but that he himself possessed divine power. So of course the leaders were considering the death penalty. The Mosaic law made both Sabbath breaking (Ex. 35:2) and blasphemy (Lev. 24:16) capital crimes. Taking God's word seriously required an earnest examination of Jesus's claims.

Jesus's claims were shocking. He knew very well what was at stake. He didn't even attempt to debate whether healing a man was truly breaking the Sabbath, as he did at other times (see Luke 14:1–6). Instead, he made things worse. He not only claimed to be the "Son of Man" prophesied in Daniel 7:13–14; he claimed to be God the Son! Jesus had no interest in lowering the stakes. He was raising them.

Let Jesus's claims sink in: he claimed to have power to raise the dead (John 5:21), authority to judge all humanity (v. 22), power to grant people eternal life (v. 24), and the same self-sustaining life that the Father has (v. 26). The leaders were not misunderstanding him. Jesus was, in fact, claiming equality with God (v. 18)—equality that, he said, the Father had given him. *And* he claimed that he deserved the same honor that was due to God the Father (v. 23). These claims are breathtaking and unnerving!

Jesus was very intentionally giving the leaders, those listening that day, and all of us who would ever hear this account, only two choices about himself: either he is God the Son, coequal with God the Father, or he is a deluded, dangerous man leading all who follow him off a spiritual cliff.

Jesus never intended to be viewed as merely another good, ethical human teacher. Either he is himself the source of eternal life (3:16) and the only way to the Father (14:6), or he has been the source of horrible destruction to millions throughout history. He leaves us no middle ground.

His question to us today is still, "Who do you say that I am" (Luke 9:20)?

SEPTEMBER 13 · JOHN 6:22-71

Eating Jesus's Flesh

JON BLOOM

JESUS'S DECLARATION that his followers must eat his flesh and drink his blood is disturbing. Everyone, including his most loyal disciples, seemed confused when he said it. It prompted many disciples to stop following him (John 6:66). It has been the subject of much debate in the church for centuries. And because of it, Christians have even been accused of cannibalism in the eating of the Lord's Supper.

But what did Jesus really mean? If we pay close attention, it's not that difficult to understand. Jesus gave us some clear clues:

- How does one work for the food that endures to eternal life? *Believe in Jesus* (vv. 27, 29).
- "I am the bread of life; whoever *comes to me* [believing] shall not hunger, and whoever *believes in me* shall never thirst" (v. 35).
- "For this is the will of my Father, that everyone who looks on the Son and *believes in him* should have eternal life, and I will raise him up on the last day" (v. 40).

- "Truly, truly, I say to you, whoever *believes* has eternal life" (v. 47).
- "Whoever *feeds on my flesh* and *drinks my blood* has eternal life" (v. 54).

Do you see it? "Whoever *feeds on my flesh* and *drinks my blood* has eternal life." "Whoever *believes* has eternal life."

For Jesus, *eating was believing; drinking was believing.* That's why he said that his words were "spirit and life" (v. 63). Jesus promised eternal life not to those who literally eat and drink from his broken body, but to those who believe in why his body was broken—to pay in full the penalty for their sin and to freely give them his perfect righteousness in exchange for their unrighteousness. This is the gospel of the New Testament. It is the priceless promise of John 3:16.

So the next time you gather with the saints in your local church to share in the simplest yet most profound of all meals, the Lord's Supper, remember: eating is believing; drinking is believing. The meal celebrates and proclaims belief. Jesus instituted it so that all of his disciples throughout all of history would remember and proclaim what they believe about his death until he comes (1 Cor. 11:23–26).

SEPTEMBER 14 · JOHN 8:48-59

If We Glorify Ourselves, Our Glory Is Nothing

JON BLOOM

THE MOST PROVOCATIVE statement in John 8, what nearly got Jesus stoned, was his claim to be Yahweh, the God who spoke to Moses out of the burning bush (Ex. 3:14). That's what Jesus meant when he said, "Before Abraham was, I am," and the leaders got his point loud and clear (John 8:58).

But for all who believe this astonishing claim, the most stunning thing Jesus said was, "If I glorify myself, my glory is nothing" (v. 54). What an extraordinary thing for Yahweh to say! These words reveal something beautiful about God and something horrible about us. And something else Jesus said shows us the escape from our horror.

Jesus's words, "If I glorify myself, my glory is nothing," reveal the beautiful humility that exists in the Godhead. Ponder this: God the Son, in whom "the whole fullness of deity dwells" (Col. 2:9), who "upholds the universe by the word of his power" (Heb. 1:3), *has no glory apart from God the Father.* The Father is the only source of true glory (Rom. 11:36), which is why the Son honors the Father (John 8:49). Even the Son humbles himself under the Father's mighty hand and trusts the Father to exalt him at the proper time (1 Pet. 5:6).

But for us these words are a horrible indictment. Jesus's perfect, humble reliance on the Father (Heb. 12:2) exposes us to be, like the religious leaders, lying "thieves and robbers" of the Father's glory (John 8:55; 10:8). Every day, we have glorified ourselves by "turning—every one—to his own way" (Isa. 53:6). We have sinned outrageously and fallen short of God's glory (Rom. 3:23), and the wages of such sin is death (Rom. 6:23).

But hear our gospel escape in John 8:51: "If anyone keeps my word, he will never see death." Our sin sentences us to death, "but the free gift of God is eternal life in Christ Jesus our Lord" (Rom. 6:23). Yahweh is *the way* that we glory-stealing sinners can be forgiven of our sin (1 John 1:9) and reconciled to the Father (2 Cor. 5:20). Each one of us who believes in Jesus, who keeps his word, "will never see death."

If we glorify ourselves, our glory is nothing and we will lose everything. But if we seek God's glory by fully trusting the Son, we will glorify the Father (Phil. 2:11) and gain everything in Christ (Phil. 3:8).

SEPTEMBER 15 · JOHN 9

What Do You See?

JON BLOOM

WHAT DID THE DISCIPLES see when they looked at the man born blind? They saw what everyone else saw: God's judgment on sin. However, it turned out that their perceptions were exactly opposite to God's purposes.

All Jews knew from the Scriptures that human suffering and death had entered the world through sin. And the Scriptures contained examples of a person's sins resulting in God's judgment, such as David's adultery and murder resulting in the disease and death of his infant son (2 Samuel 12) and Gehazi's greed resulting in his leprosy (2 Kings 5). So the Jewish theologians concluded that each person's suffering must be the result of specific sins he had committed. When an unborn child suffered, they figured either there were sins that fetuses mysteriously commit or else the parents were at fault.

That's why Jesus's disciples were curious as to whose sin had produced the man's blindness (John 9:2); it's why the Pharisees accused the man of being "born in utter sin" (v. 34). But they all seemed blind to the fact that the Scriptures, such as the book of Job, also show that God has other purposes in suffering. The irony is that Job's theologian friends had jumped to the same conclusions, and God rebuked them, saying, "You have not spoken of me what is right" (Job 42:8).

That's essentially what Jesus said in John 9:3: "It was not that this man sinned, or his parents, but that the works of God might be displayed in him." Seeing the man's blindness as God's punishment was precisely opposite to God's purposes. God made the man blind to display not his works of judgment but his works of grace. It's just that no one knew it until that day.

What do you see in the suffering around or in you? How do you interpret horrible world events? Jesus's healing of the man born blind reminds us that God's purposes in tribulation can be very different from the way they initially look to us.

Let us take great care when trying to interpret what God is doing in suffering. It might make no sense to us right now; it might appear or feel like God's judgment, or just the grinding gears of a blind, uncaring cosmos, when in reality God is preparing to display his grace in a way greater than anything we have ever imagined.

Actions Speak

JON BLOOM

THE OLD ADAGE SAYS, "Actions speak louder than words." This is true. But it's true only if our words and actions are saying different things.

In this chapter, Jesus uses words to reveal that he is the Good Shepherd who came to call his sheep from both the Jewish and the Gentile folds (John 10:11, 14, 16, 27), to lay his life down for them (v. 11), to be raised from the dead (vv. 17–18), and to give his sheep eternal life (v. 28). And once again he declares himself to be the divine Son of God, who is one with the Father and who was sent into the world by his Father (vv. 30, 36). The Jews once again show that they understand exactly what Jesus is saying, and they prepare to stone him (v. 31).

But before they can hurl the stones, Jesus asks them an unexpected and penetrating question: "I have shown you many good works from the Father; for which of them are you going to stone me?" (v. 32). The Jews respond that they don't want to stone him for his works but for his words (v. 33). So Jesus tells them that his *works are also words* (v. 38). His actions are speaking plainly, if they will just listen. He goes so far as to say that, if his works don't match his words, no one should believe his words (v. 37).

The same is true for us. No one should believe our words if our actions are saying something different. The way we live, what we actually do, testifies to what we really believe and really love. And often the most telling are the works we do when our plans are interrupted, or we face disappointment, or our weaknesses are exposed, or a threat arises, or someone else prospers, or we're called to give generously, or we must choose how to spend some precious discretionary time. These things speak eloquently of who we believe Jesus to be and how much we love him.

Jesus told people to observe his works to see if his words were true, because a "tree is known by its fruit" (Matt. 12:33). Our works are words that declare who we believe Jesus is. What are your actions speaking?

When Love Lets Us Suffer

JON BLOOM

WE OFTEN THINK that if God loves us he should spare us, or those we love, from suffering. And when he doesn't, we wonder how that can be love. In John's account of Lazarus's death and resurrection, Jesus shows us.

We start by being bewildered at Jesus's responses to Lazarus's plight. First, after hearing of his friend's illness, Jesus waited two days before going to see him. In fact, we are told that Jesus *loved* Lazarus and *therefore* he delayed the visit for two days (John 11:5–6). Therefore? That's a strange way to show love. Then, after Lazarus died, Jesus said, "I am glad that I was not there" (v. 15). Jesus was *glad* that he let his beloved friend die? That's a strange way to show love.

And here is where many people in pain misunderstand God and rail against what looks to them like God's indifference to, or maybe sadistic enjoyment in, their anguish. Even those who knew Jesus best and loved him most—his disciples, Martha, and Mary—were confused and deeply disappointed at first.

So why did Jesus delay, and why was he glad? It wasn't indifference to Lazarus's agony or gladness over his death. No, these things actually moved him to tears (v. 35). Jesus delayed and rejoiced because of what he knew God was going to do for Lazarus—and for everyone else who would ever believe in Jesus—*through* Lazarus's suffering and death.

Martha and Mary were not wrong to long for their brother's healing or to grieve when it didn't come. Disease and death are evils. But what God planned to do through this terrible event was beyond anything they could imagine. Through Lazarus's death, God would show his glory (v. 40) and reveal his Son's power over death (v. 25). Furthermore, the events surrounding Lazarus's death would actually hasten Jesus's own death (vv. 46–53), purchasing eternal deliverance from death for Mary and Martha and Lazarus and all the rest of us!

In other words, by letting Lazarus die, Jesus loved Martha, Mary, Lazarus, and millions of others in the most profound way he could. It's just that it didn't look that way at first.

That's how it is in our suffering, too. When we ask God to take away our agony and he delays, we wonder how that can be love. With Lazarus, Jesus pulled back the curtain to let us see. God withholds a joy we request only if he plans to give us, and many others, far greater joys.

SEPTEMBER 18 · JOHN 14:15-31

The Essence and Evidence of True Love

JON BLOOM

JESUS SAID, "If you love me, you will keep my commandments" (John 14:15). The unmistakable mark of the true Christian is a profound love for Jesus. And the unmistakable mark of a person who truly loves Jesus is that he keeps Jesus's commandments.

But in trying to understand the connection between love and obedience, we must avoid the huge mistake of equating obedience with love. Obeying Jesus is not the same thing as loving Jesus, but obeying Jesus *is* the most telling evidence that we love him. And the more costly the obedience, the more it says about our love. A clear illustration of this is Jesus's parable of the man who found the treasure: "The kingdom of heaven is like treasure hidden in a field, which a man found and covered up. Then in his joy he goes and sells all that he has and buys that field" (Matt. 13:44).

Here's the way it works: The man found the treasure and was captivated by its incredible beauty and worth. But the treasure demanded that the man sell everything in order to have it, so he obeyed that demand—not out of some stoic sense of duty but out of delight!

Now, compare the man in that parable with the rich man in Mark 10. The rich man, wanting eternal life, told Jesus that he had kept all of the commandments since his childhood. Jesus responded, "You lack one thing: go, sell all that you have and give to the poor, and you will have treasure in heaven; and come, follow me" (Mark 10:21). Having obeyed all those commandments, what was the one thing the man lacked? He lacked delight in Jesus and all that Jesus promised him. The treasure demanded that he sell everything in order to have it, and he could not obey that demand because that treasure did not give him joy.

The essence of our love is our delight in what we treasure. The evidence of our love is how we respond to the treasure's demands. That's why Jesus said, "If you love me, you will keep my commandments."

Ask Whatever You Wish

JON BLOOM

CAN JESUS REALLY mean what he says in John 15:7? His promise is breathtaking: "If you abide in me, and my words abide in you, ask whatever you wish, and it will be done for you."

Ask *whatever* we wish? How is this possible, when so many of our prayers seem to go unanswered? Is this promise only for super-saints?

No. The only saints Jesus chooses are weak and foolish ones (1 Cor. 1:26). They are disciples whose faith begins small (Matt. 14:31). They are people just like us. So this promise is for *us*. It is a check Jesus wants us to cash at the Bank of Heaven, where there are more than sufficient funds (2 Cor. 9:8).

But there are two conditions we must meet for this check to be valid. The first is that *we must abide in Jesus* (John 15:1–6). Jesus commands us to abide in him just as branches abide in a vine. Apart from him, we can do nothing but wither (vv. 5–6). An abiding branch has the sap of the Holy Spirit running through it. The more connected the branch, the more it receives the affections and wishes of the vine.

The second condition we must meet is that *Jesus's words must abide in us*—meaning *all* his words: "If you keep my commandments, you will abide in my love, just as I have kept my Father's commandments and abide in his love" (v. 10). Jesus loves us by telling us the truth (17:8, 26), and we love him by treasuring and therefore obeying what he says (14:15).

When our prayers seem to go unanswered, it is because we don't yet wish what Jesus wishes (James 4:3), or we don't yet share Jesus's timeline, or we haven't yet recognized that his answer has arrived in an unexpected package.

But the more we press into his two conditions (*we abide in him; his words abide in us*), the more Jesus shapes our desires and trains our discernment through the Holy Spirit. Our wishes and his wishes become increasingly the same. Therefore, increasingly, we receive whatever we wish, just like branches that receive exactly what they need from the vine.

So take this check to the Bank of Heaven. Ask whatever you wish. And in the process of redeeming the check, you'll discover that your joy springs not from Jesus *giving* you what you want but from Jesus *being* what you want.

SEPTEMBER 20 · JOHN 16:4–15

The Advantage of Jesus's Absence

JON BLOOM

HAVE YOU EVER wondered how Jesus's absence is an advantage to us (John 16:7)? What "Helper" could be better than Jesus's perfect, powerful presence and witness with us here on earth?

That's exactly how the disciples felt at the news of Jesus's departure (v. 6). What advantage could it possibly be to them for the Messiah to leave with his mission incomplete and send them a replacement? But Jesus knew it would be a huge advantage. He intended to empower their (and our) experience of his presence and global witness beyond anything they had ever imagined.

The first advantage of Jesus's physical absence is that the Helper would come to the disciples (v. 7). The Helper is the Holy Spirit, who is the "Spirit of Jesus" (Phil. 1:19). Jesus was indeed going to come to them, as he had promised (John 14:18), but rather than just being *with* them, which is all they had yet known, Jesus was going to give each disciple (including us) the deeper, more intimate experience of the Father and the Son making their home *in* him through the Spirit (14:17, 23). Each disciple would experience a personal manifestation of and communion with the triune God that could never be known as long as Jesus was physically and externally present with them.

The second advantage of Jesus's physical absence is seen in the words "convict the world" (16:8). Jesus had a worldwide mission in mind. His mission was far broader and would take far longer to accomplish than the eleven had yet comprehended. Jesus intended for billions of people to hear his gospel on multiple continents around the globe over the course of many centuries. His physical presence on earth simply would not scale to meet the needs of this mission. The mission could be accomplished only if his powerful presence was *in* millions of disciples as they took the gospel to billions around the world over many centuries.

That's why it is to everyone's advantage that Jesus is physically absent. Because of this, you as a disciple, no matter where you are, have the unspeakable advantage of the presence of the triune God dwelling in you to commune with you and empower you in your role in his Great Commission. And the global church has the advantage of Jesus's empowering presence whenever and wherever it gathers for worship (Matt. 18:20) or sends out disciples to preach the gospel (Matt. 28:20).

What Jesus Desires Most for You

JON BLOOM

JESUS HAS A DEEP, intense desire to give you something that will satisfy you more than anything else ever will. So strongly does he long for this that he prays that the Father will give it to you: "Father, I desire that they also, whom you have given me, may be with me where I am, to see my glory that you have given me because you loved me before the foundation of the world" (John 17:24).

This is the great culmination of Jesus's priestly prayer in John 17. This is why he manifested the Father's name to you (v. 6), gave you the

Father's words (vv. 8, 14), and guards you so that you will not be lost (v. 12). This is why he prays that you will be kept from the evil one (v. 15), that you will be fully sanctified (vv. 17, 19), and that you will help others to believe in him (v. 20). More than anything else, Jesus wants you to be with him forever to see and savor the glory that the Father bestowed on him from eternity past (vv. 5, 24). For he knows that this will bring you the most profound joy and pleasure that you will ever experience (Ps. 16:11).

But there is a sober implication of Jesus's fervent prayer, one you may not like at first. In fact, one day you might find yourself pleading with God to give you the opposite of Jesus's desire for you. For the answer to Jesus's prayer eventually implies your physical death.

We are right to hate death. Death is an enemy (1 Cor. 15:26), the tragic wages of our sin (Rom. 6:23). But when Jesus died for us, he paid those wages in full, and death—for the Christian—died! And now Jesus says to us, "everyone who lives and believes in me shall never die" (John 11:26). When our earthly assignment from Jesus is done (Acts 20:24), he will call us to be with him to enjoy most what we are made to most enjoy: him! Thus, death will be a "gain" for us (Phil. 1:21).

Someday, Jesus's prayer for you to be with him will overrule your prayer to be spared physical death. And when it does, you will know such joy and pleasures that you will wonder why you ever felt any reluctance to pass through the valley of shadow (Ps. 23:4).

SEPTEMBER 22 · JOHN 18:33-40

The Guilty Man Went Free

JON BLOOM

GOD WANTS US to pay attention to Barabbas. He is one of the few persons mentioned in all four Gospels.

All we know about Barabbas is that he was a "notorious" criminal (Matt. 27:16), was a known robber (John 18:40), and had committed murder during an insurrection (Luke 23:19).

No Gospel account leads us to think that Barabbas was any sort of hero to the Jewish people. In fact, in the political chess game being played between Pilate and the Jewish leaders over Jesus, Barabbas appears to be a move by Pilate to block the Jewish leaders from winning Jesus's execution. Pilate seemed to believe that Barabbas's clear guilt would highlight Jesus's clear innocence, and the common sense of justice would prevail with the crowd. But the Jewish leaders countered by coaching the crowd (Matt. 27:20), and to Pilate's surprise the people chose Barabbas (John 18:40). In the end, Pilate capitulated; the innocent man was condemned, and the guilty man went free.

And that is why God wants us to pay attention to Barabbas. God placed Barabbas in every Gospel account of the crucifixion to show us that Jesus came to lay down his life so that the guilty could go free.

In Barabbas we are to see ourselves. We all have sinned (Rom. 3:23); we all stand guilty before God. We all deserve the condemnation of eternal death (Rom. 6:23). But Barabbas is a gospel parable, and the lesson is this: "God shows his love for us in that while we were still sinners, Christ died for us" (Rom. 5:8). Our freedom from condemning guilt isn't achieved by anything we do; it is achieved by Jesus dying in our place. It is given to us as a free gift (Rom. 6:23), a gift that we receive by faith (Eph. 2:8–9). And all who receive this free gift not only are freed from the death sentence of sin; they also receive the right to become children of God (John 1:12). Barabbas is a powerful parable for those who have ears to hear.

So pay attention to Barabbas. And every time you read of him, remember this: "If the Son sets you free, you will be free indeed" (8:36).

Do Not Disbelieve, But Believe

JON BLOOM

THOMAS MAY BE unfairly labeled "Doubting Thomas." He certainly did doubt Jesus's resurrection, but his unbelief may not have been any worse than that of any other disciple. In John 20, none of the disciples (except perhaps John; v. 8) believed in Jesus's resurrection until Jesus appeared to them. But Jesus chose Thomas to confront all of our unbelief.

Why didn't Thomas believe in Jesus's resurrection? Had you asked him during the eight days when he was the last unbelieving holdout, no doubt he would have appealed to logic, historical precedent, and plain old commonsense realism. But had you asked him after he had seen Jesus, I think he would have admitted that underneath his objections was pride.

Jesus's resurrection, though seemingly incredible, was supported by credible evidence: (1) Jesus, whose words had always proven true for Thomas, had predicted that it would happen; (2) credible witnesses said it had happened, even though they endangered themselves by saying so; and (3) Jesus's body was nowhere to be found. Thomas's unbelief wasn't evidence based. He simply and stubbornly placed more authority in his own understanding than in Jesus's words or the evidence.

Pride, not evidence, is always at the root of unbelief in God. Examine your own unbelief. Is it not so? Humans have an astounding capacity for unbelief. They will even believe, despite impossible odds, that the universe is the result of blind chance, rather than believe the overwhelming evidence that a Creator exists. All our unbelief is fueled by a trust in our own judgment over God's. This was our great fall in Eden. We claimed our own wisdom to be superior to God's wisdom, and ended up becoming fools (Rom. 1:21).

Jesus's death and resurrection is the great undoing of the catastrophe of Eden. It is the genesis of the new creation, where the man who repents of his prideful and rebellious unbelief, fully trusting in God's word and not his own judgment, is forgiven and born again (John 3:3), restored to God and granted the eternal life that God originally intended for him.

Jesus's word to Thomas is a word to us all: "Do not disbelieve, but believe" (20:27). Here he confronts our prideful unbelief, whatever it is, and invites us to believe his wisdom, not ours. And since it is the one who believes in Jesus who has eternal life (3:16), let us join Thomas in responding to Jesus, "My Lord and my God!" (20:28).

SEPTEMBER 24 • ACTS 1:6-11

You Will Receive Power

JUSTIN S. HOLCOMB

MANY MEN RESONATE with the idea of having power. Think of all the movies that have powerful men at the center. These movies do well at the box office because they fulfill our desire for raw, physical power, the ability to accomplish something great no matter what kind of obstacles block our way.

This desire is reflected in the question that Jesus's disciples posed in Acts 1:6. The "kingdom" they were interested in was one of political and military power. During the time when these verses were written, the power of the Romans had dominated the Jewish world for many decades. But Israel had been occupied before, and the last time this had happened, a group of Jewish rebels had thrown out the invaders by force. The disciples wondered if Jesus was planning something just as heroic, something that would show them and the world the kind of stuff they were made of.

Fortunately, Jesus's vision of power was of a different sort. They would "receive" power, but it wasn't power for political dominance, military conflicts, or fistfights. It was the power of the Holy Spirit—God dwelling within them and transforming them. And part of this power meant being equipped to be witnesses (v. 8).

Witnessing can sound intimidating or even undesirable. But later in Acts, it becomes apparent that witnessing means being changed by God and being able to direct other people to the source of that change. In chapter 4, a crowd of listeners is astounded when they hear the witness of Peter and John, who are known to be "uneducated" and common men, but who speak with "boldness" (4:13). The fact that Peter and John overcome challenges like a lack of education (and, doubtless, their fear of public speaking!) is a testimony in itself—that God enables people of all sizes, backgrounds, ages, and temperaments to do what they otherwise cannot or will not do.

The movies with raw, physical power emphasize being strong, daring, young, or handsome, and for those who don't meet those criteria, it's easy to feel shut out. But the comfort of the power of the Holy Spirit is that it begins not with our natural abilities but with looking outside of ourselves. Just as a witness in a courtroom is most powerful when he is describing truthfully the events that he has seen or heard, the followers of Jesus are given power to speak of the transformation that God has worked in them.

SEPTEMBER 25 • ACTS 2:22-24

The Trustworthiness of Jesus Christ

JUSTIN S. HOLCOMB

AIR TRAVEL IS, by far, the safest way to travel. There are famous exceptions, of course. But they are famous because they are exactly that, the grand exceptions. By and large, 99.99 percent of all pilots succeed in bringing their passengers safely to their destination. We willingly entrust our lives to these pilots because they are required to have a rigorously proven track record before they fire up that jet engine with hundreds of people on board.

In Acts 2:22–24, Peter is making a similar claim about Jesus. He is saying that Jesus can be trusted. But this claim is not based on mere sentiment. It is based on a past track record. It's based on personal history. And there is one past deed in history that proves that Jesus is wholly and completely trustworthy: the resurrection.

For Christians, resurrection isn't just a way of expressing a spiritual truth. We believe that, in the first century, a man actually physically died, was buried in a tomb for three days, and then actually physically was raised back to life, never to die again.

If this really happened, it means that Jesus's claims about himself are trustworthy—that he can forgive our sins (Luke 5:24), that his death was not fruitless but was a ransom for many (Mark 10:45), and that in him we

326

see God himself (John 14:9). These claims are not just something to read about and nod in agreement with. Believing them changes everything. It means that, even though we may always struggle with sins we can't conquer, or a past that comes back to plague us, or disease and death, God is bringing a different reality to light.

Christianity doesn't stand or fall on subjective feelings or pragmatic how-tos, but rather on facts of history. There is no middle ground with what Peter is saying here. He is appealing to facts of history as a foundation for his audience to repent of sin and have the assurance that Jesus is able to save them. For people of the past, flying in an airplane was something one could only imagine. In the same way, Jesus underwent something that seemed impossible in order to show that his claims are by far the safest way to travel.

His resurrection paves the way for all those who trust him to look forward to a resurrection like his.

It all stands or falls on the resurrection. Do you believe it?

SEPTEMBER 26 · ACTS 4:23-31

Spirit-Filled Boldness

JUSTIN S. HOLCOMB

IN THE UNITED STATES, we have a love affair with safety. We collectively spend millions of dollars each year on home security systems to protect our living spaces. Many of us carry firearms that provide a sense of personal security. We look for the neighborhoods with the lowest crime rates and the cars with the highest safety ratings. Safety is *the* priority.

Who can blame us? What's so great about danger—coming home to a burglary, careening toward another car—especially if you can prevent it?

What makes Acts 4 so interesting is that the first followers of Jesus found themselves in just those kinds of gut-wrenching, uncontrollable situations that everyone tries to avoid. It probably never occurs to us that Christ's disciples had lived ordinary, quiet lives up until that point. Some even had families (1 Cor. 9:5). Now, for the first time, they were drawing attention to themselves. Instead of being good citizens, they were antagonizing the authorities and were being beaten and thrown into jail. But as they saw it, they were simply living in obedience to God.

Notice their response to what must have been a confusing and frightening dilemma. They did not complain, protest, or curl up in a ball of self-preservation. Rather, they prayed that God would continue to boldly work through them so that his mission could move forward. Since this Spirit-filled boldness was what led to their friends being put into custody in the first place, you might think they would tone down this type of praying, but that's not what we see. They don't seem to be thinking about themselves at all. Instead, they are okay with the pain that is part of helping to bring about God's plan.

Jesus himself repeatedly, deliberately, risked his safety during his ministry, and finally endured torture and death. He did so for the sake of "the joy that was set before him" (Heb. 12:2), the salvation of God's elect from every tribe, tongue, and nation (Rev. 7:9). The Christians who continue his mission in Acts 4 are able to pray for the same boldness because they have had a glimpse of the same joy.

Boldly living for God and others will oftentimes place you on a collision course with those who oppose him. But the staggering irony of Christianity is that if you truly want to know life, you have to be willing to lay it down (Matt. 16:25).

Are you willing to have true life?

SEPTEMBER 27 · ACTS 6:8–7:60

Stiff-Necked People

JUSTIN S. HOLCOMB

STEPHEN'S MARTYRDOM poignantly illustrates the two kinds of people in Acts: those who are led by the Holy Spirit, and those who resist him. In the first part of chapter 6, Stephen was chosen by the apostles to be a servant in the church precisely because he was full of faith and the Holy Spirit. After refuting several Jewish challengers, he was brought before the religious authorities, whereupon he criticized them for their resistance to the same Holy Spirit who was guiding his ministry.

In his witness to the Jewish leaders, Stephen drew their attention to what the Spirit did in the Old Testament and how their forefathers had continually resisted God's plan for them. He wanted the leaders to see themselves in the sordid history of God's people, and to realize that even now they might be wrong about God's plan for them. But just like their forefathers, these leaders dug in their heels and refused to listen to God's word. In Acts 7:51, Stephen summarized why this was the case: They behaved this way because they simply would not follow the lead of the Holy Spirit. They were "stiff-necked."

Stephen's listeners, who were from an agrarian economy, would immediately have understood this phrase. If a farm animal was needed to do a task it didn't want to do, how would that animal respond? It would stiffen its neck. The muscles would tighten in resistance and make the farm work difficult or impossible. Stephen was saying not only that God had given his work to different people but that the Jewish authorities had only themselves to blame for this.

Stephen's martyrdom is a sobering warning to all of us. Remember, these men were supposed to be *God's* men, and they were fully convinced that they were doing God's will. If you are wondering at this point, "How can I know that I am being led and filled by the Spirit?" you might start by asking God to empower you to do the opposite of what these men did. Ask to see in your life what Paul described as the fruit of the Spirit: "Love, joy, peace, patience, kindness, goodness, faithfulness, gentleness, self-control" (Gal. 5:22–23). This fruit is seen in the person who is willing to repent when confronted with sin. It also is seen in the person who values truth and love more than safety, and who can pray for his enemies even as they kill him for it (Acts 7:60).

The Lord Is Mighty to Save

JUSTIN S. HOLCOMB

MANY OF THE STORIES in Acts illustrate the importance of being willing to be led by the Spirit. This is especially important when it comes to evangelism.

You would probably agree that evangelism can be frustrating. We are frustrated with our lack of courage or the lack of response from our hearers. We can be frustrated when opportunities seem to be lacking or when we simply don't know what to say when someone throws us a theological curveball. We can also be frustrated because we don't know how to get started without making it awkward or embarrassing.

These feelings are to be expected: evangelism is hard! But we can find comfort in Acts 8:26–40 because it shows us the "bigger picture" of evangelism. First, it shows that evangelism isn't something that we necessarily have to plan out and execute successfully; it depends on the leading of the Spirit. We see that Philip received an explicit command from God to go to a certain location because there was someone whom God had chosen to hear the good news about Jesus. We might not hear an audible voice from God, but we can expect the Spirit to lead us. Perhaps our prayer could be something like this: "God, would you bring people into my life today who need to hear your good news and are open and willing to respond?" You might be surprised at how often God is pleased to answer this prayer.

Second, it is important to remember that God is working even before we ask. We know that he "desires all people to be saved and to come to the knowledge of the truth" (1 Tim. 2:4), and we see that God is clearly in control of saving those whom he has called. If anything is obvious from this text, it is that this was no chance encounter. God had a plan to save this Ethiopian official, and Philip was the agent whom he used to bring that plan to pass.

Being open to God's leading isn't a guarantee that evangelism will be easy or automatic; elsewhere in Acts, although the disciples were filled with the Holy Spirit, their audience turned against them and drove them out of the city (Acts 13:50–52). But it does mean that we don't need to feel pressured to perform a certain way or get certain results. God will settle the who and the how.

This should bring us great comfort. God is saving people in our day. He is mighty to save, and when he saves, all glory goes to him alone, and we receive the joy of knowing that we've been used by God.

SEPTEMBER 29 · ACTS 9:1–8

Scandalous Grace

JUSTIN S. HOLCOMB

SAUL'S CONVERSION (after which he was known as Paul) is one of the most breathtaking biblical examples of God's grace, because Paul neither knew that he needed grace nor wanted it. Up until this point in Acts, he had been growing gradually more militant against Christians. In chapter 7, he held the coats of those who stoned Stephen (Acts 7:58). In chapter 8, we see him gaining power of his own and "entering house after house," like the Gestapo, searching for evidence of this new Christian "heresy" (Acts 8:3). And then, in the beginning of chapter 9, he comes up with a new plan to legitimize hunting Christians outside the city limits (Acts 9:1–2). Paul didn't just resist the gospel; he took a perverse pleasure in destroying it.

But then God stepped into Paul's life and abruptly cut off what was an increasingly out-of-control downward spiral. Just as Paul had shattered the lives of many of God's people, God shattered Paul's pride and self-sufficiency, forcing him to seek as a blind supplicant the mercy of the people he hated. But while Paul's punishment of believers had been meant to destroy, God's punishment of Paul was meant to heal. It was the kind of loving punishment described by the prophet Hosea: "Come, let us return to the LORD; for he has torn us, that he may heal us; he has struck us down, and he will bind us up" (Hos. 6:1). And the lesson stuck. For the rest of his life, Paul dedicated himself to building up rather than tearing down.

Why God intervened with Paul is a mystery; God doesn't always explain his reasons for doing what he does. But he has revealed, from cover to cover in the Bible, that he *loves* to show up in unexpected places with unexpected mercy. He loves to shine the floodlight of his grace into the darkest corners of the world. He loves to shower his mercy and grace on the least deserving.

On people like Paul.

And people like . . . you and me.

Paul's downward spiral is easy to criticize, because hurting other people is probably the one sin that most Americans agree on (at least in theory). But there are other spirals—greed, pride, sexual sin, workaholism, self-indulgence, and self-centeredness. Some of them have innocent beginnings as love of family, or humanity, or God, but become twisted somehow. Most of them are easy to see in others but hard to see in ourselves.

If God can soften Paul's heart, he can soften ours. Ask him to reveal your sin and send his grace anew. God's merciful arm is never too short to reach you.

SEPTEMBER 30 • ACTS 10:34–43

A Gospel for All People

JUSTIN S. HOLCOMB

THE HEART OF this text is reconciliation. Reconciliation between radically diverse groups of people. Reconciliation that was necessary due to centuries of division and mistrust.

When the events of Acts 10:34–43 took place, a couple of millennia ago, non-Jewish people were coming to faith in Jesus, but it was hard for Jewish converts to Christianity to know what to do with this reality. They often believed that this new message about Jesus was only for Jewish people, or that non-Jewish converts had to become officially Jewish to be a part of this new faith. After all, hadn't God separated the Jews from all other people groups for a reason? Even though God had declared his love for all nations early in the Bible (Gen. 22:18), and the prophets had seen that God would one day be worshiped by people of every tribe and tongue (Dan. 7:14), seeing these words become a reality was a different matter.

In most places today, we don't see much of a separation between Jews and Gentiles, but if you take a minute, you can probably think of certain people whom you would rather not associate with. We often say we believe in diversity, and diversity is nice as a slogan. Slogans are easy to get behind, especially when they are kept at arm's length. Bumper stickers rarely demand much from us. But what about when "diversity" is sitting in your living room? Or sitting next to you at church? Or when "diversity" moves into your neighborhood? Or "diversity" marries your son or daughter? Or "diversity" asks something of you?

Peter's vision, which addressed the major issue of diversity in the first century, shows us how to deal with those situations. It doesn't involve feeling guilty if we aren't automatically delighted by things that are strange or different, but it shows us that God transcends our own little circles of race, behavior, personality, upbringing, politics, and even theology. Imagine what your church community would communicate to an onlooking world if it were radically diverse? If the only thing the members had in common was Jesus? It would communicate that Jesus is the true unifier. It would communicate that Christ and our allegiance to him runs so much deeper than superficial things that can divide us.

If we truly believe that the gospel is for *all*, we'll want to pursue relationships that, at times, might make some people around us question the company we keep. This is where the gospel has to lead us, just as it led Peter and the early church.

OCTOBER 1 · ACTS 13:44-49

Responding to Rejection

BRIAN J. TABB

GOD'S PLAN IS BIGGER than our personal setbacks. Initially, Paul and Barnabas enjoy a very favorable response to their ministry in Antioch in Pisidia. When the leaders of the synagogue invite them to offer a word of encouragement, Paul does not disappoint. He moves quickly through the Law, Prophets, and Psalms and powerfully articulates how God has fulfilled his promises in the death and resurrection of Jesus. The people beg them to return, and one week later "almost the whole city" gathers to hear them preach the word again (Acts 13:44). The stage is set for a citywide revival. But instead, the Jews revile and oppose the missionaries.

How might we have reacted to such rejection? Paul and Barnabas respond in a surprising way.

First, the missionaries are not intimidated but emboldened: "Paul and Barnabas spoke out boldly" (v. 46). Throughout Acts, boldness characterizes Jesus's witnesses, especially Peter and Paul (see 4:13, 31; 9:27–28; 28:31). Their boldness does not come from their strong personalities or personal resilience but from the Holy Spirit, who enables them to proclaim the truth powerfully whatever the situation.

Second, Paul and Barnabas do not take rejection personally. They do not seek to defend their reputations or nurse their bruised egos. Instead, they recognize that the Jews ultimately rejected God by thrusting aside his word (13:46).

Third, God's word orients and guides the missionaries even in rejection. They turn to the Gentiles because the Jews reject God's word (v. 46), but that doesn't mean that the Gentiles are Plan B. Rather, Jesus has commanded them to turn to the Gentiles to "bring salvation to the ends of the earth" (v. 47; quoting Isa. 49:6). Jesus is "a light for revelation to the Gentiles" (Luke 2:32). Jesus commissions the apostles as his witnesses "to the end of the earth" (Acts 1:8) and sets apart Paul for ministry to the Gentiles (9:15). Jewish opposition provides an opportunity for new, God-directed ministry among the Gentiles.

Fourth, God has appointed some to eternal life, who respond to the gospel with joy and saving faith (13:48). We must not give up when others reject or criticize us. Like Paul and Barnabas, we should continue to speak the gospel and trust that God will open hearts and grant faith.

Truth and Love

BRIAN J. TABB

THE INCLUSION OF believing Gentiles as full members of God's people was one of the most challenging theological and practical issues confronting the early church. Acts does not gloss over such difficulties but regularly highlights how believers worked through problems, resulting in the strengthening of the church and the continued spread of God's word.

Acts 15:1–35 unfolds in four main sections. First, Jewish Christians *disagree* over whether Gentile believers must keep the law and undergo circumcision to be saved (vv. 1–5). Second, church leaders gather in Jerusalem to *debate* the issue and hear testimony from Peter, Barnabas, Paul, and James (vv. 7–18) concerning God's saving work among the Gentiles that accords with Old Testament prophecy. Third, the apostles and elders *decide* not to trouble Gentile believers but to write a letter to them with four requirements (vv. 19–29). Fourth, they send Paul and others to *deliver* this letter to Gentile believers in Antioch, Syria, and Cilicia (vv. 30–35).

The church's crucial decision at the Jerusalem council reflects an unflinching concern for both truth and love. The apostles and elders stress the *truth* that God saves Gentile believers in Jesus Christ and gives his Holy Spirit to them apart from works of the Jewish law, such as circumcision and food regulations. The four requirements that Gentiles "abstain from the things polluted by idols, and from sexual immorality, and from what has been strangled, and from blood" (v. 20) likely stress that these new believers must turn from their former practices of idolatry and immorality to serve the one true God (see 1 Thess. 1:9; 4:3–5). These stipulations may also recall the Old Testament regulations for resident aliens living in the midst of Israel (Lev. 17:7, 12, 15; 18:20). At the same time, these requirements on Gentile converts demonstrate *love* and sensitivity toward conscientious Jewish believers, preserving the unity of the body of Christ.

Conflict is inescapable in relationships among families, neighbors, coworkers, and churches. When we disagree over theological or practical matters with fellow believers, some of us tend to fight for what we perceive to be the truth, while others prefer to avoid conflict and quickly pursue harmony and love. The Jerusalem council illustrates that we must hold truth and love together when working through conflicts for the sake of greater unity in Christ and greater effectiveness in mission.

Confronting Injustice

BRIAN J. TABB

IN AMERICA, the sex industry enslaves thousands of women and children, bringing much gain to their owners. Three hundred years ago, the face of slavery was an African laborer on a Southern landowner's cotton plantation. Today, slavery is a sixteen-year-old immigrant in front of a pornographer's video camera, whose "services" are paid for by thousands of anonymous online viewers in the privacy of their dorm rooms and offices. Millions of men—including countless numbers who profess to follow Christ—are addicted to Internet pornography. Not only is this a serious personal sin (see 1 Cor. 6:18–20); it also perpetuates unjust exploitation of the disadvantaged, displaced, or desperate women and girls forced into sex slavery. This situation is demonic and offensive to God, but it persists because demand is so high and business is so good.

Paul confronted a similar sort of economically motivated slavery when he came to Philippi. He and his coworkers "were met by a slave girl who had a spirit of divination and brought her owners much gain by fortune-telling" (Acts 16:16). After this girl followed Paul around for many days, he became greatly annoyed or disturbed and then commanded the demonic spirit to come out of her. Jesus "went about doing good and healing all who were oppressed by the devil" (10:38), and Paul continued this work in the authority and power of Jesus.

The slave girl's deliverance from demonic oppression had economic and social implications. Paul's good deed in Jesus's name provoked a violent response from the girl's owners because they "saw that their hope of gain was gone" (16:19). They didn't care about the slave girl but simply about her economic value, and Paul's way of salvation was not good for the bottom line. They didn't hail Paul as a hero but unjustly beat and imprisoned him as a criminal for upsetting the status quo.

Later, when Paul and his companions arrived in Thessalonica, the locals accused them of turning the world upside down by proclaiming that there is another king, Jesus (17:6–7). Where Jesus is king, his followers love others and pursue truth and justice. Where money is king, its followers treat people as commodities and exploit them for financial gain. The gospel message is good news to the disadvantaged, the displaced, and the desperate, and it threatens to turn injustice and oppression upside down.

OCTOBER 4 · ACTS 20:33–35

Work to Live and to Give

BRIAN J. TABB

WHEN PAUL MEETS with the Ephesian elders for the last time, he reminds them of *what* he taught and *how* he lived. In Philippians 3:17, Paul says, "Brothers, join in imitating me, and keep your eyes on those who walk according to the example you have in us." Similarly in Acts 20, Paul illustrates with his life what he calls the church leaders to do. Paul appeals to his impeccable integrity, his constant hardships, and his tireless gospel teaching.

Verses 33–35 contain at least three important lessons about money and work. First, Paul declares, "I coveted no one's silver or gold or apparel" (v. 33). Advertisements constantly seek to make us want more than what we have, to desire (and buy) the latest and greatest smartphone, SUV, or shoes. The opposite of idolatrous covetousness is faith-filled contentment in God's provision for our needs (see Phil. 4:11–12). Paul does not long for what other people have and thus does not use ministry for personal gain.

Second, Paul works, so that he and his companions can live: "You yourselves know that these hands ministered to my necessities and to those who were with me" (Acts 20:34). The Bible commands able-bodied

Christian men to be gainfully employed and provide for their families (1 Thess. 4:11; 1 Tim. 5:8). Paul labors at his trade as a tentmaker so that he might not burden others but might offer a model for the church to imitate (Acts 18:3; 2 Thess. 3:7–10).

Third, Paul works so that he can give to others. He says, "In all things I have shown you that by working hard in this way we must help the weak" (Acts 20:35). Christians must come to the aid of those in need, including the poor, widows, and prisoners (Gal. 2:10; Eph. 4:28; 1 Tim. 5:3; Heb. 13:3). Generosity toward others is a reflex of grace, a response to the matchless generosity of God, who gave his own Son for us. We should work to live, work to give, and be content with what God has given us.

OCTOBER 5 · ACTS 22:1-21

A Changed Man

BRIAN J. TABB

PAUL'S CONVERSION from zealous persecutor to persecuted preacher was hugely significant for the early church. Paul recounts his remarkable transformation when he defends his conduct, his gospel, and his Gentile mission before a hostile Jewish crowd (Acts 22) and King Agrippa (ch. 26). Paul's testimony in 22:1–21 makes three main points: (1) Paul, like his opponents, had been a zealous persecutor; (2) Jesus intervened in Paul's life; (3) Paul has a new identity and a new calling to mission, whatever the cost.

First, *Paul, like his opponents, had been a zealous persecutor* (vv. 3–5). Here Paul seeks to build common ground with his audience and answer the false accusations that he is teaching and acting against the Jewish people, the law, and the temple (21:28). Paul speaks to the crowd in Hebrew, addresses them as brothers and fathers, and reminds them of his impeccable Jewish credentials. He reminds them of his elite education in the law and of his unmatched zeal for God, as seen in how he had persecuted Christians (see 22:19–20).

Second, *Jesus intervened in Paul's life* (vv. 6–11). Paul actively opposed Christians until the risen Lord Jesus appeared to him. The glorious light of Jesus not only blinded Paul's eyes; it also corrected his mistaken views of Jesus and overcame his sinful opposition to the Lord and to Christians.

Finally, *Paul has a new identity and a new calling to mission, whatever the cost* (vv. 12–21). The feared persecutor is now "Brother Saul" (v. 13), a baptized believer in Jesus. The Lord has called Paul to bear witness to everyone about what he has seen and heard and also to suffer for the name of Jesus (9:15–16; 22:15). Consequently, many former friends and allies in Jerusalem reject Paul and refuse to accept his testimony.

Paul highlights his way of life before Jesus, his personal encounter with Jesus, and his transformed life as a follower of Jesus. There is simply no explanation for the drastic change in Paul's life apart from Jesus appearing to him as the glorious, righteous, risen Lord. Paul's testimony challenges his audience to reevaluate their opposition to him and to his Lord so that they might be changed themselves by the saving power of God.

The testimony of your conversion may not be as dramatic as Paul's, but it can bring glory and honor to the Savior no less so than did his. So let us seize every opportunity to share what the amazing, transformative grace of God has done.

OCTOBER 6 · ACTS 26:18

From Darkness to Light

BRIAN J. TABB

MANY BELIEVE that humanity's greatest need is effective leadership, more resources, better health care, improved education, greater cooperation, or bolstered self-esteem. Such solutions assume that our fundamental problems are ineffective governance, poverty, disease, ignorance, intolerance, or depression. In his defense before King Agrippa, Paul offers important insight into humanity's plight and the full-orbed gospel solution.

The Bible offers a devastating diagnosis of our basic plight. People have willfully and repeatedly rebelled against God, broken his law, and worshiped created things rather than the glorious Creator. Humans revel in their freedom to live as they choose and do not realize that such "freedom" is in fact bondage to Satan that will ultimately lead to ruin. The gospel of Jesus Christ alone is the comprehensive solution to our desperate condition. Acts 26:18 highlights four crucial features of biblical salvation.

First, Jesus sent Paul "to open their eyes." God must give us spiritual eyes to see Jesus as true and glorious (see 2 Cor. 4:4–6). This happened dramatically and uniquely for Paul when the heavenly Lord appeared to him on the road to Damascus. Normally, God grants spiritual sight when people encounter the Lord Jesus through faithful gospel preaching (see Acts 16:14).

Second, genuine faith involves turning "from darkness to light and from the power of Satan to God." Acts 26:20 clarifies that unbelievers "should repent and turn to God, performing deeds in keeping with their repentance." We must change our fundamental allegiance from Satan to God and begin to live to please our new king, Jesus.

Third, we must "receive forgiveness of sins." Forgiveness means that God frees rebellious human beings from their massive guilt and punishment and removes the ultimate penalty for our sins.

Finally, believers receive "a place among those who are sanctified by faith." The glorious result of forgiveness and faith is a restored relationship with God, a new family among God's redeemed people, and a sure eternal inheritance. God did not send an economist, an educator, a doctor, a politician, or a psychologist to address humanity's greatest need. He sent a Savior, who atoned for our sins by dying in our place and then rose again to be our King forever.

OCTOBER 7 · ACTS 28:30-31

Obstacles and Opportunities

BRIAN J. TABB

ACTS CONSISTENTLY presents the obstacles and opposition that believers face as surprising opportunities to proclaim the gospel. Leading witnesses like Peter, Stephen, and Paul give powerful sermons and testimonies while they are interrogated, harassed, and persecuted. Paul declares in Acts

19:21, "I must also see Rome," but on the way he faces one obstacle after another, including arrests, plots, political wrangling, a storm, shipwreck, and a poisonous snakebite. When Paul finally reaches Rome, he is placed under house arrest and chained to the soldier guarding him (28:16, 20). However, amid these challenging circumstances, Paul welcomes all who come to him and continues to preach "with all boldness and without hindrance" (vv. 30–31). Notice three important truths in the closing two verses of Acts.

First, Paul views personal obstacles as opportunities to talk about the Lord Jesus. He may be chained and confined, but he is also commissioned to testify to the gospel of God's grace (20:24). God frequently delivers Paul from dangers and threats, preserving his life so that he may testify to the facts about Jesus in Rome (23:11). But the Lord also strengthens and sustains Paul in times of suffering (26:22). Even though he is innocent of all charges, Paul is not embittered by his long imprisonment but takes it as an opportunity to bear witness to the hope that he has because of Jesus (28:17–20).

Second, Paul keeps the main thing the main thing. Acts opens by re-counting how the risen Lord Jesus appeared to his disciples for forty days, "speaking about the kingdom of God" (1:3). The book concludes with Paul in Rome, "proclaiming the kingdom of God and teaching about the Lord Jesus Christ" (28:31). Paul continues Jesus's emphasis on the kingdom of God—God's sovereign rule over his people and his world, in fulfillment of his saving promises. He also teaches about "the Lord Jesus Christ." This title stresses that Jesus is both the promised Savior ("Christ") and the divine King ("Lord").

Third, God's word is not shackled even when his people are. Paul writes, "I am suffering, bound with chains as a criminal. But the word of God is not bound!" (2 Tim. 2:9). This is the point of Acts 28:31. Paul is under house arrest, and yet he preaches about God's kingdom and King Jesus boldly and without hindrance. God turns personal obstacles into gospel opportunities.

A Hardened Heart

ROBERT L. PLUMMER

IT'S NOT UNCOMMON for older Christians to sit around and reflect on how quickly the culture has abandoned biblical principles. "When I was a kid," an older man will say, shaking his head, "people could never have imagined that homosexual behavior would be celebrated publicly like it is today."

In Romans 1, Paul teaches that the hardness of human hearts not only is the cause of God's righteous judgment but can itself be a manifestation of that judgment. The apostle describes how people have failed to rightly honor God and instead have turned to worship created things. (If writing in our day, Paul would perhaps have mentioned the idolization of sex, money, and status rather than the worship of actual physical images.) In judgment for this idolatry, God releases persons from his restraining grace and allows them to pour headlong into their wicked passions, of which homosexual lust is just one manifestation. Alongside homosexuality is found "all manner of unrighteousness, evil, covetousness, malice, . . . envy, murder, strife, deceit, maliciousness," gossip, slander, hatred toward God, insolence, arrogance, boastfulness, evil inventiveness, disobedience to parents, foolishness, faithlessness, heartlessness, and ruthlessness (Rom. 1:29–31). In other words, rampant sin not only is a basis for *future* judgment but is itself evidence of God having "given over" persons, in *current* judgment, to their sinful passions.

Multiple implications flow from this truth:

- From a national perspective, perhaps we should stop warning about God's coming future judgment and realize that his judgment is already here. The shameless flaunting of God's righteous standards in our day demonstrates minds "given over" to sin.
- In this hostile cultural environment, we must resist the temptation to be ashamed of the gospel (v. 16).

- Because only a supernatural act of God can resurrect a sinner from his spiritual death, we must pray fervently for divine intervention in our dark world.
- If we are currently behaving in a way contrary to God's word and feel no tinge of conscience, alarm bells should sound. It is a fearful thing to find our hearts cold to God. If you yourself are in such a spiritual deep-freeze, get on your knees and plead, "Lord, do not give me over to my sinful idolatry, but rather soften my hard heart to respond afresh to the truth of the gospel of your Son!"

OCTOBER 9 · ROMANS 3:9-31

The "Bad News" of the Gospel

ROBERT L. PLUMMER

IMAGINE THAT, a few days after a checkup at the doctor, you receive an urgent call from him. He says, "You have diabetes, high blood pressure, and high cholesterol. You are on the verge of death, but if you follow my instructions, there may yet be hope. Starting today, eat a vegan diet, meditate for an hour every morning, and run ten miles every afternoon. Come back and see me in two weeks."

When you return to the doctor, you confess, "I agree that the things you prescribed are good, but I am incapable of doing them."

"Excellent!" he replies. "Now you know why you must take these pills I am going to prescribe. They will do for you what you cannot do for yourself."

In Romans, Paul shows us that one of the main functions of God's law is similar to the impossible (but good) demands of this doctor. In Romans 3:20, the apostle writes, "For by works of the law no human being will be justified in [God's] sight, since through the law comes knowledge of sin." The blazing purity of God's holy law, when displayed next to a human heart, reveals our sin-stained condition. No person can ever say, "God,

I've kept your law perfectly, so I deserve to be welcomed into your presence." Rather, one of the main purposes of God's law is the "knowledge of sin" (v. 20). In other words, the law shows us how sinful we are, revealing our spiritual bankruptcy, so that we turn away from ourselves and look to Christ for our righteousness.

When you hear someone declare your desperate need for God's grace, does that statement resonate with you? Or, does it seem a bit exaggerated? The more time you spend in God's word, the more accurately you will perceive your sinfulness, and the more you will treasure the saving solution to your sinfulness—Christ.

Will you "open the books" of your life to a full spiritual audit by God's word? When that audit comes back with the bright red words "Spiritually Bankrupt" stamped on it, don't despair. As one pastor said, the bad news of the gospel is that you are far worse than you could ever imagine, but the good news is, you are more loved than you could ever hope to be. Christ lived the perfect life that you failed to live, and died the death you deserved to die. And now, by faith in him, you have a right standing before God (i.e., a righteousness) that you never could attain on your own.

OCTOBER 10 · ROMANS 4

God's "Long View" on Your Life

ROBERT L. PLUMMER

IN ROMANS 4, Paul presents Abraham as a model of the kind of faith we should have in God's Son, Jesus Christ.

Paul leaves no room for flaws in Abraham's faith. He says that Abraham "did not weaken in faith when he considered his own body, which was as good as dead (since he was about a hundred years old), or when he considered the barrenness of Sarah's womb. No unbelief made him waver concerning the promise of God, but he grew strong in his faith as he gave glory to God" (Rom. 4:19–20).

But didn't Abraham fail to believe God's promise and instead take Sarah's handmaid, Hagar, as his concubine, fathering Ishmael through her

(Gen. 16:1–6)? Didn't Abraham even laugh in unbelief when told that he would bear a son in his old age (Gen. 17:17)?

What we find in Romans 4 is not a "spin job" on Abraham's life. Instead, we have Abraham's life from God's final gracious perspective. Abraham was a flawed man—a sinner—as Paul understood himself and all humans to be (Rom. 3:23). All people "stumble in many ways" (James 3:2), but as we look at a man's whole life, does he keep turning away from sin? Does he keep looking to God as his only source of righteousness? Does he live a life of continual repentance and faith?

Over a Christian's lifetime, God progressively shapes him into the image of Jesus Christ. We can easily lose sight of this long-range plan and get mired in our daily failures. We must remember the Lord's gracious perspective on his servants' lives. God accepts us fully because of Jesus's righteousness (2 Cor. 5:21). When we do practical acts of righteousness, we should have a holy self-forgetfulness about them (Matt. 6:3; 25:37–29), realizing that God's Spirit is prompting and empowering us. These acts of righteousness are *evidences* of our filial status, not the *cause* of it.

Are you currently drowning in the remembrance of your own failures? God's plan and perspective on your life is much grander. He looks into eternity past and sees his saving love set on you before he created the world (Eph. 1:4). He looks into eternity future and sees you glorified, freed from sin in his presence, clothed in robes washed "in the blood of the Lamb" (Rev. 7:14). Even now, he leads you gently as a shepherd, not driving or scolding you. One day, when Jesus says to you, "Well done, good and faithful servant" (Matt. 25:21), the nagging memory of your failures will dissipate like the morning fog, and you will sit down to dine with Abraham, Isaac, and Jacob (Matt. 8:11).

Rejoice in Suffering

ROBERT L. PLUMMER

CHRISTIAN JOY in suffering is a repeated theme in the New Testament. In Romans 5:3–4, for example, Paul declares, "We rejoice in our sufferings, knowing that suffering produces endurance, and endurance produces character, and character produces hope." As we consider Paul's reflections on suffering in Romans 5, we are both edified and encouraged.

The suffering that Paul mentions here is not necessarily persecution for one's Christian faith. Although it is true that "all who desire to live a godly life in Christ Jesus will be persecuted" (2 Tim. 3:12), here Paul speaks of suffering quite generally. Thus, suffering in Romans 5 refers to any unpleasant effects of this broken world—illness, financial disaster, betrayal, emotional trauma, psychological struggles, or physical pain.

We do not rejoice in suffering because we are masochistic or because we stoically deny the heart-wrenching realities of suffering. Rather, we rejoice in suffering because we believe that a loving and sovereign God works behind and through these trials for our good and his glory.

Specifically, Christians affirm that suffering in our lives (overseen by the sanctifying presence of the Holy Spirit) produces "endurance," which could also be translated as "perseverance" or "steadfastness" (Rom 5:3). Over time, this endurance settles down into proven Christian character (v. 4).

As we witness the transformation God brings into our lives through suffering, we have hope. This hope is not a "pie in the sky" hope but a forward-looking confidence that the one who has begun to change us now will one day glorify us in his presence. Thus, with Paul, we can "rejoice in hope of the glory of God" (v. 2).

Have you ever known a great man of God? Think about his life. Did he perhaps go through some extreme or extended time of suffering?

If you want to become "a man after God's own heart" (see 1 Sam. 13:14), it will likely come not through extended times of prosperity but through suffering. Have you been going through hardships with a critical or despairing attitude? Hold onto God's truth, so that, with Paul, you can honestly say, "I rejoice in my sufferings."

OCTOBER 12 · ROMANS 6

A Changed Life

ROBERT L. PLUMMER

IN NATIONAL POLLS, the percentage of persons in the United States who identify themselves as "Christian" is amazingly high. And yet, when pollsters dig deeper into the lives of these self-identified "Christians," they discover that a much smaller percentage of them actually seek to follow Jesus as Lord. The term "Christian" has become so watered down that genuine Christians are constantly having to come up with new monikers or qualifying adjectives to identify "real" Christians—words or phrases such as "believers" or "evangelical" or "Bible-believing" or "regenerate."

For Paul, the idea that a person could be a genuine follower of Jesus Christ and continue to live an unchanged life was a theological impossibility. "How can we who died to sin still live in it?" Paul asks (Rom. 6:2). In verses 3–4, Paul avows that our saving trust in Jesus (expressed in baptism) unites us to our Savior's death by faith. In believing union with Christ's atoning death on the cross, we are freed from both the power and the penalty of sin. In believing union with Christ's resurrection, we experience power to live changed lives in the new age he has inaugurated.

If you were dragged into court and charged with being a Christian, would there be enough evidence to convict you? The question, though hackneyed, captures an essential Pauline and biblical teaching: genuine Christians look different because of their relationship with Jesus. Neither Paul nor the rest of Scripture denies the Christian's ongoing struggle with sin (1 John 1:8). Yet, fighting against sin is different from "living in sin" (Rom. 6:2). In Romans 6, Paul reflects the teaching of Jesus, who said, "Not everyone who says to me, 'Lord, Lord,' will enter the kingdom of heaven, but the one who does the will of my Father who is in heaven" (Matt. 7:21).

Keeping the End in Mind

ROBERT L. PLUMMER

EVERY SEMESTER, college students endure a time of testing: final exam week. They stay up late, eat poorly, and spend countless hours studying. One reason they can endure this trial is because they know their sufferings are temporary. Final exam week will end. Christmas or summer vacation is coming—with more sleep, more free time, and better food!

God has provided hope for suffering Christians by repeatedly reminding us in Scripture of our final destination. In Romans 8, Paul paints such a portrait as an antidote to despair. Paul teaches the following truths:

- We should expect suffering. We live in a broken world. Note, in verse 18, Paul does not say, "*If* you suffer . . ." The apostle assumes the reality of suffering for all people.
- Our sufferings are temporary. We live in "this present time" (v. 18), but a future age of glory, free from suffering, is assured.
- Our sufferings are inconsequential in light of the coming glory (v. 18). We should note that this shocking statement comes from a man who had experienced intense periodic suffering (2 Cor. 11:24–27), as well as an ongoing chronic suffering (2 Cor. 12:7). If you are a Christian, one day, in God's presence, you will experience no sickness, no desire or ability to sin, no death, and perfect joy, not just for a day, or five years, or eighty years, but for trillions and trillions of years—for eternity.
- Creation is our teacher, reminding us of the expectant attitude we should have (Rom. 8:19). Through things like tsunamis, earthquakes, droughts, and death, creation is crying out, "Things are not like they should be! Things are broken! God needs to fix things!" And he will! (v. 18).
- God's renewal plan includes not just humanity but the entire created order (v. 21).

- God has given us the Holy Spirit as a foretaste and promise of the coming glory (v. 23).

Christian, have you become discouraged in the face of suffering or perhaps just in the monotonous routine of your life? Ask for God's grace to walk with a consciousness of the coming glorious age. Read Romans 8 with fresh eyes, asking the Lord to plant these truths deep in your heart and mind.

OCTOBER 14 · ROMANS 9:6–23

Election and Predestination

ROBERT L. PLUMMER

IF YOU WANT to hear a heated debate, ask a diverse group of Christians to discuss the terms "election" and "predestination."

"It's not fair for God to choose some people and not others!" someone will protest.

Another will say, "I don't believe that! I believe God loves everyone and gives everyone a chance to be saved!"

Adding fuel to the fire, another Christian might chime in, "Maybe you don't believe in election because you're not elect!"

Before we find ourselves in such a theological debate, let's remember some basic interpretive assumptions we should share as we come to Romans chapters 9–11.

First and foremost, the words of the inspired apostle Paul have authority in these matters. Every creed, faith statement, confession, or personal belief must be judged by the written word of God. Not only the words of Scripture but the underlying concepts intended by the apostle must be adopted. In other words, people can define the words "election" or "predestination" in many different ways. But, finally, in Romans, we must submit our conceptions of election and predestination to Paul's exposition of these concepts.

If the Bible affirms two apparently contradictory concepts, then we must do the same. We cannot allow one concept to trump the other. So, for example, the Bible affirms God as completely sovereign over all things (Matt. 10:29), yet the Bible also teaches that God is never the author of temptation or sin (James 1:13). We must affirm such truths as a biblical paradox.

We must never use the truths of Scripture in ways that the biblical authors do not. So, for example, while the authors of Scripture affirm the believer as completely righteous in God's presence (Rom. 3:22), no biblical author teaches that it does not matter how Christians actually behave (Gal. 5:16–24). Right truths wrongly applied can result in serious distortion or even heresy.

With these interpretive ground rules in place, read afresh through Romans 9–11. What truths does Paul affirm about election and predestination? How does the apostle himself define "election" and "predestination"? Why is Paul discussing those concepts at this point in his letter? What does he want his original audience to believe or do? Where do your own beliefs (perhaps often unconscious beliefs) not match up with Paul's teaching? Where is God calling you to a deeper trust in him and his revealed word?

OCTOBER 15 • ROMANS 10:5-21

Every Christian an Evangelist

ROBERT L. PLUMMER

DID YOU HEAR about the young businessman who was delivering such an amazing PowerPoint presentation that the CEO stopped him to inquire, "What must I do to be saved?"

No? Perhaps then you've heard about the suburban dad who manicured his lawn so excellently that the neighbors flocked to his home, saying, "We come here today to declare that we also have become worshipers of your God!"

The absurdity of these two imaginary scenarios reminds us of the necessity of a Christian's verbal witness. People are not going to become Christians simply by watching us. They need to hear a word of proclamation about (a) God as holy Creator and Judge, (b) human sinfulness and the coming judgment, (c) Jesus's perfect life and atoning death, and (d) the need to respond in repentance and faith.

In Romans 10:14–15, Paul asks these searching questions: "And how are they to believe in him of whom they have never heard? And how are they to hear without someone preaching? And how are they to preach unless they are sent?"

Indeed, the answer to Paul's questions is obvious: people will not hear and believe the gospel unless someone announces it to them. God has ordained the verbal proclamation of his servants as the instrument for the spread of his gospel.

Someone will object, "Didn't Jesus say people will know we are his followers by the way we love one another?" Indeed he did (John 13:35). But he also said, "What I tell you in the dark, say in the light, and what you hear whispered, proclaim on the housetops" (Matt. 10:27). Jesus also taught, "The gospel must . . . be proclaimed to all nations" (Mark 13:10).

"I just don't feel comfortable talking about spiritual stuff," someone will object. "Can't I just invite my friends to church?"

Inviting people to church is good, but if you are not personally sharing with lost persons about God's love in Jesus Christ, then you are missing out on one of life's greatest joys. And, more fundamentally, you should ask yourself, "Am I being obedient to the Lord's instructions to make his glorious gospel known?"

OCTOBER 16 · ROMANS 11

A Father's Loving Warnings

ROBERT L. PLUMMER

IN ROMANS 11:22, Paul warns, "Note then the kindness and the severity of God: severity toward those who have fallen, but God's kindness to you, provided you continue in his kindness. Otherwise you too will be cut off."

"Be cut off"? That sounds like we can lose our salvation!

But don't forget that this warning comes in the same letter that contains "the golden chain of salvation"—Romans 8:29–30. There we read that a person who is foreknown and predestined by God to salvation will certainly respond and be justified, and the justified believer can be certain of his final glorification. Final salvation is assured!

Some Christian traditions emphasize the promises of Scripture that say Christians can never lose their salvation (e.g., John 10:28; Rom. 8:29–30; Phil. 1:6). Others emphasize the warnings of Scripture, calling fellow believers to guard themselves against the danger of apostasy (Matt. 24:10; Luke 8:13; Heb. 6:4–6). Rather than simply choosing a side and throwing proof texts at the other side, a mature Christian understanding must hold together both the promises and the warnings in Scripture—affirming both as fully true and edifying to the believer.

In fact, a warning and a promise do not necessarily contradict each other. For example, if you are teaching your daughter to ride a bike, you may say, "If you pull out into the street without looking both ways, you are going to get hit by a car and die!" At the same time, you tell your timid daughter, "Daddy's right behind you. You're going to be fine." You know that you would dive on the concrete to prevent your daughter's bike from going in front of a car. You sternly warn your daughter, even as you assure her that she is completely safe.

How much more do the warnings in Scripture come from a perfect heavenly Father who is powerful and effective in rescuing his children!

OCTOBER 17 · ROMANS 12:9–21

Sweet Revenge?

ROBERT L. PLUMMER

REVENGE SELLS. In fact, a common plotline in movies geared toward men is a heroic character enacting revenge. As we watch the story unfold, we delight to see the enemies blown up, shot, drowned, or pummeled.

One reason that we love such movies is that we love to see justice. The world is filled with injustice. We experience it daily. Our wife does not respect us. Our children do not obey us. Our boss promotes an incompetent coworker. A church member spreads malicious gossip about us. Someone breaks into our car and steals our computer. Oh, how we sometimes wish we could see people get what they deserve!

The Bible does not deny the realities of this world. We are surrounded by injustice. But in this fallen world, Christians must look to God as the ultimate Judge who will set right all wrongs. Paul instructs, "Repay no one evil for evil . . . never avenge yourselves, but leave it to the wrath of God, for it is written, 'Vengeance is mine, I will repay, says the Lord'" (Rom. 12:17, 19). King David gives us an example of such trusting restraint; he prayed for God to enact justice against Saul (Psalm 54), but he showed supernatural self-control when given the opportunity to enact vengeance himself (1 Sam. 24:1–7; 26:1–12).

Paul says we are never to enact vigilante justice, but to look to the government (police, courts, military) as God's method for dealing with injustice in society (Rom. 13:1–7). The state "bears the sword" as God's servant (v. 4).

Because human governments often fail to enact justice consistently and fairly, we must continually look to God as our ultimate vindicator. Life is not fair. We will die having never seen many injustices set right. Yet we can be sure of this: One day we will stand before our all-powerful and good King. On that day, every injustice ever committed will be either (1) justly punished or (2) declared forgiven through Christ. In our longing for justice, let us, like God, desire our enemy's repentance more than his destruction (Ezek. 33:11).

OCTOBER 18 · ROMANS 13:1–7

God on Government

ROBERT L. PLUMMER

GOD, IN HIS COMMON GRACE, has created two institutions for the ordering of society: marriage and government. Although many marriages are characterized by bitterness, unfaithfulness, and misery, that fact does not deny the essential goodness and necessity of the *institution* of marriage. Likewise, the world's political scene has many examples of corruption, ineptitude, and abuse on the national, regional, and local levels. But such widespread dysfunction does not belie the basic necessity and goodness of the *institution* of government. We need not look far to see the dire consequences of having *no* functional government, so that ordinary citizens are unable to go about their normal lives for fear of being murdered by gangs.

In Romans 13, Paul says that because "there is no authority except from God" (v. 1), Christians should obey and respect the government. For example, Christians should pay their taxes (vv. 6–7).

As you consider Paul's words in Romans 13:1–7, is God perhaps calling you to repentance in your business dealings or personal financial matters? If we fail to obey the authorities God has placed over us, what are we implicitly teaching our wives and children about their proper response to authority? Can Christians ever disobey the government? Yes, but only in cases where the government commands them to disobey God. When God's word and civil laws contradict, Christians have no choice but to obey God, not the human authorities (Acts 5:29).

Many Christians in non-Western nations face ongoing governmental persecution, while Christians in the modern West have generally not had to endure such trials. With the rapid anti-Christianization of Western society, however, it is likely that you or your children will one day have to disobey civil laws to remain faithful to God. We need not fear, however, for Jesus will give us all we need in that day of testing. He said, "For they will deliver you over to councils, and you will be beaten in synagogues, and you will stand before governors and kings for my sake, to bear witness before them. . . . And when they bring you to trial and deliver you over, do not be anxious beforehand what you are to say, but say whatever is given you in that hour, for it is not you who speak, but the Holy Spirit" (Mark 13:9, 11).

Christian Unity

ROBERT L. PLUMMER

HAVE YOU EVER had a disagreement with other Christians about a certain doctrine or behavior? Imagine living in the first century and being able to obtain an authoritative word on a debated issue from an apostle of Jesus Christ. That should settle the matter, right?

In Romans 14:5, Paul surprises us by affirming the coexistence of multiple views on the debated issue of "special days." He writes, "One person esteems one day as better than another, while another esteems all days alike. Each one should be fully convinced in his own mind."

Each one convinced in his own mind? But, Paul, I wanted you to adjudicate on this issue and tell me who is right!

In Romans 14–15, Paul teaches us that while Christians must agree on the essentials of the faith, there are other matters about which Christians will continue to disagree until Jesus returns. In admitting this, Paul is not saying that these matters are unimportant. Nor is he denying there are, in fact, answers to our questions. Yet, Paul is saying, agreement on these matters should not be viewed as a first-order issue and certainly not as one essential for salvation.

There are some things that are "of first importance," such as the death, burial, and resurrection of Jesus Christ (1 Cor. 15:3). But not all matters are of primary significance. And when we find ourselves disagreeing with fellow believers over such matters, we must never allow our disagreement to overshadow our more fundamental union with Christ, in which we both share. Such love and welcome to one another is a great privilege as believers.

As family or friends listen to your words and observe your behavior, are they gaining a broad biblical vision of what is essential in the kingdom of God? Do you reflect the nuanced maturity of Paul in your theological judgments? Or, are you perhaps drawing circles of orthodoxy so narrow as to exclude anyone who does not think exactly like you?

Building Up Others

ROBERT L. PLUMMER

IN ROMANS 14-15, Paul addresses two groups within the early church. He refers to them as "the strong" and "the weak." Apparently, these two groups differed on whether Christians should eat certain foods and observe special days. From Paul's perspective, the strong rightly understood that observing special worship days (e.g., the Sabbath), as well as eating or abstaining from various foods, were really inconsequential matters. Yet, some weak (immature) Christians, because of the prior associations of these things in their pre-Christian lives, still viewed such things as problematic. Paul says that, in such cases, mature Christians have an obligation to act in the best interest of the immature—to help them not sin against their consciences, while hopefully eventually bringing them to a proper understanding on these issues.

God has wired most men to have a strong sense of right and wrong. Not surprisingly, men often do not hesitate to step out and make public judgments on what is right or wrong. We have a harder time with the category of "the morally inconsequential." In distorted glee, we can run over the "weak," eager to show that we are right.

Very few Christians in modern Western society are dealing with the same issues as these ancient Christians in Rome. When was the last time you worried about eating meat sacrificed to an idol, or observing the Jewish Sabbath? Yet we continue to face many inconsequential matters over which Christians disagree. Depending on the people involved, this list may include such things as viewing or listening to various forms of entertainment (movies, music), wearing certain attire or jewelry, getting tattoos, consuming alcohol in moderation, or participating in the public school system.

As we face such issues in our Christian communities, let us not too quickly take upon ourselves the mantle of "strong" or mature. Are we perhaps actually the "weak" or immature one, as we try to impose our views upon the broader community? Are we the ones who need to grow up in our faith?

And, if we really are the "strong," let us remember that the spiritual health of our brothers and sisters takes priority over the exercise of our own freedoms. Our goal should not be to win an argument but to edify other believers. Or, as Paul says, "Let each of us please his neighbor for his good, to build him up" (Rom. 15:2).

OCTOBER 21 · 1 CORINTHIANS 1:18–31

The Glorious Folly of God's Grace

KEVIN CAWLEY

HUMANS UNIVERSALLY know that things are not as they should be. And we universally long for a means of escape. As Paul addresses the church at Corinth, two predominant worldviews are pursuing salvation along two radically different lines: Jews look for salvation through the military conquest of a conquering king; Greeks seek wholeness through the elegant construction of words, ideas, and well-reasoned theses (1 Cor. 1:22).

Where do you look for redemption? What do you believe is lacking in you that, if you had it, would make you complete?

The message of Christianity proclaims salvation through the death of Jesus Christ. This stands in fundamental opposition to the controlling mindsets of our world and the natural inclinations of our hearts. The gospel of Jesus isn't merely counterintuitive; Paul tells us that, apart from its being the authoritative word of God, it is utter "folly" (v. 18).

This "folly" was the clear proclamation of "Christ crucified" (v. 23) for sinners. Though the death of Jesus for sinners is considered absurd by conventional experts (v. 20), Paul assures us that Jesus's death displays the wisdom and power of God (v. 24) and offers us wisdom, righteousness, sanctification, and redemption (v. 30).

By offering salvation through what the world considers foolish, God accomplishes two things. First, through the display of his gracious mercy and glorious power, he shames the conventional wisdom of a fallen world

(v. 27). Second, by saving sinners through the sheer work of his grace, God removes all pretense for human pride.

By removing our ability to boast in his presence, God gives us an extraordinary gift. He gives us freedom from the anxiety that results from our need to boast. And he gives us the security found in making Jesus the ground of our boasting (v. 31).

Discovering that Jesus is the only legitimate ground for boasting isn't just the way we find salvation—it is the way we endure suffering and look to the future hope of glory (Rom. 5:2–3). Moreover, it's the way we are strengthened throughout the course of the Christian life (Rom. 16:25).

Worship God for the folly of his grace! Walk in the folly of his grace! Endure suffering in the folly of his grace! Be strong in the folly of his grace!

OCTOBER 22 • 1 CORINTHIANS 2

What Does It Mean to Be a "Spiritual" Man?

KEVIN CAWLEY

WHAT THE CHURCH at Corinth needed was spiritual people. Unfortunately, the Corinthian church was glutted with people who fancied themselves to be spiritual but failed to understand what constitutes true spirituality.

There is no shortage of contemporary books and sermons outlining the particulars, principles, and process of "spirituality." However, this abundance of popular resources is incapable of providing any clarity or consensus on what spirituality even is, or what makes one "spiritual."

All of the problems Paul deals with in Corinth are spiritual problems. And the good news for Corinth and for us is that God gives us spiritual solutions. That is, he provides the glorious presence of his indwelling Spirit.

The makings of a spiritual person do not consist in the possession of religious knowledge, the practice of religious rituals, or even participation in a religious community. A spiritual person, at the most fundamental level, is one who has received the Spirit of God (1 Cor. 2:12).

Being filled with the Holy Spirit, a spiritual person is controlled by the mind of Christ (v. 16). A spiritual person is able to "judge all things" (v. 15). This means the ability to engage people and ideas with a critical mind but without a critical spirit. A spiritual person is discerning. A spiritual person understands the pervasive reality of grace in his own life and in the life of the church (v. 12).

To this end, a spiritual person understands that each member of the church possesses unique gifts freely distributed by God's grace (7:7); he can delight in the administration of other people's gifts without competition or comparison, because he knows that the same Spirit gives gifts to all (12:4). Finally, a spiritual person is shaped not only by *what* Paul came teaching—but by *how* Paul came teaching (2:1–5). Spiritual people have their identity rooted in the grace of God. They discern and model the grace of God and distribute the wisdom of God.

What the church today needs is spiritual men.

OCTOBER 23 • 1 CORINTHIANS 5

Passover, Purity, and the Passion of God

KEVIN CAWLEY

ALTHOUGH PAUL'S USE of spatial and relational words like "among" and "outside" in this passage may sound like an effort to prejudicially discriminate between "insiders" and "outsiders," his words beautifully illustrate God's passion for the purity of the church.

Unfortunately, in Paul's day and in ours, the language of love and tolerance is often weaponized in a way that hurts all parties involved. A member of the Corinthian church is involved in an incestuous relationship, and the congregation, for whatever reason, has been giving its approval (1 Cor. 5:1–2). The reason for the church's acceptance of this blatant sin is unclear. But for Paul, this is an issue of the purity of the church—as well as the passion for purity that should exist among those for whom Jesus was sacrificed (v. 7). Christian love and tolerance must be defined, not by cultural trends or shifting moral standards, but by who God is and how God loves.

Because the couple at Corinth were apparently hardened in their unrepented sin, Paul calls the church to the difficult work of loving them through church discipline. Paul identifies at least five aims of church discipline: discipline aims to expose the presence of unrepented sin (v. 2), warn concerning the destructive power of sin (v. 5), awaken repentance unto salvation (v. 5), protect and uphold the purity of the church corporately (vv. 4, 6), and preserve the public witness of the gospel (v. 1).

The hope of practicing church discipline—refusing to tolerate what God demands we refuse to tolerate—is not that we destroy a member of the church. Rather, the hope is that God will mercifully destroy their desire for rebellion and their appetite for sin.

Because Christ our Passover has been sacrificed for us, let us pursue purity—both individually and collectively—for the glory of his name.

How Singleness of Devotion Shapes Singleness and Devotion

KEVIN CAWLEY

PAUL'S FIRST LETTER to the Corinthians contains a section that is, without a doubt, the text of Scripture most often quoted at wedding ceremonies both Christian and secular. But 1 Corinthians 7:25–40, obviously, is not it! (But see chapter 13!) In fact, the likelihood of chapter 7 being read at any wedding is extremely low. But the degree to which this passage should shape our approach to marriage in general, as well as how we think about getting married and being married specifically, is tremendous.

Contemporary views of marriage, even within the church, range from hindrance to be avoided to right and entitlement to be demanded. Marriage for the Corinthians was much different. Marriages were arranged. Couples were engaged ("betrothed"; 7:25) at a very young age and entered marriage almost as soon as they entered puberty. But Paul's thoughts on marriage in these verses may have been as unpopular in his day as in ours: "I think that in view of the present distress it is good for a person to remain as he is. Are you bound to a wife? Do not seek to be free. Are you free from a wife? Do not seek a wife" (vv. 26–27).

Though all of Paul's life and teaching was certainly shaped by his expectation of the final "day of the Lord" (1 Cor. 5:5; 1 Thess. 5:2; 2 Thess. 2:2), it is likely that his instruction here was influenced primarily by the "present distress" within Corinth. History indicates a cataclysmic grain shortage in the region of Corinth during this time. Accordingly, Paul's comments probably involve giving direction about decision making in light of this existing crisis.

The historical moment facing the Corinthians should not cause us to miss the deeper import of Paul's apostolic exhortation. That is, Paul exhorts the Corinthians and us to orient the totality of our lives around our devotion to Jesus and his impending return. We must "live as if not . . ." (see 1 Cor. 7:29–31). Paul is saying that, whether we choose to marry or not, we must not let marriage—or anything—compromise the urgency of our devotion to the Lord. Christ must be our all (Col. 3:11).

OCTOBER 25 · 1 CORINTHIANS 8

Does Knowledge or Love Determine Your Dinner?

KEVIN CAWLEY

"THERE IS NO such thing as a unicorn!"

"There are no monsters in your closet!"

Statements like these are basic truths that we *know*—we have heard them since we were young, and they have done much to shape our behavior. The adult versions of these truisms are obviously more sophisticated, but our basic pattern in all of life is to embrace a premise and then develop practices that are consistent with it.

This is what the Corinthian Christians were doing with regard to the issue of eating meat that had been sacrificed to idols: "Idols aren't real!" they said. Or, "There is only one true and living God; any statue or object purporting to be another 'god' is just make-believe" (see 1 Cor. 8:4). With these true premises in place, they felt free to make sacrificial meat a part of their diet.

Paul had probably taught the Corinthians the truths that formed their "knowledge" concerning idolatry (vv. 1, 4). But Paul wants now to challenge them based on a deeper premise. What makes someone a Christian is not *what* they know, but *whom* they are *known by* (v. 3). *Jesus* makes you a Christian, not your great knowledge about spiritual matters. Being known by Jesus transforms us from the inside out. Whereas academic knowledge can make us arrogant, knowing Jesus makes us loving.

Of course, objects made by human hands are not gods. But some people don't possess this knowledge. Some are navigating their world by a different set of premises—different ethical and worldview landmarks and points of orientation (v. 7). Their consciences are shaped not by the transforming knowledge of God but by the premise that idols are real gods. If they see a fellow Christian eating meat that has been sacrificed to idols, it might lead them astray. Therefore, those who have a more secure relational knowledge of God (v. 3) should be willing to forgo controversial activities such as eating sacrificial meat rather than try to convince someone of the superiority of their "knowledge" about such matters (v. 13).

This is voluntary self-denial for the benefit of another. What Paul exhorts the Corinthians to do regarding this particular cultural issue is a small picture of the kind of self-denial Jesus offered on the cross for our benefit.

Do you know there is no such thing as an idol? What about the person with whom you are sharing a meal? How does love affect your menu choice?

OCTOBER 26 • 1 CORINTHIANS 10:23-33

Who Picks What We Eat for Dinner?

KEVIN CAWLEY

STROLL THROUGH almost any urban center and you will encounter an increasingly common phenomenon: an innovative Bohemian restaurant inhabiting the walls of what was once a place of worship. In the ancient world and in Corinth, however, places of worship *were* restaurants. Temples sacrificed animals. And temples sold the meat of sacrificed animals. What was sold in the market often came from the temples. It is understandable, then, that Paul now returns to the issue of meat sacrificed to idols, after already addressing it in chapter 8.

Though unwitting consumption of sacrificial meat is rarely a modern concern, we constantly encounter similar ethical dilemmas. How do we respond in potentially sticky situations? How do we apply the wisdom of the Spirit of God (2:6–16) and live as the "temple" of God (3:16)? How do we put into practice a passion to glorify God in all things (10:31) specifically when it comes to things like dietary choices? Can a Christian consume meat that has been offered in sacrifice to an idol? Well, it depends.

On the one hand, everything in the universe belongs to God (vv. 25–26). Therefore, Christians are free to eat whatever is offered to them. On the other hand, there are instances where a Christian eating meat sacrificed to an idol in the presence of an unbeliever could cause confusion. In both instances, Paul contends, our course of action is clear.

The key to eating meat or abstaining from eating meat rests not in the origin of the meat but in the spiritual good of the one who is serving it to you or with whom you are dining. The ethic of the New Testament often moves away from simple binary equations ("eat this; don't eat that") and instead bases moral decision making on the worship of God and the spiritual welfare of others. This is the essence of the Great Commandment applied to all our decision making (Matt. 22:36–40).

In all we do—eating, drinking, and everything (1 Cor. 10:31)—let us strive to orient all our actions in such a way that God is glorified through self-denying love of neighbor.

How to Take Communion

KEVIN CAWLEY

COMMUNION. THE LORD'S SUPPER. THE EUCHARIST. This sharing of bread and wine is a symbolic meal in which Christians remember the loving sacrifice of Jesus on behalf of sinners. The meal was instituted by Jesus as a celebration. In fact, the word "eucharist" simply means "to give thanks," reflecting the words Jesus spoke over the meal as he instituted it with his disciples (1 Cor. 11:24).

The Eucharist is a symbol—a reenacted drama—representing God's glorious plan of redemption. Therefore, the context in which we share this meal should be characterized by celebration, unity, and integrity. Though Paul's audience at Corinth and many churches today place communion within the context of a shared common meal, the purpose of the Eucharist is not sustenance but remembrance and celebration. And Paul reminds us that we should make a concerted effort to ensure that all participants in the Eucharist feel both welcome and unified.

Many things can jeopardize the unity of this celebration. Paul highlights two of them.

First, the Corinthians were organizing their meal in such a way that class divisions were highlighted by something as simple as when people were able to arrive for the celebration. Wealthier people in the church, who either didn't have to work or had flexible work schedules, could arrive earlier than the working class. Instead of waiting for everyone to arrive—making the Eucharist the central feature of the meal—these wealthy Christians made their appetites and their culinary enthusiasm the central feature. Consequently, latecomers found scant portions of food and wine. In fact, the wine that was supposed to symbolize Jesus's blood was apparently being used by the early arrivers to get drunk (v. 21)!

Second, while some in Corinth were mindlessly ignoring the needs of their poorer brothers and sisters, others were ignoring their own needs. Failing to "examine" oneself (v. 28) or "judge" oneself "truly" (v. 31) refers to the failure of certain people to see themselves as needing the grace of God represented in the bread and the wine.

The cure for divisions that threaten both corporate unity and individual spiritual health is to remember Jesus! The glorious Son of God, who offered himself as a sacrifice, mercifully pours out the grace of God to sinners without discriminating on the basis of race, gender, or economic class.

So, how should we take communion? Focused on Jesus! Meditating on his body and his blood. Together!

How Self-Pity and Self-Sufficiency Destroy the Body

KEVIN CAWLEY

THE CHURCH IS NOT a social club or a provider of philanthropic services. The church is nothing less than the body of Christ (1 Cor. 12:27). Paul highlights throughout this section the glorious reality that the church is not simply a collection of individuals but a living organism—a community arranged and assembled according to the loving purposes of God.

The Corinthian church, much like our churches today, struggled with division, disputes, competition, and jockeying for superiority among its members. The answer to this struggle is not the obliteration of identity through uniformity (v. 14) but an emphasis on the unity of the body through the work of the Spirit (v. 13).

The unity of the church is under the constant threat of two enemies: self-pity and self-sufficiency.

Self-pity tempts us to believe, "Because I'm not like them, I'm not useful." Paul lovingly exposes the emptiness of this thinking and the fallacy of its logic (vv. 15–18). Self-pity is *pride inverted*. In the church, we can look at others' gifts and esteem them to be more valuable than our own, leading us to reason, "I *deserve* to be valuable like that." Self-sufficiency is the opposite of self-pity. Self-sufficiency says, "Because you're not like me, you're not useful." (v. 21).

Both of these versions of pride compromise God's glorious design for the body and cripple its health and function. When we attempt to conform the church body to our own arrogant desires, the individual takes precedence over the community, and the church becomes deformed, resembling a single-celled organism more than a complex, divinely ordered body (v. 19).

God's glorious design for the church means that, instead of comparing and competing, we are empowered to care for one another (v. 25). Instead of demanding that our importance be acknowledged, or diminishing our importance, we can rest in God's sovereign apportionment of our gifting and our place in the body (v. 18). We can joyfully embrace our mission of spreading the fame of the Head of the body—the one from whom we grow (Col. 2:19) and the one who is preeminent over all things (Col. 1:18).

OCTOBER 29 · 1 CORINTHIANS 13

Future Hope and Present Love

KEVIN CAWLEY

THIS IS ONE of the most familiar chapters of the Bible, even for people unfamiliar with Christianity and the church. Stripped from its context, it is seen as a poetic meditation on love that is as humanly impossible as it is lyrically beautiful. But Paul never intended this section of his letter to function as a solitary meditation on romantic love. Instead, he placed this chapter within the broader context of his address to the Corinthian church.

The Corinthians were failing to embody love (1 Cor. 13:1–3). They were boasting in the power of their spiritual gifts and the intensity of their zealous devotion. They were deficient in using their gifts to embody the heart of God—flaunting them rather than using them to build up the body and serve one another in love (12:25–26). In contrast to the narcissism and selfishness of the Corinthians, Paul describes the nature and character of supernatural love (13:4–7).

We regularly find ourselves in the same predicament as the Corinthians. Focused on manifestations of the supernatural power of God or on our feelings of devotion to him, we miss the heart of love and therefore miss everything (see Paul's emphasis on "nothing"; vv. 2–3). The way to become loving people in the present, Paul contends, is to focus *now* on the *future* reality of the kingdom of God.

Demonstrating the loving care of a pastor (4:15), Paul is doing three things in 1 Corinthians 13. He elevates the vital role that love plays in the Christian life. He describes the essence of love. And he shows us the pathway to embodying the supernatural love he describes.

The first step down this pathway is to abandon the emotional patterns of children (13:11). Children will fight over utterly insignificant objects and ideas. Maturity, Paul contends, brings with it the emotional ability to put aside transient, insignificant fixations, and instead value what is supreme and significant. Paul's point is hardly subtle: spiritual children fight over things like tongues and prophecy; the spiritually mature focus on that which remains—love (v. 13).

The second, and ultimate, step to embodying supernatural love is to look to the future hope of the consummation of the kingdom of God. Presently, Paul notes, we see the future of God's glorious kingdom in a mirror (v. 12). Not only are mirrors dim, but they also present reality to us in a distorted, inverted, or inaccurate way. Paul is convinced that directing our hope to the day when we will see fully, know fully, and be known fully will enable us *now* to manifest the love that will be perfect and complete *then*.

OCTOBER 30 · 1 CORINTHIANS 15:50-58

The Mundane Application of Our Glorious Future Hope

KEVIN CAWLEY

THEOLOGY GIVES birth to doxology. That is, when we give ourselves to thinking about the person of God and meditating on his wondrous works, we cannot help but soar in worship and adoration. We see an example of this in the conclusion of Paul's letter to the church in Rome (Rom. 16:25–27). And we see it here in his letter to the church in Corinth.

In the beginning of this penultimate chapter, Paul rehearses the essence of the gospel (1 Cor. 15:1–4), confirms the numerous eyewitnesses of the resurrected Christ (vv. 5–11), declares the certainty and the power of the resurrection (vv. 12–34), and anticipates questions regarding the nature of resurrected bodies (vv. 35–50) and the bodily transformation of those who remain alive when Jesus returns (vv. 51–53). Quoting Hosea 13:14 as proof of the victorious power of the resurrection (1 Cor. 15:54–56), Paul bursts forth into praise: "Thanks be to God, who gives us the victory through our Lord Jesus Christ" (v. 57).

Considering the life-transforming, universe-altering, glorious new-creation power of Jesus, Paul's words of adulation are entirely fitting.

But what is also fitting is that Paul did not conclude his letter here. Life in the church at Corinth was characterized by immense transformation and serious struggles. Theology begets worship, to be sure. But worship produces and shapes our action. Paul's "therefore" (v. 58) illustrates that worship of God is not incompatible with or somehow "above" daily, practical obedience and seemingly mundane fidelity.

The details of *how* our present labor will be significant in the age to come (v. 58) are about as clear as *how* God will transform mortal bodies into immortal and imperishable (vv. 35–54). Like the transformation of our bodies, what *is* certain and clear to us is *that* our labor will not be in vain.

The Lord Jesus Christ conquered death and will share the fullness of his resurrection life with us in the new heavens and new earth. Therefore, be steadfast! Work with all the strength that God supplies (2 Cor. 9:8; 1 Pet. 4:11), knowing that your labor is not in vain (1 Cor. 15:58).

The God of All Comfort

JASON C. MEYER

IT IS HARD TO overestimate the importance of the word "comfort" in this passage. It occurs only thirty-one times with this meaning in the New Testament, and ten of those occurrences are found in this paragraph alone. Bible commentator Scott Hafemann rightly calls these verses the "paragraph of comfort."[11]

Men, this word is for you. If you prize strength, then you should prize this word. "Comfort" in contemporary English may sound soft, but "comfort" in Paul's day meant "to strengthen." A return to Paul's meaning would actually take us back to the original meaning of the English word, because it comes from the Latin root *fortis*, meaning to fortify or to strengthen.

Biblical comfort is divine deliverance. Humanity despairs in weakness when we are "utterly burdened beyond our strength" (2 Cor. 1:8). Comfort is a "but God" moment of divine intervention (see Eph. 2:4). Battered and broken souls find rest in the comforting shelter of his strength. Comfort moves the weak and weary from despair to doxology. Here is the paradigm: desperation (2 Cor. 1:8) brings dependence (v. 9), which leads to deliverance (v. 10) and then culminates in doxology or thanks (see v. 11).

Comfort is not just something God gives; it is something he *is*. To comfort is part of his character. He is called the "God of *all* comfort" (v. 3) and the God "who comforts the downcast" (7:6). When God's children are comforted, they too become comforters (1:4). God can use others to be the *face* of comfort (like Titus in 7:6), but God is still the *source* of comfort.

Men, cry out to the God of all comfort to come to you in your affliction. When you are comforted, become a comforter. Sometimes God's comfort rescues the believer out of affliction (2 Cor. 1:8–11), while at other times the comfort sustains the believer in the affliction so that they can "patiently endure" it (v. 6). Comfort is not a tranquilizer shot to numb the pain of affliction; it is a steroid shot that gives the strength necessary to push past the pain so that we can reach the finish line. Comfort is not the nap after the Thanksgiving turkey; it is the burst of adrenaline after the triple espresso at Starbucks.

Avoid the Devil's Ditches

JASON C. MEYER

PAUL ASSUMES that we know Satan's deceitful schemes: "We are not ignorant of his designs" (2 Cor. 2:11). Which raises a very big question: do we know what tricks the enemy of our souls has up his sinister sleeves?

Satan is an opportunistic opponent. He uses against us our tendency to fall into extremes. The Corinthians veered off into two different ditches. In 1 Corinthians, Paul rebuked them for the first ditch of not knowing when to *start* discipline. They had to deal decisively with the man caught in sexual immorality, or sin would spread like leaven (1 Cor. 5:1–7). In 2 Corinthians, however, Paul had to rebuke them for falling into the opposite ditch: not knowing when to *stop* discipline and *start* restoration (2 Cor. 2:5–11).

These texts highlight a common denominator in the designs of Satan. C. S. Lewis, in *Mere Christianity*, noticed the same pattern:

> He always sends errors into the world in pairs—pairs of opposites. And he always encourages us to spend a lot of time thinking which is the worse. You see why, of course? He relies on your extra dislike of the one error to draw you gradually into the opposite one. But do not let us be fooled. We have to keep our eyes on the goal and go straight through between both errors. We have no other concern than that with either of them.[12]

Men, avoid the devil's ditches! Keep your eyes on the path of life found in the gospel. It is paved with joys that are full and pleasures that last forever (Ps. 16:11). Satan knows that unforgiveness is one way to leave that path, and so he seeks to use it against us (2 Cor. 2:10). This issue is immensely important for men because anger is such a common struggle we share. Anger that lasts too long will cause the heart to spoil and go sour. Unresolved anger gives Satan an "opportunity"—a place (Eph. 4:27). Unresolved anger is like a room prepared for Satan's extended stay.

But faith gives him the eviction notice, because unforgiveness is unbelief. Unforgiveness acts as though someone else's sin is bigger than Christ's sacrifice. Faith takes the reconciliation accomplished at the cross and applies it to real-life wrongs. Men, do you have any open door of unforgiveness and unresolved anger in your life? Slam the door shut through faith and forgiveness.

NOVEMBER 2 • 2 CORINTHIANS 3

You Become Like What You Behold

JASON C. MEYER

"AND WE ALL, with unveiled face, beholding the glory of the Lord, are being transformed into the same image from one degree of glory to another. For this comes from the Lord who is the Spirit" (2 Cor. 3:18).

Ongoing transformation is part of a process that can be summed up in one word: Christlikeness. God has ordained that every Christian will be conformed to Christ's image (Rom. 8:29a). The rest of the verse explains why this will happen: so that Christ will be "the firstborn among many brothers" (Rom. 8:29b). In other words, God has ordained that Christlikeness will be the unifying factor in the family of God. We all must have a family resemblance to Christ, so that he will have first place in the family.

Our text here in 2 Corinthians shows *how* sanctification happens. If sanctification is Christlikeness, then the key question is, how does one become Christlike? Verse 18 of chapter 3 says we become Christlike *by beholding Christ*. In fact, seeing the glory of Christ is what converts us (4:6), sanctifies us (3:18), and glorifies us (1 John 3:2).

Why do we become Christlike by beholding Christ? Answer: we watch what we love, and as we watch we become like what we watch. For example, I did not have to be forced to watch Michael Jordan play basketball. It was natural because I loved what I saw. I wanted to be like him. So I watched him and I became like Mike. It probably goes without saying that I never came close to being as good as he was; my playing style became more like his, not my ability! And I was not alone. It became more common, in those days, to see kids on the basketball court with their tongues sticking out—they were trying to be like Mike!

If you become what you watch, then the question is, "Men, what are you watching?" Internet pornography or trashy TV allows trash to fill your soul. Beholding Christ brings the bright light of Christ to every dark corner. We have been set free to see! Let us fix our gaze on the glory of Christ.

NOVEMBER 3 · 2 CORINTHIANS 4:7–18

How Not to Lose Heart

JASON C. MEYER

PAUL UTTERS WORDS that sound unattainable: "So we do not lose heart" (2 Cor. 4:16). The disturbing truth of living in a fallen world is that there are always good reasons to lose heart. Losing heart is a natural knee-jerk response to earthly losses. Men are not impervious to pain. Pretending to be invulnerable is pathetic and ridiculous—like trying to eat from a fake fruit basket. Be real, not fake!

Being real with our losses, however, does not mean we will lose heart. Losing heart involves buying the lie that those losses are all there is. Don't let your losses trick you into thinking you are losing everything. Here is the secret for not losing heart: there are always good reasons to lose heart, but the reasons to take heart *are always bigger and better and longer lasting.*

Paul offers a more excellent way for looking at life's losses: *walk by faith, not by sight* (5:7). The things we see by sight are real, but temporary. The things we see only by faith are both real and eternal. Looking at present losses is a prescription for losing heart. Fix your eyes by faith on the unseen and eternal (4:18).

In 2 Kings 6, when the Syrian army surrounds Elisha and his servant, it looks like they have no chance. What are two people against a whole army? But physical sight was deceiving in this case. So Elisha prayed that his servant would start seeing the unseen. "So the LORD opened the eyes of the young man, and he saw, and behold, the mountain was full of horses and chariots of fire all around Elisha" (2 Kings 6:17). Elisha's servant thought he had good reasons to lose heart, but Elisha helped him see that there were better reasons to take heart. Paul is like Elisha, and he is helping the Corinthians learn to see the things that can be seen only by faith.

We must distinguish between our *felt* needs and our *forever* needs. The gospel guarantees that our forever needs are fully met, but the Lord also uses present sufferings as the sharp whittling tool that actually produces future glory (2 Cor. 4:17). Future glory so outweighs present sufferings that it will make all the sorrows of this present age seem like a mere "watch in the night" (Ps. 90:4).

NOVEMBER 4 · 2 CORINTHIANS 5:11–21

The Glorious Exchange

JASON C. MEYER

THE BIBLE IS a story of reconciliation. Humanity needs to be reconciled because we rebelled against God and the relationship was severed by sin. Reconciliation is the restoring of that relationship. The *message* of reconciliation confronts us in 2 Corinthians 5:20: "Be reconciled to God." The *method* of reconciliation comes in verse 21—as a price paid and a gift given.

First, look at the price paid: "For our sake he made him to be sin who knew no sin" (v. 21a). God sent his sinless Son to be our substitute. Faith looks at Christ on the cross and sees him suffering for our sins, not for his own—for he was sinless. Wrath was poured out in full *on Christ,* so the debt is paid in full *by Christ.*

Second, look at the gift received. Verse 21b calls it "the righteousness of God." In Christ, we receive what we could never have earned. We have a right standing with God only because, by faith in Christ, we receive his righteousness as a gift. Paul speaks elsewhere of the "gift of righteousness" (Rom. 5:17).

Maybe an illustration will help. Imagine you need a perfect score on a test in order to get into heaven. As sinners, we all get failing scores. "None is righteous, no, not one" (Rom. 3:10). Our test scores earn us eternal death (Rom. 6:23). How could anyone receive the gift of eternal life? So, God sends his Son. He takes on flesh and becomes like us in every way so that he can take the same test. Jesus gets a perfect score. Receiving Christ by faith means we are united to him, which means that what is his becomes ours and what is ours becomes his. Do you see what this means? He pays the penalty for our failing score on the cross, while his perfect score opens up heaven for us. Theologians sometimes call this "double imputation": our sin imputed to Christ; his righteousness imputed to us. We can't be good enough to bring salvation within our reach; but with Christ on our side, we can't be bad enough to put salvation out of reach.

Salvation cannot be earned—only received or rejected.

The Conversion of Your Wallet

JASON C. MEYER

SAM HOUSTON (1793–1863) was a colorful soldier and politician and is best known for helping to bring Texas into the United States. He surprised everyone when he became a Christian. He surprised everyone *even more* when after his baptism he said he wanted to pay half of the local minister's salary. When someone asked him why, he responded, "My pocketbook was baptized, too." The conversion of our wallets should be included in our conversion to Christ. The extent of our generosity tests whether or not we know the grace of Christ.

The word "test" or "prove" is one of the linchpin terms in this section of 2 Corinthians (8:2, 8, 24; 9:13). It means "testing in order to form a judgment or conclusion." A person's claim is tested and approved (if they pass the test) or disproved (if they fail the test).

The Macedonian church had "a severe test of affliction" (8:2). They passed the test and became a paradigm of giving: (1) God's grace came down (v. 1); (2) abundant joy welled up (v. 2); and (3) a wealth of generosity flowed forth (v. 2). Now Paul tells the Corinthians that it is their turn to take the test (v. 8). They should excel in giving so that they can prove that their love is genuine (vv. 7–8). Giving is the proof of knowing gospel grace (vv. 8–9). Paul says that generosity gives proof of "your confession of the gospel of Christ" (9:13).

If Christians *represent* Christ, then their giving will *reflect* Christ's giving. When the chance to give comes, can you imagine Christ closing his heart and giving nothing? Preposterous! Look at what he gave in 2 Corinthians 8:9: "For you know the grace of our Lord Jesus Christ, that though he was rich, yet for your sake he became poor, so that you by his poverty might become rich." Sacrificial giving (v. 8) flows from the sacrifice of Christ (v. 9). Therefore, a call to believe the gospel and a call to give cannot be separated. Men, if your wallets took the witness stand, would they speak for, or against, your confession of Christ?

NOVEMBER 6 • 2 CORINTHIANS 11:1–15

Know Your Enemy

JASON C. MEYER

THE BIBLE HAS unsettling things to say about Satan. He prowls around like a roaring lion desiring to devour us (1 Pet. 5:8). The word Peter uses for "devour" is the word that appears in the Greek translation of the Old Testament for what the fish did to Jonah (Jonah 1:17). Gulp, and gone! But how does Satan devour anyone? He can devour people only by drawing them away from Christ. That is why Peter says we resist Satan by faith (1 Pet. 5:9). Faith lays hold of Christ, while Satan seeks to lead away from Christ.

Paul gives precisely the same summary. Satan's aim is to lead us away from Christ (2 Cor. 11:3). He does this in subtle ways, so that we embrace a clever deception rather than respond with an outright denial of Christ. It is a doctrinal attack, because he seeks to lead our "thoughts" about Jesus "astray." Satan produces a cunningly counterfeit version of Jesus to draw the Corinthians away from a "sincere and pure" devotion to the real Jesus.

It is a familiar scene in movies for the bad guys to replace the right briefcase with one that looks similar but has contents that are totally different.

Paul calls the Corinthians' discernment into question because they have put up with counterfeit versions of Jesus, the Spirit, and the gospel (v. 4). Some in Corinth had grabbed the wrong briefcase!

Why were they not able to detect the differences? Answer: the messengers are skilled with their deceptive speech (v. 6). The contrast is between cunning speech and truthful speech. Satan, the master of disguise and lies, is the opposite of Jesus, who is truth incarnate. Paul sets up the same point of comparison between the false apostles and himself: skill in speaking (how *well* something is spoken) versus accuracy of speech (how *true* something is that is spoken). Paul admits that he may be "unskilled in speaking" in contrast to the servants of Satan, but he blows them out of the water in terms of "knowledge" (v. 6).

The way that people are trained to catch a counterfeit is not by studying all the possible ways of distorting something but by carefully studying the real thing. In the same way, we protect ourselves from counterfeit christs by knowing the real Jesus better than we know anything or anyone else.

NOVEMBER 7 · 2 CORINTHIANS 12:1-10

The Sufficiency of Grace

JASON C. MEYER

PAUL WAS NOT a humble man; he was a *humbled* man. He needed to be humbled because he was naturally proud. Even heavenly visions did not humble him. He was not humbled *by them;* he needed to be humbled *because of them* (2 Cor. 12:1–7). It is ironic that these visions made Paul proud—after all, they were visions of God's greatness, not Paul's greatness. But pride can even take great visions and falsely translate them into a self-exalting message of how great we are for receiving them. Great gifts mean that the Giver is great, not the receiver.

God's gracious answer to this problem was a painful thorn. Paul regarded it as a bad thing and asked three times that the Lord would remove it (v. 8). But God said no, because the bad thorn served a good purpose. Think about that statement for a second. God gave Paul chronic pain.

Why? Paul needed *chronic pain* because his real problem was *chronic pride*. He needed to be humbled. Therefore, Paul received another vision: not a vision of heavenly glory but a revelation of all-sufficient grace (v. 9).

Paul's response was to begin to boast about his weakness (v. 9). What a crazy response! Why would he possibly want to draw attention to something so unflattering? Paul knew that his weakness was the best backdrop against which God's strength could stand out. People would see neither God nor Paul rightly if Paul got credit for God's strength.

We need to see who we really are so that we can see our real need. I remember reaching this point in an adoption process. I had literally done everything that I could. I had made all the phone calls and filled out all the paperwork and had written all the emails. I am ashamed to say that it was not until that point that I started praying more. God mercifully brought the lesson home to me. I never had felt so helpless and so out of control. God mercifully showed me the mess I am always in: the way I was feeling *at that time* was the way I was *all the time*. Even though it was always true, it was not always felt. Control is such an illusion. It is good for us to feel viscerally how dependent we are. Seeing ourselves rightly as weak is a prerequisite for prizing God's strength.

NOVEMBER 8 · GALATIANS 2:15-21

A New Identity

MICHAEL REEVES

HOW DO YOU tend to think of yourself? Popular? Successful? Strong? Nerdy? Ugly? A failure?

In whatever way you answer that question, you'll almost certainly find that, normally, you define yourself by what you do, or by how you think others see you. The trouble is, it's a way of thinking that leaves you horribly vulnerable to the ups and downs of life: when you're doing well, you feel like a champion; but when things go wrong, maybe you just fall apart.

Even worse, that's the approach we instinctively take with God. When you go to church and pray, you feel quite sure that God must love you.

When you don't, you feel sure that he doesn't! And so your religious performance becomes the bone-shaking rollercoaster ride of your walk with God: up and down you go, all depending on *you.*

How utterly wonderful, then, is Paul's solution for the believer: "I have been crucified with Christ. It is no longer I who live, but Christ who lives in me" (Gal. 2:20). Christians are not people who yo-yo in and out of God's favor, depending on how they're doing. Christians are people who are united to Christ. We are described as the body of Christ (1 Cor. 12:27), meaning that what happened to his body happened to us. He went through all the condemnation our sin deserves; we went through it with him. He was crucified; we were crucified with him. Our identity as hell-bound sinners was killed on the cross, and we have been raised with him to enjoy his new life, beyond all condemnation.

What happy confidence that gives! All my many failures do not define me, nor do my acts of goodness: I have been crucified with Christ, and now *he* is my identity. Every day, I stand before God—and I can talk to him—not on the basis of my own righteousness or performance but on the basis of Christ's. I don't flit in and out of God's love; I'm kept there, for my righteousness is "the same yesterday and today and forever" (Heb. 13:8).

NOVEMBER 9 • GALATIANS 3:15–29

No Second-Class Citizens

MICHAEL REEVES

ONE GOOD INDICATION that the gospel has failed to get into the bloodstream of a church is this: the church will have its own class system. There will be a clear elite or inner priesthood. It could be the preacher who is given special dispensation; it could be those with particular gifts; it could simply be the wealthy and powerful who get treated differently. In such churches, you know the gospel is being sidelined, because nothing levels people like the gospel.

The reason the gospel levels everyone is that it is a *promise.* God gives eternal life, not to those who earn it by their behavior and adherence to the law but to those who believe in Jesus (Gal. 3:21–22). Every Christian, however gifted or godly, stands condemned in himself or herself by the law: "All our righteous deeds are like a polluted garment" (Isa. 64:6). We have eternal life and righteousness *only* as an astonishing and undeserved gift.

That means there can be no second class in Christ's church, for no one is left with anything to boast in except Christ. The most brilliant and talented, the most mature and Christlike, together with the roughest and most unreconstructed young convert: all stand before God only and ever because of Christ. That is why "there is neither Jew nor Greek, there is neither slave nor free, there is no male and female" (Gal. 3:28). For us, Christ is all: all our boast, all our glory.

The godliest senior saint remains as much a debtor to grace as the struggling young believer. The tempted teenager who trusts in Jesus is as much a child of God as the greatest heroes of the faith. "In Christ Jesus you are all sons of God, through faith" (v. 26), and our Father in heaven has the same fatherly love toward all his family.

NOVEMBER 10 · GALATIANS 4:1-7

The Highest Blessing

MICHAEL REEVES

IT IS A VERY ODD thing that the apostle Paul does in this passage: in the middle of this letter to the Galatians, written all in Greek, he slips in this one Aramaic word, "Abba" (Gal. 4:6). The word simply means "Father," and yet immediately after writing "Abba" he then writes the word "Father" in Greek. "Abba! Father!" He writes the same word in two different languages. Why?

Clearly, Paul is thinking of the time when, in the garden of Gethsemane, Jesus was talking to his Father. There, in that private moment, Jesus called him "Abba, Father" (Mark 14:36). With that poignant allusion, Paul holds out to us the breathtaking truth that we Christians are all given the very relationship with the Father that Jesus has always enjoyed.

In other words, when Paul writes that we have received "adoption as sons" of God (Gal. 4:5), he isn't imagining that we are given the status of being "okay, sort-of-acceptable" to God. We are given the matchless status of *the* perfect and utterly beloved Son: never to be forgotten, never to be disowned, never to be unloved. Christian, you could have no better standing with the Almighty! The Spirit of Comfort that the Son has always enjoyed has been shared with us, assuring us of our Father's tenderness toward us and care for us.

And that is just what fills us with such happiness in God: assured by the Spirit that we have the Son's own status before the Father, we find ourselves filled with confidence and delight in so wonderful a God. Knowing and enjoying his love, an answering love wells up in us as the Spirit who is breathed into us creates in us a deep and passionate heart-cry: "Abba! Father!"

No longer slaves, but beloved sons and heirs of the most glorious and generous God! Think on that today, and cry out to him as a cherished and honored son should.

NOVEMBER 11 · GALATIANS 5:16-26

How to Grow

MICHAEL REEVES

IT IS VERY EASY to read Galatians 5:22–23 as a challenge. You can read it, gear yourself up, and think, "Right. *Love*: okay, I should be nicer. *Joy*: I must smile more. *Peace*: I must stop yelling at other drivers," and so on. All of which completely misses Paul's point—that these beautiful characteristics of love, joy, peace, patience, and so forth, are "the fruit *of the Spirit*." Paul isn't writing a self-help manual or giving us a list of goals to strive for in the steam of our own zeal for self-improvement. He is describing what a person looks like when he walks by the Spirit.

It is a beautiful description: the person who walks by the Spirit will be loving, joyful, peace-filled, patient, kind, good, faithful, gentle, and self-controlled. So how can we get to be like that?

Throughout the book of Galatians, Paul consistently and tightly connects "the Spirit" and "faith" (see, for example, Gal. 3:1–6, 14). That's because the Spirit's work is to uncoil us from our pitiful self-dependence and create in us a loving trust in God. Directing our gaze to Jesus, helping us to understand Scripture, and waking us up to see the glory of God in all creation, he opens our eyes to see God's beauty and turns our hearts to want God more than anything else. And in drawing us to love God, he brings us to find our joy and peace in God, as Christ always has (see John 4:34). That is, the Spirit makes us like Jesus, the one, above all, who walks by the Spirit.

If you would be characterized by the fruit of the Spirit, don't focus so much on trying to produce the fruit; focus on God. Cry out for a heart that trusts and desires him more; seek to know him better in his word; spend your life communing with him. Then, just as Moses reflected the Lord's glory when he talked with him (Ex. 34:34–35), so you will begin to glow with Christlikeness (2 Cor. 3:18). You will become like the one you love.

NOVEMBER 12 · EPHESIANS 2:1–10

Our Greatest Problem

ERIK THOENNES

WHAT IS THE biggest problem we humans face? Depending on whom you ask, you will get many different answers. Racism, poverty, lack of education, religious extremism, or gender inequality will all get mentioned as the core human dilemma, along with many other suggestions.

"You were dead" (Eph. 2:1). Paul shocks his readers; there is no question as to what he thinks our biggest problem is! As children of Adam, we are born spiritually dead, without hope, and unable to resuscitate ourselves. This is our nature. As "children of wrath" (v. 3), we are born that way and lack the resources within ourselves to find life. The image is severe. We are not knocked out, incapacitated, tied up, or merely in need of a little more time or education or social assistance. Better parents or teachers or politicians won't solve our problem. Dead men can do nothing to save themselves. We must look well beyond ourselves for the solution.

If verse 1 brings the reader up short, perhaps verse 4 does so even more. But the hopelessness of verse 1 stands in stark contrast to the hope of verse 4. There is a turning point here; one little conjunction alerts us that God has not only changed human history but has solved the problem of death as well: "*But* God, being rich in mercy, because of the great love with which he loved us, even when we were dead in our trespasses, made us alive together with Christ" (vv. 4–5). God intervened as only he could and as we desperately needed him to. There is only one solution to death. We were dead; he made us alive in Christ. Because of Christ's resurrection, we are revived.

The emphasis is on God's powerful initiative. Only God has the power to raise the dead. Only Christ's death and resurrection make it possible. We must see ourselves as dead before we can find life through God's gift of grace. "For by grace you have been saved through faith. And this is not your own doing; it is the gift of God, not a result of works, so that no one may boast" (vv. 8–9). Yet, how often we try to add our own good works to God's gift, and then boast in ourselves. Let us not be guilty of circumventing God's resuscitation plan. Let us rest in his solution to our spiritual deadness. Praise God that, because of his extravagant mercy, he brought us back from the dead and made us his workmanship, for his glory.

NOVEMBER 13 · EPHESIANS 3:14–21

A Prayer for Strength in the Inner Man

ERIK THOENNES

WHAT IS THE best thing you can do for someone? With all the needs and desires people have, what is the greatest service you can perform on their behalf? There is nothing more important than praying for people. In the middle of his efforts to help the Ephesians understand the gospel better, Paul breaks into a heartfelt, eager prayer for them.

In Ephesians 3:14–21, Paul picks up where he left off in 3:1 and continues his teaching on God's astounding work in unifying all people under the authority of Christ. When he ponders God's worldwide work of redemption, he is inspired to bow his knees in humble adoration and worship of God (v. 14). God's work of redemption demonstrates that every family on the earth finds its identity in God the Creator.

This posture of humility before God naturally leads to prayer, which is an expression of our dependence on God. Paul's preaching turns to prayer in recognition that only God is able to bring the heart transformation needed in the lives of the Ephesians. Any ministry not grounded in prayer will have a shaky foundation and will lack any lasting significance.

Paul's prayer is for inner strength that comes through the power of the Holy Spirit (v. 16). Men tend to pay a lot of attention to their physique. Bodily strength is often seen as a sign of manliness. But inner strength is far more important. The Spirit-empowered strength of our "inner man" defines us far more significantly than the size of our biceps.

As the indwelling Spirit works in our inner man, he mediates the presence of Christ. Although Christ dwells in all believers, as our faith grows, his presence becomes more evident to us as well as to others. And this presence always shows itself in our being ever more "rooted and grounded in love" (v. 17). Paul's desire for us to understand the breadth, length, height, and depth of God's love points to the incomprehensible magnitude of his benevolence toward sinners. Our love for God increases in direct proportion to our understanding of his love for us. We love him because he first loved us (1 John 4:19).

Prayer then turns to praise as Paul contemplates the depth of God's love for us in Christ. This praise results in glory being ascribed to God in the church, which is the place on earth where God is to be most glorified (Eph. 3:21).

A Radical New Way to Live

ERIK THOENNES

IN THIS PASSAGE, Paul urges us "no longer" to "walk," or live, "as the Gentiles do" (Eph. 4:17), in ignorance and futility of mind. The phrase "no longer" indicates that he is referring to our manner of life before we came to faith in Christ, and the reference to "Gentiles" means anyone living outside the household of faith. Such people—including us, before conversion—are "alienated" from God, with "darkened" understanding, callousness, sensuality, greed, and impurity (vv. 18–19). But when we "learned Christ" (v. 20), everything changed. When we were taught the truth in Jesus, we put off our old self and its lifestyle, and put on the new self after the likeness of the true, righteous, and holy God who saved us (v. 24). Now, with nothing to prove, no image to maintain, no need to impress, we are able to live with truthfulness and grace.

So many men today seem to have anger problems. Road rage, domestic abuse, violent crime, and brawls in bars and on ball fields are predominantly male behaviors. When we "learned Christ," however, we learned to keep our anger in check and keep the devil at bay (vv. 26–27). Honesty and hard work become a way of life, which enables generosity toward our neighbors (v. 28). Our words, which once were used for self-exaltation, are now used for gracious edification. Sinful attitudes like bitterness, wrath, anger, slander, and malice are now replaced with godly traits like kindness, goodness, and forgiveness. These are not merely moral virtues accomplished through self-will. They are the result of our new identity, grounded in the gospel, because we now realize that God in Christ has forgiven us (v. 32).

This radically new way of living is the work of the Holy Spirit, who has "sealed [us] for the day of redemption" (v. 30). He graciously brings the power to be freed from our "former manner of life" (v. 22), which was bitterly empty, so that we can now await the return of Christ, when we will all be perfectly conformed to his image (Rom. 8:29).

Walk Wisely

ERIK THOENNES

THROUGHOUT HIS LETTERS, Paul uses many contrasting images to teach us about our new life in Christ. Here in Ephesians 5:6–17, as the new nature replaces the old one, light replaces darkness. "For at one time you were darkness, but now you are light in the Lord. Walk as children of light" (v. 8). The believer himself was once called darkness, but his identity has changed and he is now called light. The word "light" reminds us that Jesus said, "I am the light of the world. Whoever follows me will not walk in darkness, but will have the light of life" (John 8:12). As "sons of disobedience" we were deceived, walking in darkness and deserving of God's wrath (Eph. 5:6). When we trust Christ, we become children of light, and our lives bear the fruit of the light, which is "all that is good and right and true" (v. 9).

Light and darkness cannot occupy the same space. Either we are in the dark, unsure of what might trip us up, or we are in the light, able to see potential dangers and avoid them. The radical shift from darkness to light brings life change. Thanksgiving replaces impurity. Filthy, foolish talk and crude joking have no place. "Do not become partners" with ungodly people, we are told (v. 7). We are to "walk as children of light" (v. 8), saying no to sin and yes to holiness. Walking in the light includes accountability and confession with other men who desire to expose sin and live faithfully. Walk carefully. Walk wisely. Walk in the light.

The light exposes the "unfruitful works of darkness" (v. 11), revealing their emptiness and allowing a man "to discern what is pleasing to the Lord" (v. 10). Once we know what is pleasing, we have a choice as to whether we will walk wisely, "making the best use of the time" (v. 16). Every hour presents a choice of whether we will live for ourselves or for God's kingdom purposes. When we are filled with the Spirit, our lips are filled with worshipful singing and our hearts are filled with melody to the Lord. Then we are able to fulfill the main reason for our existence—to worship God and "proclaim the excellencies of him who called you out of darkness into his marvelous light" (1 Pet. 2:9).

Spiritual Warfare in the Life of a Man

ERIK THOENNES

DO YOU REALLY BELIEVE in the spiritual realm? Do you believe there is a battle raging for the souls of men? It is hard to imagine that this is true if we are living in relative comfort and ease. But no matter our earthly situation, we need to think and live like soldiers.

In this passage Paul is likely getting to the main point he wanted to make all along in Ephesians. He frames the Christian life in light of the cosmic spiritual battle that is always going on, but of which we are often unaware. Here spiritual forces of good and evil are clear and present, and their presence requires a wartime mentality. This war necessitates four imperatives: (1) be strong; (2) put on the full armor of God; (3) stand firm; (4) pray at all times.

Jesus delivered the decisive blow in the battle against the powers of darkness on the cross, but the battle still continues, and it is a matter of life and death, with eternal consequences (Eph. 6:12). The source of our strength and confidence in this conflict is always found in Christ (1:19–20). We fight fearlessly because God "has delivered us from the domain of darkness and transferred us to the kingdom of his beloved Son" (Col. 1:13). Because of this, we are able to obey the main command of this passage, which is to "stand firm" (Eph. 6:13). The armor imagery is from the prophet Isaiah, who describes God as a warrior dressed for battle and defending his people (Isa. 11:4–5). With God leading the way into the fray, and with us wearing the armor he provides, we cannot lose.

We need to be prepared for the conflict, armed with God's truth both proclaimed and lived out (Eph. 6:14). Our lives should be marked by the righteousness that is ours in Christ, and with faith in what God provides. This enables us to resist the schemes of the devil that would otherwise take us down. Ungodly behavior, doubt, and despair from within, and persecution and false teaching from the outside are deadly enemies, but they cannot stand against us when God is fighting for us. The salvation and word of God are powerful enough to protect us and to enable us to go on the offensive as well (v. 17). Then we too can pray for boldness to be faithful ambassadors, even if we are in chains like Paul.

NOVEMBER 17 • PHILIPPIANS 2:1-11

Christ's Infinite Downward Journey

ANDREW M. DAVIS

SOMETIME BEFORE GOD put Adam in the garden of Eden, Satan fell in love with his own beauty and became ambitious—what today we might call upwardly mobile. He thought he could ascend to take God's place on the throne of the universe, and thus began his rebellion. But the omnipotent God defeated him and cast him down to earth (Isa. 14:12–15). Then, at the tree of the knowledge of good and evil, Satan lured Adam into a similar pattern of rebellion—of prideful upward mobility. When Adam sinned, he corrupted his heart by elevating himself above God and all other creatures. Adam's sin-cursed race has lived in that pride ever since. We arrogantly push ourselves forward in rivalry and conceit; in pride we consider ourselves and our agendas far more important than anyone else's.

The gospel of Christ changes that for all eternity. This amazing passage shows how Jesus Christ, the Son of God, willingly embarked on an infinite downward journey, from the glorious throne of God to a lowly human body, and further downward to a life of servanthood and eventually death, even death on a cross. This downward journey won us our salvation, forgiveness for all our selfishness and our prideful jockeying for our own interests. The text says plainly that, because of Christ's downward journey, God highly exalted him and bestowed on him the name that is above every name (Phil. 2:9). Someday, every single created being in the universe will bow the knee before Christ and acknowledge that he is Lord, to the glory of God the Father (vv. 10–11). This astonishing downward journey of Christ is directly opposed to Satan's self-exaltation, and to ours.

As Christian men, Paul commands us to have this mind of humility among ourselves, which is ours in Christ Jesus (v. 5). We are to seek to go downward in our lives, to find ways to serve others, to consider other people better or more important than ourselves. We are to learn how to die to ourselves so that others may live for God. This heart attitude is rightfully ours by our new birth in Christ. It is for us to embrace it and live it out. If we do, we also will be exalted by the hand of our Father, though not to the highest place. That belongs to Christ alone!

NOVEMBER 18 · PHILIPPIANS 3:1-11

Exchanging Counterfeits for the True Masterpiece: Christ

ANDREW M. DAVIS

IN 1937, a skillful Dutch art forger named Han van Meegeren completed his counterfeit masterpiece, *The Supper at Emmaus*, a work supposedly by Johannes Vermeer. This forgery deceived the experts and sold for millions of dollars. Imagine the shock of discovering that a "masterpiece" you bought for a fortune was worthless!

But that is nothing compared to the shock many will have on judgment day when they discover that what they valued most in life was not only worthless but offensive to God, and that they will be condemned eternally for believing the lie. Men struggle to evaluate properly the true treasures of life. False treasures abound: human praise, possessions, sensual pleasures, professional achievements, and so forth. But far more dangerous to our souls is the allure of false religious systems that offer the treasure of counterfeit self-righteousness, a forged ticket to heaven.

The apostle Paul was deeply concerned that the Philippians would be duped by the counterfeit treasure of self-righteousness that the "dogs" (false teachers of Jewish legalism; see Galatians and Acts 15:1) were peddling.

Paul claimed to be the greatest achiever of Jewish self-righteousness of his generation. But his masterpiece of righteousness, painted by brushstrokes of self-effort, was exposed as a forgery by the light of Christ's heavenly glory on the road to Damascus. Knocked to the ground by this blinding light, Paul asked for the first time the question that would drive him the rest of his life: "Who are you, Lord?" (Acts 9:5). Paul exchanged the counterfeit of self-righteousness for the true masterpiece: Christ. At that moment, he realized that all his righteousness was "rubbish" (Phil. 3:8) and that all he needed was the gift of perfect righteousness through faith in Christ.

Once that massive change occurred in Paul's heart, knowing Christ better and better became the driving ambition of his life. The foretaste of heavenly fellowship with Jesus left Paul both deeply satisfied and ever thirsty for more. The purpose of his life was to learn how to suffer and die like Christ did, so that he could live the resurrection life that Christ was living in heaven.

So, what is the priceless masterpiece of your life? What ambition drives you on, day after day? And by what means do you expect to stand accepted by God on judgment day? These things are all answered by Paul here in one word: Christ!

A Treasure Chest of Eternal Joy

ANDREW M. DAVIS

EDMOND DANTÈS'S heart was beating wildly as he opened the huge oak chest on the Mediterranean island of Monte Cristo. The treasure map given him by his friend and fellow prisoner, the Abbé Faria, had proved genuine. As his eyes gazed inside the great chest and he saw a thousand gold ingots, rare jewels, pearls, diamonds, and gold coins—worth over thirteen million francs—he knew he was instantly one of the wealthiest men on earth.

So it went in *The Count of Monte Cristo*, written by Alexandre Dumas more than a century and a half ago. But that was fiction, and it fed people's worldly dreams. There is a true treasure chest of infinite value awaiting anyone who opens the book of Philippians. Paul concludes his epistle by laying line upon line of sparkling commands on his hearers. These commands are not burdensome but delightful, the equivalent of directions on the Abbé Faria's map.

Paul begins by pleading with two hardworking women, Euodia and Syntyche, to agree in the Lord. Just as it was time for these bickering women to forgive and be restored to sweet fellowship, perhaps there is someone you also need to forgive.

Then Paul gives the most famous command in the letter: "Rejoice in the Lord always; again I will say, rejoice" (Phil. 4:4). Since the resurrection of Christ, joy in the Lord in all circumstances is more than just possible—it is our rightful inheritance! By the Spirit, we live in constant anticipation of the day when we will be in the presence of the Lord, where there is "fullness of joy" and "pleasures forevermore" (Ps. 16:11).

From this comes a heart demeanor of "reasonableness," or gentleness, because "the Lord is at hand" (Phil. 4:5). A Christian man knows how to moderate his strength, using just the right touch to achieve his godly purpose. He also has a supernatural peace that surpasses all understanding, because he has learned to entrust all his anxieties to God in prayer. Finally, his mind feeds on only the highest-quality thoughts: whatever is true, honorable, just, pure, lovely, commendable, excellent, worthy of praise (v. 8). Such a man walks in the pattern of godly living exemplified by Paul, courageously inviting others to follow his own example as well.

This staggering heart-wealth is found only by faith in Jesus. This is the richest possible life a man can live. If you are Christ's, this treasure chest is yours!

He Is the Main Thing

SAM CRABTREE

ALL HEARTS WORSHIP SOMETHING. The heart tends to worship what amazes it. Godly hearts worship the most amazing thing, which is also the Main Thing. Christian men find it entirely fitting and pleasant to supremely value the supremely valuable.

Absolutely nothing is greater than, or more important than the Main Thing. Today's text is among the most sweeping, universal, glorious, and Christocentric passages in the Bible. Five times this text uses the phrase "all things." Of all things vying for consideration, Christ is the Main Thing. As the Main Thing, Christ is not in a tie with anything or anyone else, and there is no close second.

He is the image of the invisible! The invisible has an image? Yes! Images are to be seen, so look! Gaze! That's what wise men do. They look seeingly, not blindly. In some measure, wise men see aspects of the vast unseen.

See this: Jesus is not merely the echo of God; he *is* God. Nothing is lacking in Jesus that would thereby disqualify him as almighty God:

> Jesus said to him, "Have I been with you so long, and you still do not know me, Philip? Whoever has seen me has seen the Father. How can you say, 'Show us the Father'?" (John 14:9)

The fullness of God dwells in Jesus bodily, the immaterial expressed in the material, the transcendent in the immanent.

What's behind all creation? Jesus! Jesus himself never came into existence; he was never in a prior condition of nonexistence. "All things were made through him, and without him was not any *thing* made that was made" (John 1:3). "Things" include thrones, dominions, forces, realms visible and invisible, with all their ranks and including all the individuals in those ranks, including family lines producing the men reading these words.

Nothing is self-made. Plainly, anything that came into existence was not there to bring itself into existence. Nothing can launch its own existence, for it is not there to do the launching. It can't have capabilities, because it's not there to have them. Therefore, *made* things rightly and gladly bow to their Maker. And so must we.

NOVEMBER 21 • COLOSSIANS 2:6-15

Rooted and Established

SAM CRABTREE

ACCORDING TO THIS remarkable text, what is a man to do with Jesus? We must first receive him. We must walk in him. We are to be rooted in him, established in faith in him. We should learn of him ("just as you were taught") and be built up in him. We must never fail to thank him. Our ideas should align with his. Don't be taken captive by knowledge according to human tradition and elemental spirits, and not according to Christ. Use Christ as the plumb line to measure all else. Be filled in him. Be buried with him in baptism. Recognize his cancellation of the record of trespasses. And be certain to hail him for his decisive work on the cross.

But we must be careful. This text is not chiefly about what we are to do with Jesus, but what he has done and is doing for us. In him, and for our sake, is found all the fullness of deity in a human body—miraculous condescension and incarnation! He fills us and circumcises our hearts of flesh. He takes us with him in death and burial and raises us from the dead with him. He accomplishes forgiveness of all our trespasses and cancels the record of debt standing against us, setting it aside, nailing it to the cross. And he disarms all rulers and authorities, putting them to shame.

So, if we connect the two lists above, we see that we receive him because he first comes to us. We walk in him because he first fills us. We thank him because he first does so much for us. In other words, the things we do are on account of the things he does. He acts first. His work is decisive. Ours is responsive. "We love [him] because he first loved us" (1 John 4:19).

A man's heart does not interact with Jesus in such ways without first receiving him as Lord (see Col. 2:6). "Lord" means boss or master or owner. Men with great hearts see themselves as owned by Another.

The Word of Christ

SAM CRABTREE

HEARTS OF MEN! Attention! Here come your marching orders. This passage posts a substantial array of straightforward commands.

We are told to set our minds on the things that are above, and to seek them. We are encouraged to put to death what is earthly in us—sexual immorality, impurity, passion, evil desire, covetousness, idolatry. We must give no place to anger, wrath, malice, slander, or obscene talk. We must never lie to one another. Rather, we should put on compassion, kindness, humility, meekness, and patience—bearing with one another and forgiving each other. We are to put on love and let the peace of Christ rule in our hearts. Be thankful. Teach and admonish one another. Sing psalms and hymns and spiritual songs. Do everything in the name of the Lord Jesus. Wives, submit to your husbands. Above all, let the word of Christ dwell in you richly.

Although this is a men's devotional Bible, I left "wives, submit to your husbands" in the list, because believing men are part of the bride of Christ and are to submit to him. Submission can be difficult. These are hard things. These are impossible things apart from enabling grace.

One of the things on the above list is essential to all the others. Though easily overlooked, this is the key to seeking things that are above, setting your mind there, putting to death what is earthly in you, not lying, putting on compassion, forgiving, loving, letting the peace of Christ rule in your hearts, and being thankful. This is the absolutely crucial key for teaching and admonishing one another well. It's the last item on the list: letting the word of Christ dwell in you richly. The *word* is the key. The Scriptures play a fundamentally important role in strengthening a man's heart to not go off the rails. Without the word dwelling in a man, he will not sustain his pursuit of any of the other things listed. Wise men recognize this, and therefore permeate themselves with Scripture.

Grief Shot Through with Hope

J. J. SEID

PAUL WANTS TO infuse the Thessalonians' grief with hope. He wants to free them from their mistaken belief that those who died "in Christ" (1 Thess. 4:16) have missed the opportunity to participate in the resurrection. He gives them truths to cling to that will guard them from hopelessness. They will know that they have understood Paul's teaching when they are able to "encourage one another" by sharing his words of assurance (v. 18).

Paul says, in effect, "Don't you see, brothers, what massive significance the death and resurrection of Jesus has for the funeral of the fellow believer you just attended?" (see v. 14). If we are "in Christ" (v. 16), then nothing can ever dictate our *future prospects* more than Jesus's *past performance* on our behalf. Even as the thief on the cross was "led away to be put to death with him" (Luke 23:32), so too our old selves were "crucified with him" (Rom. 6:6). In light of this settled fact, Paul can elsewhere similarly conclude that "if we have been united with him in a death like his, we shall *certainly* be united with him in a resurrection like his" (Rom. 6:5).

Grief without hope is what happens when you have death without resurrection. As Christians, we grieve because death is still a reality, but we grieve *in hope* (1 Thess. 4:13) because the cross means that death won't get the last word. The death and resurrection of Jesus means that someday even death will die (1 Cor. 15:25–26). In the words of the seventeenth-century poet John Donne, "One short sleep past, we wake eternally, and death shall be no more; Death, thou shalt die."[13]

Death is a trauma, a tearing, a ripping apart of what ought not be separated. But not for the Christian. The cruel agony of the cross of Jesus has transmuted death into something beautiful. Death for the Christian is no longer just a departure; it is also an arrival. No longer just a tearing, but also a mending. At "the coming of the Lord" (1 Thess. 4:15), all things will be made new, and our exile from Eden and from God's presence will be permanently repaired. The dead in Christ *will* rise (v. 16) and will *always be with* the Lord (v. 17). Not a separation, but a *union.* Not a divorce but a *wedding.* If we are "in Christ," then death is a doorway into a banquet hall where a table is laid for the marriage supper of the Lamb (Rev. 19:6–9). True, we still grieve, Paul says, but our grief is filled with hope (1 Thess. 4:13).

The Christian Life Is Growth Downward

J. J. SEID

FOLLOWING HIS WORDS of encouragement to the Thessalonians, Paul said, "Therefore encourage one another" (1 Thess. 4:18), and he then repeats those very words in 5:11, adding that they should also submit to their elders, cultivate peace, be patient with everyone, never repay evil for evil, rejoice at all times, pray in all situations, and give thanks in all circumstances (vv. 12–18). This long string of ethical exhortations can seem overwhelming—even downright unrealistic. What's the solution?

At the end of this long string of *therefores,* Paul provides a beautiful *because* as one of the means by which we can begin to obey his instructions. What hope do we have that we can *therefore* begin to rejoice more than we despair, pray more than we panic, give thanks more than we grumble? *Because,* Paul assures us, the God of peace himself is up to something in our lives, changing us from the inside out, until the time when he will finally "sanctify you completely" (v. 23). As we partner with him in this transformation project, we'll find that what we think, say, do, and desire will slowly start to look more and more like Jesus (v. 23).

But how do we increasingly partner with the Father in this change project? Paul says in verse 23 that we will find ourselves slowly looking more and more *like* Jesus as we look more and more *to* Jesus. The Father is faithful to keep his promises (v. 24). He who did not spare his own Son (Rom. 8:32), how will he not also transform our lowly bodies to be like Jesus's glorious body (Phil. 3:20–21)? "He will surely do it" (1 Thess. 5:24).

As we look forward in confident expectation to that great day, we will be protected from despair and resignation in our fight against our remaining sinful desires.

As J. I. Packer has pointed out, growth in the Christian life is growth downward—growth in humility, awareness of our frailty, and awareness of our need of grace. As we grow downward in increasing awareness of just how wide the gap is between our holy status and our sinful attitudes and actions, we are in danger of wavering in our resolve to keep striking at the sin that remains. Paul encourages us more and more to take God at his word about our position, our progress, and our ultimate purification.

In so doing, we'll find ourselves able to increasingly "act like what we are"—striking at our sin and stirring up our affection for Jesus. As we place our confident expectation in God to keep his promises (1 Thess. 5:24), we'll become increasingly pure as Jesus is pure (1 John 3:3).

NOVEMBER 25 • 2 THESSALONIANS 2:13–17

The Good News of Jesus's Performance on Our Behalf

J. J. SEID

WE CAN HAVE confidence in God's certain, undeserved, future favor toward us because he chose us and called us (2 Thess. 2:13–14) *precisely so that* we someday soon "may obtain the glory of our Lord Jesus Christ" (v. 14). But not only can we rest secure in his love for us because it rests on his initiation instead of ours; we can also feel secure because God's love for us rests on his undeserved favor instead of on our performance. Paul reminds us that God loved us (v. 13) "through grace" (v. 16). Not only did God love us *first*; God loved us *undeservedly*.

World-class athletes compete with a confidence that almost seems to border on certainty as to the outcome of the contest. *Almost.* If *that* level of imperfect confidence can lead to great athletic performance, how much more can the *certainty* of God's future, undeserved favor energize us, encourage us, and give us perseverance to "stand firm" (v. 15) in the truth of what we have believed—and as a result be established in "every good work and word" (v. 17)! In other words, as God comforts our hearts by reassuring us of our security in his love (v. 16), we'll increasingly find ourselves working *from* our acceptance by God rather than *for* our acceptance by God.

As men who all too often base our identity on our performance, we've all experienced the crippling, paralyzing fear of failure. And worse, we've all experienced the shame, discouragement, and hopelessness that often accompany the stark reality of past failure. But the humble confidence we'll need to repent and increasingly be busy about "every good work" (v. 17) won't come from propping ourselves up with self-talk, or putting our confidence in the approval of other people. Instead of the performances that prop up our pride, and the failures that paralyze our pride, the good news of Jesus's performance at Calvary on our behalf guarantees that we won't experience rejection when we someday see God face to face. Rather, we will joyfully "obtain the glory of our Lord Jesus Christ" (v. 14).

NOVEMBER 26 · 1 TIMOTHY 2

Pray for All People

TODD WILSON

WHEN PAUL THINKS about priorities for the local church, prayer tops the list. Whatever else a church does, it must be a praying church if it is to be a faithful church. That's why Paul instructs Timothy "that supplications, prayers, intercessions, and thanksgivings be made for all people" (1 Tim. 2:1).

Yet notice the expansive, evangelistic intent of these prayers. When the church prays, it needs to be with a heart for the world and a vision for the nations. Prayer that's focused only on local matters doesn't qualify as praying in any New Testament sense.

Yes, the people of God should petition their heavenly Father for favor with the powers that be, so that the church can enjoy the freedom to flourish as the people of God (v. 2). But this isn't an excuse to pray for a comfortable middle-class existence, free from the worries and cares of the world.

No, as Paul explains, our prayers must be expansive and evangelistic because this reflects the heart of the One to whom we pray. "God our Savior," Paul reminds us, "desires all people to be saved and to come to the knowledge of the truth" (vv. 3–4). It is good and right, then, to pray big, sweeping prayers for the salvation of others—because this is God's heart as well. We must never forget that this man who encourages us to pray that others might be saved is the very man who declared, "My heart's desire and prayer to God for [the nation of Israel] is that they may be saved" (Rom. 10:1).

But not only is this true of God's heart; it is rooted in his very nature as the *one* true God. "For there is one God," Paul says (1 Tim. 2:5). And because there is one God, and not many gods, *everyone* must look to him for salvation. More than that, because there is only "one *mediator* between God and men, the man Christ Jesus," we can look nowhere else to find deliverance from our sins. Jesus Christ is our only hope—and not only *our* only hope, but the whole world's only hope as well. So let us pray without ceasing and praise God for the fruit it bears.

NOVEMBER 27 · 1 TIMOTHY 6:11–21

Fight the Good Fight of Faith

TODD WILSON

BEFORE CLOSING his first letter to Timothy, Paul offers one last word of exhortation to his young protégé: "Fight the good fight of the faith" (1 Tim. 6:12). The fight of faith is the foundation of godliness; we will not make strides in our pursuit of Christlikeness without putting up a good fight—*the fight of faith*. Needless to say, there is no role for passivity in Paul's concept of the Christian life.

Paul, of course, wants Timothy to understand the stakes involved here: The fight of faith is the path to final salvation, which is why Paul charges Timothy to "take hold of . . . eternal life" (v. 12). We cannot do an end run around the life of faith and hope to find our eternal reward on the last day.

Here, Jesus is our example par excellence. Remember the warfare he waged throughout the course of his earthly ministry, not least in the final days of his life. He was betrayed by associates, falsely accused by kinsmen, mocked mercilessly before Pontius Pilate—all of which would have been profound tests of faith and good reasons to throw in the proverbial towel. But, Paul reminds us, even in the face of extreme odds and imminent death, Jesus "made the good confession" (v. 13). He fought the fight of faith—and won!

Now this mantle falls to Paul and Timothy—and to anyone who would confess the name of Christ. We are to follow in the footsteps of Jesus and "keep the commandment unstained and free from reproach until the appearing of our Lord Jesus Christ" (v. 14). This is a rallying cry—to fight the good fight till the end.

Yet not in our own strength. There is a "blessed and only Sovereign" (v. 15) who is Lord of the nations and Lord of our lives. To him, and him alone, we look for nourishment and strength in the throes of battle, even in the face of disappointing setbacks or temporary defeats. It is through his power that we are being guarded and preserved by faith "for a salvation ready to be revealed in the last time" (1 Pet. 1:5). The King of kings and Lord of lords is able to keep us to the end. "To him be honor and eternal dominion. Amen" (1 Tim. 6:16).

NOVEMBER 28 · 2 TIMOTHY 1:3–18

Guard the Deposit Entrusted to You

TODD WILSON

IN HIS MOST PERSONAL and pastoral letter, the apostle Paul calls on his young protégé Timothy to "guard the good deposit entrusted to you" (1:14). Nothing is more important than that, not only for Timothy but for us as well.

Timothy, however, is waffling a bit. Ministry hasn't been easy. Perhaps he's fatigued by the labor; doubtless, he's intimidated by the challenge. And yet shrinking in fear and cowardice isn't a viable option. Instead, Paul encourages Timothy to do just the opposite: "Fan into flame the gift of God" (v. 6). Don't go backward, but forward! Don't take your foot off the accelerator; press down even harder.

Yet not in your own strength. No, God has gifted Timothy, and us, with "a spirit not of fear but of power and love and self-control" (v. 7). But more than that, we have Paul's unwavering apostolic example, which shouldn't cause us to cower but should engender confidence within us. Just as Paul perseveres through thick and thin, so too should we—with the same sort of confidence that he has in the God who "is able to guard until that day what has been entrusted to me" (v. 12).

We are to follow Paul's example even as we proclaim Paul's gospel. It won't be easy, but it will be worth it. Some Christian workers find the task to be more than they bargained for, and thus turn away, as Paul knew only too well. "You are aware," he tells Timothy, "that all who are in Asia turned away from me, among whom are Phygelus and Hermogenes" (v. 15). Surely, for the battle-worn apostle, simply uttering these words brought back painful memories. Yet, notwithstanding the ways in which the church may have failed the apostle, God never did and never would.

Furthermore, there are others like faithful Onesiphorus, who didn't avoid Paul but embraced his ministry of hardship and suffering. They are the ones who refresh the hearts of the saints even as they labor on behalf of the Savior. They're also the ones sure to find mercy from the Lord on that day!

NOVEMBER 29 · 2 TIMOTHY 2:14-26

A Worker Approved by God

TODD WILSON

THERE'S AN OLD adage that goes something like this: "There are a million ways to fall down, but only one way to stand up straight." When it comes to the life of ministry, the apostle Paul would likely say the same. An *approved worker* is Paul's vision for those who follow in Christ's footsteps. But it isn't an easy calling. There are challenges innumerable and temptations everywhere. Hence, Paul's simple charge to Timothy: "Do your best to present yourself to God as one approved, a worker who has no need to be ashamed, rightly handling the word of truth" (2 Tim. 2:15).

For Paul, the secret to ministry success is in how you handle God's word. If you play fast and loose with Scripture, your ministry will eventually unravel like a cheap sweater. And if you get sidetracked by any number of petty distractions—what Paul calls "irreverent babble"—you can count on getting yourself off track and eventually swerving away from the truth.

In order to be useful to the Lord, we need to give ourselves wholly to *his* service, not our own. Vessels for honorable use, Paul reminds Timothy, are those that have been "set apart as holy" (v. 21). They're individuals whose lives have been brought, by the grace and Spirit of God, into alignment with God's word, so that they are truly "useful to the master of the house, ready for every good work" (v. 21).

When it comes to the rough-and-tumble of ministry, however, Paul knows full well where perhaps the greatest temptation lies: it is in becoming hotheaded when you encounter opposition. This is why he admonishes Timothy, "Flee youthful passions" (v. 22). Paul doesn't intend this primarily as a call to avoid sexually illicit thoughts or actions, though of course such are out of place for the people of God. Rather, what Paul has in mind is a person who has a hot temper and short fuse, someone who lacks self-control and thus is ready to "go off" on another person who gets in his face or stands in his way. Of course, these sorts of individuals are part and parcel of any gospel-oriented ministry; you will face opposition. But, Paul pleads with Timothy, when you face this sort of pushback, take the moral high ground as the Lord's servant: don't be quarrelsome, but kind. In short, don't lose your head, but keep your cool. Besides, this kind of measured, gracious, and grace-dependent response may be the very thing the Lord uses to bring the opposition to repentance and thus to a knowledge of the truth (v. 25).

The Root of Maturity

JOHN D. HANNAH

A COMMAND OR exhortation given without a clear and compelling reason rarely generates authentic obedience. After all, we all seek our own good and cannot do otherwise; the only way to live unselfishly is out of a rich sense of what we ourselves have received from God in the gospel.

Earlier in Titus 2, Paul gave clear instructions regarding the conduct of both older men (2:2) and younger men (vv. 6–8). But he is also careful not to leave us without compelling reasons for our good conduct. We see this in his use of the word "for" in verse 11. Paul couldn't have been clearer in making the point that the foundation of moral obedience is the wonder of God's saving grace, through which we were transferred from the kingdom of darkness to the kingdom of light.

First, this "grace" (v. 11) that has appeared in the coming of Christ Jesus "trains" us for righteousness (v. 12). Grace, then, is more than a principle by which we are saved; it is also the power and divine strength by which we are progressively sanctified and enabled "to live self-controlled, upright, and godly lives in the present age" (v. 12).

Second, this grace has awakened us to the realization that this world is a "shadowland," that there is a world of reality far greater, and more fulfilling, than the best that this age has to offer. This grace has reoriented our spiritual priorities, has given us new goals, and has instilled Christ-exalting perspectives on all of life.

Finally, the apostle reminds us that this grace has appeared in and through the life, death, and resurrection of the greatest figure in all of history, Jesus Christ. He gave his life to redeem us from the pit of sin and to make us a people for his possession, a new people devoted to the sort of works that display his worth and honor his name.

Is your daily experience characterized by the values of God's kingdom or by the spirit of this present age? Has the new life you have in Christ brought changes in your relationships with others? Are you a man living in light of God's redemptive and transformative mercies? In what ways can you say this is so? What issues are there that still need to be addressed?

DECEMBER 1 · TITUS 3:4-7

We Must Never Forget

JOHN D. HANNAH

THERE ARE SOME things in life that we count so precious that forgetting them is precarious and potentially disastrous. Think of a forgotten appointment, birthday, or anniversary. However, there is something far more important that we must never forget, and that is the wonder of our acceptance by God. The foundation of all moral instruction in the Holy Scriptures is the marvel that God has forgiven our sins. Thus we are motivated less by divine threats than by reminders of God's great love. The Bible does not make demands of us without the provision of power to obey. This book is the story of God's gracious supply that makes fulfilling his demands possible. It is in this that we discover the root of obedience.

Our passage alerts us to three wonderful acts of God in our lives. First, God sovereignly chose to be gracious toward broken, twisted people like you and me (Titus 3:4). Thus our lives of obedient response ought to be grounded in heartfelt gratitude for such breathtaking grace.

Second, he justified us by his grace through faith in the work of Christ in our place on Calvary's tree. This glorious salvation was applied to our hearts by the work of the Holy Spirit in granting us rebirth and in opening the eyes of our heart to God's free gift of life through his Son. Salvation is a work of the great triune God in providing Jesus Christ as a substitute for us, in renewing our hearts by the Spirit, and in the Father declaring us to be his washed, forgiven, forever children (vv. 5–6).

Third, because the great divine Judge has declared us righteous, we are now his children, heirs according to his promises and full of hope (v. 7).

How thrilling! Can you focus on what God has done for you in Christ and remain unappreciative or unchanged? How does God's saving grace affect your perspective on life, money, marriage, vocation, and your numerous social relationships? Are there old habits to change, or attitudes to forsake, or new kinds of actions to embrace? God's saving grace is more than a principle on which to meditate; it is a power that brings change.

The Great Heart of Great Men

SAM CRABTREE

THE GREATEST MEN commend the greatest things. Paul commends specific qualities in Philemon. That's what healthy hearts do with the good deeds of men: commend them. It is the pattern of wise and generous hearts to give commendations—regularly, habitually, generously, truthfully, gladly. Paul commends Philemon for many things:

- his love for Jesus Christ
- his love for the saints
- his faith toward Jesus Christ
- his sharing of his faith
- his refreshing of the hearts of the saints
- his consenting to good plans
- his considerate partnership
- his ability to refresh Paul's heart in Christ
- his obedience
- his going above and beyond as a second-miler, doing more than asked
- his anticipated hospitality

All of the good patterns in Philemon's life are owing to the grace of Jesus. When Paul hears of good things in the life of Philemon, he thanks *God*. In fact, any and all commendable qualities originate in and echo Christ Jesus. Christ is doing good things in us, and wise hearts strive to come into full awareness and appreciation of Christ for working those things.

Good men commend good things. Bad men commend bad things. Empty men commend empty and worthless things. When wise, masculine, biblical hearts spot something commendable, they don't merely notice it; they *say* something about it. For dads to do more fault-finding than affirming is a gross imbalance that costs relational capital down the road and leads to painful regrets.

The story of Philemon is a portrayal of the gospel—forgiveness paving the way for reconciliation. In this account we see an offended party, an offender, a human mediator, and another mediator, behind the scenes, who pleads the cause of the offender at great personal cost. That's what Jesus does for all believers: "Treat him as you would treat me" is alien righteousness; and "if he has offended you, charge it to my account" is substitutionary atonement (see v. 18).

In manly love, Paul is imitating Jesus. Great men aim to do the same.

The Question of God

TOM NELSON

FROM THE EARLIEST days of our lives, we men are curious and questioning creatures. We are explorers, adventurers seeking to discover, to know, and to understand who we are and the nature of the world around us. But no question is more inviting to our heart and stretching to our mind than the question of God. Who is God? What is God like? How can we know him?

It is not surprising, then, that the opening verses of Hebrews focus on Jesus, the One to whom our deepest questions about God inevitably point, and the One through whom those questions are ultimately answered. Unlike God's revelation in the past, Jesus has now uniquely made God known to us, by becoming one of us. Describing the role of Jesus of Nazareth in redemptive history and in creation, the author of Hebrews gives a compelling glimpse of the Son of God's nature and redemptive work on our behalf.

Like an athletic hall of fame display, Jesus's glorious posture of deity is presented here for us both to see and to marvel at. This very Jesus is the "exact imprint of [God's] nature, and he upholds the universe by the word of his power" (Heb. 1:3). The apostle Paul employs similar words, describing Jesus as the one by whom and through whom all things were created (see Col. 1:16). Jesus's glorious posture of sinless humanity is also on display for us in these opening verses of Hebrews. Jesus is the One whose atoning and finished work on the cross has satisfied the righteous wrath of a holy God and made complete provision for our sin (Heb. 1:3). Is it any wonder, then, that the writer of Hebrews will remind us repeatedly throughout his brilliant treatise that this Jesus is *more excellent* than even the angels or any other earthly or heavenly creature?

What questions about God are stirring in your mind today? What longings are beckoning your heart? Every question we ask about God and every desire of our hearts inevitably leads us to Jesus and to the good news of the gospel. Will you look to Jesus? Will you trust him? Will you follow him? There is no greater adventure than knowing, loving, and following Jesus.

DECEMBER 4 · HEBREWS 2

Are You Adrift?

TOM NELSON

AS A YOUNG BOY, I remember a seasoned fisherman saying, "A boat adrift is a boat heading for danger." Over the years I have learned that, like boats, men also can drift. In tranquil or turbulent water, without an anchor we drift; and the longer we drift, the farther off course we become. We drift in our friendships and our marriage. We drift in our work. Most perilously, we drift in our relationship with Christ and the gospel faith that we cherish.

The writer of Hebrews addresses the peril of gospel drift by encouraging us to "pay much closer attention" to the gospel message we have heard (Heb. 2:1). The deceptive subtlety of spiritual peril is reinforced by the nautical metaphor of drifting. We don't wake up in the morning thinking of how we can drift from Christ and the gospel, yet not one of us is immune from losing sight of who Jesus is as our Creator and Redeemer and thus "neglecting such a great salvation" (v. 3).

How do we avoid the peril of spiritual drift? In Hebrews 2 we are reminded that our crucified and risen Savior is there to keep us from drifting and to help us stay firmly anchored to him. We must continually preach the good news of the gospel to ourselves, remembering that Jesus is our "merciful and faithful high priest" (v. 17). Jesus is the One who has made provision for our sin, and who is there to help us when we face suffering in the pain of our bodies, in the heartache of our relationships, in our stinging failures, and in the shattering of our dreams. Jesus, who faced every temptation we do, though he did not sin, is there to help us in our temptation (v. 18).

So what sets you adrift? Is your honest doubt morphing into willful disbelief? Are your heartfelt disappointments with others and even God setting you adrift? What about the peer pressure you are experiencing at school or at work? Are you drifting, or are you anchored? If you are not firmly anchored to Jesus, you are drifting away from him. Keep your eyes on Jesus. Keep preaching the gospel to yourself. Feed your heart and mind daily with the truths of holy Scripture. Stay tethered to other gospel-transformed men, who will help you stay on course. Pay close attention to what matters most.

DECEMBER 5 · HEBREWS 4

Experiencing True Rest

TOM NELSON

WHEN YOU THINK of rest, what comes to mind? Perhaps catching up on sleep or watching your favorite sports team. Yet the biblical idea of rest speaks to the good life we were originally created to live, a life of intimacy, wholeness, purpose, and delight. Amid life's seemingly endless responsibilities, the exhausting demands of work, and the painful struggles of a fallen world, how do we experience true rest?

The writer of Hebrews wants us to firmly grasp that true rest is not a divine afterthought but an integral aspect of God's perfect creation design. God resting on the seventh day of creation paints a beautiful picture of pure and joyful delight in his Trinitarian being and his creation (Gen. 2:2; Heb. 4:4). Sabbath rest is now something we experience in and through the grace gift of gospel faith. "For we who have believed enter that rest" (v. 3). True rest is something Jesus, our "great high priest" (v. 14), has made possible for us to experience through his sinless life, atoning death, and death-defeating resurrection.

In Hebrews 4 we encounter one of several warning passages prompting us toward honest self-reflection. We must take seriously the ever-present threat of the unbelief of hardened hearts (v. 7) and "disobedience" (v. 11) that keeps us from experiencing true rest. What is the true condition of your heart today? Is your heart hardening? Is there a willful disobedient sin, a heart idol you are looking to instead of Jesus to find true rest?

Jesus invites you to find the true rest for which your heart longs. "Come to me, all who labor and are heavy laden, and I will give you rest. Take my yoke upon you, and learn from me, for I am gentle and lowly in heart, and you will find rest for your souls" (Matt. 11:28–29). Employing the metaphor of a yoke, Jesus wants us to know that following him leads to true rest. When we take Jesus's yoke of apprenticeship and learn from him how to live our lives like he would if he were us, we increasingly learn the rhythms of true Sabbath rest. Echoing Jesus's words, the author of Hebrews invites us to "draw near to the throne of grace, that we may receive mercy and find grace to help in time of need" (Heb. 4:16). Let us draw near to the One who created true rest, the One who has redeemed us to experience true rest not only now, but for all eternity.

DECEMBER 6 · HEBREWS 6:13-20

A Promise You Can Count On

TOM NELSON

WE ALL MAKE PROMISES, but do we keep them? We promise our boss to have a project done by a specific date. We enter into a contract promising to pay our mortgage every month. We even promise to be faithful in a vow of marriage. We also encounter in life the stinging pain of broken promises. A marriage vow not kept. A work contract not fulfilled. A word of promise that proves hollow. It is easy for our hearts to become cynical. In moments of shattering disillusionment, we wonder if there is a promise we can truly count on, a promise keeper we can truly trust.

In Hebrews 6 we are pointed to the promise keeper we can completely trust. We are given a flashback in human history to the big promise God made to Abraham, saying, "Surely I will bless you and multiply you" (Heb. 6:14). Through Abraham's descendants, God's plan of redemption would unfold in human history (Gen. 12:2–3). Even though Abraham waited a long time, in faith he remained "fully convinced that God was able to do what he had promised" (Rom. 4:20–21).

Abraham banked his entire life on God's promise. But what about us? Can we still count on God's promises? The promise made to Abraham is the promise made to all who share the faith of Abraham (Rom. 4:16). Seeking to fortify our gospel faith, the author of Hebrews reminds us of God's "unchangeable character" and encourages us to "hold fast to the hope set before us" (Heb. 6:17–18). A promise is only as good as the one who makes it, and God certainly makes good on his promises. Though we too, like Abraham, wait, our hope in God's promise need not waver, for through the eyes of faith we look to Jesus, the one whose high priestly work on the cross has made the way for us to be reconciled to God. When gospel faith is securely tethered to the promises of God, our spiritual formation is deepened.

If you have embraced the gospel, you have "a sure and steadfast anchor of the soul" (v. 19). Because of Christ, you not only have the power to keep the promises you make; you have confidence, security, and peace in the ultimate promise keeper. Bank your life on God's promise in Christ.

Good to Great

TOM NELSON

THE GOOD CAN keep us from the great, but what about the old? Whether due to simply a comfortable familiarity or a secure feeling of rootedness from the past, it is easy to cling to the old rather than embrace the new. The new offered to us may be a hobby to explore, a friendship to foster, or a recent technology to purchase. Going from good to great often means recognition that the new way is better than the old way.

In Hebrews 8 we are encouraged to leave behind the old and look to the new. The new and better way is Jesus, whose new covenant is secured by his completed priestly sacrifice on our behalf. The old covenant, embedded in the law, was good (Rom. 7:12), but the new covenant of gospel grace is *great*. Comparing the old with the new, the Hebrew writer asserts, "Christ has obtained a ministry that is as much more excellent than the old . . ." (Heb. 8:6). The prophet Jeremiah had spoken of how the good old covenant anticipated the great new covenant that was to come (Jer. 31:31–34). The new covenant would be much better, much more excellent. But why?

The new covenant says a resounding "No!" to our work on behalf of God and says a grateful "Yes!" to God's work on our behalf. The new covenant makes possible a new heart, an internal transformation, and not mere external conformity to a prescribed code of conduct. The intimacy our hearts long for becomes a reality. The new covenant means that our sins are not only covered; they are forgiven and remembered no more. What extraordinary good news! The old may be good, but the new is great. The night before he would shed his blood on the cross, the Lord Jesus celebrated the new covenant he was bringing to fruition. Jesus said, "For this is my blood of the [new] covenant, which is poured out for many for the forgiveness of sins" (Matt. 26:28).

What freeing and hopeful words Jesus uttered to all who would follow him! The good news of the gospel is the great news of a new covenant and a new way, not of law but of grace. Jesus has made it possible for us to go from good to great, but we must say good-bye to the old that is now obsolete (Heb. 8:13) and embrace the new and better way.

DECEMBER 8 · HEBREWS 9:11-28

Once for All

TOM NELSON

THERE ARE A LOT of things we do once a year. We celebrate birthdays and anniversaries. We enjoy Christmas and other holidays with our families. We settle our tax bill with the government. We experience much of life through the rhythms of yearly repetition. Yet we also experience once-in-a-lifetime moments like the birth of a child, graduation from college, or the declaration of wedding vows. While once-a-year moments are important, once-in-a-lifetime moments often bring with them a greater sense of significance.

The writer of Hebrews reminds us of this very thing as we encounter in chapter 9 a riveting contrast between something that occurred once a year and something that occurred once for all. One day each year, God's covenant people in the Old Testament experienced the Day of Atonement. On that day, the high priest took the blood of a sacrificed animal and made atonement for his sins and the sins of the people. But now because of Jesus, what was once a year is now once for all. Speaking of Jesus and his high priestly work on the cross, the writer of Hebrews declares the good news: "He entered once for all into the holy places, not by means of the blood of goats and calves but by means of his own blood, thus securing an eternal redemption" (Heb. 9:12). Not wanting us to miss the importance of Jesus's once-and-for-all sacrifice for sin, the writer repeats this thought: "But as it is, he has appeared once for all at the end of the ages to put away sin by the sacrifice of himself" (v. 26).

Hebrews points us to a secure gospel faith, one based not on our performance, merit, or feeling, but on Jesus's perfect and complete sacrifice on our behalf. Nothing can be added to it or subtracted from it. Jesus paid it all, once for all. When we let this transforming truth soak into our hearts and minds, a microburst of joyous gratitude and humble confidence erupts. The payment for your sins was very costly, but Jesus paid it all with his precious blood. Today, wrap your heart and mind around the good news that Jesus not only paid it all; he paid it *once* for all. What a good, glorious Savior you serve!

DECEMBER 9 · HEBREWS 10:19-25

Finding Intimacy by Drawing Near

TOM NELSON

FEW THINGS BRING greater joy to our lives than close relationships. The joy of a satisfying marriage or a deepening friendship is hard to describe or fully fathom. On the other hand, our relationships can be a source of great loss and heartache. Few things put greater hopelessness in our hearts than an imploding marriage or an unraveling long-time friendship. The pain we experience often leads us to guard our wounded hearts in the unsatisfying shallows of superficiality and individual isolation. Intimacy is something we long for yet also fear. Why?

In a pristine garden long ago, the intimacy we once had with God and with our fellow humans was vandalized and corrupted when sin and death entered God's good world. Loneliness, alienation, isolation, and despair have now become our heart companions, replacing the joyful intimacy of true community that God had intended for us to experience.

The writer of Hebrews speaks good news into our deepest heart longings. The good news of Jesus's atoning death and completed priestly sacrifice has now made it possible for us to experience true intimacy both with God and with others. The gospel brings hopeful reconciliation in our relationship with God and with our fellow man (2 Cor. 5:18). In Hebrews 10, we are encouraged collectively as brothers in Christ to draw near to God and to each other in the transforming power and grace of gospel faith. In verse 22 we hear the glorious invitation to experience a restored intimacy in Christ: "Let us draw near with a true heart in full assurance of faith."

In verse 24 we are invited to experience restored community in Christ: "Let us consider how to stir up one another to love and good works." The gospel calls us to draw near to Christ and to draw near to one another.

Are you experiencing deeper and deeper intimacy with the true Lover of your soul? Is your heart increasingly knitted to other followers of Jesus whom you are seeking to encourage in their faith? You were not only created with community in mind; you have been redeemed with a *new* community in mind: the local church. A greater intimacy with God and others awaits you in the local church that Christ has called you to, until that day yet in the future when our Lord will return for his bride. The author of Hebrews reminds us that that day is drawing near. Are you drawing near to Jesus? Are you drawing near to others who follow him?

DECEMBER 10 · HEBREWS 11

Believing Is Seeing

TOM NELSON

WHEN YOU HEAR the word "faith," what pops into your mind? For many, faith is the wishful thinking we cling to when we have exhausted all other means of knowing at our disposal. For others, faith is something we deeply feel, a set of beliefs that is part of our religious traditions.

So what is faith? The writer of Hebrews grapples with this question in an entire chapter devoted to the subject of faith and its transforming power on men and women throughout biblical history. In verse 1, we discover a bedrock definition of faith. "Now faith is the assurance of things hoped for, the conviction of things not seen." Faith, properly understood, is not something we cling to as a last resort; rather, it is the first thing we look to.

We often think that, in order to truly believe, we must first see; but here the author of Hebrews asserts that in order to truly see, we must first believe. Through the eyes of faith, we see in ways we could not otherwise see. Faith opens our eyes to see as God sees. Faith also allows us to truly please God. "And without faith it is impossible to please him, for whoever would draw near to God must believe that he exists and that he rewards those who seek him" (Heb. 11:6). From Abraham to David and beyond, God's people of old pleased God by trusting him as they looked to the future promise of Messiah Jesus. Properly understood, gospel faith is how we truly see, how we please God, and how we live the life we were designed and redeemed to live. The apostle Paul writes, "I have been crucified with Christ. It is no longer I who live, but Christ who lives in me. And the life I now live in the flesh I live by faith in the Son of God, who loved me and gave himself for me" (Gal. 2:20).

Are you pleasing God by placing your faith in Jesus? Are you living each day in the joy and power of gospel faith? Are you looking at all of life through the eyes of faith? Seeing is not believing, but believing is seeing.

The Race of Faith

TOM NELSON

TO RUN A RACE WELL, we must train well. Not even the most physically fit person decides one day to go out and run a marathon without spending extensive time preparing for it. Athletes know that, the longer the distance of the race, the more endurance is required. This is the timeless truth the writer of Hebrews wants to impress on those who are running the race of gospel faith.

What will help you finish the race of faith well? Hebrews 12 informs us that, to run the race of gospel faith, we need to keep two truths in mind; in the power of the Holy Spirit, we must *eliminate* and *concentrate*: First, we must eliminate anything that hinders us from running well. In verse 1, we read, "let us also lay aside every weight, and sin which clings so closely." Running the race of faith requires that we address those things that clutter our lives and weigh us down, as well as sinful attitudes and actions. Faith training requires the discipline of elimination.

Second, faith training requires the discipline of concentration. In verse 2 we read, ". . . looking to Jesus, the founder and perfecter of our faith, who for the joy that was set before him endured the cross, despising the shame, and is seated at the right hand of the throne of God." Running well requires that we keep our eyes on the One who has perfectly run the race of faith before us, and also that we keep our eyes fixed on the finish line, where Jesus is, seated at the right hand of the throne of God.

Running the race of faith is not merely about trying harder; it is also about training better. We do not run the race of faith alone. Jesus invites us to take up our cross and follow him (Mark 8:34), to enter his yoke of apprenticeship and learn from him (Matt. 11:29).

Are you running well the race of gospel faith? Are you merely trying harder, or are you training better? What do you need to eliminate in your life that is weighing you down, distracting you, or ensnaring you? How might you better concentrate on loving, knowing, following, and serving Jesus? To run the race of faith well, we must train well.

DECEMBER 12 • JAMES 1:19-27

Don't Just Hear—Do!

GREG GILBERT

THERE'S A HUGE difference between hearing the word of God and doing it. In fact, just to hear God's word has no spiritual value at all. You have to *do it*—follow it, obey it—for there to be any good in it for you. You can listen to sermons, read the Bible, and do your devotional reading every day, but if you don't obey God's word, you're not really accomplishing much at all.

That's James's message in 1:19–27. There are some texts in the Bible that are difficult to understand, ones that you really have to analyze in order to grasp their meaning. There are others, though, that just punch you right between the eyes, and this is one of those. There's no doubt about what James is saying. Simply hearing God's word is not enough. You have to do what it says.

Verses 19–20 can seem a bit random here. If James's point is that we as Christians need to hear and obey God's word, what are these verses about hearing, speaking, and getting angry doing? The answer is that they are paving the road for James's exhortation to receive and do the word. After all, much of our trouble in really hearing and then really doing God's word comes because we ourselves are too eager to speak our own opinions, too slow to hear God's voice in his word, or too full of anger, agitation, irritation, and distraction to give it the attention it deserves.

What today is keeping you from really hearing—and then doing—God's word? Are you distracted by work, family, your task list, phone calls to make, vacations to plan, appointments to keep, and, "Aaarrrgghh! It all just gets away from me!"? Are there things that you have come to value more than you value God's word? Are you discontented with where God has you in life right now? Any and all of that can contribute to our natural tendency to let our church attendance, our devotions, and our reading of Scripture become rote and lifeless.

Take some time today to determine what might be keeping you from doing God's word—from (as James says in verses 26–27) being careful about your words, caring for those in need, and not falling into friendship with an ungodly world. Don't look in the mirror and then forget what you've seen (vv. 23–24); look deeply into the word of truth, obey it, and see how God will bless you—not just in the hearing but in the doing! (v. 25).

DECEMBER 13 · JAMES 2:14-26

Living Faith

GREG GILBERT

JAMES IS A REALLY simple book. Chapter by chapter, James unfolds what the life of a Christian ought to look like after he is born again through the gospel of Jesus Christ. This is what a Christian does: He bears up under trials (James 1:2–3). She's a doer of God's word, not just a hearer (vv. 22–25). She doesn't show partiality (2:1–7). He keeps his tongue under control (3:1–12). This passage is no exception to that simplicity. Even if some of its details cause us difficulty, the main point is blindingly clear: Your "faith" (if it can even be called that, James means) is dead and meaningless unless it results in godly action.

The structure of the passage is not difficult. James lays out his principle in 2:14, then illustrates it in verses 15–17. Verses 18–19 deal with an objection to his point, and then in verses 20–26 he gives two examples from the Old Testament. Many Christians have explained some of the more difficult details here, so we won't take time to do that. The most important thing to realize, however, is that James uses the word "faith" in two very different senses. On the one hand, he uses "faith" to refer to *living, saving, real* faith (v. 22); but he also uses the same word "faith" to refer to a *dead, false, useless* faith (vv. 14, 17, 20, 26). Being able to distinguish which "faith" James is talking about in any given verse is the key to getting this passage right.

Once you do, what James is saying becomes very clear: A real, saving, living faith will produce godly works. Now, James is not saying that we have to add works to our faith in order to make it alive. That would be like saying you have to tape a plant onto a seed in order to make the seed alive. No, James is saying that, just as a living seed will produce a plant, so living faith will produce godly action. And just as a seed that doesn't produce a plant is dead, so faith that doesn't produce works is dead.

Simply calling yourself a Christian, or simply having made a decision at some point to follow Jesus, is not worth anything. A "faith" that does nothing is dead. Growing up in a Christian home is not enough; going to church is not enough. A real, vital, genuine faith in Jesus will express itself in a life of godly works. Take some time today to examine your heart and make sure that your faith is living and active, and then give thanks to God for the fruit you see!

DECEMBER 14 · JAMES 3:1–12

Bombs and Trip Wires

GREG GILBERT

EVERYONE KNOWS THAT, despite the playground taunt, words *can* hurt you just as badly as sticks and stones. In fact, if James has anything to say about it, sticks and stones have *nothing* on the tongue, which, he says, is "set on fire by hell" itself! (James 3:6).

Apparently the churches to which James wrote were being rocked by fights and controversies, especially among people who were jockeying for leadership, in which they were using their tongues—that is, their words—to wreak enormous havoc in the church. So James launches a full frontal assault on the tongue, describing just how evil it can be. In fact, he seems amazed that so much trouble could be caused by such a small thing. Like a bit in a horse's mouth or a rudder on a ship, the tongue is a small thing that exerts great power. It's like a fire that sets a forest ablaze (v. 5), a world of unrighteousness (v. 6), and though humans have managed to tame every other kind of beast, James says, the tongue remains wild and unbridled (vv. 7–8). Not only so, but it's the fountain of exactly the kind of double-mindedness James talked about in chapter 1. One minute the tongue can be singing praises to God, and the next minute it can be forming words meant to destroy a brother or sister in Christ.

You don't have to live very long in the world—or in the church—to know that the tongue has fearsome power to destroy relationships. The world is littered with the remains of marriages and friendships and parent-child relationships that have been pulverized to dust by the tongue. Not only so, but the damage the tongue does can be incredibly subtle. Like a terrorist laying booby traps, Satan can use what we say to lay webs of offense and accusation that, when they explode, can destroy entire families or groups of friends, or even churches. When you speak ill of others, gossip, backbite, or tear down, you are helping Satan lay bombs and trip wires that, many times, remain unseen until they explode. And then it blows up all at once, in an explosion of, "Well, you said, and he said, and she said . . . !"

If that's true, then so is what James says in verse 10—that among Christians, "these things ought not to be so." Keep a guard on your tongue today. Consider where you might be laying unseen trip wires that Satan could use to destroy relationships, friendships, your marriage, or even your church. Be a person who's not laying bombs but rather who is working hard to disarm them.

Does God Want to Answer Prayer?

GREG GILBERT

I WAS WITH a group of friends recently when one of the young kids ran up to his dad and said, "Daddy, can I have a cookie?"

Almost without even thinking, the dad responded, "Yes, of course, Buddy. Of course you can have a cookie."

Immediately a hundred objections flew into my own mind, but as I thought about it, I *loved* that dad's response. He genuinely *wanted* to give his son what he asked for.

That's the main idea of this section of James. God is like that dad, eager to answer his children when they pray. Some of the details can get a little tricky, and we won't take time to deal with them here. The important thing, however, is that James is not saying there's a special "prayer of faith" or holy sacrament that will *always* heal people of illness; rather, he is saying something similar to what John said in 1 John 5:14–15: "If we ask anything according to his will . . . we have the requests that we have asked of him." God is sovereign. He alone determines how he will answer prayer, and a "prayer of faith" is precisely a prayer that recognizes his sovereignty, not one that believes it can somehow *force* God to act. It's a prayer that's prayed in the confidence that God will give us what we ask for when those things are in accordance with his will.

James's point is simple and profound: our God hears prayer, and he answers it. "Prayer is powerful," we often say, but what we really mean is that *God* is powerful, and he *wants* to answer prayer. So be a person of bold prayer. Pray for people who are suffering. Pray for people who are thriving. Pray for people who are sick. Ask God to do specific, big things, and then live in the expectation that he will answer.

Why is it that the Bible's strong statements that God *will* answer prayer so often bother us and make us feel the need to qualify them? I think it's because we tend to approach prayer with the expectation that it's *most* likely that God *won't* grant our requests, even that he doesn't really *want* to, and we end up pleasantly surprised when he does. But what if that's all wrong? What if we prayed with the real expectation that he *wants* to give us good things? Today, let's approach God as the loving Father he is, with a recognition that, of course he might say no to our requests, but the confidence that, in his great love, he *wants* to say, "Yes, of course!"

DECEMBER 16 • 1 PETER 1:13–16

Tempted to Look at Pornography?

ANDREW DAVID NASELLI

YOU MAY BE TEMPTED to conform to the evil desires you had before you became God's child—perhaps looking at pornography or getting drunk or loving money or slandering others or being lazy and gluttonous. In light of God's saving grace (1 Pet. 1:1–12), what should you do instead?

Peter's counsel in 1 Peter 1:13 is to "set your hope fully on the grace that will be brought to you at the revelation of Jesus Christ." Confidently expect and eagerly await the day when Jesus will return and finish the saving work that he has already begun in you, so that you will no longer sin.

That is why John Newton, the former slave-trader who wrote the song "Amazing Grace," encapsulated the Christian life in this pithy statement: "I am not what I ought to be. . . . I am not what I wish to be. . . . I am not what I hope to be. . . . Yet . . . I am not what I once was . . . and by the grace of God I am what I am."[14] And by the grace of God you will become what you ought and wish and hope to be. That grace is future. And God tells you to set your hope on it.

How? By "preparing your minds for action" and "being sober-minded." Roll up the shirtsleeves of your mind, and be fully alert, disciplined, and intentional in how you think. View sin as what it really is, and view God as who he really is. When you conform to sinful passions like viewing pornography, you are as sensible as someone who caresses a deadly spider in the dark, thinking it is harmless and cuddly. If you think that sin is attractively glamorous and that God is boring, then you are not sober-minded but, essentially, drunk. Avoid whatever numbs your mind to God.

Instead of conforming to "the passions of your former ignorance," be like God. His moral character is the standard for how you should behave, so reflect it. Be pure. Be separate from evil. "In *all* your conduct" (v. 15). Why? Because God is holy. And you are his child.

DECEMBER 17 • 1 PETER 3:7

How to Treat Your Wife

ANDREW DAVID NASELLI

GOD DIRECTLY TELLS husbands how to treat their wives: "Live with your wives in an understanding way." God then explains how and why:

- *How* should you live with your wife in an understanding way? By "showing honor" to her.
- *Why* should you honor your wife? (1) "Since" she is an heir "with you of the grace of life" and (2) "so that your prayers may not be hindered."

So if you are a husband, you should ask yourself, "How can I better live with my wife in an understanding way? How can I better honor her?" Here are some diagnostic questions to help you do that:

1. How often do you ask your wife, "How can I better live with you in an understanding way? How can I better honor you?" Or stated negatively, "Are there ways in which I am *not* living with you in an understanding way? Are there ways in which you feel like I am not honoring you?" If you are wise, you'll ask her that regularly and assure her that you will receive her answer humbly and graciously, responding neither defensively nor offensively.

2. How well do you know your wife? What does she need and want from you? You can't live with your wife in an understanding way if you don't know very much about her. You should know your wife better than anyone else. What makes her tick? What does she like and dislike? What are her deepest fears and aspirations?

It is shameful if you know and care more about players on your favorite football team than you do about your wife. Do you delight to *study* your wife?

3. What are you intentionally doing to get to know your wife better? Do you regularly plan to set aside time to have unhurried, distraction-free conversations? Does she feel like you are deeply interested in her and her world? Do you draw out what is in her heart with thoughtful questions?

4. Do you treat your wife in a harsh or domineering way? Do you think of her or treat her as less important than you?

5. Can you name specific ways that you regularly honor your wife (privately and publicly) in ways that make her *feel* honored?

DECEMBER 18 · 1 PETER 4:12

Expect Persecution

ANDREW DAVID NASELLI

WHEN YOU EXPERIENCE persecution for being a Christian, you may be tempted to ask, "Why is this happening to *me*? This is shocking. I can't believe this. It's strange." No, it shouldn't be surprising, and it isn't strange. Christians experience persecution. You should be surprised if you *don't* experience it.

You may live in a culture where you think it is unusual for non-Christians to persecute Christians. But 1 Peter 4:12 says not to be surprised when others persecute you for your faith.

What exactly is persecution? Is it only extreme hostility and violent treatment, perhaps even imprisonment or death? No, even in places such as America that seek to uphold religious freedom, Christians experience persecution every day. It may not occur as often, consistently, or intensely as it occurs in other places. There are different levels of persecution.

Persecution can be as simple as harassing, shaming, mocking, vilifying, or slandering people because they believe what the Bible teaches about an issue (e.g., God created the universe, including Adam and Eve; faith alone in Jesus alone is the exclusive way to salvation; those who reject Christ will suffer eternal conscious torment in hell; marriage is between one man and one woman, and any sex outside of marriage is sin). Persecution in that sense is what *all* Christians experience to at least some degree: "All who desire to live a godly life in Christ Jesus will be persecuted" (2 Tim. 3:12). Jesus warned, "If they persecuted me, they will also persecute you" (John 15:20). It's normal for non-Christians to hate followers of Christ.

So expect persecution. "Do not be surprised" at it, "as though something strange were happening to you" (1 Pet. 4:12).

DECEMBER 19 · 2 PETER 3:11, 14

Why Does God Tell Us What's Going to Happen in the Future?

ANDREW DAVID NASELLI

GOD DOES NOT discuss the end times in 2 Peter 3 merely to satisfy your curiosity. His purpose is practical: in light of this future destruction when Jesus returns, you should live in a holy and godly way now (2 Pet. 3:11, 14). To live in an unholy, ungodly way now is foolish, just as it would be foolish to invest all of your money in a company that you know is going to crash in the near future.

God tells you throughout the Bible what is going to happen in the future. You might wish for even more specific details, but the amount he has disclosed is substantial. Some end-times specialists confidently chart out precise timetables for end-time events. One danger is that you may become so preoccupied with the timing of these events that you neglect to focus on the main purpose for which God disclosed those events to you.

The Bible's teaching about the end times (theologians call it "eschatology") has three essentials. The first two essentials are events, and the third answers the "So what?" question:

1. Jesus won the victory over sin, death, and hell at the cross and empty tomb.
2. Jesus will return to earth personally, bodily, and gloriously to consummate his righteous rule.
3. Therefore, Christians (who currently live in between Jesus's two victories) should live in light of Jesus's imminent return.

Jesus's two victories parallel D-Day and V-E Day in World War II: a decisive battle has determined the war's outcome, but more battles remain to end the war. Christians confidently expect that God will vindicate himself and his people and re-create "new heavens and a new earth" (2 Pet. 3:13; Isa. 65:17; 66:22; Revelation 21).

So the primary purpose of eschatology is ethical. In other words, God tells us about what's going to happen in the future in order to motivate us to *live* a certain way right now: "Since all these things are thus to be dissolved, what sort of people ought you to be in lives of holiness and godliness. . . . Therefore, beloved, since you are waiting for these, be diligent to be found by him without spot or blemish, and at peace" (2 Pet. 3:11, 14).

DECEMBER 20 · 1 JOHN 2:1-8

True Light for a True Life

ROBERT W. YARBROUGH

"THE TRUE LIGHT is already shining" (1 John 2:8). What does that mean? It means that Christ has come. That changes everything for those who follow him. When we follow Christ,

- He deals with our sin problem (v. 1). He is our "advocate" in the presence of God. This does not mean sin is acceptable. It means Jesus is the "propitiation for our sins" (v. 2); he bore God's wrath in our place, making God's forgiveness possible.
- We can embrace God's commandments (v. 3). Questions of right and wrong are not always a murky gray: the commands of Christ and Scripture give us clear direction.

- We hear the truth about ourselves. Verse 4 says that if we do not keep God's commandments, we are liars, even if we say, "I know him." Truth sometimes hurts, but self-deception can do great damage.
- God perfects his love in us (v. 5a). This does not mean we become perfect. It means that our lives increasingly exhibit Christlike traits and instincts.
- We gain the assurance that God accepts us; we come to "know that we are in him" (v. 5b). The continuing popularity of J. I. Packer's book *Knowing God* points to the human hunger to come into a relationship with one's Maker and Redeemer. Following Christ makes this possible.
- Christ shows the way for us to live as he lived (v. 6). His life gives guidance, inspiration, and oversight for ours.
- We gain a unified sense of God's expectations. They involve an old-yet-new commandment (vv. 7–8): The Old Testament taught love for God and for people (Deut. 6:5; Lev. 19:18). Jesus renews and intensifies this greatest of all commandments. He lived out perfect love for God as well as for other humans. He calls and enables us to do the same.

Thus "the darkness" of human self-centeredness and animosity toward others "is passing away" (1 John 2:8). True light gleams into and from the lives of those who know God through faith in Jesus. Our lives are not muddled, tasteless, or meaningless; they are, rather, engaged, enriched, and true.

Conquering Cain, Confessing Christ

ROBERT W. YARBROUGH

ONE OF THE FIRST big events in the Bible is the sin of Adam and Eve (Genesis 3). As promised, this called forth God's curse (Gen. 3:14–19). As if to illustrate this new normal for humankind, the next big event is Cain's slaughter of his brother Abel (Genesis 4).

First John 3:12 warns us against being like Cain, and with good reason. There's some Cain in all of us. Who has never struck another person in anger? If nothing else, as children we performed violent acts. We were little and weak then, so injury may not have resulted. But if we had known how and been stronger, the outcome might have been grave or even fatal.

Siblings may get so angry with each other that they feel like lashing out and sometimes do. So much for brotherly love! Parents lose their temper and smack down their children in rage. Children in retaliation and disrespect may snarl and curse the mother and father who gave them life. Cain-like contempt crops up outside our "loving" families, too. Street gangs are vehicles for organized expression of lawlessness and anger. Fraternities and sororities may be "respectable," but they can also be hotbeds of arrogant exclusivism, racism, and even physical violence related to hazing.

How about the backstabbing that goes on in many (most?) workplaces? How about management contempt for workers? What about the workingman's rage toward the company's executives with their lavish incomes, stylish suits, and soft hands?

Some of us not only know all about the myriad settings of human resentment and rage: we give in to it ourselves. Perhaps we have even inflicted bodily harm on another person, whether premeditated or on impulse. Maybe we are just waiting to do it again. No wonder many churches observe a time in worship called the "Kyrie," wherein they pray, "Lord, have mercy!" As sons and daughters of Cain, we all need it.

First John 3:11–24 sets forth a better way: we are to "love the brothers" (v. 14). As Christ laid down his life for others, so do we (v. 16). We don't just talk about mutual care; we exercise it (v. 18). This arises "by the Spirit whom he has given us" (v. 24). Goodness rooted in Jesus and his commandment (v. 23) causes the Cain-impulse to dwindle, replaced by love for God, for persons created in his image, and especially for fellow Christ-followers.

DECEMBER 22 · 1 JOHN 4:7-21

Tapping into God to Find Life's Meaning

ROBERT W. YARBROUGH

PSYCHIATRIST VIKTOR FRANKL survived Nazi death camps and wrote a book entitled *Man's Search for Meaning*. We have a drive to find meaning in life even amid cruelty and pain. Men seek that meaning in many places: sports, work, family, adventure, hobbies, travel, vice, and more. What gives our life significance, in God's sight?

The answer lies in the simple word "love." But not just any love: John speaks of a love that is from God. This love is exercised by the one who "has been born of God and knows God" (1 John 4:7). What are some symptoms of embracing this love? One symptom is that we "live through him" (v. 9). The Son of God, at God's right hand, mysteriously empowers our earthly lives as we trust in him. His vitality and will take shape in our lives through our union with him.

Another symptom: the quality of our love is defined by the cross. "Propitiation" in verse 10 refers to Jesus's suffering on the cross for our salvation. "In this is love," John writes. As Jesus's self-giving love takes shape in our lives, we might want to reread 1 Corinthians 13, to see how we're measuring up.

A third symptom of embracing God's love is love for one another. This refers especially to fellow Christ-followers, though like Jesus we are called to be gracious to all people. "If God so loved us, we also ought to love one another" (1 John 4:11). The logic is compelling when one considers the sacrifice of the Son of God for us.

Another symptom: freedom from the fear of judgment day (vv. 17–18). Many people live in denial of death and what may lie beyond this life. God's love as shown in Christ affirms liberation from death's terrors. Terror takes flight if we live through the one who conquered death.

Men invest their lives in all kinds of pursuits, many of them noble and commendable. But the greatest need, the deepest drive, and the highest prize is knowing and showing God's love as demonstrated in his Son. Lives take on eternal meaning as love gives new depth to our relationships, new definition to our pursuits, new direction in our decisions, and new reality to our sense that, in living our lives by faith in Jesus (see v. 15), we are drawing something pure, sweet, and eternal from God.

DECEMBER 23 · 2 JOHN 4–11

Overcoming Hindrances to Pleasing God

ROBERT W. YARBROUGH

AT THE CORE OF 2 John is a pleasant picture: the elder John rejoices that members of the church to which he writes are obeying the truth that the Father commands (v. 4). It is always delightful when God's people care for each other (v. 5), living out what God and his word set forth (v. 6).

But John also lists some hindrances to pleasing God. First he speaks of *deceivers* (v. 7). These people are teaching that Jesus Christ did not come "in the flesh." They do not build their lives on the fact of Christ's incarnation. A faulty view of Christ's person and work can lead to faulty behaviors and loyalties. Our view of Christ should be expanding and challenging us to ever more authentic lives in him.

A second hindrance is *devaluation* of God's gifts through Christ. Verse 8 speaks of what Christians "have worked for," which leads to "a full reward." John refers to things like heeding the gospel's good news, repenting of sin, trusting in Christ, and fulfilling his will in dedicated service. It is possible to take lightly the benefits of saving faith that are granted to us by God's magnificent grace. When we do, we may find these benefits have slipped from our grasp.

A third hindrance is posed by *deviators* (v. 9). Apostles like John spread a "teaching of Christ" which, when believed, created fellowship between Father, Son, and sinner (see 1 John 1:3). In John's time, and still today, people both outside and inside the church deviate from apostolic (biblical) teaching. This may take the form of denying what Scripture teaches about God, Jesus, the human plight, heaven and hell, and much else. It may take the form of advocating practices that Scripture forbids. Anyone taking such steps "does not have God" (2 John 9)—a chilling thought.

A fourth hindrance takes the form of *deniers*—those who do "not abide in the teaching" (v. 9) that John upholds. This describes would-be church leaders whose doctrine and practices do not line up with the apostolic message and the Bible as a whole. We should not "greet" (treat as Christian brethren in good standing) religious leaders who undercut scriptural teaching.

Four hindrances—but in naming them, John shows confidence that we can avoid and overcome them. Pleasing God is the reward for avoiding hindrances by heeding his commands.

DECEMBER 24 · 3 JOHN 5-12

Walking in the Truth

ROBERT W. YARBROUGH

THIRD JOHN IS very brief, but one word stands out by its frequent appearance. That word is "truth" (vv. 1, 3, 4, 8, 12). Why is truth so important to the elder John as he jots this note to his friend Gaius? Why is it still important today, for those who follow Christ?

Truth is a basis for joy. When we see others "walking in the truth" (see vv. 3, 4), it encourages us. To walk in the truth means to live a life pleasing to God in all respects. When those around us walk in truth, it encourages us to do likewise. It glorifies God. And it brings joy to all those who love him.

Truth centers our lives on the spread of the gospel. It unites people. Verse 8 expresses the aim of being "fellow workers for the truth." Early Christian missionaries went forth spreading the truth about Christ

(vv. 3–7). When we unite with servants of the gospel, it elevates our lives. It refines us, delivers us from self-fixation, and focuses our gaze on God's amazing work all around the world. It brings deep fellowship and fruitful collaboration for the sake of the truth.

Truth displaces error. John writes about Diotrephes, a man important in his own eyes (v. 9). John intended, upon his next visit, to confront Diotrephes and put an end to the divisions he was causing (v. 10). How often does selfishness, desire for power, and the resulting tensions mar the life of a church? How often do these ills hinder Christian witness?

John writes that he loves his friend Gaius "in truth" (v. 1). This means with integrity. Where truth is honored, the Lord Jesus, who *is* truth (John 14:6) and who *pointed* to the truth (John 18:37), is honored. For "everyone who is of the truth listens to" Christ's voice (John 18:37).

In every age there are those who are skeptical of Christian claims. Jesus himself met with opposition to his person, his mission, his message, and even his miraculous works, as amazing as they were. But some saw in Jesus the truth. Some still embrace truth as it is in Jesus (see Eph. 4:21). Rather than give up on truth or even mock it as some always will, we are called to seek, stand up for, and serve the truth that Christ has revealed.

DECEMBER 25 • JUDE 20–21

Three Ways to Keep Yourselves in God's Love

ANDREW DAVID NASELLI

IF YOU ARE A CHRISTIAN, then God "keeps" you (see Jude 1, 24). He preserves you in his love so that nothing can separate you from him (John 6:37–40; 17:11–12; Rom. 8:28–39; 1 Thess. 5:23; 1 Pet. 1:3–5; 1 John 5:18).

And *you* are responsible to continue in the faith. Not only does God keep you; God commands you, in community with the other believers in your church, to "keep yourselves in the love of God" (Jude 21; see John 15:9–10). He tells you to do this in three ways:

1. Keep yourselves in God's love by "building yourselves up in your most holy faith." What is this "faith"? It is "the faith" that verse 3 says you must "contend for." The faith is the content of Christian belief as Christ and his apostles handed it down. It includes foundational teachings such as Christ's atoning death in the place of sinners, his resurrection, salvation by grace alone through faith alone in Christ alone, Christ's second coming, and—especially in Jude's situation—the holy lifestyle that flows from God's grace in Christ. So you build yourselves up on that foundation (i.e., the faith) by growing doctrinally strong. You should feel God's love for you more intensely as you understand the faith more deeply.

2. Keep yourselves in God's love by "praying in the Holy Spirit." Pray in a way that the Spirit stimulates, guides, and infuses (Rom. 8:26–27; Eph. 6:18). God himself should move you to pray and then direct and energize *what* you pray, according to his will. Regularly praying like this guards you in God's love.

3. Keep yourselves in God's love by "waiting for the mercy of our Lord Jesus Christ that leads to eternal life." Expectantly anticipate and live in light of God's future deliverance when Jesus returns (2 Pet. 3:11–14). That (rather than loving this present evil age) will keep you in God's love.

DECEMBER 26 · REVELATION 2:1–7

Jesus Knows It All

JAMES M. HAMILTON JR.

THE RISEN CHRIST appears to John in the fullness of his resurrection glory and speaks to him (Rev. 1:10–20). For whom would you expect Jesus to be concerned? What do you think he would say? What might be the first issue Jesus raises? What would be his primary concerns?

Jesus loves his bride, the church, and he wants his church to walk in the greatest commandment, as can be seen from the first thing out of his mouth when he begins to address the churches. By addressing seven churches, Jesus has representatively addressed all churches: each of these seven letters (chs. 2–3) concludes with a call, for the one with ears, to hear what the Spirit says to the churches. So while Revelation 2:1–7 is directed specifically to the church in Ephesus, it also speaks to anyone with an ear to hear, in any church—both then and now.

Do you feel that your church is obscure? Or if you're in a larger church, do you wonder if anyone ever notices what you do? Look at the words of Jesus in 2:2: "I know your works." He knows us. He knows what we do. He knows our sacrifices and vigilant efforts. Do we need anyone else's recognition? Isn't it enough that *he* knows?

He also knows where our hearts are, and the Lord Jesus loves us enough to want what is best for us: himself. Moreover, he will not allow our enjoyment of what is best to be halfhearted. Jesus wants the full measure of devotion from us—that first, fervent love (see 2:4)—because he wants his own joy for us, that our joy may be full (John 15:11). Jesus knows that true joy comes from self-sacrificial love (Heb. 12:2), and he knows that, what we love best, we give the most for. The amount we are willing to sacrifice to gain something is a direct reflection of how much we value it. Jesus wants the first love of his bride to correspond with the truth that he is of ultimate value to her.

Jesus wants what is best for his bride: himself. And he wants to give what is best to her, as can be seen from his promise that the one who conquers will eat from the tree of life in God's paradise. Those who love Jesus as they should will enjoy God's presence in a new and better Eden.

DECEMBER 27 • REVELATION 5

The Lion and the Lamb

JAMES M. HAMILTON JR.

BEHOLD THE GLORY of Christ in Revelation 5. In chapter 4, John described God the Father, seated on the throne, worshiped by the heavenly host. Could anything add fervor to the praise the Father receives from the heavenly host? Jesus can. Could anything take the eyes of heaven off the Father? Jesus does. Is there anyone worthy of being worshiped alongside the Father in heaven? Jesus is.

Christ is glorious in the way he fulfills the Old Testament. Note the elder's interpretation of the Old Testament in Revelation 5:5. The reference to the Lion of the tribe of Judah comes from the blessing of Judah in Genesis 49:8–12, and the reference to the Root of David comes from Isaiah 11. The elder announces that those passages are fulfilled in Jesus. If you don't read such Old Testament passages as being fulfilled in Jesus, you're not reading them the way the elders in heaven do.

Christ is glorious in paradox. The elder announces in Revelation 5:5 that Jesus is the Lion who has conquered, and then John sees him in verse 6 as the Lamb standing as though slain. Jesus the Lion conquered by becoming the slain Lamb. And look at the Lamb: he has seven horns. Horns in the Bible represent military might, and seven is a biblical number for fullness and completion. Jesus is a Lamb, an animal to be sacrificed, endowed with the fullness of military might: he was not slain because he was weak. Having the full power of omnipotence at his disposal, he freely laid down his life. No one took it from him (John 10:17–18).

Is it any wonder that those who were praising the Father in Revelation 4:4–11 direct their praise to the Son in 5:8–12? You will not regret joining "every creature in heaven and on earth" in ascribing "blessing and honor and glory" to "him who sits on the throne and to the Lamb" (v. 13).

DECEMBER 28 · REVELATION 7:9-17

God Our Tabernacle

JAMES M. HAMILTON JR.

ISRAEL'S EXODUS from Egypt and pilgrimage through the wilderness to the Land of Promise informs much of what John describes in Revelation 7:9–17. The death of Jesus fulfilled the death of the Passover lamb at the exodus, and the redeemed in Revelation 7, who are not just from Israel but from all nations, have washed their robes in the blood of Jesus the Lamb (v. 14).

The pilgrimage through the wilderness stands between the fulfillment of Passover at the cross and the fulfillment of the Land of Promise in the new heaven and new earth. During the Old Testament Feast of Tabernacles (or Booths), the people of Israel celebrated the way God provided for them in the wilderness, and they worshiped him with palm branches (Lev. 23:40). The redeemed in Revelation 7 have palm branches (v. 9) because they are celebrating the way God preserved them on their pilgrimage through the wilderness after the cross, on the way to the new and better Land of Promise.

God's people "serve him day and night in his temple" (v. 15) because Jesus "made us a kingdom, priests to his God and Father" (Rev. 1:6; see Ex. 19:6). When John writes that the one who sits on the throne "shelters" them with his presence (Rev. 7:15), that word "shelters" could be rendered "tabernacles over"—God tabernacles over his people, himself protecting them from the striking sun and scorching heat (v. 16).

Moses shepherded God's flock through the wilderness to the Land of Promise after the exodus, and through him God gave his people manna from heaven and water from the rock. Now that Jesus has fulfilled the exodus by his death and resurrection, "the Lamb in the midst of the throne will be their shepherd, and he will guide them to springs of living water" (v. 17), and "they shall hunger no more, neither thirst anymore" (v. 16; see John 4:10–14; 6:35; 7:37–39).

We are like the Israelites in the wilderness on the way to the land promised to us, the new heaven and new earth. God the Father is our Tabernacle (Rev. 7:15), and Jesus the Lamb is our Shepherd (v. 17), giving us the Spirit as the living water that keeps us alive (John 7:37–39; see Psalm 23), giving us himself as the bread of life (John 6:35), and promising that, when our journey is over, "God will wipe away every tear" (Rev. 7:17).

Conquering Satan by the Blood of the Lamb

JAMES M. HAMILTON JR.

THE DRAMA OF REVELATION 12 can be difficult to discern from the apocalyptic symbolism, but its unfolding is powerfully encouraging: the woman and the dragon are both referred to as signs, to be understood symbolically (vv. 1, 3). The conflict between the woman and the serpentine dragon (v. 9) dramatizes Genesis 3:15. The snake intends to devour the individual seed of the woman at the moment of his birth (Rev. 12:4). This individual seed of the woman is King Jesus, as can be seen from the reference to his ruling all nations in the language of Psalm 2:8–9 (Rev. 12:5).

The earthly career of Jesus is summarized in 12:5, with everything from his birth to ascension evoked by the fact that he is born, delivered from the dragon, and caught up to God in heaven. Then God preserves the woman from the dragon (vv. 6, 13–17), and the woman becomes the mother not only of the Messiah but of the people of God, as can be seen from the reference to "the rest" of her seed in verse 17.

On the basis of Christ's victory over the serpent through his life, death, and resurrection (v. 5), Michael the archangel is able to drive Satan and his angels from the heavenly field of battle (vv. 7–12). Whereas, prior to the cross of Christ, Satan could accuse Job (e.g., Job 1:9–11) and Joshua the high priest (Zech. 3:1) before God in heaven, because of what we read about in Revelation 12:5, Satan's accusations no longer have standing in the heavenly court: "The accuser of our brothers has been thrown down" (v. 10) and God's people have conquered him "by the blood of the Lamb and by the word of their testimony" (v. 11). Satan has a "short" time (v. 12) to wage war on those who "hold to the testimony of Jesus" (v. 17), but God delivers and nourishes his people (vv. 13–16).

Satan has no standing before God to accuse those who conquer him by the blood of the Lamb (vv. 10–11). He has been thrown out of heaven because of what Christ accomplished (vv. 7–9; see John 12:31). Are you plagued by guilt? Confess your sin, repent, and refer every satanic accusation to the blood of the Lamb, which washes white as snow.

DECEMBER 30 · REVELATION 15

What True Worship Looks Like

JAMES M. HAMILTON JR.

THE AUDIENCE OF REVELATION has been called to be faithful unto death (Rev. 2:10), and the slaughter of the faithful has been depicted (13:10, 15). John now relates a scene he saw in heaven (15:1) that shows his audience what lies beyond death for those who are faithful. Revelation 15 opens (v. 1) and closes (vv. 5–8) with descriptions of the seven angels who will pour out the final seven bowls of God's wrath in Revelation 16, assuring the faithful that the wicked will not escape God's justice. Revelation 15:2–4 depicts the martyrs in heaven worshiping God as they await his justice and their own resurrection, which happens in Revelation 20:4–6. The book thus assures the faithful that, if they are martyred, they will worship God in heaven (15:2–4) and will rise from the dead to reign with Christ (20:4–6).

The sea of glass that John sees in 15:2 is the same sea of glass he saw before the throne of God in 4:6. The sea is mingled with fire because God is about to judge his enemies in the outpouring of the bowls of wrath (ch. 16). John says he saw those who had conquered the beast (15:2), recalling the brothers who loved not their lives even unto death (12:11). Not only did they conquer the beast; they conquered "its image and the number of its name" (15:2), recalling the image of the beast (13:14), the execution of those who would not worship the image (v. 15), and the number of the name of the beast (vv. 16–18). These who have been slain, the faithful unto death, are "standing beside the sea of glass" (15:2), which means that they are before the throne of God in heaven (4:6).

The description of these martyred faithful singing the song of Moses and the song of the Lamb in 15:3 means that they sing the fulfillment of the Exodus 15 victory song that celebrated God's redemption of his people at the exodus from Egypt. The Lamb of God, Jesus, has fulfilled the patterns of the exodus as the true Passover Lamb whose death has set in motion the new exodus.

The words of praise in Revelation 15:3–4 celebrate God's incomparable power, his holy justice, his rightful rule over all nations, and the reality that the salvation he has wrought in Christ reveals his righteousness and will draw all nations to worship him.

DECEMBER 31 · REVELATION 21:1-8

Heaven on Earth

JAMES M. HAMILTON JR.

IN REVELATION 21:1-8, John depicts God's purposes for the ages finally coming to pass. Before sin entered the world, the Lord walked with man in the garden in the cool of the day (Gen. 3:8). When all is complete, he will again dwell with those who are his people, and he will be their God (Rev. 21:3). On that day he will have healed their hurts, removed their pain, and sanctified their sorrow (v. 4). No more death, pain, or mourning. No more sea, because the sea has been the place from which the great dragon summoned up the beast (12:17–13:1). Heaven and earth will be made new, and the holy city will be like a bride adorned for her husband (21:1–2).

There can be no better hope than this, which is why it is what politicians and dreamers and philosophers and emperors have promised and sought across the ages. God will bring it to pass. He promises to do so; his word is trustworthy and true (v. 5). To those who thirst for peace, harmony, justice, and purity, God promises to freely give the water of life (v. 6).

Who gets to enjoy the goodness that God creates when the former things have passed away (v. 4) and all is made new (v. 1)? Those who conquer, which is what Jesus called the churches to do in Revelation 2–3 and what those who "loved not their lives even unto death" achieved in 12:11. The conquerors will inherit the new Land of Promise as sons of God (21:7).

What keeps people from conquering, defeating them and disqualifying them from the enjoyment of all that is desirable? Cowardice, unbelief, abomination, murder, sexual immorality, sorcery, idolatry, and lying (v. 8).

What will the disqualified inherit? Their portion is the second death in the lake of fire and sulfur (v. 8).

Is there any hope for those who have thus disqualified themselves? Revelation teaches that those who have conquered are those who have been freed from their sins by the blood of Jesus (1:5), who "have washed their robes and made them white in the blood of the Lamb" (7:14), who have held fast to the testimony of Jesus (12:17). Throughout Revelation, John is clear that following Christ means turning from sin, resisting temptation, and enduring persecution. As the book culminates with the resurrection of the righteous (20:4–6), the new heaven and new earth (21:1–22:5), and the promise that Christ is coming soon (22:6–21), John shows what Paul put so well: "The sufferings of this present time are not worth comparing with the glory that is to be revealed to us" (Rom. 8:18).

Notes

1. William Cowper (1731–1800), "God Moves in a Mysterious Way," 1774.
2. J. R. R. Tolkien, *The Hobbit* (New York: Ballantine, 1966), 270.
3. See James Montgomery Boice, *Joshua: An Expositional Commentary* (Grand Rapids, MI: Baker, 1989), 83.
4. Augustine, *Confessions* I.1.
5. Thomas Goodwin, *The Glories of Christ Set Forth in His Mediatorial Character* . . . (London: J. Bennett, 1818), 351.
6. Jonathan Edwards, "Union with Christ," in *The Miscellanies: Entry Nos. a–z, aa–zz, 1–500, in The Works of Jonathan Edwards,* vol. 13, ed. Harry S. Stout (New Haven, CT: Yale University Press, 1884), 183–184.
7. C. S. Lewis, "Is Theology Poetry," in *The Weight of Glory and Other Addresses,* rev. ed. (New York: HarperCollins, 1980), 131.
8. "How Firm a Foundation," from Rippon's *Selection of Hymns,* 1787, author unknown.
9. C. S. Lewis, *The Last Battle* (New York: Macmillan, 1956), 171 (chapter 15).
10. Thomas Watson, *The Doctrine of Repentance* (1668; repr., n.p.: Blessed News Publishing, 2019), 83.
11. Scott Hafemann, *2 Corinthians,* NIV Application Commentary (Grand Rapids, MI: Zondervan, 2000), comment on 2 Corinthians 1:3–11.
12. C. S. Lewis, *Mere Christianity* (New York: Macmillan, 1952), 160.
13. John Donne (1571–1631), "Death, Be Not Proud" (Holy Sonnet 10).
14. John Newton, quoted in *The Christian Spectator,* vol. 3 (1821), 186.

Index of Scripture References

(italic typeface denotes featured texts)

Joshua

Judges

Ruth

Go Deeper in Your
Study of God's Word

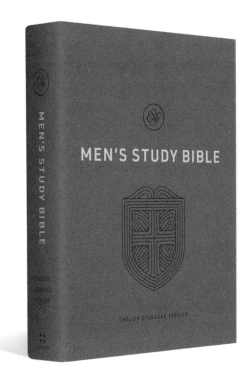

The *ESV Men's Study Bible* is designed to encourage men and draw them into deeper, more purposeful time with the Lord. It features 12,000 theologically rich study notes, 14 life application articles, a devotion for every day of the year, and content from more than 100 leading pastors and Bible scholars.

For more information, visit **crossway.org**.